THE JURISPRUDENTIAL LEGACY OF
JUSTICE RUTH BADER GINSBURG

The Jurisprudential Legacy of Justice Ruth Bader Ginsburg

Edited by

Ryan Vacca and Ann Bartow

NEW YORK UNIVERSITY PRESS

New York

NEW YORK UNIVERSITY PRESS
New York
www.nyupress.org

Please contact the Library of Congress for Cataloging-in-Publication data.
ISBN: 9781479817856 (hardback)
ISBN:9781479817894 (library ebook)
ISBN: 9781479817870 (consumer ebook)

New York University Press books are printed on acid-free paper, and their binding materials
are chosen for strength and durability. We strive to use environmentally responsible suppli-
ers and materials to the greatest extent possible in publishing our books.

Manufactured in the United States of America

10 9 8 7 6 5 4 3 2 1

Also available as an ebook

To the memory of Justice Ruth Bader Ginsburg, without whom Ann and many of the authors who contributed chapters to this collection may not have been able to go to law school or become law professors. She made the world a better place for everyone, especially women.

—AB & RV

To Ryan Burke,
Your brilliance, love, and support inspire me.

—RV

To my brilliant, kind and just generally amazing son Casey Bartow-McKenney.

—AB

CONTENTS

PREFACE

When news of Associate Justice Ruth Bader Ginsburg's death on September 18, 2020, became public, co-editor and co-contributor Ryan Vacca began considering the effect this might have upon copyright law, a field in which Justice Ginsburg had notable impact during her time on the bench. He contacted co-editor, co-contributor, and colleague Ann Bartow with the idea of collaborating on a short essay about Ginsburg's copyright law jurisprudence, and she readily agreed to it. It was a way to mourn and honor this pathbreaking individual, who at one point in her career was a law professor herself, with an overview of her impact on a subject area we have devoted our lives to studying, teaching, and reforming.

Once we started writing, we realized that the fifteen or so pages we initially planned were inadequate to describe the significant impact Justice Ginsburg had on copyright law, mostly within the United States but even internationally. She expressed strong opinions about copyright law issues in her written opinions, and not all of them could be described as reflecting a liberal ideology. On balance, she favored the Goliaths of copyright litigation more frequently than the Davids. And we had a lot to say about that, so our short essay turned into a lengthy law review article.

Even though we passionately disagreed with some of Justice Ginsburg's copyright law opinions, we were impressed with the depth and detail with which she analyzed each dispute. We found immersing ourselves in the writings and life of Ruth Bader Ginsburg so interesting that we decided to invite legal scholars in other subject areas to write essays about Ginsburg's jurisprudence and to compile them into the book you currently have before you.

We chose the legal subject areas of the chapters in consultation with Supreme Court observers and professional colleagues. We were fortunate to attract a brilliant lineup of contributing authors, whose participation was a source of inspiration and pride. We hope you learn a lot from the contributions included here, and readers can incorporate the wisdom they contain into their own careers—including writing, teaching, and legal practice.

Ryan Vacca and Ann Bartow
Concord, New Hampshire

Introduction

Opening Statement

Ruth Bader Ginsburg started her legal career as a firebrand feminist attorney who advanced the cause of women's equality, using legal tools to pursue equal citizenship and full participation in society for all women. Though she was not a person who sought the spotlight, her work brought a lot of attention. Her judicial career began when she was appointed to the United States Court of Appeals for the District of Columbia Circuit in 1980 by President Jimmy Carter. Once on the bench, Judge Ginsburg was well respected by her colleagues and considered to be a centrist.[1] In fact, she voted with her Republican-appointed colleagues more frequently than her Democrat-appointed ones.[2] She was not even remotely considered a firebrand jurist in those days.

In 1993, President Bill Clinton nominated her to the United States Supreme Court. She was nominated and confirmed to the Court, in part, because of her moderate, balanced, and thoughtful jurisprudence while serving on the D.C. Circuit.[3] When Clinton nominated her, he knew he needed the approval of Republicans. Judge Ginsburg's reputation as a moderate who exercised judicial restraint fit the bill.[4] This was reflected in her opening statement during her confirmation hearing:

> Let me try to state in a nutshell how I view the work of judging. My approach, I believe, is neither liberal nor conservative. Rather, it is rooted in the place of the judiciary, of judges, in our democratic society. The Constitution's preamble speaks first of "We, the People," and then of their elected representatives. The judiciary is third in line and it is placed apart from the political fray so that its members can judge fairly, impartially, in accordance with the law, and without fear about the animosity of any pressure group. In Alexander Hamilton's words, the mission of judges is "to secure a steady, upright, and impartial administration of the laws." I

would add that the judge should carry out that function without fanfare, but with due care. She should decide the case before her without reaching out to cover cases not yet seen. She should be ever mindful, as Judge and then Justice Benjamin Nathan Cardozo said, "Justice is not to be taken by storm. She is to be wooed by slow advances."[5]

Soon after joining the Supreme Court, Justice Ginsburg became more culturally visible than other Justices. She developed into an iconic member of the Court who penned passionate opinions in high-profile cases and wore eye-catching, festive neckwear atop her judicial robes.[6] She acquired a humorous and affectionate nickname—"The Notorious R.B.G."—and became a prolific subject of merchants and crafters who produced objects like dolls, quilts, and mittens bearing her likeness, sometimes featuring RBG signifiers such as her famous "dissent collar." By the time of her passing, she was once again viewed as a firebrand.

During her four decades on the bench, Justice Ginsburg heard cases and wrote opinions concerning a great many legal subjects. She had to become a quick expert in subjects ranging from environmental law to tax law, from copyright law to the death penalty, from voting rights to administrative law—and everything in between. She also had to absorb and mediate a litany of political questions embedded in the legal disputes before the Court.

Following Justice Ginsburg's death in 2020, we did a big-picture inventory of her copyright jurisprudence.[7] As we read and reread her copyright opinions, listened to oral argument recordings, learned about her life on and off the bench, and perused her enormous body of scholarship and speeches from her days as a law professor, lawyer, and jurist, we detected several jurisprudential themes running through Justice Ginsburg's copyright analyses and animating her opinions, and we wrote a lengthy law review article about them. The exercise was so useful to our thinking about copyright law that it sparked the genesis of this book.

This edited collection brings together the efforts of twenty-seven terrific legal scholars who examined and described Justice Ginsburg's jurisprudential contributions to each author's area of expertise. These amazing thinkers have written chapters that paint a rich and nuanced portrait of RBG's jurisprudential legacy. As you read these essays, you'll learn that Ginsburg's opinions were sometimes driven by large structural concerns such as federalism and separation of powers, that she often preferred to develop the law in any given area incrementally, and that her foundational beliefs about gender equality were not always consistently reflected in her opinions. Themes such as predictability, contextual analysis, pragmatism, access to justice, efficiency, and recognition of institutional capacity limitations all surfaced in her written opinions. Finally, the essays also explain that while serving on the bench Ruth Bader Ginsburg brought empathy, compassion, and humanity to legal interpretation.

NOTES

1 Rebecca Barnhart & Deborah Zalesne, *Twin Pillars of Judicial Philosophy: The Impact of the Ginsburg Collegiality and Gender Discrimination Principles on Her Separate Opinions Involving Gender Discrimination*, 7 N.Y. City L. Rev. 275, 283–85 (2004).

2 Jeffrey Brandon Morris, Calmly to Poise the Scales of Justice: A History of the Court of the District of Columbia Circuit 320 (2001).

3 *See* Mark Silverstein & William Haltom, *You Can't Always Get What You Want: Reflections on the Ginsburg and Breyer Nominations*, 12 J. L. & Pol. 459 (1996); Barnhart & Zalesne, *Twin Pillars of Judicial Philosophy*, at 283 (2004).

4 Jane Sherron De Hart, Ruth Bader Ginsburg 307 (2018).

5 *Nomination of Ruth Bader Ginsburg, to Be Associate Justice of the Supreme Court of the United States: Hearing Before the S. Comm. on the Judiciary*, 103rd Cong. 51 (1993).

6 Tessa Berenson, *Portraits of Ruth Bader Ginsburg's Favorite Collars and the Stories Behind Them*, Time (Dec. 3, 2020), https://time.com.

7 Ryan Vacca & Ann Bartow, *Ruth Bader Ginsburg's Copyright Jurisprudence*, 22 Nev. L.J. 431 (2022).

1

Gender and the Law

Revisiting the Legacy of a Feminist Icon

DEBORAH L. BRAKE

Justice Ginsburg attained celebrity status in her later years as the voice of feminism from the bench, but her influence on law and gender was not always so venerated. For much of her career, feminist scholarly criticism of her gender jurisprudence was sharp. Critics called the approach "formal equality," pointing out that it benefited those women most similarly situated to men. The criticism echoed that leveled against her strategy as a litigator representing male plaintiffs. In recent years, Justice Ginsburg's legacy has been burnished by a fresh interpretation crediting it with a more robust vision of gender equality than previously appreciated. This chapter contends that, while far from radical, the Justice's gender jurisprudence is the product of a jurist committed to minimizing the role of gender as a site of social and economic oppression.

Although Justice Ginsburg's impact on gender equality can fill a book on its own, this chapter focuses on identifying and explaining three core themes: an antipathy toward gender stereotypes embedded in law; a vision of gender equality that transcends formal equality; and a recognition of the centrality of reproductive freedom to women's equality. Each of these themes has been advanced, albeit imperfectly, by Justice Ginsburg's career as a litigator and a jurist.

Anti-stereotyping Above All

Justice Ginsburg's views on the harms of sex-based classifications, and the stereotypes that underlie them, were formed before she became a jurist and followed her to the bench. The anti-stereotyping principle at the heart of her approach has often been maligned as a thin version of equality. But it has proven to be strong medicine for challenging legally enforced gender conformity and the gender binary.

Some feminist scholars questioned the strategy of making gender stereotyping the cornerstone of constitutional gender equality. Mary Becker famously indicted the leading constitutional law cases applying heightened scrutiny to gender, the culmination of the Ginsburg litigation strategy, for targeting irrational generalizations instead of women's subordination.[1] Becker's critique was not merely that this approach failed to address the ways women were differently situated from men due to systemic disadvantage. Becker's indictment went further, arguing that the gender-blind model deepened gender inequality by reinforcing the gendered patterns that hurt women. Catharine MacKinnon was also scathing in her review of the model of equality most often associated with the RBG brand, which she regarded as a hollow assimilation that helped those women most closely situated to men, thereby reinforcing male dominance.[2] The emphasis on sex-based classifications left out many issues contributing to women's economic and social inequality, such as welfare, domestic violence, rape, and poverty.

While these critiques remain forceful, more recent feminist scholarship has been kinder to RBG's anti-stereotyping principle.[3] There is more than a hollow liberty at the core of the anti-stereotyping principle.[4] The breadwinner/homemaker dichotomy is problematic not only because it interferes with liberty (men's as well as women's) but also because it reinforces a hierarchy of gender power.[5] The breadwinner role is privileged precisely because it is associated with masculinity.

Recall, for example, *Weinberger v. Wiesenfeld*,[6] one of the gems in Ginsburg's litigation career with the ACLU. The plaintiff's wife was deceased, but the Social Security Act denied widowers the survivors' benefits automatically granted to widows. It took some explaining to convince the Supreme Court that the statute harmed the *women* (who were already deceased) whose spouses were denied benefits. On the surface, the statute *favored* women, since female beneficiaries—surviving spouses of deceased husbands—automatically received benefits. Only by focusing on the dual roles reflected in the statute did the harm to women come into focus. The law operated as a de facto subsidy to male wage-earners, whose families would have more resources upon their death.[7] As Martha Chamallas explained, the Court could not have understood the harm in these cases without implicitly recognizing the devaluation of women workers.[8]

The role of male plaintiffs in the foundational gender cases has also been criticized. As a litigator, Ginsburg represented more men than women,[9] a move critics saw as a cynical tactic to appeal to male judges. Ginsburg herself viewed *Craig v. Boren*,[10] the case adopting intermediate scrutiny in a challenge to a state law barring young men from purchasing low-alcohol beer, as something of an embarrassment—despite her collaboration with the plaintiffs' attorneys challenging the law.[11] As sex discrimination law developed, cases brought by male plaintiffs played a central role. Before Justice Ginsburg joined the Court, *Mississippi University for Women v. Hogan*[12] was decided in favor of a male plaintiff's challenge to a state nursing school's exclusion of male applicants. Writing the opinion for the Court, Justice Sandra Day O'Connor closely tracked the core Ginsburg insight that gender stereotypes are a double-edged sword: even when targeting men, they also hurt women. Justice O'Connor pointedly observed that excluding men from nursing depresses women's wages.[13] When it came time for Justice Ginsburg to write the Court's opinion in a later challenge to sex-based admissions in higher education (*United States v. Virginia*, addressing the issue at the Virginia Military Institute, or VMI), she leaned heavily on Justice O'Connor's opinion in *Mississippi University for Women*.[14]

Elaborating the harms to men from gender stereotyping can now be understood as a precursor to socio-legal studies in the field of masculinities.[15] One core precept of masculinities theory is that men, while privileged by gender, pay a price for that privilege. Though men benefit as workers from the premium afforded male breadwinners, they bear a cost to the quality of their relationships, health, and lives outside of work. Relatedly, the price men pay for gender privilege is interconnected to the oppression of women. For example, lifting sex-based restrictions blocking men's access to jobs gendered feminine ("women's jobs") helps women in those jobs by raising wages and status.[16] Finally, masculinities scholars teach that, while men as a group have power over women, not all men share equally in male privilege. The cases Ginsburg litigated on behalf of male plaintiffs reflected the unevenness of male privilege; they included a primary caretaker to an elderly mother, a stay-at-home father, and husbands of higher-earning wives.[17]

Exposing sex discrimination's harms to both men and women resists framing gender equality as a zero-sum game, a "battle of the sexes" in which men lose if women advance. The zero-sum framing rests on an overly simplistic understanding of gender bias and promotes a narrative that invites backlash: if women's equality goes "too far," men lose. This lesson remains urgent, as backlash threatens to unravel feminism's gains.

One of the most transformative insights generated by Ginsburg's anti-stereotyping project is that gender stereotyping is predicated upon a polarized, binary understanding of sex. Unsettling gender stereotypes destabilizes the gender binary. Ginsburg's agenda to obtain heightened scrutiny of gender classifications opened the door to using anti-stereotyping theory to challenge the gender policing underlying antigay and antitrans bias.[18] The Supreme Court's 2020 decision in *Bostock v. Clayton County*,[19] recognizing sexual orientation and transgender discrimination as encompassed by Title VII's ban on sex discrimination, stops short of a wholesale destabilization of the gender binary. But it is a step in that direction made possible by Ginsburg-style skeptical scrutiny of sex-based classifications and the stereotypes underlying them.[20]

Yet there are limits to the transformative power of placing such an emphasis on gender stereotyping. One such limitation stems from the primacy of gender in this approach, as a single axis of bias, and the neglect of intersectional oppression. Gender stereotypes do not operate independently of race and class, and not all women are subject to the same gender stereotypes. Separate spheres ideology and the cult of domesticity (the stereotype underlying the breadwinner/homemaker dichotomy) was always racially specific. Women of color have always been expected to work—indeed, enslaved Black women were forced to work by violence and terror—and were never "protected" from the hardships of labor to preserve a revered maternal role. Challenging the gendered assumptions underlying the breadwinner/homemaker dichotomy did not necessarily dismantle the stereotypes most harmful to women of color or poor women.

Another problematic dimension of reliance on gender stereotyping as the building block of sex discrimination law is that it leaned heavily on the analogy to race discrimination. Ginsburg's litigation strategy built the case for heightened scrutiny explicitly on the comparison to race. As a Justice, Ginsburg relied on the analogy to advance the tough intermediate scrutiny standard elaborated in her VMI opinion, citing *Sweatt v. Painter*, a precursor to the rejection of "separate but equal" for racial segregation.[21] The race-sex comparison was effective in moving the law closer to strict scrutiny. But the analogy is flawed in its implicit assumption of discrete race/sex categories, the premise that each can be understood as a singular identity unmarked by the other and the implicit assumption of a shared history of oppression. Constitutional law might have had a firmer foundation for dismantling gender oppression if it had been predicated on a deeper historical analysis of gender and the Constitution.[22]

Nevertheless, this criticism should be evaluated in historical context. The very first Title VII case decided by the Supreme Court, *Phillips v. Martin Marietta*,[23] was brought by lawyers with the NAACP Legal Defense Fund. Even though the plaintiff, Ida Phillips, was white, the civil rights community understood that a narrow interpretation of Title VII as applied to sex would eviscerate the statute's ban on race discrimination.[24] Their argument pressed the race-sex analogy to warn that permitting the different treatment of women based on a characteristic in addition to sex (in this case, discrimination against women with young children) would have equally pernicious consequences for race discrimination.[25] Situating the argument historically may not fully rehabilitate the analogy. But its role in building the case for heightened scrutiny is as much a product of the limits of legal reasoning and precedent as it is a failure of imagination by the architects of sex discrimination law.

Not Formal Only: A Gender Equality with Substance

The gender equality at the heart of Justice Ginsburg's jurisprudence has always had a substantive core. Justice Ginsburg's model of equality allows room for some gender-conscious uses of law to address gender disadvantage, with antisubordination as the ultimate goal. The anticlassification approach was a means to an end—that of uprooting the gender hierarchy that subordinated women—not merely an end in itself.[26] In the VMI decision, perhaps the opinion that best captures Justice Ginsburg's gender jurisprudence, "skeptical" scrutiny expressly permits sex-based classifications tailored to remedying women's disadvantages. She threaded the needle as carefully as the Court's precedents would allow, writing:

"Inherent differences" between men and women . . . remain cause for celebration, but not for denigration. . . . Sex classifications may be used to compensate women "for particular economic disabilities [they have] suffered," to "promot[e] equal employment opportunity," . . . [and] to advance full development of the talent and capacities of our Nation's people. But such classifications may not be used, as they once were, to create or perpetuate the legal, social, and economic inferiority of women.[27]

The line between reinforcing and remedying women's oppression is crucial and yet has proven far more difficult to discern in concrete cases than this formulation admits. There is a tension, perhaps never fully resolvable, in the push for equal treatment founded on a disdain for gender stereotypes and the acknowledgement that gender matters and may sometimes be taken into account.

The main difficulty with this formulation is in determining when the goal of antisubordination demands a departure from the equal treatment norm. It was easy to see that VMI's exclusion of women did nothing to rectify women's social and economic inferiority. But in cases with more plausible claims of doing so, Ginsburg, as a litigator, took a hard stance against sex classifications, making it difficult to see the boundaries of what she would accept in the name of substantive equality as a jurist. The one case that Ginsburg argued before the Supreme Court and lost, *Kahn v. Shevin*,[28] upheld a state property tax exemption for widows. The Court viewed the different treatment of widows and widowers as "reasonably designed to further the state policy of cushioning the financial impact of spousal loss upon the sex for which that law imposes a disproportionately heavy burden."[29] Arguing for the plaintiff, a widower who had relied on his wife's income for support, Ginsburg agreed that women generally face greater economic burdens after the loss of a spouse, but she argued that the state should provide benefits to needy spouses regardless of gender.[30] She did not view the Florida law as affirmative action (which she supported). Rather she viewed the special treatment for widows as predicted on the breadwinner/homemaker stereotype, which the Florida law reinforced.[31]

A stronger case for upholding sex classifications to remedy women's disadvantage might be made in *Schlesinger v. Ballard*,[32] decided the year after *Kahn*. Described by Ginsburg as "a tangled, idiosyncratic case,"

the case turned on whether the United States Navy could give servicewomen extra years to compile a record for promotion to compensate for
the combat restrictions that made it tougher for servicewomen to secure
promotion.[33] Even here, Ginsburg held steadfast to the equal treatment
approach. Although the combat restrictions were not directly at issue,
Ginsburg would have had the Court review the underlying restrictions
instead of upholding the piecemeal compensatory treatment layered
upon discrimination.[34] Disagreeing, the Court upheld the classification
as a measure targeting the reality (not the mere stereotype) of the disadvantages women faced in military service. Ginsburg viewed the decision
as a capitulation to discrimination against women in the military. While
it is possible to view her perspective as ensconced in formal equality, in
fact, hers was the more radical view.

Another case conventionally understood as posing the formal equal-
ity/substantive equality dilemma also found Ginsburg on the equal
treatment side. In the early 1980s, the Court took a case that divided the
women's rights community over whether the Pregnancy Discrimination
Act allowed pregnant workers to be treated more favorably than employees with other medical conditions. Ginsburg sided with the equal treatment advocates—but not out of a rigid adherence to formal equality.
Rather she favored extending the favorable treatment of pregnancy to all
workers with medical conditions. She believed that permitting more favorable treatment for pregnancy would end up penalizing women. Real
reform, she believed, could come only from improving the treatment of
all workers with conditions affecting work capacity.

During her career as a litigator, the one instance where Ginsburg
approved of a sex-based classification that came before the Court was
the federal government's use of a catch-up provision allowing women
to subtract more low-earning years in calculating social security benefits. On this, Ginsburg agreed with the Court that the statute's narrowly
tailored sex-based classification compensated women for lower wages
without reinforcing harmful stereotypes.[35] This position fit with her
support for affirmative action to remedy disadvantages stemming from
discrimination.[36]

An important limitation to Justice Ginsburg's embrace of a substantive model of equality, however, was her vacillating approach to remedying discrimination. As a litigator, Ginsburg pressed for curing inequality

by extending the more favorable treatment to similarly situated members of the disadvantaged sex. But as a Justice, she did not always opt for leveling up. The issue came to the forefront in a case decided in 2017, *Sessions v. Morales-Santana*.[37] The Court, in an opinion authored by Justice Ginsburg, struck down a sex-based classification in the federal immigration and naturalization statute saddling U.S. citizen fathers with more onerous requirements for conferring citizenship on their nonmarital children born overseas. The statute imposed a longer U.S. residency requirement on citizen fathers than on similarly situated citizen mothers, treating the sex of the parent as a proxy for inculcating American cultural values. By striking down the classification, the Court advanced the anti-stereotyping principle at the heart of Justice Ginsburg's jurisprudence.[38] But when it came to remedying the discrimination, Justice Ginsburg explained that the equal protection violation could be cured by either extending the more favorable treatment to the children of citizen fathers or ending it for the offspring of citizen mothers. Because she believed Congress intended to end, rather than extend, the more favorable treatment in the event it was ruled unconstitutional, Justice Ginsburg opted for ending the privilege. This left the plaintiff and others similarly situated with a victory more symbolic than real.

As a Justice, Ginsburg lacked a principled theory for when to level up and when to level down. The determination in *Morales-Santana* boiled down to legislative intent. Writing before she reached the bench, Ginsburg opined that leveling down is appropriate when doing otherwise would affect a large group and impose hefty costs, especially on private parties.[39] But this approach fails to consider whether leveling down exacerbates the harm of the underlying inequality.[40] Instead of grappling with the harms of stigma, subordination, and retaliation for challenging inequality, the Justice defaulted to formal equality, assuming that the harms of discrimination can be sufficiently cured with a gender-blind rule.

Justice Ginsburg's gender equality jurisprudence, despite its limitations, continued to have force in her later years. One of her crowning achievements was her dissent in *Ledbetter v. Goodyear Tire and Rubber Company*.[41] Technically a procedural ruling on the statute of limitations, the Court's decision that Title VII's short limitations period begins running the moment gender bias infects a pay-setting decision prompted Justice Ginsburg to rebuke the majority for its formalism and inattention to the lived realities of employees. She railed against the injustice of preventing workers from challenging ongoing pay discrimination, which may have been impossible to discover sooner. Reading her dissenting opinion from the bench, Justice Ginsburg sparked a resurgence of the equal pay movement, culminating in the first piece of legislation signed by President Barack Obama, which amended Title VII to override the Court's decision.[42] Although Justice Ginsburg has been criticized for too readily pulling back from the edges of popular opinion to avoid backlash,[43] in this instance she used her platform to mobilize equal pay advocates to press Congress to better address the institutional practices that depress women's wages.[44]

Linking Women's Equality and Reproductive Freedom

Yet another defining feature of Justice Ginsburg's gender equality jurisprudence is her recognition that women's equality and women's reproductive control are fundamentally and inextricably connected. As a litigator, Ginsburg saw no daylight between equal opportunity in the economic and social spheres and reproductive freedom. While at the ACLU, she supported a case brought by a pregnant teacher challenging a school board policy requiring pregnant teachers to take a leave of absence.[45] The Court decided the case on procedural due process grounds, holding that the rule created an irrebuttable presumption of incapacity, with no opportunity for an individual to demonstrate otherwise. But in her amicus curiae brief, Ginsburg pressed a sex equality rationale, invoking the equal protection clause as the basis for women's reproductive rights. In her view, the right to have children and the right not to have children were flip sides of the same coin.

Admittedly, Ginsburg's litigation strategy did not place abortion rights at the center of the docket. The Ford Foundation, a key funder of the ACLU, would not support litigation challenging abortion restrictions.[46] But no such constraint applied to pregnancy discrimination, which Ginsburg understood as central to reproductive freedom. As she explained in the nomination process, she would have preferred the Court address the abortion right in her own case, *Struck v. Secretary of Defense*,[47] which was on the docket the same term as *Roe v. Wade*.[48] Captain Susan Struck challenged the Air Force's directive, after learning of her pregnancy, that she either have an abortion or leave active duty. Struck refused to have an abortion and challenged the rule. Observing that men could father children while continuing to serve, Ginsburg argued that the freedom to choose—either to have or not have—a child is crucial to women's equality. The case had been headed to the Supreme Court until the Air Force waived the rule, mooting the case and leaving *Roe* as the vehicle for the landmark abortion ruling.

Justice Ginsburg's scholarly criticism of *Roe* dogged her in the women's rights community, causing some to question her nomination to the Court. The substance of Ginsburg's criticism, however, did not disagree with the fundamental importance of women's reproductive freedom. Rather, she believed sex equality was the better framework for capturing the problems with abortion restrictions. Perhaps antiabortion activists understood the significance of her critique better; they feared that, if confirmed, she might succeed in securing abortion rights under the Equal Protection Clause.[49]

Many of Justice Ginsburg's opinions reveal her understanding of the centrality of pregnancy and reproductive freedom to sex equality. In 1974, the Court issued its infamous ruling in *Geduldig v. Aiello*,[50] holding that pregnancy discrimination is not a form of sex discrimination against women. The Court never repudiated that opinion, which has continued to haunt the case law, and Justice Ginsburg seized every chance to lambast its obtuseness. Dissenting in *Coleman v. Maryland Court of Appeals*,[51] Justice Ginsburg faulted the Court for failing to see how the Family Medical Leave Act (FMLA) self-care provision furthered the equal protection rights of women denied pregnancy leave at work. The Court placed the FMLA's guarantee of medical leave outside Congress's power to enforce the Fourteenth Amendment, rendering it unconstitutional as applied to state employers in suits for damages. But in Justice Ginsburg's view, the law's guarantee of gender-neutral self-care leave protected women's equal opportunity at work during and after pregnancy without making women singularly more costly to employ. As she explained, the freedom to have children without being penalized as workers is crucial for women to have "a more egalitarian relationship at home and at work."[52]

The ghost of *Geduldig* also surfaced in *AT&T v. Hulteen*,[53] in which the Court refused to allow retired women to challenge the continuing effects of pregnancy discrimination, even though the employer's discriminatory denial of service credit for pregnancy leave resulted in reduced pension benefits. Justice Ginsburg again dissented, excoriating the Court for its continued adherence to *Geduldig* as the correct measure of pregnancy discrimination. She viewed the Court's continued missteps, first in deciding *Geduldig* and then in adhering to its logic even after Congress enacted the Pregnancy Discrimination Act in 1978, as a fatal failure to see how "societal attitudes about pregnancy and motherhood severely impeded women's employment opportunities."[54]

Justice Ginsburg's dogged determination and urgency in pushing the Court to overrule *Geduldig* was prescient. Far from a dead letter, *Geduldig* returned with a vengeance in the Supreme Court's 2022 decision in *Dobbs v. Jackson Women's Health Organization*,[55] pulling the rug out from under a constitutional right to abortion. Justice Alito's opinion for the Court relied on *Geduldig* to slam the door on an equal protection theory that might have supported an alternative rationale for abortion rights even after overturning *Roe*.[56] Justice Ginsburg clearly foresaw this danger all along, as she made sex equality the centerpiece of her work on reproductive rights.

Both as a litigator and a jurist, Justice Ginsburg recognized that the gender stereotype she had long contested—that women are naturally suited to motherhood and have a primary duty to family life—leads directly to restrictions on abortion. Justice Ginsburg's most notable abortion opinion is her dissent in *Gonzales v. Carhart*, in which a slim majority of the Court upheld the federal statute (provocatively titled "The Partial Birth Abortion Act") banning a common late-term abortion procedure.[57] In Justice Kennedy's opinion for the Court, the woman-protective rationale that Justice Ginsburg had long railed against came home to roost. Justice Kennedy insisted, without empirical support, that women would come to regret their decision to have the procedure. On this view, women's natural affinity for motherhood leaves them vulnerable to psychological harm from abortion. The regret thesis rests upon the same stereotypical naturalization and reverence for motherhood that lies behind the sex-based classifications Justice Ginsburg spent her career dismantling. Justice Ginsburg's dissent skillfully exposed the archetypal views of motherhood lying at the heart of the Court's rationale. Behind restrictions on abortion are familiar, long-standing judgments about women's maternal roles and an insistence that women accede to motherhood's demands. The idealization of motherhood is a double-edged sword indeed.

Conclusion

Although Justice Ginsburg's jurisprudence on gender has been faulted for being tactically driven and insufficiently substantive, she was pre-scient in taking the long view. Pragmatic, yes, but formalistic, no. The skeptical approach to gender stereotyping at the heart of Justice Gins-burg's jurisprudence remains relevant to a modern vision of gender justice. In particular, Justice Ginsburg's linkage of sex equality with reproductive freedom is especially relevant at this moment, when *Dobbs* has opened the door to a cascade of reactionary new laws that deprive women of control over their reproductive lives. As Justice Ginsburg rec-ognized all along, there is no equality for women without reproductive freedom. We will never know whether, had Justice Ginsburg remained on the Court, she might have persuaded enough Justices to ground the abortion right in equal protection doctrine, or at least to keep the door open to this possibility. Surely she would have relished the opportunity to try.

NOTES

1 *See* Mary Becker, *Patriarchy and Inequality: Towards a Substantive Feminism*, 1999 U. CHI. LEGAL F. 21.

2 *See* Catharine A. MacKinnon, *Reflections on Sex Equality Under Law*, 100 YALE L.J. 1281, 1296–97 (1991) ("Until this model based on sameness and difference is rejected or cabined, sex equality law may find itself increasingly unable even to advance women into male preserves—defined as they are in terms of socially male values and biographies. . . . As a result, when sex inequality is most extreme . . . it drops off the sex inequality map."). In later writings, MacKinnon clarified that the fault lies with the Court's rendering of the theories advanced by Ruth Bader Gins-burg and not in her theories or arguments per se. *See* Catharine A. MacKinnon, *A Love Letter to Ruth Bader Ginsburg*, 31 WOMEN'S RTS. L. REP. 177, 181 (2010) ("The Supreme Court accepted only certain parts of those briefs—specifically, the abstract analysis that supported the conventional 'sameness' approach to equal-ity"); *id.* at 183 ("Knowing that gender hierarchy socially exists is what impels [Ginsburg's] gender neutrality as a legal solution, whether or not that understand-ing has impelled the Court's embrace of it.").

3 *See, e.g.*, Cary Franklin, *Inventing the Traditional Concept of Sex Discrimination*, 125 HARV. L. REV. 1307 (2011); Stephanie Bornstein, *Degendering the Law Through Stereotype Theory, in* THE OXFORD HANDBOOK ON FEMINISM AND LAW IN THE UNITED STATES (Oxford Univ. Press, Deborah L. Brake, Martha Chamallas & Verna Williams eds. forthcoming 2023).

4 *See* Naomi Schoenbaum, *The Case for Symmetry in Antidiscrimination Law*, 2017 WIS. L. REV. 69.

5 *Cf.* Ruth Bader Ginsburg, *Gender and the Constitution*, 44 U. CIN. L. REV. 1, 41–42 (1975) (discussing the persistence of the breadwinner/homemaker dichotomy).

6 420 U.S. 636 (1975).

7 Not all of the Justices were convinced. Califano v. Goldfarb, 430 U.S. 199, 239 (1977) (Rehnquist, J., dissenting).

8 *See* Martha Chamallas, *Deeping the Legal Understanding of Bias: On Devaluation and Biased Prototypes*, 74 S. CAL. L. REV. 747 (2001).

9 *See* Deborah Jones Merritt & Wendy Webster Williams, *Transcript of Interview of U.S. Supreme Court Associate Justice Ruth Bader Ginsburg, April 10, 2009*, 70 OHIO ST. L.J. 805, 814 (2009).

10 429 U.S. 190 (1976).

11 Amy Leigh Campbell, *Raising the Bar: Ruth Bader Ginsburg and the ACLU Women's Rights Project*, 11 TEX. J. WOMEN & L. 157, 237 (2003).

12 458 U.S. 718 (1982).

13 *Id.* at 728.

14 United States v. Virginia, 518 U.S. 515 (1996).

15 *See generally* ANN C. McGINLEY, MASCULINITY AT WORK: EMPLOYMENT DISCRIMINATION THROUGH A DIFFERENT LENS (2016); MASCULINITIES & THE LAW: A MULTIDIMENSIONAL APPROACH (Frank Rudy Cooper & Ann C. McGinley eds. 2012).

16 *See* Martha Chamallas, *Exploring the "Entire Spectrum" of Disparate Treatment Under Title VII: Rules Governing Predominantly Female Jobs*, 1984 U. ILL. L. REV. 1, 9.

17 Franklin, *Inventing the Traditional Concept*, at 84–87.

18 *See* Martha Chamallas, *Of Glass Ceilings, Sex Stereotypes and Mixed Motives, in* WOMEN AND LAW STORIES (Elizabeth M. Schneider & Stephanie M. Wildman eds. 2011) (discussing gender stereotyping theory as a precursor to postmodern feminist theorizing on gender).

19 140 S. Ct. 1731 (2020).

20 *See* Bornstein, *Degendering the Law*.

21 *Virginia*, 518 U.S. at 553. *See also id.* at 532 n.6 (stating that the Court has "thus far reserved most stringent judicial scrutiny for classifications based on race or national origin," leaving open the possibility that it might yet extend strict scrutiny to sex); Harris v. Forklift Systems, 510 U.S. 17, 25–26 n.1 (1993) (Ginsburg, J., concurring) (stating that Title VII requires the same analysis for sex and race discrimination and observing: "Indeed, even under the Court's equal protec-

tion jurisprudence, which requires 'an exceedingly persuasive justification' for a gender-based classification, it remains an open question whether 'classifications based upon gender are inherently suspect.'") (citations omitted).

22 *See* Reva B. Siegel, *She the People: The Nineteenth Amendment, Sex Equality, Federalism, and the Family*, 115 HARV. L. REV. 945 (2002).

23 400 U.S. 542 (1971).

24 Martha Chamallas, *Mothers and Disparate Treatment: The Ghost of Martin Marietta*, 44 VILL. L. REV. 337, 341 (1999).

25 *Id.* at 347–48.

26 Ruth Bader Ginsburg & Barbara Flagg, *Some Reflections on the Feminist Legal Thought of the 1970's*, 1989 U. CHI. LEGAL FORUM 9.

27 *Virginia*, 518 U.S. at 533–34 (citations omitted).

28 416 U.S. 351 (1974).

29 *Id.* at 355.

30 Brief for Appellants at 31, Kahn v. Shevin, 416 U.S. 351 (1974) (No. 73–78), 1973 WL 172384.

31 *Id.*

32 419 U.S. 498 (1975).

33 Ruth Bader Ginsburg, *Gender in the Supreme Court: The 1973 and 1974 Terms*, 1975 S. CT. REV. 1, 4 (1975).

34 *Id.* at 7; Ruth Bader Ginsburg, *Sexual Equality Under the Fourteenth and Equal Rights Amendments*, 1979 WASH. U. L.Q. 161, 165–66 (criticizing the *Ballard* decision for leaving undisturbed the underlying discrimination against women in the military).

35 *See* JANE SHERRON DE HART, RUTH BADER GINSBURG: A LIFE 264 (2020).

36 *See, e.g.*, Gratz v. Bollinger, 539 U.S. 244, 298 (2003) (Ginsburg, J., dissenting).

37 137 S. Ct. 1678 (2017).

38 Justice Ginsburg dissented from the Court's ruling in two prior cases upholding differently formulated statutory preferences for citizen mothers in the conferral of citizenship on children born overseas. *See* Nguyen v. INS, 533 U.S. 53 (2001); Miller v. Albright, 523 U.S. 420 (1998).

39 Ruth Bader Ginsburg, *Some Thoughts on Judicial Authority to Repair Unconstitutional Legislation*, 28 CLEV. ST. L. REV. 301, 318–19, 323–24 (1979).

40 For a discussion of how leveling down can exacerbate, rather than remedy, the harms of inequality, see Deborah L. Brake, *When Equality Leaves Everyone Worse Off: The Problem of Leveling Down in Equality Law*, 46 WM. & MARY L. REV. 513 (2004); Tracy Thomas, *Leveling Down Gender Equality*, 42 HARV. J. LAW & GENDER 177 (2019). *See also* Rebecca Aviel, *Rights as a Zero-Sum Game*, 61 ARIZ. L. REV. 351 (2019) (arguing that leveling down weakens public support for equality rights).

41 550 U.S. 618, 643 (2007) (Ginsburg, J., dissenting).

42 Lilly Ledbetter Fair Pay Act of 2009, Pub. L. No. 111–2, 123 Stat. 5 (2009).

43 *See* Sally Kenney, *Backlash Against Feminism: Rethinking a Loaded Concept, in* THE OXFORD HANDBOOK OF FEMINISM AND LAW IN THE UNITED STATES (Oxford Univ. Press, Deborah L. Brake Martha Chamallas & Verna Williams eds. forthcoming 2023).

44 *See* Martha Chamallas, *Past as Prologue: Old and New Feminisms*, 17 MICH. J. GENDER & L. 157, 160 (2010) (describing Justice Ginsburg's *Ledbetter* dissent as "her finest hour").

45 Cleveland Bd. of Educ. v. LaFleur, 414 U.S. 632 (1974) (invalidating Ohio school board rule requiring pregnant teachers to take a leave of absence).

46 *See* Aryeh Neier, *How Ruth Bader Ginsburg Got Her Start at the ACLU*, ACLU. ORG, www.aclu.org.

47 460 F.2d 1372 (9th Cir. 1972).

48 *See* Olivia B. Waxman, *Ruth Bader Ginsburg Wishes This Case Had Legalized Abortion Instead of* Roe v. Wade, TIME MAG., Aug. 2, 2018, www.yahoo.com.

49 Cary Franklin, *The Anti-Stereotyping Principle in Constitutional Sex Discrimination Law*, 85 N.Y.U. L. REV. 83, 84, 162 (2010).

50 417 U.S. 484 (1974).

51 566 U.S. 30, 45 (2012) (Ginsburg, J., dissenting).

52 *Id.* at 65.

53 556 U.S. 701 (2009).

54 *Id.* at 718 (Ginsburg, J., dissenting).

55 142 S. Ct. 2228 (2022).

56 *Id.* at 2246 (citing and quoting from *Geduldig* for the proposition that "[t]he regulation of a medical procedure that only one sex can undergo does not trigger heightened constitutional scrutiny unless the regulation is a "mere pretex[t] designed to effect an invidious discrimination against members of one sex or the other").

57 550 U.S. 124, 169 (2007) (Ginsburg, J., dissenting).

2

Administrative Law

The Feminist State(s) of Ruth Bader Ginsburg

KALI MURRAY

It is a truism that the sparkly, glittery persona of her later years as "The Notorious R.B.G." obscures the ways in which Justice Ruth Bader Ginsburg was a traditional appellate judge. Indeed, an initial review of her administrative law opinions exhibits a kind of conservatism. Ginsburg appears to have accepted the theoretical claim that the administrative state is legitimated through the expertise of agency actors in her opinions that directly address core administrative law doctrine. For example, when she utilized the *Chevron*[1] framework, she did not question the parameters of the doctrine; in fact, she frequently offered significant deference to agency interpretations based on statutory authority.[2]

Even in areas of controversy, Ginsburg often applied the precedent as it was already presented in a given matter. For example, during her tenure on the United States Court of Appeals for the District of Columbia Circuit, Ginsburg, writing for the majority in *Schor v. Commodity Futures Trade Commission*,[3] held that the Commodity Futures Trade Commission, an administrative agency, had no authority to entertain common-law contract and tort claims when it examined trading disputes. In an opinion[4] that was overturned by the Supreme Court, Ginsburg adhered to the controversial textual framework of *Northern Pipeline Construction Co. v. Marathon Pipe Line Co.*,[5] which stated that the text of Article III of the Constitution demanded that significant restraints be placed on the ability of Congress to assign what had typically been adjudicative power to administrative agencies. Ginsburg's opinion in *Schor* is a template to her jurisprudence in administrative law. She carefully applied the precedent before her, attentive not to roil the constitutional waters. In this, Justice Ginsburg's approach to administrative law sharply contrasted with other Justices during her tenure. Recent administrative law has been blessed (or cursed?) with any number of Justices, among them Justices Antonin Scalia, Stephen Breyer, and Elena Kagan, who have substantial expertise and interest in its doctrinal formation. Ginsburg's seeming jurisprudential caution in administrative law seems unique for modern constitutional law.

This chapter, however, contends that, despite this caution, we can look outside of "administrative law" writ small and instead use a number of other types of evidence—her constitutional law jurisprudence, her series of briefs before the Supreme Court during her work as a self-consciously feminist lawyer, and her scholarship on the roles of Congress within the political order—to see the ways in which Ginsburg's jurisprudence offers an absolutely vital insight into a subject that does not often receive significant attention in administrative law: the question of the state within feminist theory. Modern administrative theory and law often presume, without question, the rationality of the state; feminist theory (and other critical theory) must grapple with the ways in which the state *might not be rational* at all. Thus, the project of feminist theory in administrative law is often twofold: first, the state must be tested for its rationality; and second, the state must reconstruct itself as a rational actor.

The administrative law jurisprudence of Ruth Bader Ginsburg can be seen in a different light when it is connected to a larger project of conceiving the (feminist) state from a normative perspective. Ginsburg's contribution to administrative law emerges when we see how she engaged with the fundamental problem of the state, both in her challenge to its rationality and its reconstitution through active interplay among social movements, legislatures, and judges. The first section of this chapter outlines the feminist project of reconceiving the administrative state in both micro-level and macro-level models. The second section explores how the administrative law jurisprudence of Ruth Bader Ginsburg reflects and furthers the debate of the feminist project in two ways: by reframing the individual before the state, and by reconceiving the role of Congress within the administrative state. A brief concluding section summarizes these issues in perspective.

Feminist State(s)

Feminist theory has always contemplated what governance would look like in an ideal state. For instance, Charlotte Perkins Gilman in her utopian novel *Herland*[6] envisioned a governing system composed of all female councils organized at the local level. These local councils, when confronted with a decision, would sit down together and come to a decision through extensive conversation.[7] Any decision of the local council could then be appealed to the High Council, which Gilman described as being "held among the wisest of them all."[8]

Gilman's concept of such state-making through council prefigures two key elements that would preoccupy Ginsburg in her contributions to administrative theory. Gilman boldly specified that her ideal state places a new set of actors—women—leading the political decision-making. We might pass this over very quickly today; but in 1915, writing "imagining a world where they [women] ran the whole government [was] radical, provocative and inspiring."[9] Gilman's interest in how individual women engaged in the state is an example of what I have termed elsewhere "micro-level administrative law," which is "interested in how the law shapes an individual's encounters with agencies of the administrative state."[10] Second, Gilman was also interested in what I have termed elsewhere "macro-level administrative law,"[11] "which concerns itself with examining macro-level relationships between agencies and the legislative, executive, and judicial branches of government."[12] The female council becomes the site of state action because of the institutional nature of its conversations. Indeed, Gilman predicted what would become a central feature of feminist practice, the work of "consciousness raising," which held as its ideal the expectation that conversations would lead to a reformation of individual and political conceptions of femininity, becoming the basis of state practice.

Gilman's work prefigures how modern feminist theory offers new ways to engage with *micro-level* and *macro-level* models of administrative law. This section first considers how feminist theory conceives of micro-level relations between the state and the individual, then considers how feminist theory conceives of macro-level administrative law—the appropriate set of institutional relations between agencies and the legislative, executive, and judicial branches. In examining how modern feminist theory can be used to engage with micro-level and macro-level administrative, this section considers how adding the lens of gender can help to illuminate theoretical challenges associated with both models. Linda Brush, in *Gender and Governance*,[13] produced a syncretic summary of these important strands of feminist theory by taking what she called a "gender lens" perspective. Brush contended that we should view states and social policies through two distinct lenses: what she terms the "governance of gender" and the "gender of governance."[14] These two gender lenses are useful mechanisms of categorization within administrative law, as they map comfortably with administrative law as it is constructed as micro and macro levels and further offer utility in understanding a feminist theory of the state from a descriptive perspective because these lenses offer a way to reconcile different competing theories.

Micro-level administrative law grapples with the fundamental question: how should the individual stand before the state? The intersection between self and statehood is prototypically a concern of micro-level administrative law insofar as it attempts to map the relationship between the individual self and the state.

Feminist theory complicates this question by highlighting how central gender is to how an individual engages with the state. Linda Brush named this process the "governance of gender," which describes "the ways states and social policies set the rules and circumstances under which we become women and men and accept or reject the different and unequal life chances assigned to us."[15] The administrative state can assign gender identity through often unremarked acts such as the issuance of birth certificates, marriage certificates, and driver's licenses. The private curation of self is thus interpenetrated by the state curation of self. Additionally, the state can also intersect with other social contexts in which gender identity is formed, including social contexts that maintain selfhood, a sacred identity and sacred rituals, and family structures. The state can reinforce the governmentality of other sites of governance by the surveying of population dynamics or the surveillance of productive capacity.[16] Thus, the state is jointed with other acts of *governmentality* over gender, thereby making the exercise of gendered power "a positive social presence that operates in all aspects of life and exerts itself in all directions, creating a variety of different relationships other than those

within the domination-subordination dynamic of traditional conceptions."[17] The intertwining of the state with other areas of gendered governmentality may compromise the rationality of the state actor, given a
social commitment to imposing a patriarchal order over women. Catharine MacKinnon, the most prominent theorist of this claim, contends
this intertwining of the state means "[t]he law sees and treats women the
way men see and treat women . . . and [thus], the liberal state coercively
and authoritatively constitutes the social order in the interest of men as a
gender, through its legitimating norms, relation to society, and substantive policies."[18]

In contrast to micro-level administrative law, macro-level administrative law is concerned with how the law legitimates the exercise of
bureaucratic mechanisms. Thus, a macro-level perspective would consider how the state itself internalizes gender roles into its intramural
institutional dynamics. Linda Brush termed this lens the "gender of governance," which interrogates "the variable degree to which assumptions
about masculinity and femininity, male privilege and female penalty,
structure the logic, determine the personnel, influence the budget, and
otherwise organize the institutions and practices of the state."[19] The gender of governance lens consequently maps onto the concerns of macro-
level administrative law because it is concerned with how relationships
function between different formal and informal dimensions within the
administrative state. The gender of governance also suggests that the
state legitimates itself because it is a site of conflict over differing conceptions of gender and the subsequent social policies that emerge from
the state. A state can legitimate itself by paying close attention to the
ways in which informal sites of governance, and formal sites of government, work together to produce political meaning within a given society.
This feminist idea of state is less methodologically coherent than the
other visions, since contours of this theory are explored in different dis-
ciplines including law, philosophy, and social science.[20] Consequently,
this feminist perspective seeks to interrogate the disciplinary ways in
which concepts, including those that are related to gender, are governed
at formal and informal sites. The state draws power from its simultaneous ability to produce bureaucratic actions, maintain the gendered
status of its citizens, and serve as a forum where contested meanings of
gender are debated.

The Feminist Administrative State(s) of Ruth Bader Ginsburg

Understanding the pivotal contributions of Ruth Bader Ginsburg to administrative law arises when her jurisprudence is situated against feminist theory and its reexamination of the state in law. This section first considers how her career in activism in the 1970s was deeply involved in exposing the governance of gender from a micro-level perspective. It then considers how her administrative law jurisprudence offers a different way to conceive of Congress's legitimation within a structural conception of the administrative state.

The Individual Stands Before the State: RBG'S Rhetoric of Individuality Before the State

A core assumption of micro-level administrative law is to manage the ways that an individual stands before the state; Ruth Bader Ginsburg's obvious contribution to micro-level administrative law was her steady work of challenging the gender classifications made by the state between 1970 and 1980.[21]

Other chapters in this book discuss this fertile period of work, but this chapter isolates her work in uncovering the ways in which the state curation of identity interfered with the individual curation of female identity. In this element of her work (like in many other areas), Ruth Bader Ginsburg served to popularize the foundational contribution of Pauli Murray by actualizing the ways in which the state curation of the feminine self interfered with the individual curation of the feminine self.[22]

Ginsburg's creative theoretical praxis in the 1970s was built on the groundbreaking article by Pauli Murray and Mary Eastwood titled "Jane Crow and the Law."[23] In the article, Murray and Eastwood described two key assumptions that need to be challenged before one can "attempt[] to formulate any principle of equal protections of the laws."[24] The first assumption was that equal rights for women would be tantamount to seeking "identical treatment with men."[25] Instead, Murray and Eastwood maintained that women as individuals seek "equality of opportunity" without "barriers built upon the myth of a stereotyped women" and "freed of choice to develop their maternal and familial functions primarily, or to develop different capacities at different stages of life, or to pursue some combination of these choices."[26] The second assumption was that the inherent difference between men and women did not imply "inequality or inferiority" but "made necessary the application of different principles to women than to minority groups."[27] Murray and Eastwood also challenged that assumption, arguing that "[w]hen the law distinguishes between 'the two great classes of men and women,' gives men a preferred position by accepted social standards, and regulates the conduct of women in a restrictive manner having no bearing on the maternal function, it disregards individuality and relegates an entire class to inferior status."[28] Murray and Eastwood's assertation of feminine individuality was necessary to an understanding of equality because it is a fundamental recognition of personhood, which is a prerequisite of citizenship.[29]

Ginsburg's work in the 1970s can be seen as a crucial elaboration of Murray and Eastwood's two key assumptions that, for a claim of equality to be made in a constitutional sense, the compromised state curation of feminine identity had to be dismantled. Ginsburg employed two strategies to break this compromised state curation of feminine identity. First, she repeatedly invoked the idea that state claims as to female identity were "myths" or "lore."[30] For example, her amicus brief in *Craig v. Boren*[31] contended:

> This case involves more than an impermissible sex/age differential. It also involves the lore relating to women and liquor—a combination that has fascinated lawmen for generations. The legislation at issue is a manifestation, with a bizarre twist, of the erstwhile propensity of legislatures to prescribe the conditions under which women and alcohol may mix. In recent years, however, outside Oklahoma, such legislation has been relegated to history's scrap heap.[32]

Focus on the persuasive language of irrationality in *Craig*: "lore," "fascinated," "manifestation," "bizarre," "propensity." Ginsburg's repetition of the truly bizarre undermines the states' claim to a rational curation of female identity; indeed, it sets up a new binary: the irrational state versus the rational woman.

The making of the rational woman was itself a radical act. Law and politics often presumed that women lacked the rationality to be considered capable of legal decision-making. A famous case that rendered a woman an irrational actor is *In re Strittmater's Estate*,[33] in which the court determined that a woman was acting under an insane delusion because she gifted her estate to the National Woman's Party (an organization that advocated for the passage of the Nineteenth Amendment and the Equal Rights Amendment). *Strittmater* makes the belief in a feminist state itself evidence of irrationality.

Second, Ginsburg repeatedly attacked the state curation of female identity by deploying once again the rationality of the state, through its use of stereotypes to classify men and women through the law. For example, in *Kahn v. Shevin*,[34] Ginsburg attacked the utility of granting property tax exemptions to widows but not to widowers by noting that granting "property tax exemptions to widows but not to widowers[] reflects a familiar stereotyping of sex roles: a woman left alone by the death of her husband is thought economically disabled; a man is believed to suffer scant financial loss upon the death of his wife, and even to be relieved of the burden of supporting her."[35] Ginsburg's deployment of a stereotype differed from her invocation of myth or lore; stereotypes are not necessarily de facto irrational. Rather, the state use of stereotypes[36] obscures the individuality of a woman who can support herself and the man who cannot support himself.[37] Ginsburg's rhetorical deployment of myths and stereotypes should be understood as a strategic choice: if state curation of identity rests on its own problematic assumptions, then a fundamental part of equality is the ability of individuals to define themselves on their own terms.

Ginsburg's contribution to micro-level administrative law is often poorly understood. This perception, of course, is based on the fact that her appellate work in the 1970s primarily raised constitutional grounds rather than administrative grounds. However, to the extent that Ginsburg sensitively explored how state curation of female identify rested on irrational grounds, her advocacy needs to be incorporated more fully into mainstream administrative law scholarship.

The Interplay of the Administrative State

A primary claim of macro-level administrative law is that the legitimacy of the administrative state rests on the role played by Congress in delegating its lawmaking authority to an administrative agency. If, however, we deploy the gender of governance lens, Ruth Bader Ginsburg's administrative law jurisprudence also suggests that Congress draws its legitimacy in the administrative state because Congress itself needs to be understood as a site of conflict over differing conceptions of gender and the subsequent state curations of identities that flow from them.

The crucial term to understand RBG's approach to administrative law is "interplay." That is, she viewed the process of coming to a political consensus on difficult issues as a shared process between social movements ("the people") and what she termed the "political branches" (Congress, the president, and courts).[38] This view is most famously expressed in her conclusion that *Roe v. Wade*[39] was wrongly decided on a medical framework rather than on a sex-equality framework. After reviewing the events that led to *Roe*,[40] Ginsburg concluded that "[t]he political process was moving in the early 1970s, not swiftly enough for advocates of quick, complete change[,] but majoritarian institutions were listening and acting. Heavy-handed judicial intervention was difficult to justify and appears to have provoked, not resolved conflict."[41] Ginsburg's interplay is a way to capture and disrupt a separation of powers framework that is typically used in constitutional theory, which maintains that constitutional change must be managed through a careful balance among the three branches.

Her interplay framework interposes an additional actor: the advocate, who inspires constitutional change through activism. The relationship between informal actors and formal institutions is therefore dynamic insofar as political institutions are constantly shifting between formal and informal modes. Ginsburg's understanding of the importance of interplay between different institutional entities appears to have had an impact on her views of administrative law in two key respects.

First, Ginsburg emphasized the primacy of Congress in establishing the institutional goals of the administrative state. Ginsburg's deference to Congress within administrative law is unusual, but it is consistent in several ways. For instance, Ginsburg argued for significant deference to the use of broad standards enacted through congressional language.[42]

A typical case in which Ginsburg asserted congressional primacy was *Digital Realty Trust Inc. v. Somers*, in which the Supreme Court considered whether a whistleblower who failed to report a claim to the Securities and Exchange Commission (SEC) had recourse to the antiretaliation provisions of the 2010 Dodd–Frank Wall Street Reform and Consumer Protection Act (Dodd-Frank Act).[43] In her majority opinion, Ginsburg stated that a whistleblower had to report a claim to the SEC in order to claim protections associated with the antiretaliation provisions of the Dodd-Frank Act. This framed the opinion in light of what Ginsburg characterized as a set of choices made by Congress in response to the financial crisis of 2008. Namely, Congress identified a problem of employment discrimination related to whistleblowers,[44] Congress included clear definitional language that limited the scope of the Dodd-Frank antiretaliation provisions to a whistleblower who had reported to the SEC,[45] and Congress identified the SEC as the agency to regulate within this particular area.[46] Although the litigant was attacking the regulations issued by the agency, Congress became the dominant player in *Digital Realty*.

Second, Ginsburg encouraged a dialogic relationship between the political branches and the judiciary. In a law review article titled "The Intercircuit Committee,"[47] Ginsburg argued that Congress, instead of establishing a new secondary national court specifically to address circuit splits not taken up by the Supreme Court, should instead develop an Intercircuit Committee that could take a "legislative second look" at issues that have emerged. Ginsburg and co-author Peter Huber argued that a legislative Intercircuit Committee offered significant advantages over an additional appellate court for two key reasons. First, the membership of the Committee could be varied to include members of Congress, retired judges, law professors, and other public officials. With its broader membership, this committee could more swiftly respond to emerging circuit splits than the slower judicial branch.[48] Second, the committee would serve as a "gap filler; its business would examine court decisions construing federal statutes and to draft bills to resolve actual or potential conflicts."[49] Initially, Ginsburg and Huber's solution signals once again Ginsburg's placement of Congress as the primary mover within the administrative state. Moreover, it suggests once again her commitment to dynamic lawmaking insofar as the committee's heterogeneous composition would make it likely to be both more representative and responsive to shifting interpretations of the law.

Ginsburg's ongoing commitment to the concept of interplay between social movements, the political branches, and the judiciary should be explicitly connected to a gendered construction of the state: the governance of gender. Particularly, Ginsburg's (somewhat) instinctual approach is consistent with what Teresa Kulawik[50] identified as a "feminist discursive institutionalism." Ginsburg's administrative law jurisprudence "conceives of gender as a relevant analytical factor";[51] which supports a view that "the intersections between public and private are taken seriously";[52] sees "social and political orders as relational networks and temporal processes";[53] and interprets governance as "a mode of ruling to which discursive political process and knowledge production are central."[54] Uncovering Ginsburg's feminist predilections, then, invigorates our understanding of her administrative law commitments.

Conclusion

The totality of Ruth Bader Ginsburg's contributions to the development of law in the United States is still being considered. This chapter is a start in an assessment, first of Ruth Bader Ginsburg's contribution to administrative law, and second its relationship to a feminist theory of the state.

Why is this important? Initially, Ginsburg's connections to feminist theory writ large are often poorly understood. To connect her with feminism's larger project, however, illuminates the important role she granted in her jurisprudence to promoting feminine individuality as a necessary precondition to the full citizenship of women. Moreover, Ginsburg's contributions to the broader question of how to conceive of the feminist (states) helps to generate further questions. How should the law conceive of the interplay between the state and informal actors? How should the law incorporate this interplay into its formal dimensions? If the feminist state is built through discourse, what are the benefits and, more important, the limits of discursive legitimation?

To conclude, Ginsburg's jurisprudential treatment of the state is an important one. Ultimately, for Ginsburg the state must not act in ways that interfere with the fundamental project of female individuality and autonomy. To reference Vivian Gornick in her examination of "The Solitude of Self," Elizabeth Cady Stanton's last speech, we must give women the means to participate in every part of life, because as much as women would like "to be protected and supported, not how men desire to have them do so, they must make the voyage of life alone."[55]

NOTES

1 Chevron, U.S.A., Inc. v. Nat. Res. Def. Council, Inc., 467 U.S. 837, 839–40 (1984).

2 A review of Justice Ginsburg's decisions under the *Chevron* framework reflects a relatively deferential view to agency interpretations. Dig. Realty Trust, Inc. v. Somers, 138 S. Ct. 767, 782 (2018) (holding under *Chevron* framework, the statutory language was clear and therefore, deference was not owed); Mellouli v. Lynch, 135 S. Ct. 1980, 1985 (2015) (interpretation is not owed deference under *Chevron* because it would undermine regulatory scheme); E.P.A. v. EME Homer City Generation, LP, 572 U.S. 489, 514 (2014) (upholding agency interpretation of statute); Sebelius v. Auburn Med. Ctr., 568 U.S. 145, 157 (2013) (upholding agency interpretation of statute under *Chevron*); Watters v. Wachovia Bank, N.A., 550 U.S. 1, 41 (2007) (agency acted outside the scope of *Chevron* framework); Alaska Dep't of Env't Conservation v. E.P.A., 540 U.S. 461, 468 (2004) (applying *Skidmore* deference to agency interpretation issued in a manual); Lopez v. Davis, 531 U.S. 230, 242 (2001) (upholding agency interpretation of statute under *Chevron* framework); Regions Hosp. v. Shalala, 522 U.S. 448, 457–64 (1998) (upholding agency interpretation of statute under *Chevron* framework); U.S. v. O'Hagan, 521 U.S. 642, 675–76 (1997) (upholding agency interpretation of statute under *Chevron* framework); Holly Farm Corp. v. N.L.R.B., 517 U.S. 392, 403 (1996) (upholding agency interpretation of statute under *Chevron* framework); NationsBank of North Carolina, N.A., v. Variable Annuity Life Ins. Co., 513 U.S. 251, 263 (1995) (upholding agency interpretation of statute under *Chevron* framework).

3 Schor v. Commodity Futures Trading Comm'n, 740 F.2d 1262, 1264 (D.C. Cir. 1984), *cert. granted, judgment vacated sub nom.* Conticommodity Servs., Inc. v. Schor, 473 U.S. 922 (1985), and *cert. granted, judgment vacated*, 473 U.S. 922 (1985).

4 *Id.* at 1269–74.

5 Northern Pipeline Constr. Co. v. Marathon Pipe Line Co., 458 U.S. 50 (1982).

6 CHARLOTTE PERKINS GILMAN, HERLAND (1915).

7 *Id.* at 19–20

8 *Id.* at 256.

9 Desirina Boskovich, *Early Feminist Utopias, from Gilman's Herland to Rokeya's Sultana Dream*, in LOST TRANSMISSION: THE SECRET HISTORY OF SCIENCE FICTION AND FANTASY 14 (Desirina Boskovich ed. 2019).

10 Kali Murray, *Charles Reich's Unruly Administrative Law*, 129 YALE L.J. FORUM 714, 716 (March 16, 2020).

11 *Id.*

12 *Id.*

13 LINDA BRUSH, GENDER AND GOVERNANCE 34–35 (2003).

14 *Id.*

15 *Id.*

16 *Id.* at 35.

17 Vanessa Munro, *On Power and Domination: Feminist and the Final Foucault*, 2 EUR. J. OF POL. THEORY 79, 82 (2003).

18 Catharine MacKinnon, *Feminism, Marxism, Method and the State: Towards a Feminist Jurisprudence*, 8 SIGNS 635, 644 (1983).

19 BRUSH, GENDER AND GOVERNANCE at 34–35.

20 Kali Murray & Esther van Zimmeren, *Dynamic Patent Governance in Europe and the United States: The* Myriad *Example*, 19 CARDOZO J. INT'L & COMP. L. 287, 297–313 (2011) (examining formal and informal dimensions in patent governance); Deborah Rhode, *Feminism and the State*, 107 HARV. L. REV. 1181, 1191–92 (1994) (examining the institutional policy agenda on a range of issues); Nancy Fraser, *Rethinking the Public Sphere: A Contribution to the Critique of Actually Existing Democracy*, 25 SOCIAL TEXT 56–80 (1990) (explaining the Habermasian critique of the public sphere and offering a feminist re-reading of the same).

21 For a through description of Ginsburg's work during this period, *see* Amy Leigh Campbell, *Raising the Bar: Ruth Bader Ginsburg and the ACLU Women's Rights Project*, 11 TEX. J. WOMEN & L. 157 (2002).

22 KALI MURRAY, A POLITICS OF PATENT LAW: CRAFTING THE PARTICIPATORY PATENT BARGAIN 103 (2013) (examining the role of praxis, the relationship between law craft, ideology, and social movements in creating change through the participatory patent bargain).

23 Pauli Murray & Mary O. Eastwood, *Jane Crow and the Law: Sex Discrimination and Title VII*, 34 GEO. WASH. L. REV. 232 (1965).

24 *Id.* at 239.

25 *Id.*

26 *Id.*

27 *Id.*

28 *Id.*

29 Nicole Gombay, *"There are mentalities that need changing": Constructing Personhood, Formulating Citizenship, and Performing Subjectivities on a Settler Colonial Frontier*, 48 POL. GEOGRAPHY 11, 13 (2015) ("One must first be deemed a person before being deemed a citizen, which, in turn, gives individuals access to specific resources. Since understandings of both personhood and citizenship can shift, so too do the resources to which one has access.").

30 *See, e.g.*, Reply Brief of Appellant at 2–3, Reed v. Reed, 404 U.S. 71 (1971) (No. 70–4), 1971 WL 133598 ("The *myth* that women are inherently disqualified for full participation in public life as independent persons is no longer acceptable. Yet this Court's silence has deferred recognition by the law that women are full persons, entitled as men are to due process guarantees and the equal protection of the laws. The time to break the vicious cycle which sex discriminatory laws create is overdue. If a legislature can bar a woman from service as a fiduciary on the basis of once popular, but never proved, assumptions that women are less qualified than men are to perform such services, then the *myth* becomes insulated from attack, because the law deprives women of the opportunity to prove it false.").

31 Craig v. Boren, 429 U.S. 190 (1976).

32 Motion of the American Civil Liberties Union for Leave to File Brief Amicus Curiae and Brief Amicus Curiae, Craig v. Boren, 429 U.S. 190 (1976) (No. 75–628), 1976 WL 181333, *18.

33 In re Strittmater's Estate, 53 A.2d 205 (N.J. Ct. App. 1947).

34 Kahn v. Shevin, 416 U.S. 351 (1974).

35 Brief for Appellants, Kahn v. Shevin, 416 U.S. 351 (1974) (No. 73–78), 1973 WL 172384, *4; Brief for Appellees, Edwards v. Healy, 421 U.S. 772 (1975) (No. 73–759), 1974 WL 185825, *12 ("In *Reed v. Reed*, and *Frontiero v. Richardson*, this Court declined to perpetuate approval of legislative line-drawing based on gross generalization about the roles of men and women in the community. In *Reed*, the apparent premise of the legislature was that, in general, men have more business experience than women. *Frontiero* concerned, as this case does, the assumption that women are destined for the care of husbands, home and children, men for participation in the world outside the home. *Hoyt* rested on a lump judgment of the same order, that 'woman is still regarded as the center of home and family life.' Because the decision in *Hoyt* is impossible to reconcile with the new direction signaled in *Reed* and *Frontiero*, the court below determined that it was not obliged to follow 'the outgrown dogma.' State tax classifications apart, it is now plain that similarly situated adult men and women are constitutionally entitled to evenhanded treatment by the law, and that 'it is manifestly unfair to indulge in generalities when speaking of women, which no one would think of using when referring to men.'") (internal citations omitted).

36 Lawrence Blum, *Stereotypes and Stereotyping: A Moral Analysis*, 33 PHIL. PAPERS 272–73 (2004).

37 Brief for Appellants, Kahn v. Shevin, 416 U.S. 351 (1974) (No. 73–78), 1973 WL 172384, *5–6.

38 Ruth Bader Ginsburg, *On Women Becoming Part of the Constitution*, 6 MINN. J. OF LAW & INEQUALITY 7, 25 (1988).

39 Roe v. Wade, 410 U.S. 113 (1973).

40 Ruth Bader Ginsburg, *Some Thoughts on Autonomy and Equality in Relation to Roe v. Wade*, 63 N.C. L. REV. 375 (1985).

41 *Id.* at 385–86.

42 *See, e.g.*, Alaska Dept. of Env't Conservation v. EPA, 540 U.S. 461, 484 (2004) (Ginsburg, J.) (interpreting Environmental Protection Agency's authority in light of the "notably capacious terms" contained in its authorizing statute).

43 Dig. Realty Trust v. Somers, 138 S. Ct. 767 (2018).

44 *Id.* at 774 ("Congress sought to protect whistleblowers from employment discrimination.").

45 *Id.* at 777 ("Congress placed a government-reporting requirement in § 78u–6(h), but not elsewhere in the same statute. Courts are not at liberty to dispense with the condition—tell the SEC—Congress imposed.").

46 *Id.* ("Congress authorized the SEC 'to issue such rules and regulations as may be necessary or appropriate to implement the provisions of [§ 78u–6] consistent with the purposes of this section.' § 78u-6(j).").

47 Ruth Bader Ginsburg & Peter W. Huber, *The Intercircuit Committee*, 100 HARV. L. REV. 1417 (1987).

48 *Id.* at 1433

49 *Id.* at 1432.

50 Teresa Kulawik, *Staking the Frame of a Feminist Discursive Institutionalism*, 5 POL. OF GENDER 262–63 (2009).

51 *Id.* at 262.

52 *Id.*

53 *Id.*

54 *Id.*

55 VIVIAN GORNICK, UNFINISHED BUSINESS: NOTES OF A CHRONIC RE-READER 98–99 (2020) (assessment of Elizabeth Cady Stanton's "The Solitude of Self").

3

Arbitration

Consent, Not Coercion

JILL I. GROSS

It is no secret that the modern Supreme Court loves arbitration, both as a docket-cleaner and an efficient dispute resolution process. Justice Ruth Bader Ginsburg did, too, but only when it resulted from parties' freely given consent to opt out of litigation and instead use arbitration to resolve a dispute. Throughout her years on the Court, Justice Ginsburg respected arbitrator decision-making and interpreted the Federal Arbitration Act (FAA)[1] to strictly limit judicial intervention in arbitration processes. As the years went by, however, she grew increasingly disillusioned with arbitration when parties with weaker bargaining power were forced to arbitrate pursuant to an adhesive arbitration agreement.

In arbitration, parties consent to submit their dispute to a third-party neutral who hears from all parties and imposes a binding decision, or award, on the disputants.[2] Fundamentally, arbitrators derive their authority to impose an outcome from the parties' consent to "trade[] the procedures and opportunity for review of the courtroom for the simplicity, informality, and expedition of arbitration."[3] Courts will review arbitrators' awards only on very limited grounds and typically only when a losing party demonstrates fundamental unfairness in the process.

Americans have used arbitration to resolve commercial disputes since the founding of the country. In 1925, Congress enacted the FAA to reverse judicial hostility to enforcing arbitration agreements by deeming them "valid, irrevocable and enforceable" absent a successful common law–based challenge to the enforceability of any contract.[4] Since the 1980s, the Supreme Court has interpreted the FAA to reflect a "national policy favoring arbitration" and has enforced arbitration agreements as written.[5] The Court also has held that, pursuant to the U.S. Constitution's

Supremacy Clause, the FAA applies in state as well as federal courts and preempts any conflicting state law or rule that either singles out arbitration agreements for special treatment or disfavors arbitration as a means to resolve disputes (this is known as the "FAA preemption doctrine").[6]

During her twenty-seven years on the Supreme Court, Justice Ginsburg authored thirteen opinions involving arbitration or interpreting various sections of the FAA.[7] During her first sixteen years, she authored five majority opinions, one concurrence, and one opinion concurring in part and dissenting in part. These opinions reflect her well-known academic passion for civil procedure, her endorsement of arbitration, and her support of the FAA, including the Court's FAA preemption doctrine.[8] In contrast, during her final decade on the Court, Justice Ginsburg authored five (and joined other) dissenting opinions and one concurring opinion, all of which sharply criticized the Court's expansive interpretation of the FAA to validate adhesive predispute arbitration agreements in the consumer and employment settings, especially when coupled with a class action waiver.

This chapter explores Justice Ginsburg's chronological move from majority opinion author to strident dissenter when interpreting the FAA. In some ways, the move reflected broader ideological shifts on the Court. However, her evolution cannot be explained simply by these shifts, as more liberal iterations of the Court had also strongly endorsed the FAA. Though loyal to the fundamental principle that "[a]rbitration is a matter of 'consent, not coercion'"[9] throughout her arbitration-related opinions, Justice Ginsburg ultimately disagreed with the way the Court defined "consent" when the agreement to arbitrate was adhesive. As a result, by the end of her time on the Court, Justice Ginsburg's favorable view of arbitration as a dispute resolution process yielded to her growing disenchantment with—and indeed disdain for—mandatory arbitration clauses.

The FAA Preemption Doctrine

Justice Ginsburg joined the Court in the fall of 1993, right in the middle of the Court's development and expansion of the FAA preemption doctrine. In her very first arbitration-related opinion as a Supreme Court Justice, she demonstrated her strong support of the FAA as a powerful federal statute that displaced conflicting state laws. In *Doctor's Associates v. Casarotto*,[10] the Court held that the FAA preempted a Montana notice statute requiring that arbitration agreements be typed in underlined capital letters on the first page of the contract. Writing for the majority, Justice Ginsburg held that the arbitration clause in a franchise agreement was enforceable because the FAA was not "compatible" with the Montana law, which singled out arbitration agreements for special treatment.[11] Instead, the Montana law had to yield to the FAA's policy mandate to put arbitration agreements on equal footing with all other contracts.[12]

In *Casarotto*, Justice Ginsburg expanded the scope of FAA preemption by distinguishing the Court's prior 1989 holding that the FAA did not preempt a California law that "called for arbitration to be stayed pending the resolution of a related judicial proceeding" in *Volt Information Sciences, Inc. v. Board of Trustees*.[13] Instead, the *Casarotto* opinion limited *Volt* to its facts by characterizing the state law at issue as "procedural," because it "determined only the efficient order of proceedings; it did not affect the enforceability of the arbitration agreement itself."[14] Thus, Justice Ginsburg established a version of the FAA preemption doctrine dictating that the FAA displaced any state rule, whether procedural or substantive, that disfavored arbitration as a dispute resolution process.

Fifteen years later, in the 2008 opinion *Preston v. Ferrer*,[15] Justice Ginsburg reasserted her support for the FAA preemption doctrine. In *Preston*, the Court ruled in favor of a compelled arbitration of a fee dispute between "Judge Alex" and his lawyer, who allegedly was acting as a talent agent without registering under California's Talent Agencies Act (TAA). The Court held that the FAA preempted a provision of the TAA that required an administrative forum for resolution of disputes arising under the TAA and thus enforced the arbitration agreement between the parties.[16] Both *Preston* and *Casarotto* (and numerous other majority opinions she joined in this time frame) exemplify Justice Ginsburg's alignment with the Court's construction of the FAA as a powerful federal statute that limits the ability of states to regulate any arbitration agreement "involving commerce."[17]

However, as perhaps an unanticipated consequence of the Court's expansion of the FAA preemption doctrine, corporations increasingly inserted predispute arbitration clauses in adhesive consumer and employment agreements, and the Court enforced those adhesive arbitration agreements against virtually any legal challenge. This development in the "business-to-consumer" world clashed with Justice Ginsburg's liberalist instinct to protect the powerless. Not surprisingly, a few years after *Preston*, Justice Ginsburg joined the liberal bloc in Justice Breyer's dissent (along with Justices Sotomayor and Kagan) when the Court's conservative majority used the expanded FAA preemption doctrine to enforce class action waivers in arbitration provisions. The majority held that any state law declaring these waivers per se unconscionable conflicted with the purpose of the FAA to treat arbitration agreements like any other contract.[18] As a result, consumers subject to these agreements were deprived of the ability to pursue small dollar value claims, which the dissent viewed as deeply problematic.

In her final years on the Court, Justice Ginsburg thought the Court should rein in the FAA preemption doctrine, but by then it was too late. In *DIRECTV, Inc. v. Imburgia*,[19] a consumer sued DIRECTV, a satellite television provider, to recover fees that allegedly violated California law. The customer agreement contained a predispute arbitration clause stating that, if the "law of your state" made class arbitration waivers unenforceable, then the entire arbitration provision was unenforceable.[20] Lower courts refused to enforce the arbitration clause, reasoning that California law rendered the provision unenforceable. The Supreme Court reversed, concluding that the California law was an obstacle to Congress's intent in enacting the FAA and was therefore preempted. As a result, the Court enforced the arbitration clause and class action waiver.[21]

Justice Ginsburg strongly disagreed and authored the dissenting opinion. Describing the Court's role in facilitating companies' insertion of class action waivers combined with predispute arbitration clauses in adhesive contracts, she wrote:

> It has become routine, in a large part due to this Court's decisions, for powerful economic enterprises to write into their form contracts with consumers and employees no-class-action arbitration clauses. The form contract in this case contains a Delphic provision stating that "if the law of your state" does not permit agreements barring class arbitration, then

the entire agreement to arbitrate becomes unenforceable, freeing the aggrieved customer to commence class-based litigation in court. This Court reads that provision in a manner most protective of the drafting enterprise. I would read it, as the California court did, to give the customer, not the drafter, the benefit of the doubt. Acknowledging the [preemption] precedent so far set by the Court, I would take no further step to disarm consumers, leaving them without effective access to justice.[22]

Justice Ginsburg termed the majority's ruling a "dangerous first," recalling that, "in the more than 25 years between *Volt* and this case, not once has this Court reversed a state-court decision on the ground that the state court misapplied state contract law when it determined the meaning of a term in a particular arbitration agreement." Citing legal scholarship critiquing the many perils of mandatory arbitration clauses,[23] Justice Ginsburg argued that the Court "misread the FAA to deprive consumers of effective relief against powerful economic entities that write no-class-action arbitration clauses into their form contracts."[24]

She strenuously objected that the Court's expansion of the FAA in *Imburgia* went too far, declaring: "Congress in 1925 could not have anticipated that the Court would apply the FAA to render consumer adhesion contracts invulnerable to attack by parties who never meaningfully agreed to arbitration in the first place." In her view, the FAA preemption doctrine she supported—and indeed helped expand earlier in her term—had reached its limits.

The Role of Federal Courts in Regulating and Supporting Arbitration

Justice Ginsburg's FAA opinions in her earlier years on the Court also reflect her efforts to define the role of federal courts in the fast-developing law of arbitration. Before Justice Ginsburg joined it, the Court already had recognized the FAA's anomalous cast as a federal statute creating a substantive right to enforce arbitration agreements as written, although not providing a basis for federal jurisdiction to enforce that right.[25] In *Vaden v. Discover Bank*,[26] an affiliate of Discover Bank sued a cardholder in state court to recover an outstanding credit card balance. Neither the claims nor the cardholder's counterclaims arose under federal law. Invoking the arbitration clause in the cardholder agreement, Discover Bank moved to compel arbitration in federal court under FAA section 4. Justice Ginsburg ultimately wrote a 5–4 majority opinion in this dispute that resolved a circuit split and interpreted the FAA's key provision authorizing motions to compel a reluctant party to arbitrate. The majority concluded that a federal court may "look through" a section 4 petition to determine whether it is predicated on a controversy that "arises under" federal law. Justice Ginsburg wrote that section 4 of the FAA authorized a federal court to take jurisdiction on a petition to compel arbitration only if the underlying merits controversy set forth in the complaint would have qualified for federal jurisdiction.[27] In so ruling, the majority approved the "look through" approach to federal court jurisdiction.[28] In the *Vaden* case, because Discover Bank's claim for the balance due on Vaden's account was entirely state-based, the Court ruled that the district court did not have jurisdiction to hear the petition. Nonetheless, by endorsing look-through jurisdiction under the FAA for future cases, Justice Ginsburg ensured that federal courts would have a role, though perhaps limited, in enforcing the FAA's substantive right.

In contrast to *Vaden*, Justice Ginsburg's earlier nonmajority, arbitration-related opinions reflected her views that a federal court's role is limited when losing parties seek to disturb an arbitration panel's award. For example, in *Major League Baseball Players Association v. Garvey*,[29] a dispute involving a baseball player's challenge to a labor arbitration award, the Court reversed the Ninth Circuit's vacatur of the award because it had decided the merits of the underlying case, improperly substituting its judgment for the arbitrator's and barring further proceedings. Justice Ginsburg concurred in the judgment and somewhat mysteriously wrote: "I agree with the Court that . . . the Ninth Circuit [in this case] should not have disturbed the arbitrator's award. Correction of that error sets this case straight. I see no need to say more."[30] Her concurrence reinforced her view that grounds to challenge a commercial or labor arbitration award are narrow and that federal courts do not have the power to vacate an award simply because they disagree with the merits of the panel's decision.

In *Stolt-Nielsen S.A. v. AnimalFeeds International Corp.*,[31] parties to a shipping agreement disagreed about whether their arbitration clause, which said nothing about class arbitration, authorized a class proceeding. The parties then entered into a supplemental agreement authorizing the arbitration panel to decide that issue, and the panel ruled that the clause allowed class arbitration.[32] After appeals, the Court held that the arbitration panel exceeded its powers by construing a silent arbitration clause to authorize class arbitration.[33] Instead, the panel "imposed its own policy choice," subjecting the award to vacatur under the FAA.[34]

Justice Ginsburg dissented, arguing that the FAA does not permit a court to overturn an arbitration award simply because it disagrees with the outcome. By deciding the merits of the clause-construction dispute, the majority engaged in de novo review, thus usurping the function of the arbitrator.[35] This opinion is consistent with her long-standing view that courts should respect, not disturb, arbitration awards, especially where, as here, the parties clearly empowered the arbitrators to construe the clause.

A final early Ginsburg opinion on arbitration, *Green Tree Financial Corp.-Alabama v. Randolph*,[36] previewed her concerns about adhesive arbitration agreements. In *Randolph*, a mobile home purchaser brought a class action suit against the lender alleging its financing agreement violated federal consumer protection statutes. Invoking the contract's arbitration clause, Green Tree moved to compel arbitration. The district court compelled arbitration, but the appeals court reversed, holding the arbitration clause was unenforceable because the named plaintiff asserted she could not afford the arbitration filing and process fees.[37]

The Supreme Court reversed again, holding that, when a consumer agrees to resolve claims by arbitration, she must proceed with arbitration unless she can demonstrate that she cannot vindicate her legal rights in arbitration. Because the plaintiff merely speculated, but did not prove with affirmative evidence, that arbitration costs could run high, the Court concluded that the appeals court erred in declaring the arbitration clause unenforceable.[38]

Justice Ginsburg concurred with the majority that the order compelling arbitration was a "final decision" within the meaning of section 16 of the FAA and thus immediately appealable, and she concurred with the judgment to vacate the lower court's decision. However, she dissented from the Court's decision to even consider the case.[39] She disagreed with placing the burden on the consumer to come forward with information about the costs of arbitration: "In these circumstances, it is hardly clear that Randolph should bear the burden of demonstrating up front the arbitral forum's inaccessibility, or that she should be required to submit to arbitration without knowing how much it will cost her." She noted that, "[a]s a repeat player in the arbitration required by its form contract, Green Tree has superior information about the cost to consumers of pursuing arbitration."[40] Instead, she would have remanded the case to the district court to develop the record further on the costs of an arbitration.

FAA Supremacy Is Limited in Coercive Settings

Justice Ginsburg's early concerns about adhesive arbitration agreements mushroomed in her remaining decade on the Court, when the composition of the Court turned more conservative and the Court's FAA jurisprudence seemingly converted the FAA into a "super-statute." Though the Court had already been stating for many years that, in principle, the FAA may yield to a "contrary Congressional command," it had never found that a particular federal statute superseded the FAA. Instead, the Court required express language indicating congressional intent to disallow an arbitral forum for resolution of a particular statutory right.[41]

Justice Ginsburg invoked this "contrary congressional command" doctrine to attempt to limit the impact of the FAA. For example, in *CompuCredit Corp. v. Greenwood*,[42] the Court held that language in the Credit Repair Organizations Act (CROA) providing consumers with a right to sue yields to a predispute arbitration agreement, as the phrase "right to sue" was not specific enough to indicate congressional intent to deem CROA claims nonarbitrable.[43]

Justice Ginsburg, the lone dissenter, disagreed, writing instead that the FAA clashed with the consumer-protective CROA. In her view, the "right to sue" under the statute was nonwaivable—as the right to sue means the right to litigate in court. She criticized the majority, writing that

> [t]he Court today holds that credit repair organizations can escape suit by providing in their take-it-or-leave-it contracts that arbitration will serve as the parties' sole dispute-resolution mechanism. . . . If the Act affords consumers a nonwaivable right to sue in court, as I believe it does, a credit repair organization cannot retract that right by making arbitration the consumer's sole recourse.[44]

Six years after *CompuCredit*, Justice Ginsburg was again unsuccessful in convincing a majority of Justices to limit the reach of the FAA when it deprived consumers or employees of rights arising under a federal statute. In *Epic Systems Corp. v. Lewis*,[45] a conservative 5–4 majority ruled that the National Labor Relations Act (NLRA),[46] which secures for employees the right to engage in concerted activities for their "mutual aid or protection,"[47] does not render arbitration clauses with class action waivers unenforceable. The Court rejected the plaintiffs' views that the statutory protection of concerted activities included the right to sue as a class to vindicate statutory rights.

In her lengthy dissenting opinion, which was joined by Justices Breyer, Sotomayor, and Kagan, Justice Ginsburg called the majority opinion "egregiously wrong." She referred to the "extreme imbalance once prevalent in our Nation's workplaces, and Congress' aim in [federal labor statutes] to place employers and employees on a more equal footing." In that historical context, she argued, the FAA, "sensibly read, does not shrink the NLRA's protective sphere." Noting that "the Court has repeatedly recognized the centrality of group action to the effective enforcement of antidiscrimination statutes," she concluded that "employees' [NLRA] rights include the right to pursue collective litigation regarding their wages and hours," and therefore "the employer-dictated collective-litigation stoppers, i.e., 'waivers,' are unlawful."[48]

While her critique was policy-based, her tone telegraphed outrage. She suggested that the conservative Court had weaponized the FAA to suppress federal statutory rights of consumers and employees with weaker bargaining power. No longer a strong supporter of limiting the power of courts to police the FAA, Justice Ginsburg argued that the Court should not have applied the statute to an arbitration agreement that was coercive rather than consensual.

In *Epic Systems*, Justice Ginsburg urged the Court to construe the FAA so as not to infringe on employees' rights under federal labor laws. Eight months later she authored a short, somewhat cryptic concurring opinion in *New Prime Inc. v. Oliveira*.[49] In *Oliveira*, she agreed with the majority's view that the FAA's employment exclusion applied to independent contractors, writing merely to declare that the Court should look at a word's general meaning at the time Congress enacted the specific statute.[50]

"Arbitration Is a Matter of Consent, Not Coercion"

In her final arbitration-related opinion, Justice Ginsburg's disdain for mandatory arbitration could not be clearer. *Lamps Plus, Inc. v. Varela*[51] is a case about a hacker who obtained tax information of over 1,300 employees of a light fixture company and filed fraudulent federal income tax returns in their names. An employee brought a class action against the employer for negligence and other claims. Lamps Plus moved to compel arbitration, invoking the arbitration clause in the standard employment agreement. After the district court and Ninth Circuit both construed the arbitration clause to allow for class arbitration, the Supreme Court reversed. The 5–4 majority held that the arbitration agreement was ambiguous as to whether the parties agreed to class arbitration and that courts may not infer from an ambiguous agreement that parties have consented to arbitrate on a class-wide basis.[52]

Justice Ginsburg's dissent warned "how treacherously the Court has strayed from the principle that 'arbitration is a matter of consent, not coercion.'"[53] Citing her own dissent four years earlier in *Imburgia*, she accused the Court of "deploy[ing] the law to deny to employees and consumers 'effective relief against powerful economic entities.'"[54] In her view, the Court had weaponized the FAA "consent requirement" by requiring an affirmative demonstration of consent to class procedures, yet requiring no real consent for an employee to "agree" to arbitration as a "take-it-or-leave-it condition of employment" or for a consumer "given no genuine choice in the matter."[55] The majority thus "hobbled the capacity of employees and consumers to band together in a judicial or arbitral forum."[56]

Justice Ginsburg concluded by arguing that mandatory arbitration clauses deprive consumers and employees of important statutory rights. She reminded the majority of the premise in her *Epic Systems* and *Imburgia* dissents: that Congress intended the FAA to apply only to arbitration agreements arising in commercial contexts between merchants of equal bargaining power. She then decried the Court's recent FAA decisions, which in her view improperly expanded the FAA far beyond its intended scope and eroded any meaningful consent requirement. This, in turn, led to the proliferation of mandatory arbitration clauses in adhesive consumer and employment settings, thereby "thwart[ing] 'effective access to justice' for those encountering diverse violations of their legal rights."[57]

Justice Ginsburg likely did not know that these would be her final written words about the majority's interpretation of the FAA:

> When companies can "muffl[e] grievance[s] in the cloakroom of arbitration," the result is inevitable: curtailed enforcement of laws "designed to advance the well-being of [the] vulnerable." "Congressional correction of the Court's elevation of the FAA over" the rights of employees and consumers "to act in concert" remains "urgently in order."[58]

In her final words about arbitration, not unlike her entire career as a lawyer, activist, and jurist, Justice Ginsburg urged congressional reform to protect the weak.

Conclusion

Justice Ginsburg's authored opinions in the area of arbitration span almost her entire tenure on the Court: her first was issued in 1996, her last in 2019. Viewed chronologically, these opinions demonstrate her growing disdain for mandatory arbitration in any adhesive contractual setting. In particular, she strongly disagreed with the Court's direction in interpreting the FAA to deprive consumers or employees of the right to proceed in arbitration on a class-wide basis to vindicate their statutory rights. Yet that direction seems to have been a natural extension of Justice Ginsburg's own language.

But did she evolve, or did the Court evolve around her? Likely it was a combination of both. It is well known that, in that time period, the Court grew more conservative. Like many arbitration scholars, Justice Ginsburg grew increasingly concerned about how corporate America was using the Supreme Court's FAA jurisprudence to its advantage. She had an idealized version of arbitration as a process between two freely consenting, commercial entities, but her early concerns expressed in *Randolph* came true: companies inserted conditions in their adhesive arbitration agreements to effectively strip consumers and employees of important rights.

Through this lens, Justice Ginsburg's arbitration jurisprudence was less formalistic and increasingly aimed at fairness to the weaker bargaining party. Rather than focus on the text of the FAA itself, as she did in her earlier FAA opinions, she emphasized that the underlying purpose of the statute was to put commercial arbitration contracts on equal footing with all other contracts, not to suppress claims of the weak. But the majority of the Court was focused on textualist statutory interpretation, not fairness. In the end, Justice Ginsburg could not hide her disappointment in the way powerful entities hijacked her own arbitration jurisprudence to exploit the disadvantaged.

NOTES
The author greatly benefited from feedback from participants in the 2021 Park City Writer's Workshop, a Haub Law summer 2021 workshop, and the AALS ADR 2021 Works-in-Progress Conference. I am also grateful for the excellent research assistance of Diana Balaj, Haub Law Class of 2022.

1   9 U.S.C. §§ 1 *et seq.* (2018).
2   *See* IMRE STEPHEN SZALAI, OUTSOURCING JUSTICE: THE RISE OF MODERN ARBITRATION LAWS IN AMERICA 7 (2013).
3   *See, e.g.,* Mitsubishi Motors Corp. v. Soler Chrysler-Plymouth, Inc., 473 U.S. 614, 628 (1985).
4   The FAA's key substantive provision, section 2, declares that a written agreement to arbitrate existing or future disputes arising out of a "maritime transaction or a contract evidencing a transaction involving commerce" is "valid, enforceable and irrevocable, save upon such grounds as exist at law or in equity for the revocation of any contract." 9 U.S.C. § 2.
5   Southland Corp. v. Keating, 465 U.S. 1, 10 (1984).
6   Volt Info. Scis., Inc. v. Bd. of Trs. of Leland Stanford Junior Univ., 489 U.S. 468, 477 (1989); *see also* Perry v. Thomas, 482 U.S. 483, 488–89 (1987) (holding the FAA preempted a California statute requiring wage collection actions to be resolved in court).
7   I could locate no opinions Justice Ginsburg authored during her time on the D.C. Circuit court of appeals that interpreted a provision of the FAA or expressed a view about arbitration, other than some dicta describing arbitration as a process to resolve labor grievances.
8   *See* Jeffrey W. Stempel, *Tainted Love: An Increasingly Odd Arbitral Infatuation in Derogation of Sound and Consistent Jurisprudence,* 60 U. KAN. L. REV. 795, 856 (2012) (stating "*Casarotto* reads like an opinion written by a court in the sway of arbitration and wishing to promote it in spite of legitimate countervailing state goals").
9   *See* Lamps Plus, Inc. v. Valera, 139 S. Ct. 1407, 1420 (2019) (Ginsburg, J., dissenting); DIRECTTV v. Imburgia, 577 U.S. 47, 62 (2015) (Ginsburg, J., dissenting); Stolt-Nielsen S.A. v. AnimalFeeds Intl. Corp., 559 U.S. 662, 681 (2010) (Ginsburg, J., dissenting); *see also* Air Line Pilots Ass'n v. Miller, 523 U.S. 866 (1998) (Ginsburg, J.) (holding that non-union pilots challenging union fees for representing

them before management could not be compelled to exhaust the arbitration remedy provided in the collective bargaining agreement before resorting to federal court since they were not parties to that agreement); C&L Enterprises, Inc. v. Citizen Band Potawatomi Indian Tribe of Oklahoma, 532 U.S. 411 (2001) (Ginsburg, J.) (holding that an Indian tribe waived its tribal immunity by entering into an unambiguous, nonadhesive agreement with a construction company that it drafted providing for arbitration of disputes arising out of the contract and reasoning that the contract represented the tribe's express consent to arbitration as a means of resolving disputes).

10 517 U.S. 681 (1996).

11 *Id.* at 683.

12 *See id.* at 688.

13 *Id.* (distinguishing *Volt Info. Scis.*, 489 U.S. at 478–79).

14 *Casarotto*, 517 U.S. at 682.

15 552 U.S. 346 (2008).

16 *Id.* at 360.

17 9 U.S.C. § 2.

18 *See* AT&T Mobility LLC v. Concepcion, 563 U.S. 333 (2011).

19 577 U.S. 47 (2015) (Ginsburg, J., dissenting).

20 *Id.* at 50.

21 *See id.* at 58–59.

22 *Id.* at 59–60 (Ginsburg, J., dissenting).

23 *See, e.g.*, Judith Resnik, *Diffusing Disputes: The Public in the Private of Arbitration, the Private in Courts, and the Erasure of Rights*, 124 YALE L.J. 2804 (2015); Jean R. Sternlight, *Tsunami*: AT&T Mobility LLC v. Concepcion *Impedes Access to Justice*, 90 OR. L. REV. 703 (2012).

24 *Imburgia*, 577 U.S. at 67 (Ginsburg, J., dissenting).

25 *See* Moses H. Cone Mem'l Hosp. v. Mercury Constr. Corp., 460 U.S. 1, 25 n.32 (1983).

26 556 U.S. 49 (2009).

27 *Vaden*, 556 U.S. at 66.

28 *Id.* at 62.

29 532 U.S. 504, 512 (2001) (Ginsburg, J., concurring).

30 *Id.* at 512 (Ginsburg, J., concurring).

31 559 U.S. 662 (2010).

32 *Id.* at 668–69.

33 *Id.* at 675–77.

34 *Id.* at 677.

35 *Id.* at 693–96 (Ginsburg, J., dissenting). She also dissented on procedural grounds, arguing that the panel's "partial construction clause award" was not immediately appealable. *Id.* at 692 (Ginsburg, J., dissenting).

36 531 U.S. 79 (2000) (Ginsburg, J., concurring).

37 *Id.* at 82–84.

38 *Id.* at 92.
39 *See id.* at 96 (noting that, "[a]s I see it, the Court has reached out prematurely to resolve the matter in the lender's favor.") (Ginsburg, J., concurring).
40 *Id.*
41 Shearson/American Express Inc. v. McMahon, 482 U.S. 220, 226 (1987).
42 565 U.S. 95 (2012).
43 *Id.* at 104.
44 *Id.* at 110–11 (Ginsburg, J., dissenting).
45 138 S. Ct. 1612 (2018).
46 29 U.S.C. §§ 151 *et seq.*
47 *Id.* at § 157.
48 *Lewis,* 138 S. Ct. at 1633–49 (Ginsburg, J., dissenting).
49 139 S. Ct. 532 (2019).
50 *Id.* at 544 (Ginsburg, J., concurring) ("Looking to the period of enactment to gauge statutory meaning ordinarily fosters fidelity to the 'regime . . . Congress established.'").
51 139 S. Ct. 1407 (2019).
52 *See id.* at 1412–19.
53 *Id.* at 1420 (Ginsburg, J., dissenting) (quoting Stolt-Nielsen S.A. v. AnimalFeeds Intl. Corp., 559 U.S. 662, 681 (2010)).
54 *Id.* (Ginsburg, J., dissenting) (quoting DIRECTV, Inc. v. Imburgia, 577 U.S. 47 (2015) (Ginsburg, J., dissenting)).
55 *Id.* at 1420–21 (Ginsburg, J., dissenting) ("Today's decision underscores the irony of invoking 'the first principle' that 'arbitration is strictly a matter of consent[]' . . . to justify imposing individual arbitration on employees who surely would not choose to proceed solo.").
56 *Id.* at 1421 (Ginsburg, J., dissenting).
57 *Id.* at 1422 (Ginsburg, J., dissenting).
58 *Id.* (Ginsburg, J., dissenting) (internal citations omitted).

4

Bankruptcy

The Scholar, the Harmonizer, and the Institutionalist

MARY JO WIGGINS

When delivering remarks in which she described the work of the United States Supreme Court, Associate Justice Ruth Bader Ginsburg noted:

> The federal law on which we rule may be the Constitution itself. More often, however, we deal not with constitutional questions, but with ordinary laws governing a wide range of areas, for example, statutes governing bankruptcy, federal taxation, intellectual property, environmental protection, pensions, and provision of health care.[1]

As a longtime scholar and teacher of bankruptcy law, I am not surprised that Justice Ginsburg listed bankruptcy *first* on her list of "ordinary laws." For most of her twenty-seven years on the Court, the number of bankruptcy filings nationwide was significant, reaching a historic peak of 1.5 million in 2010.[2] Justice Ginsburg wrote the majority opinion in seven major bankruptcy cases,[3] and she either wrote or joined a dissenting opinion in nine other bankruptcy and bankruptcy-related cases.[4] These opinions, of course, resolved discreet legal questions of great interest to bankruptcy lawyers and their clients. The opinions also revealed much about Justice Ginsburg's approach to her work as a jurist.

In this chapter, I examine how Justice Ginsburg's judicial perspectives resonated both within and beyond the field of bankruptcy law, a field I have taught and published in for over three decades. More specifically, I show how Justice Ginsburg connected her bankruptcy opinions to her exemplary jurisprudential aspirations and, even more important, how she joined this "ordinary" law to the broader foundations of the American legal system.

I explicate three overarching themes in Justice Ginsburg's bankruptcy jurisprudence. First, her opinions reflected an interpretive methodology that blended textual and contextual analysis, displayed exacting rigor, and embraced a strong preference for predictability, uniformity, and restraint. Second, her opinions displayed deep appreciation for the critical task of harmonizing bankruptcy law with foundational legal concepts and doctrines outside the bankruptcy context. Finally, Justice Ginsburg's bankruptcy opinions evinced strong fidelity to Supreme Court precedent, including respect for the proper allocation of jurisdictional power and authority among the federal courts. I conclude by connecting these recurring themes in Justice Ginsburg's bankruptcy opinions to her larger jurisprudential values and commitments.

Interpretive Methodology

Justice Ginsburg's bankruptcy opinions often blended meticulous analysis of the specific words of the United States Bankruptcy Code (the Code) with disciplined attention to its broader statutory design, thereby avoiding the pitfalls of both rote textualism *and* unprincipled contextualism. Moreover, her bankruptcy opinions displayed a preference for legal uniformity and predictability over chaotic flexibility and fuzzy uncertainty. Perhaps the best example of these admirable tendencies was her opinion in *Associates Commercial Corp. v. Rash*.[5] The issue was what definition of "value" applies under section 506(a) of the Code when a chapter 13 debtor elects the "cramdown" option under section 1325(a)(5)(B). The chapter 13 cramdown option allows a debtor to retain important property in which a secured creditor has an interest by proposing to pay the creditor a statutorily determined amount. The Court had to decide whether the valuation standard under section 1325(a)(5)(B) was foreclosure value (i.e., the amount the creditor would obtain at a foreclosure sale) or replacement value (the cost the debtor would incur to obtain a like asset for the same proposed use). The applicable valuation standard plays a vital role in equitably balancing debtors' retention rights with secured creditors' state law remedies. Justice Ginsburg, writing for the majority, held that the "value" of property retained via cramdown must be replacement value.[6]

Justice Ginsburg started her analysis by parsing the very first sentence of section 506(a). This analytical starting point led to a distinction that was critical to a proper resolution of the issue: the distinction between what must be evaluated (i.e., the creditor's interest in the collateral) and how to value that interest (the proper valuation standard). Justice Ginsburg then analyzed section 506(a) as a whole. This logical and systematic progression through section 506(a) in its entirety allowed the Court to reach a crucial understanding of what chapter 13 "bankruptcy cramdown" means, both legally and practically. Without such an understanding, there was a substantial risk that the Court would have undermined a statutory scheme that Congress undertook with care.

Justice Ginsburg expertly recognized that section 506(a) had to be interpreted against the backdrop of federal bankruptcy law's replacement of the secured creditor's state law rights with the cramdown option. The rigor with which Justice Ginsburg undertook the statutory analysis in *Rash* was impressive. Moreover, she displayed a keen understanding of the proper role of state law in relation to federal bankruptcy law and of bankruptcy's unique charge to displace state law when legally required.

The debtor had urged the Court to adopt a rule that would allow bankruptcy courts to split the difference between replacement and foreclosure value or, alternatively, use a case-by-case method. Justice Ginsburg rejected such a muddle, stressing that her analysis demonstrated why it was unnecessary. This preference for uniformity and predictability in adjudication had parallels to Justice Ginsburg's approach in another major opinion she wrote: *Petrella v. Metro-Goldwyn-Mayer, Inc.*[7] *Petrella* was not a bankruptcy case. It instead dealt with the interaction of the federal copyright statute with the equitable defense of laches. Justice Ginsburg, writing for the majority, rejected an attempt to create a porous opening for the use of laches in the context of certain copyright law damage claims. *Petrella* held that laches could not be invoked to bar relief on a copyright infringement claim brought within the copyright statute's three-year limitations period.[8] One of Justice Ginsburg's concerns in *Petrella*, as in *Rash*, was ensuring that a federal statute would be uniformly applied as Congress intended.[9]

Justice Ginsburg concluded her opinion in *Rash* by convincingly explaining that replacement value is a fairer standard for creditors because of the asymmetrical economic risks for creditors that cramdown generates. Her well-grounded explanation on this point challenged the suggestion that she could be reliably counted upon to side with debtors over creditors in cases that came before the Court.[10]

Justice Ginsburg's disciplined approach to statutory interpretation in bankruptcy was further exemplified by two other majority opinions she wrote: *Kawaauhau v. Geiger*[11] and *Harris v. Viegelahn*.[12] The Court held in *Geiger* that section 523(a)(6)'s exemption from discharge for debts for willful and malicious injury was confined to debts arising from intentional torts.[13] In *Harris*, the Court decided that a debtor who initially files a chapter 13 bankruptcy petition but then converts to chapter 7 is entitled to return of any postpetition wages not yet distributed by the trustee appointed by the bankruptcy court under chapter 13.[14] Justice Ginsburg used well-established rules of statutory construction to supplement her deliberate textual analysis in *Geiger*. Moreover, she declined the creditor's attempt to advance a policy argument external to the text and structure of the Code, explaining that the Court must follow the Code as written and leave amending the Code to Congress. In *Harris*, Justice Ginsburg's straightforward reading of section 348(f)(1)(A), combined with her reference to section 348(e)'s role in the overall statutory scheme for converted cases, underscored the extent to which the Fifth Circuit used result-oriented reasoning rather than statutory logic when it reached a different result. What tied *Geiger* and *Harris* together was Justice Ginsburg's fidelity to the words of the Code *and* her clear appreciation for the larger statutory design at work.

This is not to suggest that all of Justice Ginsburg's statutory analyses were equally compelling. One opinion that was less persuasive than *Rash*, *Geiger*, and *Harris* was her dissent in *Schwab v. Reilly*.[15] *Schwab* dealt with a trustee's or a creditor's need to object to a debtor's claimed exemption to preserve the estate's right to retain the excess value. Exemption laws allow debtors to retain property, or the value of property, that would otherwise go to the estate usually up to a certain dollar limit. A bankruptcy trustee will normally object to such a claimed exemption if she contends that the exemption does not apply to that particular item of property or if the debtor has declared an exemption for a dollar value not allowed.[16] The trustee seeking to object successfully must follow specific procedural steps. If the trustee misses a step or is not timely, the trustee's right to object to the exemption will usually be deemed waived.[17] For a variety of practical reasons having nothing to do with fraud or misconduct, it is not unusual for the actual value of property to exceed the value stated in a debtor's initial disclosure forms when it comes time for the trustee to dispose of, or otherwise assert an interest in, the property.

The Court held that no objection is required to preserve the estate's ability to recover value in the asset beyond the dollar value the debtor declared.[18] Justice Thomas based the majority opinion on: (1) a persuasive statutory analysis of the interplay of sections 522(l), 522(b), and 522(d); (2) a sound conclusion that *Taylor v. Freeland & Kronz* did not require an objection; and (3) a strong conviction that requiring an objection in this situation would shift the policy balance too far in favor of debtors. Justice Ginsburg anchored her dissent on what she understood to be prevailing procedural practice and her concern that the majority opinion would be unfair to debtors by exposing them to prolonged uncertainty in cases of delayed trustee action.

Justice Ginsburg's dissent failed to convince for three reasons. First, the force of her statutory analysis was weaker than the majority's because her analysis turned on unpersuasive claims about the role that a debtor's estimate of "current market value" plays under the Code. Second, the majority made central to its analysis the critical distinction in bankruptcy exemption law between the debtor's *interest* in property and the property *itself*, a distinction that Justice Ginsburg did not appear to prioritize. Third, under the foundational principles of exemption law, value in an asset beyond the dollar value allowed by state or federal exemption law belongs to the estate, not the debtor. Therefore, absent fraud or trustee waiver, the rules in bankruptcy should facilitate rather than thwart the estate's recovery of that value. While Justice Ginsburg's fears about instances of trustee delay were not trivial, the more realistic incentive has been for trustees to act quickly to preserve the estate's rights. Moreover, even in situations where property becomes subject to a delayed exemption challenge, most debtors will continue to have options under the Code for retaining property that is critical to the debtor's fresh start.[19]

Harmonizing Bankruptcy Law with Legal Concepts Outside Bankruptcy

The United States Bankruptcy Code operates alongside state common law, state statutory law, and other doctrines and concepts of long-standing pedigree and authority. Therefore, judges who decide bankruptcy cases should understand and appreciate nonbankruptcy doctrines, concepts, and policies to reach correct results and render decisions that will withstand rigorous scrutiny. In her bankruptcy opinions, Justice Ginsburg made abundantly clear her prodigious knowledge of many substantive and procedural touchstones throughout the American legal system, and she seamlessly harmonized bankruptcy law with foundational touchstones. *Howard Delivery Service, Inc. v. Zurich American Insurance Co.*[20] and *Kontrick v. Ryan*[21] are excellent examples of this harmonization.

In *Howard*, the Court had to decide whether section 507(a)(5) included claims for unpaid premiums on a policy purchased by an employer to cover its workers' compensation liability. If the claims qualified under section 507(a)(5), the workers' compensation carrier would have received priority payment over general unsecured claims in the employer's bankruptcy. If the claims did not qualify under section 507(a)(5), then the carrier would be paid alongside general unsecured claims, usually at no more than pennies on the dollar. A creditor in bankruptcy is almost always better off having a priority claim than not. The Court held that the premiums owed by the employer to the workers' compensation carrier did not fit within the section 507(a)(5) priority.[22]

Justice Ginsburg's statutory analysis in *Howard* displayed a superb understanding of the larger statutory scheme at work in section 507(a)(4) (i.e., the priority provision for claims of certain employees) and section 507(a)(5). Yet what gave *Howard* more lasting resonance was Justice Ginsburg's insistence on elucidating what she called "the essential character of worker's compensation regimes."[23] Justice Ginsburg explained that, while section 507(a)(5) has an employee focus because it gives priority to unsecured claims for contributions to employee benefit plans, workers' compensation plans have an employer focus. The employer selects the carrier and pays the premiums. The plan is designed to help the employer reduce the risk of large tort judgments and associated litigation. Moreover, as she noted, employers are required to have workers' compensation plans. Although Justice Ginsburg relied on chestnuts of bankruptcy policy in building the case for her decision, it was her desire and ability to integrate the Code's commitments with the foundational purposes of workers' compensation schemes that made the result in *Howard* compelling rather than merely supportable.

In *Kontrick*, the issue was whether a debtor who did not raise the time limitation contained in Rule 4004 of the Federal Rules of Bankruptcy Procedure (FRBP) before the bankruptcy court reached the merits of the creditor's objection to discharge forfeited the right to rely on FRBP 4004. The Court held in the affirmative, thereby dashing the attempt of an inattentive debtor to thwart a creditor's discharge objection by arguing that the objection was not timely.[24] The core of Justice Ginsburg's reasoning in *Kontrick* started with her acknowledgement that subject matter jurisdiction comes from Congress, pursuant to the Constitution and related federal statutes. Properly understood and applied, a court's subject matter jurisdiction cannot be expanded to account for the parties' litigation conduct. By contrast, the time constraints applicable to objections to discharge come from the FRBP, which do not create or withdraw federal jurisdiction. Justice Ginsburg reasoned that the FRBP are *claims processing rules* that can, in fact, be forfeited if the party asserting the rule waits too long to raise the claim. The formal distinction between subject matter jurisdiction and claims processing rules is one that civil procedure and federal court scholars would have at the ready. It is safe to say that most bankruptcy scholars (myself included) would need a moment to reorient themselves to the difference. Yet Justice Ginsburg expertly weaved the dynamics of bankruptcy discharge litigation with the complexities of federal procedural law in a way that ultimately strengthened the durability of both.

Fidelity to Precedent and the Proper Allocation of Jurisdictional Power

In addition to fulfilling its role as the final interpreter of the Constitution's text and of federal statutes, including the Bankruptcy Code, the Supreme Court interprets judicially created doctrines within the federal courts. One of these doctrines is the so-called probate exception to federal court jurisdiction. The probate exception holds exclusively for state probate courts the probate or annulment of a will and the administration of the decedent's estate. The probate exception also means that federal courts are not charged with disposing custodial property in state probate court. Since bankruptcy courts are federal courts and are sometimes called upon to adjudicate claims involving probate-related issues, there are occasions where the proper scope of the probate exception becomes an issue in bankruptcy.

The Supreme Court issued two decisions while Justice Ginsburg was on the Court that involved the now-deceased model and actress Anna Nicole Smith (Smith) and the estate of J. Howard Marshall II (Marshall), who at the time of his death was married to Smith. One of these cases, *Marshall v. Marshall*, involved the proper scope of the probate exception.[25] In *Marshall*, the Court had to decide whether the United States Court of Appeals for the Ninth Circuit properly invoked the probate exception when it held that the exception barred the district court of federal jurisdiction over a counterclaim for tortious interference with a gift that Smith expected from her deceased husband. Smith's counterclaim was against E. Pierce Marshall (Pierce), J. Howard Marshall's son. Writing for the majority, Justice Ginsburg held that the Ninth Circuit had misapplied the probate exception and thus the district court's assertion of jurisdiction was proper.[26] Although the specific issue in *Marshall* had more to do with federal court jurisdiction than with any specific provision of the Code, the Court's decision had bankruptcy implications because Smith filed for bankruptcy while Marshall's estate was being administered in a Texas probate court.

Justice Ginsburg began the majority opinion with a revealing quote from Chief Justice John Marshall in *Cohens v. Virginia*:

> "It is most true that this Court will not take jurisdiction if it should not: but it is equally true, that it must take jurisdiction if it should. . . . We have no more right to decline the exercise of jurisdiction which is given, than to usurp that which is not given."[27]

Justice Ginsburg's homage to Chief Justice Marshall's perspective signaled an interest in guiding the lower federal courts toward her view of the proper balance between aggressive and timid federal court authority.

Justice Ginsburg next proceeded with a scholarly elucidation of the history of the probate exception as a creature of judicial evolution, noting that, while lower courts had enlarged the scope of the exception, the Supreme Court had narrowed it, most notably in *Markham v. Allen*.[28] In criticizing the Ninth Circuit's holding, which read the exception broadly so as to deny federal courts any power to entertain any probate-related matters, she displayed abundant concern for the correct allocation of judicial authority between state probate courts and federal courts. She concluded that the probate exception did not bar federal courts from adjudicating matters outside the strictures of estate administration as long as the matter was otherwise within federal jurisdiction.

Turning to Smith's claim against Pierce, Justice Ginsburg reasoned that, since Smith was pursuing an in personam claim for tortious interference with a gift or inheritance, her claim was properly within the jurisdiction of a federal court and not barred by Texas law. Justice Stevens, concurring in part, thought Justice Ginsburg's reasoning on this point was cogent,[29] but the significance of her reasoning goes beyond its legal persuasiveness. Justice Ginsburg's reasoning in *Marshall* revealed her to be an unapologetic federal court institutionalist. She insisted on identifying and applying a deep and robust understanding of federal court jurisdiction, one that allows federal courts to decide matters they are, historically and practically, well-suited to adjudicate. Her understanding of federal court jurisdiction was not only more accurate than the Ninth Circuit's; it had greater potential to further the smooth and proper functioning of the lower federal courts. At the same time, Justice Ginsburg's approach clearly evidenced respect for advancing the traditional design and objectives of state probate law.

Another important aspect of Justice Ginsburg's opinion in *Marshall* concerned her efforts to ensure that the Court adhered to its own prior precedent on the scope of the probate exception. Justice Ginsburg's trenchant analysis of *Markham* provided a firm and transparent footing on which to rest the exception going forward. This was especially crucial because, as noted earlier in this chapter, the probate exception derives not from a statute or the Constitution's text but from judicial origins. This made it all the more critical that the Court be scrupulous in adjudicating its own precedent.

The other Supreme Court decision that involved Smith and Pierce was *Stern v. Marshall*.[30] The issue in *Stern* was whether a bankruptcy court had statutory and constitutional authority to enter final judgment on the same counterclaim as in *Marshall*. The Court held 5–4, with Chief Justice Roberts authoring the majority opinion, that the bankruptcy court had federal statutory authority to enter final judgment but that it did not have Article III constitutional authority to do so.[31] Justice Breyer wrote the dissenting opinion, joined by Justices Ginsburg, Kagan, and Sotomayor. The dissenters framed the issue as whether the bankruptcy court had jurisdiction to adjudicate the counterclaim. They would have found jurisdiction under both the federal statute and the Constitution. The dissenter's approach obviously did not carry the day. *Stern* significantly curbed the jurisdictional power of bankruptcy courts to decide matters not squarely and unequivocally within the majority's very narrowly defined statutory and constitutional core. Bankruptcy courts and litigants are still paying the price in terms of increased delay, cost, and inefficiency.

Justice Ginsburg's decision to join the dissent in *Stern* provided further evidence of her exceedingly strong commitment to ensuring that the Court rigorously interpret and apply its own precedent. In *Marshall*, Justice Ginsburg took seriously the Court's prior effort in *Markham v. Allen* to restrain lower federal courts from using the probate exception to deprive federal courts of jurisdiction they ought sensibly to have. In *Stern*, the dissenters meticulously explained how and why the majority misapplied and failed to follow its prior decisions, suggesting serious doubts about the soundness of the majority opinion. In the wake of renewed concern about the current Supreme Court's uneven performance when it comes to fidelity to prior precedent as well as the Court's own process norms, the dissenters' scrupulous and transparent approach compares favorably to several of the current Court's recent pronouncements.[32]

In addition to offering a compelling argument rooted in Supreme Court precedent, the *Stern* dissent firmly anchored bankruptcy court jurisdiction to its legislative purpose, as that purpose was reflected in the original design of the bankruptcy system. Under that constitutional framework, the resolution of Smith's counterclaim in bankruptcy court was crucial to maintaining a uniform bankruptcy system that advances legislative ends. In this case, those ends include a working bankruptcy system that funnels most disputes that involve the insolvent debtor, including counterclaims such as Smith's, into a single, specialized forum so that stability and order can be the norm for a comprehensive resolution of the debtor's financial distress.

Justice Ginsburg's wise sensitivity to the foundational role of legislative purpose was also on display in *Ritzen Group Inc. v. Jackson Masonry LLC*, Ginsburg's final majority opinion on a bankruptcy issue.[33] The issue in *Ritzen* was whether a creditor's motion for relief from the automatic stay initiated a distinct proceeding terminating in a final, appealable order when the bankruptcy court ruled dispositively on the motion. A creditor's motion for relief from stay is often the most consequential early motion in a bankruptcy case. In some cases, if the creditor wins, the property that had been subject to the stay will usually be seized immediately and the debtor's prospects for truly effective bankruptcy relief may be dashed. Alternatively, the debtor may be subjected to litigation from that creditor that will divert time and attention away from the critical early stages of a bankruptcy proceeding.

Justice Ginsburg, writing for the majority, held that the adjudication of a relief from stay motion results in a final, appealable order when the bankruptcy court grants or denies relief.[34] The practical consequence of *Ritzen* was that it expedited the final resolution of an exceedingly important and interconnected issue in many bankruptcy cases (i.e., the disposition of property or the expediting of pending nonbankruptcy litigation) prior to the final winding up of the bankruptcy case. More fundamentally, what was key to Justice Ginsburg's adroit reasoning in *Ritzen* was her acknowledgement of the uniqueness of bankruptcy adjudication. She wrote: "The ordinary understanding of 'final decision' is not attuned to the distinctive character of bankruptcy litigation. A bankruptcy case encompasses numerous 'individual controversies, many of which would exist as standalone lawsuits but for the bankrupt status of the debtor.'"[35] The "distinctive character" of bankruptcy adjudication can be traced to the same source that fueled the dissenters' reasoning in *Stern*: legislative efforts, rooted in the Constitution, to create and maintain a well-functioning federal bankruptcy system. Without the ability to bring certainty and finality to the adjudication of relief from stay motions, delay and stagnation would be the order of the day in bankruptcy cases. Justice Ginsburg's ability to recognize the benefits to the bankruptcy process of the efficient disposition of stay motions was central to vindicating the larger legislative purpose.

Conclusion

Each Supreme Court Justice brings a unique personal history, professional outlook, and judicial philosophy to his or her work on the Court, and the issues the Court adjudicates are intricate, challenging, and cover vast stretches of legal terrain. Despite these complexities, I have shown that it is possible to find recognizable traces of Justice Ginsburg's broader jurisprudential commitments in the bankruptcy cases she authored or joined. This is particularly so when it comes to her known views on what constitutes good opinion writing, what it means to be an effective judge, and her conception of the ideal judicial voice.

In describing her preferred style of opinion-writing, Justice Ginsburg wrote: "I prefer and continue to aim for opinions that get it right and keep it tight without undue digressions or decorations, or distracting denunciations of colleagues who hold different views."[36] Justice Ginsburg's bankruptcy opinions showed an unwavering commitment to accuracy and concision. Her methodology has been particularly vital for the positive advancement of bankruptcy law and adjudication. Bankruptcy practitioners and scholars appreciate Justice Ginsburg's use of analytical methods and reasoning that conformed expertly to well-understood doctrines and concepts. Her approach has been instrumental to furthering both fairness and efficiency, as well as successfully integrating the Bankruptcy Code with many laws external to it. Even more important, Justice Ginsburg's decisional methodology has helped ensure the long-term value of contractual and legal entitlements throughout bankruptcy, commercial, and debtor-creditor law.

In describing her conception of judicial efficacy, Justice Ginsburg wrote that "the effective judge . . . strives to persuade, and not to pontificate. She speaks in a moderate and restrained voice, engaging in dialogue with, not a diatribe against, coequal departments of government, state authorities, and even her own colleagues."[37] Justice Ginsburg's bankruptcy opinions reflected the voice of both a scholar and a persuader. She was learned and supremely professional. She eschewed an imperious or incendiary tone, choosing instead to teach the relevant bankruptcy doctrines, explain how the doctrines applied to the case before the Court, and defend her conclusions with compelling logic rather than dismissive rhetoric. Among other positive effects, Justice

Ginsburg's scrupulous and controlled voice enhanced the Court's institutional credibility with bankruptcy academics as well as with the bench and bar.

At the 1993 Madison Lecture at New York University, Justice Ginsburg reflected upon what it meant to be a "good judge." In doing so, she summoned the advice of her teacher and friend, Professor Gerald Gunther, who at the time was finishing a biography of Judge Learned Hand. According to Justice Ginsburg, Professor Gunther advised her:

> [The good judge] is open-minded and detached . . . heedful of limitations stemming from the judge's own competence and, above all, from the presuppositions of our constitutional scheme; th[at] judge . . . recognizes that a felt need to act only interstitially does not mean relegation of judges to a trivial or mechanical role, but rather affords the most responsible room for creative, important judicial contributions.[38]

This chapter has detailed precisely how Justice Ginsburg's bankruptcy jurisprudence embodied fidelity to the aim of balancing judicial imaginativeness with institutional probity. Generations of bankruptcy scholars, practitioners, and others will unquestionably benefit from her thoroughgoing devotion to being a "good judge." Indeed, it seems that Justice Ginsburg did her most extraordinary work with this very ordinary area of law.

NOTES

1 RUTH BADER GINSBURG, WITH MARY HARTNETT & WENDY W. WILLIAMS, MY OWN WORDS 201 (Simon & Schuster, 2016).

2 *See* STATISTA, *Annual Number of Bankruptcy Cases Filed in the United States from 2007 to 2020, by Chapter,* STATISTA, http://statista.com.

3 *See* Assocs. Com. Corp. v. Rash, 520 U.S. 953 (1997); Kawaauhau v. Geiger, 523 U.S. 57 (1998); Kontrick v. Ryan, 540 U.S. 443 (2004); Howard Delivery Serv. Inc. v. Zurich Am. Ins. Co., 547 U.S. 651 (2004); Marshall v. Marshall, 547 U.S. 293 (2006), Harris v. Viegelahn, 575 U.S. 510 (2015); Ritzen Grp. Inc. v. Jackson Masonry LLC, 140 S. Ct. 582 (2020).

4 *See* Travelers Indem. Co. v. Bailey, 557 U.S. 137 (2009); Schwab v. Riley, 560 U.S. 770 (2010); Stern v. Marshall, 564 U.S. 462 (2011); Hall v. U.S., 566 U.S. 506 (2012); Baker Botts LLP v. Arasco, 576 U.S. 121 (2015); Puerto Rico v. Franklin California Tax-Free Trust, 136 S. Ct. 1938 (2016); Spokeo v. Robins, 578 U.S. 330 (2016); Midland Funding LLC v. Johnson, 137 S. Ct. 1407 (2017); Rotkiske v. Klemm, 140 S. Ct. 355 (2019).

5 *Rash*, 520 U.S. 953 (1997).

6 *Id.* at 956.

7 Petrella v. Metro-Goldwyn-Mayer Inc., 572 U.S. 663 (2014).

8 *Id.* at 667.

9 *Id.* at 681.

10 *See* William Rochelle, *Homage to RBG: The Advocate for Consumers and Debtors*, www.abi.org (Sept. 28, 2020).

11 Kawaauhau v. Geiger, 523 U.S. 57 (1998).

12 Harris v. Viegelahn, 575 U.S. 510 (2015).

13 *Geiger*, 523 U.S. at 59.

14 *Harris*, 575 U.S. at 513.

15 Schwab v. Riley, 560 U.S. 770 (2010).

16 Or if the debtor committed fraud or other misconduct.

17 *See* Taylor v. Freeland & Kronz, 503 U.S. 638 (1992).

18 *Schwab*, 560 U.S. at 770.

19 *See* 11 U.S.C. § 524 and 11 U.S.C. § 722.

20 Howard Delivery Serv., Inc., v. Zurich Am. Ins. Co., 547 U.S. 651 (2004).

21 Kontrick v. Ryan, 540 U.S. 443 (2004).

22 *Howard*, 547 U.S. at 655.

23 *Id.* at 662.

24 *Kontrick*, 540 U.S. at 447.

25 Marshall v. Marshall, 547 U.S. 293 (2006).

26 *Id.* at 299–300.

27 *Id.* at 298–99.

28 *Id.* at 299.

29 *Marshall*, 547 U.S. at 315 (Stevens, J., dissenting).

30 Stern v. Marshall, 564 U.S. 462 (2011).

31 *Id.* at 469.

32 For example, the lawyer and legal commentator Jennifer Rubin opined in 2021: "If the justices are no longer bound by precedent, rewrite statutes at their will and don't even bother to present their full legal reasoning in many cases, the public should draw the conclusion that they are not acting as judges but as partisan surrogates." Jennifer Rubin, *The Supreme Court Has Only Itself to Blame*, WASHINGTON POST (Sept. 23, 2021), www.washingtonpost.com.

33 Ritzen Grp. Inc. v. Jackson Masonry LLC, 140 S. Ct. 582 (2020).

34 *Id.* at 586.

35 *Id.*

36 GINSBURG, MY OWN WORDS at 212.

37 *Id.* at 229.

38 *Id.* at 247.

5

Citizenship and Immigration Law

Through Her Opinions

M. ISABEL MEDINA

When Ruth Bader Ginsburg joined the Supreme Court, the plenary power doctrine was understood to vest Congress with almost unreviewable power in drawing lines with regard to acquisition of citizenship and immigration.[1] In cases like *I.N.S. v. Chadha* and *Landon v. Plasencia*, the Court signaled that framework constitutional doctrines such as separation of powers and due process would be enforced in the immigration context,[2] but other cases, like *Fiallo v. Bell*, left unsettled whether constitutional norms uniformly applied.[3] A storm of litigation was about to unleash itself on the U.S. legal system, prompted by legislation enacted in response to concerns about terrorism and migration to the United States, unauthorized migration, and increasingly aggressive enforcement of laws already in place.[4]

In the multitude of cases challenging a vast expansion of deportation and detention of noncitizens in the United States, Justice Ginsburg steered a course that solidly repudiated the view that noncitizens were not entitled to constitutional protections such as protection against gender discrimination and access to meaningful judicial review. Justice Ginsburg delivered death blows to a federal statute that facially discriminated on the basis of gender—an acquisition of citizenship statute that imposed a greater burden on men who wanted to transmit U.S. citizenship to their children than was placed on similarly situated women, who were able to transmit U.S. citizenship to their children much more quickly.[5]

Justice Ginsburg's opinions consistently demonstrated her commitment to constitutional rights–based protections for all persons present in the United States. This is evident through her application of framework constitutional norms and principles of statutory construction with her consistently methodical, well-developed contextual analysis, rooted in a commitment to judicial restraint while working, often, for transformative change. This chapter explores Justice Ginsburg's key majority, concurring, and dissenting opinions in citizenship and immigration law, and the extent to which they changed the course of U.S. immigration and citizenship law, all working within her moderate views about the role of judicial review in the constitutional scheme.

Striking Down Gender-Based Discrimination in Federal Citizenship Statutes

From the earliest days of our constitutional republic, citizenship statutes reflected deeply racist and gendered stereotypes, embedded particularly in the acquisition of citizenship provisions.[6] Long after most federal statutes had abandoned facially discriminatory provisions on the basis of gender, federal citizenship statutes continued to discriminate between U.S. citizen biological mothers and U.S. citizen biological fathers regarding their ability to pass on U.S. citizenship to their children born abroad. Children of U.S. citizens born abroad stand at a peculiar junction: by statute they are citizens at birth as long as their U.S. citizen parents have satisfied the statutory requirements that were the law at the time of the child's birth abroad, even if the requirements involved conduct after the child's birth.[7] If the statutory requirements are not satisfied, however, they are not citizens at all.[8] The statutory provisions applied different requirements depending on whether both parents were U.S. citizens, if only one of the parents was a U.S. citizen, and whether the parents were married. If they weren't married and only one parent was a U.S. citizen, the statute differentiated between women and men, imposing very light requirements on the children of women U.S. citizens but much heavier burdens if the parent was a man. The gender differential was explicit; the impact on children of color, born from the union of a citizen father and noncitizen mother of color, was not.

Miller v. Albright came before the Court in 1998, Justice Ginsburg's sixth year on the Court and two years after her majority opinion in *United States v. Virginia*, striking down the exclusion of women for admission to Virginia Military Institute.[9] *Miller v. Albright* involved a challenge to the difference in treatment between nonmarital children born abroad based on whether their U.S. citizen biological parent was a woman or a man.[10] The statutory scheme made it possible for the children of U.S. citizen women born outside of marriage, to gain citizenship at birth if the mother had resided in the United States continuously for one year at any time before the child's birth.[11] The children of U.S. citizen men born outside marriage, however, like Lorelyn Penero Miller, had to establish that their fathers had taken a number of additional steps—here, formal legitimation before she turned eighteen—to acquire citizenship at birth.[12] The statutory scheme did not require any showing of support or custody by the mother for the child to acquire citizenship at birth. Few U.S. citizens were aware of the critical importance of the statutory requirements that applied to transmission of citizenship to their born-abroad children, and the Millers were no different than most American families—the knowledge often came too late to satisfy the formal requirements.

Penero Miller was born in the Philippines in 1970 to an unmarried Filipino woman and U.S. citizen man, Charlie Miller. Her biological father, however, failed to formally acknowledge paternity. When the United States denied her request to be certified as a U.S. citizen on the grounds that her father had failed to comply with the additional requirements for transmission of U.S. citizenship imposed on nonmarital children of U.S. citizen fathers, Charlie Miller secured formal legitimation, a "voluntary paternity decree" from a Texas court in 1992 declaring him to be the biological and legal father of Lorelyn Penero Miller. The United States again rejected recognition of her U.S. citizenship because the legitimation had not occurred before she turned eighteen, as required by the statute. Had Miller Penero's U.S. citizen parent been her mother, rather than her father, she would have been recognized as a U.S. citizen, since the statute placed no requirements of this type on biological mothers.

Charlie Miller and his daughter challenged the difference in treatment as gender discrimination without justification in violation of their respective rights to equality implicit in the Fifth Amendment Due Process Clause. A federal district court in Texas held that the father lacked standing and transferred the case to the District of Columbia. That court dismissed the claim on standing grounds, reasoning that, even if Miller Penero suffered injury, courts could not grant her a remedy because federal courts lacked power to grant citizenship. On appeal, the D.C.

Circuit held that the daughter had standing but that the difference in treatment between unmarried U.S. citizen mothers and fathers was justified because it promoted the child's ties to the United States.

The Court emerged from consideration of the case seriously fractured. An opinion authored by Justice Stevens and joined only by Chief Justice Rehnquist announced the judgment of the Court: the difference in treatment between nonmarital U.S. citizen mothers and U.S. citizen fathers was justified.[13] Two other opinions, one by Justice O'Connor and one by Justice Scalia, concurred in the judgment. Justice O'Connor's opinion, joined by Justice Kennedy, rested on the standing issue: because the difference in treatment was between mothers and fathers, not sons and daughters, the daughter lacked standing to assert the father's equal protection claim. In Justice O'Connor's view, only the parent, not the child, was treated differently on the basis of gender with regard to transmission of citizenship; the child would be asserting a third-party claim, and in this case there was no reason to prevent the father from asserting his own claims. The fact that the father had been wrongly dismissed from the litigation did not affect the matter—he should have appealed![14] Miller Penero's claims presented neither gender discrimination nor a claim of discrimination on the basis of legitimacy, and thus it would be subject to rational basis scrutiny. "[A]ny reasonably conceivable state of facts that could provide a rational basis for the classification" sufficed; the statute was sustainable under that standard.[15]

Justice Scalia's concurring opinion, joined by Justice Thomas, reasoned that the claim had to be dismissed because the Court lacked the power to confer citizenship "on a basis other than that prescribed by Congress."[16] In Justice Scalia's view, it didn't matter whether the statute was subject to heightened scrutiny or rational basis scrutiny; in either case, the Court could not grant citizenship to Miller Penero if the terms of the statute did not, so the claim had to be dismissed. If the noncitizen could not satisfy the conditions in the statute, she remained a noncitizen because courts lacked the power to vest citizenship. Justice Scalia's opinion reflected the view that Congress has plenary power over immigration and citizenship.

Justice Ginsburg's dissent, joined by Justices Souter and Breyer, provided the historical context for the use of gender in transmission of citizenship laws, establishing that Congress historically had used gen-

der to disadvantage women or mothers, not to benefit them.[17] Justice
Ginsburg acknowledged that the gender distinction could be viewed as
a "benign preference" for women; but historically, citizenship transmission laws had discriminated against citizen mothers, not citizen fathers.
Not until 1934 did Congress place U.S. citizen mothers and fathers on
equal footing in transmission of citizenship without regard to the marital status of the parents. At that time, Congress imposed an additional
burden on children of five years' residence in the United States prior
to their eighteenth birthday. In 1940, however, Congress distinguished
between citizen mothers and citizen fathers with regard to children born
outside marriage. This history, Justice Ginsburg noted, cast doubt on
the government's justification for the gender line: the connection between mother to child contrasted to the "distant or fleeting father-child
link." The justification reflected generalizations and stereotypes about
gender—"the way women (or men) are"—and thus, consistent with
gender discrimination cases, could not support differential treatment of
men and women. That more mothers of children born abroad actually
raised their children than fathers did not justify distinguishing between
mothers and fathers categorically, according to Justice Ginsburg. Congress could distinguish between parents who take responsibility for their
children and those who do not, regardless of whether they were mothers or fathers. If Congress desired to promote the opportunity for U.S.
citizen parents to foster and encourage close ties to the United States, it
could do so without reference to gender.

Almost twenty years later, in *Sessions v. Morales-Santana*, the Court
struck down the difference in treatment between U.S. citizen nonmarital
mothers and fathers with regard to the physical presence requirement
in the statute.[18] In the interim, the Court had considered the gender
differentials in two other cases: *Nguyen v. I.N.S.*,[19] involving the parental acknowledgement and legitimation requirement imposed only on
fathers, not mothers; and *Flores-Villar v. United States*,[20] involving the
differential physical presence requirement also at issue in *Sessions v.
Morales-Santana*. In both cases, the Court purported to apply heightened scrutiny to statutory provisions that facially discriminated on the
basis of gender but nonetheless upheld the discriminatory schemes: in
Nguyen, with a 5–4 majority; and in *Flores-Villar*, with the Court split
evenly (and thus, no actual opinion from the Court).

It was not only the gender differential that drove these cases but also the increasing importance of the issue to numerous children of color born abroad to U.S. citizen parents, children who lacked familiarity with the language or culture of the country of their actual birth. Perhaps thoroughly integrated as Americans, they would find themselves caught in the grip of the detention and removal practices that gained popularity in the United States in the 1990s.[21] The acquisition of citizenship cases thus reflected the government's zealous enforcement of removal sanctions on mixed-status American families, mostly families of color.

The demise of the statutory gender differential came in a case challenging the greater physical presence requirement imposed on U.S. citizen fathers compared to mothers. The only statutory requirement imposed on nonmarital children to derive U.S. citizenship from their biological U.S. citizen mothers at birth was that the mother reside in the United States for one year at any time before the child's birth.[22] Nonmarital children of U.S. citizen fathers, however, had to show that their father had resided in the United States for ten years. At least five of those years had to be after their father turned fourteen—the same period of physical presence required for marital children born abroad of mixed citizenship status parents to acquire citizenship at birth.[23] This requirement was impossible for Luis Morales-Santana to establish, since his father had left the United States to take up employment in the Dominican Republic twenty days short of his nineteenth birthday.[24] Morales-Santana was born in the Dominican Republic in 1962 before his parents married in 1970. The family moved back to Puerto Rico in 1975, when Morales-Santana was thirteen, and by 1976 they resided in New York.

In 2000, the United States initiated removal proceedings against Morales-Santana as a noncitizen on the basis of several criminal convictions in 1995. Immigration courts rejected his claim that he could not be deported because he had acquired U.S. citizenship at birth as a child born abroad of a U.S. citizen parent. He asserted that the government's refusal to recognize his citizenship because his father, as opposed to his mother, was a U.S. citizen violated the equal protection guarantee of the Fifth Amendment Due Process Clause. Where his father spent twenty days of his youth determined whether Morales-Santana was a U.S. citizen and therefore not removable from the United States; but the stark difference between the result in his case as opposed to if his citizen parent had been a woman presented a gender differential that was difficult for the government to defend.

Justice Ginsburg's opinion emphasized citizenship laws' long history of subordination of women and the overbroad and archaic stereotypes about women as mothers and men as fathers embedded in the difference in the physical presence requirement. Laws that reflected the view that women are the "natural" parent, and men are not, perpetuated the stereotypes and were "stunningly anachronistic."[25] To the extent the requirement of physical presence was justified because it "ensured that a child born abroad has a connection to the United States of sufficient strength to warrant conferring citizenship at birth," Justice Ginsburg reasoned, a difference in the term of years required for the U.S. citizen mother and the father ultimately rested on the assumption that nonmarital fathers, as opposed to nonmarital mothers, would not accept parental responsibility and that they "care little about, indeed are strangers to, their children."[26] Justice Ginsburg noted that the statutory scheme allowed children born abroad of U.S. citizen nonmarital mothers to acquire citizenship at birth with no ties to the United States. There simply was not a close fit between the asserted actual interest and the difference in treatment.

Similarly, the government's other asserted interest—reducing the risk that children born abroad of a U.S. citizen mother would be stateless—was simply not supported by the evidence. Little evidence existed to suggest that Congress had concerns about statelessness in enacting the provision. Further, at the time, many countries made it more difficult for nonmarital mothers than fathers to pass on citizenship to their child. The biological mother in those countries was not entitled to pass on citizenship to her child if the child was born outside of marriage. Thus, children of U.S. citizen men and noncitizen women born outside of marriage faced the highest risk of statelessness. Additionally, international entities seeking to end statelessness globally had made a central premise of the campaign the elimination of gender discrimination in citizenship or nationality laws. In this context, Justice Ginsburg reasoned, it made no sense to recognize the risk of statelessness as justification for gender discrimination in citizenship laws.

Equality rested on identifying and dismantling the overbroad and archaic stereotypes reflected in the statutory treatment of women and men as parents. The proper remedy appeared simple: strike down the more burdensome treatment of fathers and accord them the same treatment extended to mothers. This remedy would have recognized Morales-Santana as a U.S. citizen from birth. It would have achieved formal and substantive equality for Morales-Santana and U.S. citizen nonmarital mothers and fathers.

Instead, the Court struck down the one-year physical presence requirement and extended the more burdensome physical presence requirement accorded to nonmarital fathers and mixed citizenship status marital parents to nonmarital mothers. Justice Ginsburg, writing for a six-justice majority, noted there were reasons to "leave it to Congress to select . . . a physical-presence requirement . . . uniformly applicable to all children born abroad with one U.S.-citizen and one alien parent, wed or unwed."[27] The Court appeared concerned that applying the one-year physical presence requirement to unwed fathers would result in more favorable treatment to nonmarital children born abroad than to children born abroad of married parents with mixed citizenship. The statute required children born of a citizen parent and a noncitizen parent to satisfy the longer physical presence requirements imposed on nonmarital fathers.[28] Arguably, the statutory treatment of mixed citizenship marital children should have been irrelevant to the question of the remedy for unconstitutional gender discrimination between nonmarital mothers and fathers. Justice Ginsburg justified the result on the grounds that extending the reduced physical presence requirement granted to noncitizen mothers to nonmarital fathers would turn the exception into the rule; this result, in the view of the majority, did not appear consistent with congressional intent. The decision ended this facial gender discrimination in citizenship law and forced federal immigration agencies to minimize the use of gender stereotypes to deny citizenship to the children born abroad of U.S. citizen parents.[29] The complete elimination of the gender and racial stereotypes reflected in the statutory framework that informs U.S. citizenship law will have to come from Congress.

A Changing Docket: The Importance of Immigration Statutes and Enforcement Imperatives Before the Court in the 21st Century

In Justice Ginsburg's first term, the Supreme Court did not issue any signed opinions in cases on citizenship or immigration law.[30] In her last term, the Court issued eight signed opinions on immigration issues. Her opinions in these cases reflected her careful and firm adherence to principles of equality and liberty, including as they applied to non-citizens, and her principled approach to statutory text and structure, to precedent, and to judicial restraint, when appropriate, to the extent it preserved judicial independence.

Congress enacted substantial restrictions in federal judicial review of immigration decisions in 1996 legislation.[31] After a flood of habeas corpus challenges filed in district courts throughout the country, Congress amended the provisions in the Real I.D. Act of 2005.[32] In *Kucana v. Holder*, Justice Ginsburg wrote the majority opinion, rejecting the government's argument that all discretionary immigration decisions were rendered impervious to federal court review under the statute.[33] She reasoned that interpreting the statute to apply to administrative decisions rendered discretionary by the United States Attorney General would represent an expansion of the bar to judicial review not warranted by the statutory framework erected by Congress.

Similarly, in *Vartelas v. Holder*, Justice Ginsburg again wrote for the majority, which held that the 1996 changes to statutory provisions concerning when permanent residents returning to the United States would face the possibility of removal actions did not apply retroactively.[34] The case involved a lawful permanent resident originally from Greece who traveled to Greece to visit his parents. He had been a long-term resident of the United States, and in 1994 he pleaded guilty to conspiracy to make or possess counterfeit securities, a conviction that for immigration purposes constitutes a crime of moral turpitude. He was sentenced to four months' incarceration and two years' supervised release.

Prior to 1996, legal doctrines protected Vartelas's ability to travel abroad for brief periods of time without running the risk of having the government subject him to removal proceedings. Changes in the law, however, allowed immigration officers to treat a returning permanent resident as someone asking for "admission" and thus place him in removal proceedings. It wasn't until 2003, after several trips abroad to see his parents, that immigration officers stopped him and subjected him to removal on the basis of the 1994 conviction. The Court rejected the government's argument that the 1996 changes could be applied retroactively to convictions that predated the enactment of the Illegal Immigration Reform and Immigration Responsibility Act of 1996 (IIRIRA). The Court instead held that the law in place at the time of the person's conviction with regard to the effect of brief trips abroad governed. *Vartelas* restored the ability of permanent residents to travel abroad for brief periods of time without endangering their status and ability to reside in the United States if their convictions predated IIRIRA. Justice Ginsburg's opinion relied on established principles of statutory interpretation, an approach consistent with judicial restraint, to curtail the impact of the 1996 law on the lives of permanent residents.

In the same year she wrote for the majority in *Vartelas*, Justice Ginsburg dissented in *Kawashima v. Holder*, a case involving removal of a married couple, both permanent residents, who had been convicted of submitting a false income tax return.[35] The case involved the expanding definition of what offenses constituted aggravated felonies for removal purposes. For immigration purposes, "aggravated felonies" are defined under federal immigration law and may include offenses that would not be considered aggravated felonies in other contexts. Persons who have been convicted of aggravated felonies for immigration purposes are barred from qualifying for most forms of relief regarding removal from the United States. The majority found that, because the offenses involved deceitful conduct, they could be treated as an aggravated felony for immigration purposes.

Justice Ginsburg's dissent stressed principles of statutory construction that required the Court to interpret the statute in a way that did not render other statutory prohibitions superfluous. She urged a method of analysis that protected noncitizens from overzealous and expansive applications of removal statutes while relying on traditional methods of statutory interpretation, consistent with judicial restraint. In cases involving criminal offenses and immigration, she relied on the rule of lenity to interpret the statutes consistently with their plain language to narrow the reach of the statutes in rendering noncitizens removable from the United States.

Conclusion

The extent to which well-settled constitutional norms apply to nonciti-zens in the United States, particularly in the context of immigration, is contested and unsettled.[36] In her last full term on the Court, Justice Ginsburg wrote a powerful dissent in *Hernandez v. Mesa*. This was a dis-pute in which the Court held that parents of a Mexican youth killed in a cross-border shooting by a Border Patrol officer firing from U.S. terri-tory could not bring a *Bivens* action. A *Bivens* action is an implied cause of action against federal officials for violations of a person's civil rights,[37] in this case for violations of their son's Fourth and Fifth Amendment rights. Justice Ginsburg's dissent focused on the long-standing principle that "rogue U.S. officer conduct falls within a familiar, not a 'new,' *Biv-ens* setting."[38] She argued that application of the norms that informed the Court's analysis of whether a *Bivens* claims was available to liti-gants yielded a result different from what the majority concluded. She observed that "had the bullet hit Hernandez while he was running up or down the United States side of the embankment," his parents would have been free to pursue a *Bivens* claim.

Justice Ginsburg's legacy on the Court and American society was shaped by her firm and unwavering commitment to equality and liberty, adhering to a judicial philosophy that valued restraint, at times achiev-ing transformational change. In her opinions, as well as in the many other opinions she joined, Justice Ginsburg consistently recognized that noncitizens in the United States were entitled to constitutional protec-tions, including in the context of removal proceedings. These cases make clear her unwavering commitment to the Constitution as a vehicle for the protection and attainment of liberty and equality, whether the per-sons seeking that protection were citizens or noncitizens.

NOTES

1 GERALD L. NEUMAN, STRANGERS TO THE CONSTITUTION: IMMI-
   GRANTS, BORDERS, AND FUNDAMENTAL LAW (1996). *See* Matthew J. Lindsay, *Disaggregating Immigration Law*, 68 FLA. L. REV. 179, 187–94 (2016); Kevin

R. Johnson, *Los Olvidados: Images of the Immigrant, Political Power of Noncitizens and Immigration Law and Enforcement*, 1993 BYU L. REV. 1139 (1993); Stephen H. Legomsky, *Immigration Law and the Principle of Plenary Congressional Power*, 1984 SUP. CT. REV. 255 (1984); Hiroshi Motomura, *The Curious Evaluation of Immigration Law: Procedural Surrogates for Substantive Constitutional Rights*, 92 COLUM. L. REV. 1625 (1992).

2   I.N.S. v. Chadha, 462 U.S. 919 (1983) (interpreting the bicameral and present-ment clauses to bar a one-house legislative veto of agency deportation orders as inconsistent with separation of powers); Landon v. Plasencia, 459 U.S. 21 (1982) (permanent resident returning from brief trip abroad has a right to due process, even in the context of an exclusion hearing).

3   Fiallo v. Bell, 430 U.S. 787 (1977) (upholding statutory preference for marital, legit-imated, or nonmarital children of citizen or permanent resident biological mother but denying the same to nonmarital children of biological fathers and rejecting a claim that the gender discrimination violated the equal protection guarantee of the Due Process Clause). The year before, a majority of the Court had decided *Craig v. Boren*, 429 U.S. 190 (1976), holding that gender was a semisuspect clas-sification subject to intermediate scrutiny.

4   *See* Teresa Miller, *Citizenship & Severity: Recent Immigration Reforms and the New Penology*, 17 GEO. IMMIGR. L.J. 611, 619–20, 632–42 (2003); Jennifer Chacon, *Commentary: Blurred Boundaries in Immigration: Unsecured Borders: Immigra-tion Restrictions, Crime Control and National Security*, 39 CONN. L. REV. 1827, 1831–33, 1851–52 (2007); Kevin Johnson, *Symposium: Law and the Border: Open Borders?*, 51 UCLA L. REV. 193, 196 (2003); *see also* Howard S. Myers III, *Im-migration Law: An Examination of America's Immigration System at a Time of Un-certainty America's Immigration Policy—Where We Are and How We Arrived: An Immigration Lawyer's Perspective*, 44 MITCHELL HAMLINE L. REV. 743, 768–71 (2018); Jennifer M. Chacon, *Overcriminalizing Immigration*, 102 J. CRIM. L. & CRIMINOLOGY 613, 631–39 (2012); Ingrid V. Eagly, *Prosecuting Immigration*, 104 NW. U. L. REV. 1281 (2010).

5   Sessions v. Morales-Santana, 137 S. Ct. 1678 (2017).

6   *See* JOAN HOFF, LAW, GENDER, AND INJUSTICE: A LEGAL HISTORY OF U.S. WOMEN (1991); CANDICE LEWIS BREDBENNER, A NATIONALITY OF HER OWN: WOMEN, MARRIAGE, AND THE LAW OF CITIZENSHIP (1998); IAN HANEY LOPEZ, WHITE BY LAW: THE LEGAL CONSTRUCTION OF RACE (1996); Kristin A. Collins, *Illegitimate Borders: Jus Sanguinis Citizenship and the Legal Construction of Family, Race, and Nation*, 123 YALE L.J. 2134 (2014); M. Isabel Medina, *Derivative Citizenship: What's Marriage, Citizenship, Sex, Sexual Orientation, Race and Class Got to Do with It?* 28 GEO. IMMIGR. L.J. 391, 395–417 (2014); Rose Cuison Villazor, *The Other Loving: Uncovering the Federal Government's Racial Regulation of Marriage*, 86 N.Y.U. L. REV. 1361, 1390–97 (2011); Nancy K. Ota, *Paper Daughters*, 12 WASH. & LEE J. CIVIL RTS. & SOC. JUST. 41, 54–57 (2005); Leti Volpp, *Divesting Citizenship: On Asian American*

History and the Loss of Citizenship Through Marriage, 53 UCLA L. REV. 405, 453–58 (2005); Leti Volpp, *"Obnoxious to Their Very Nature": Asian Americans and Constitutional Citizenship*, 8 ASIAN L.J. 71, 83–85 (2001).

7 8 U.S.C. § 1401(c), (g) and § 1409. *See* Rogers v. Bellei, 401 U.S. 815 (1971) (upholding a statutory requirement that the child born abroad be physically present in the United States continuously for at least five years after age fourteen and before the age of twenty-eight; if the child did not satisfy the requirement, he/she lost citizenship).

8 *Sessions*, 137 S. Ct. 1678 (2017); Flores-Villar v. United States, 564 U.S. 210 (2011); Nguyen v. I.N.S., 533 U.S. 53 (2001).

9 518 U.S. 515 (1996).

10 523 U.S. 420 (1998).

11 8 U.S.C. § 1409(c).

12 8 U.S.C. § 1409(a).

13 Miller v. Albright, 523 U.S. 420 (1998).

14 *Id.* at 445–52 (O'Connor, J., concurring).

15 *Id.*

16 *Id.* at 452–59, 453 (Scalia, J., concurring).

17 *Id.* at 460–71 (Ginsburg, J., dissenting).

18 *Sessions*, 137 S. Ct. 1678 (2017).

19 533 U.S. 53 (2001) (upholding a gender differential that required the father to formally legitimate the child prior to the child turning eighteen).

20 564 U.S. 210 (2011).

21 Chacon, *Overcriminalizing Immigration* at 632.

22 8 U.S.C. §1409(c) (2012).

23 8 U.S.C. §1407(a) (2012).

24 8 U.S.C. §601(g) (1940 ed.) was made applicable to unwed U.S. citizen fathers by 8 U.S.C. § 1409(a). The Court has held that the date of a child's birth determines which statutory provisions apply to their acquisition of citizenship claim. Currently, the statutory provisions require only a five-year period of physical presence prior to the child's birth. 8 U.S.C. § 1401(g) (2012).

25 137 S. Ct. at 1693.

26 *Id.* at 1695.

27 *Id.* at. 1686.

28 *Id.* at 1686, 1700–01; 8 U.S.C. § 1401(a)(7) (1958 ed.) currently 8 U.S.C.§ 1401(g) (2012); Medina, *Derivative Citizenship* at 432–34. In fact, section 1401(a)(7) made no reference to marriage; the provision applied to all children born of mixed citizenship status parents. The statutory provision to introduce gender and marital status was the one imposing additional burdens on the biological fathers but easier terms for the biological mother. Medina, *Derivative Citizenship* at 403–04.

29 The Department of Homeland Security does not apply *Morales-Santana* retroactively to children born before 2017. Children born before 2017 continue to benefit from the one-year presence requirement if their U.S. citizen parent was a woman rather than a man. *See* 12 USCIS-Policy Manual Chapter 3, www.uscis.gov.

30 *Supreme Court Cautious, Pragmatic*, CQ ALMANAC 310–14 (50th ed. 1994), http://library.cqpress.com.

31 Illegal Immigration Reform and Immigrant Responsibility Act of 1996, Pub. L. No. 104–208, 110 Stat. 3009 (restricting review of discretionary decisions, decisions in cases of noncitizens who had committed an extensive number of criminal offenses); and Anti-Terrorism and Effective Death Penalty, Pub. L. No. 104–132, 110 Stat. 279 (1996) (eliminating judicial review of removal or noncitizens convicted of certain criminal offenses). *See* Michelle R. Slack, *No One Agrees . . . But Me? An Alternative Approach to Interpreting the Limits on Judicial Review of Procedural Motions and Requests for Discretionary Relief After* Kucana v. Holder, 26 GEO. IMMIGR. L.J. 1 (2011).

32 Real I.D. Act of 2005, Pub. L. No. 109–13, 119 Stat. 231 (May 11, 2005).

33 Kucana v. Holder, 558 U.S. 233 (2010).

34 Vartelas v. Holder, 566 U.S. 257 (2012).

35 Kawashima v. Holder, 565 U.S. 478 (2012).

36 Maryam Kamali Miyamoto, *The First Amendment After* Reno v. American-Arab Anti-Discrimination Committee: *A Different Bill of Rights for Aliens?* 35 HARV. C.R.-C.L. L. REV. 183 (2000).

37 Bivens v. Six Unknown Fed. Narcotics Agents, 403 U.S. 388 (1971).

38 Hernandez v. Mesa, 140 S. Ct. 735, 753 (2020).

6

Civil Procedure

The Institutional Pragmatist

ELIZABETH G. PORTER AND HEATHER ELLIOTT

Justice Ginsburg is widely revered for her contributions to the law of gender equality and reproductive rights, as well for her incisive dissents in pivotal voting rights cases from *Bush v. Gore* to *Shelby County v. Holder*. In contrast to her deserved fame in these areas, the Justice's contributions to the field of civil procedure are less well known. This is hardly surprising; procedure is not exactly an Instagrammable topic. But procedure has always been central to the Justice's approach to law. Justice Ginsburg's first postclerkship job was at Columbia's Project on International Procedure,[1] for which she co-authored a study on Swedish civil procedure.[2] Later she taught civil procedure for seventeen years as a law professor.[3] And while on the Court, Justice Ginsburg wrote a substantial number of opinions on civil procedure and federal jurisdiction. In fact, she once said, "I'd write all the procedure decisions for the Court if I could."[4]

The significance of Ginsburg's focus on civil procedure might be obscure to many Americans, but it has long been perfectly clear to civil rights lawyers, who have fought to increase access to courts for marginalized members of society by pushing for robust discovery and flexible use of tools such as class actions. The centrality of procedure has also been perfectly clear to corporate defendants, who continue to implement long-range strategies aimed at reducing litigation exposure through the narrowing of procedural rules.[5] Inevitably, the Supreme Court has played a deciding role in this protracted conflict between those who seek to expand access to justice and those who are focused on closing the courthouse door to claims they believe are meritless.

In cases implicating this long-simmering tension, Justice Ginsburg was not the iconoclast that she is sometimes perceived to be. To the contrary, her procedural jurisprudence was defined by evenhanded restraint, pragmatism, and an abiding faith in the coordinate branches of the federal government and in state governments and state courts. Federalism is often associated with conservative legal thought, but Justice Ginsburg's civil procedure decisions undermine that oversimple assumption. Indeed, her commitment to separation of powers and federalism was not in tension with her views in the areas of equal protection or reproductive rights. To the contrary, Justice Ginsburg's civil procedure oeuvre was wholly consistent with her broader belief that courts should play a deliberate, consistent, and restrained role in upholding—and symbolizing—the rule of law.

Justice Ginsburg and the Separation of Powers

Justice Ginsburg wrote many opinions in the areas of civil procedure and federal jurisdiction that reflect her larger commitment to ensuring that the democratic branches of the federal government were constrained by the courts only when necessary. As Linda Greenhouse put it, the Justice had "a liberal vision of a muscular and broadly inclusive Constitution coupled with a pragmatist's sense that the most efficacious way of achieving the Constitution's highest potential as an engine of social progress is not necessarily through the exercise of judicial supremacy."[6] This section limns several procedural and jurisdictional opinions that fit this mold.

Jurisdiction is about the power of *courts*. In deciding jurisdictional questions, the Supreme Court sets the boundaries of its own power and the power of lower courts. Yet the Supreme Court is not the sole authority in such questions. To the contrary, above certain minima, the Constitution grants Congress authority to expand or contract federal judicial jurisdiction through statutes.[7] Justice Ginsburg's decisions in this area demonstrate a keen awareness that, if courts patrol the borders of their jurisdiction too aggressively, they can obstruct Congress's constitutional authority to regulate that jurisdiction. Her decisions evince consistent respect for this dual decision-making authority.

For example, writing for the majority in *Ruhrgas AG v. Marathon Oil Co.*[8] and *Sinochem International Co. v. Malaysia International Shipping Corp.*,[9] Justice Ginsburg gave federal courts a choice among which threshold jurisdictional question to resolve first, whether subject-matter jurisdiction, personal jurisdiction, forum non conveniens, or the like. Thanks to these cases, a court can now forgo a tricky subject-matter jurisdiction question in favor of, for example, an easier personal jurisdiction question. Many would argue that this results in ultra vires action: if a court addresses a personal jurisdiction question without ensuring its subject-matter jurisdiction,[10] it acts beyond its authorized powers, just as it would if it resolved a merits question before a subject-matter jurisdiction question.[11]

Justice Ginsburg, however, perceived that Congress's control, within the bounds of the Constitution, is limited to regulating subject-matter jurisdiction, while many other threshold questions remain within the province of the judicial branch. Requiring that subject-matter jurisdiction *always* come before any other threshold question would require courts to always resolve questions about the margins of their power, even if exceptionally difficult—precisely the kinds of questions that might risk judicial overreach. By permitting courts to opt instead for dismissal on easier personal-jurisdiction grounds, Justice Ginsburg created a way for courts to leave tricky subject-matter jurisdiction questions for another day, thereby preserving Congress's primacy over that jurisdiction.[12]

Similarly, in *Holmes Group, Inc. v. Vornado Air Circulation Systems, Inc.*,[13] Justice Ginsburg chided the majority for failing to take Congress's jurisdictional choices into account. The case asked whether a patent counterclaim arising in a federal case must be appealed to the Federal Circuit. Applying the well-pleaded complaint rule, the majority said it did not because the rule did not consider counterclaims and the complaint did not contain a claim based on patent law. Justice Ginsburg criticized this reasoning for privileging court-centric procedural rules over Congress's constitutional authority to regulate patents, asserting:

> The sole question presented here concerns *Congress'* allocation of adjudicatory authority among the federal courts of appeals. At that appellate level, *Congress* sought to eliminate forum shopping and to advance uniformity in the interpretation and application of federal patent law. . . . I would . . . give effect to *Congress'* endeavor to grant the Federal Circuit exclusive appellate jurisdiction at least over district court adjudications of patent claims.[14]

A similar respect for the democratic branches lies behind Justice Ginsburg's opinion for the Court in *Friends of the Earth v. Laidlaw Environmental Services (TOC), Inc.*[15] In that case, the Court held that environmental plaintiffs had Article III standing to sue over water pollution because the defendant violated its Clean Water Act permit, causing injury to the plaintiffs, who averred that the pollution decreased the aesthetic and recreational value of the river to them. The dissenting Justices would have required a more demanding judicial inquiry into whether the alleged permit violations caused actual harm to the plaintiffs absent a showing of harm to the environment and whether the legislative remedy redressed that harm. Justice Ginsburg, writing for the majority, recognized that such an independent judicial inquiry replaced Congress's judgment of harm and remedy with the Court's, violating separation of powers.[16] The Court, Justice Ginsburg wrote, should not "raise the standing hurdle higher than the necessary showing for success on the merits."[17]

Justice Ginsburg's solicitude for the other branches also arises in decisions under the Federal Rules of Civil Procedure (FRCP). While cases interpreting the FRCP do not involve congressional intent as often or as directly as jurisdictional cases do, the Court is sometimes asked to square the application of a Rule with Congress's intent in another statute.

For example, in *Arbaugh v. Y&H Co.*, the Justice deferred to Congress's construction of Title VII's numerosity requirement, which provides that only employers with more than fourteen employees need to comply with federal antidiscrimination laws. The defendant contended that numerosity was a jurisdictional requirement that could be raised at any time, even on appeal, and even by courts sua sponte.[18] If, instead, the numerosity requirement was an element of the plaintiff's claim, the defendant should have raised it in a Rule 12(b)(6) motion to dismiss for failure to state a claim and had waived the issue by failing to raise it before the trial had ended.[19] Justice Ginsburg, writing for a unanimous Court,[20] noted that "[n]othing in the text of Title VII indicates that Congress intended courts, on their own motion, to assure that the employee-numerosity requirement is met."[21] Although "Congress could make the employee-numerosity requirement 'jurisdictional,'" it had not clearly done so, and the Court, rather than "constricting . . . Title VII's jurisdictional provision, . . . le[ft] the ball in Congress' court."[22]

Justice Ginsburg's focus on congressional intent was not partisan. In *Mayle v. Felix*,[23] for example, the Court faced the question of whether Felix's amended habeas petition related back to his initial habeas petition. Justice Ginsburg, writing for the Court, noted that Congress had imposed a strict one-year time limit on habeas petitions in the Anti-Terrorism and Effective Death Penalty Act (AEDPA).[24] Even though the relation-back provisions of FRCP 15(c) applied to habeas petitions,[25] Justice Ginsburg emphasized "Congress' decision to expedite collateral attacks by placing stringent time restrictions on" such petitions[26] and rejected Mr. Felix's argument for failure to relate back.[27] If the Court allowed relation back in cases where, as here, the amended petition asserts a new ground for relief based on facts differing in time and type from the original pleading, then "AEDPA's limitation period would have slim significance."[28]

In a similar analysis, Justice Ginsburg emphasized congressional authority in *Tellabs, Inc. v. Makor Issues & Rights, Ltd.*[29] Writing for the majority, she emphasized that "Congress enacted the Private Securities Litigation Reform Act of 1995 (PSLRA) . . . [a]s a check against abusive litigation by private parties."[30] Because "[e]xacting pleading requirements are among the control measures Congress included in the PSLRA," the statute affects the FRCP's pleading standards. Unlike FRCP 8(a) and 9(b), the PSLRA requires the plaintiff to "state with particularity facts giving rise to a *strong inference* that the defendant acted with the required state of mind."[31] Congress did not, however, define "strong inference."

In resolving the ambiguous term, the Court held that the PSLRA's "twin goals"—"to curb frivolous, lawyer-driven litigation, while preserving investors' ability to recover on meritorious claims"[32]—were best fulfilled "only [when] a reasonable person would deem the inference of scienter cogent and at least as compelling as any opposing inference one could draw from the facts alleged."[33] "Congress, as creator of federal statutory claims, has power to prescribe what must be pleaded to state the claim, just as it has power to determine what must be proved to prevail on the merits."[34]

Justice Ginsburg and Federalism: Is This Conflict Really Necessary?[35]

In addition to her respect for the coordinate branches of the federal government, Justice Ginsburg's decisions evinced deep respect for the role that state courts and state legislatures play in our democracy. She did not subscribe to a toggle-switch federalism wherein state and federal powers operate in distinct and competing spheres of authority; rather, she embraced the cooperative relationship between the two systems. Her approach emphasized the ability of state courts to interpret federal law while simultaneously recognizing that the converse is also true: federal courts must—and are competent to—adjudicate issues that bear directly or closely on state-law questions. In her words: "Federal and state courts are complementary systems for administering justice in our Nation. Cooperation and comity, not competition and conflict, are essential to the federal design."[36]

Gasperini v. Center for Humanities—a thorny *Erie* case—aptly illustrates Justice Ginsburg's commitment to giving effect to state law.[37] Precisely because it accurately captures the cognitive dissonance of the *Erie* doctrine, *Gasperini* is not for the faint of heart. Invoking diversity jurisdiction, Gasperini, a photographer, sued the Center for Humanities in federal court in New York, alleging that the Center had lost 300 of his valuable photographic slides. A jury awarded him a hefty $450,000, which was $1,500 per slide. The defendant appealed, arguing that a New York statute empowered appellate courts to review and remediate excessive jury verdicts. Over Gasperini's objection, the Second Circuit applied that New York law and ruled that the verdict "materially deviate[d] from what is reasonable compensation." On petition to the Supreme Court, the Center for Humanities defended the Second Circuit's application of what it argued was *substantive* New York law. Defending the verdict, Gasperini urged that, in federal court, the Seventh Amendment's Reexamination Clause barred *procedural* appellate review of a jury's fact-finding power.

The New York statute at issue straddled the line between substance and procedure. Rather than choosing one characterization over another, Justice Ginsburg's majority opinion sought a middle way. Explaining that "the principal state and federal interests can be accommodated," the

Court held that the federal *district* court could constitutionally apply the New York "deviates materially" standard, although the New York statute was written to empower review by state appellate courts. To prevent trenching on the Seventh Amendment, federal appellate review would be confined to a more circumscribed check for abuse of discretion. In other words, Justice Ginsburg's opinion repackaged a state law aimed at appellate review into a form of district court review. This reframing aimed to preserve the New York legislature's intent to limit excessive jury verdicts while purporting to steer clear of the Seventh Amendment's restrictions on reexamination of jury findings. In dissent for three justices, Justice Scalia disagreed, writing:

> [T]he people of the State of New York may well be correct that such a rule contributes to a more just legal system. But the practice of federal appellate reexamination of facts found by a jury is precisely what the People of the several States considered not to be good legal policy in 1791. Indeed, so fearful were they of such a practice that they constitutionally prohibited it by means of the Seventh Amendment.[38]

Justice Ginsburg's quest in *Gasperini* to give full effect to state law within the constraints of the *Erie* doctrine and the Seventh Amendment embodied her venturesome approach to accommodating both state and federal interests rather than choosing a single victor. But the long-term impact of this approach on the *Erie* doctrine is unclear. In a fractured decision a decade after *Gasperini*, involving yet another New York law in a diversity suit, Justice Scalia's views on *Erie*—that it was less accommodating of state law and far simpler to apply—won the day, at least as a technical matter, thanks to a concurring vote by Justice Stevens. In this case, *Shady Grove Orthopedic Associates, P.A. v. Allstate Insurance Co.*,[39] the question was whether a federal court should give effect to a New York law that prohibited class actions seeking to recover a "penalty" such as statutory interest. Writing for a plurality, Justice Scalia rejected application of the law, holding that Rule 23 is the sole method for evaluating whether a class action can be maintained in federal court.[40] Justice Ginsburg's dissent for four justices criticized the plurality's "relentless" reading of Rule 23. She declared: "I would continue to interpret Federal Rules with awareness of, and sensitivity to, important state regulatory policies."[41]

Other procedural decisions written by Justice Ginsburg echo this sensitivity to the dignity and legitimacy of state courts. In the context of a suit challenging the constitutionality of a state tax, Justice Ginsburg's deference to state courts found easy purchase. In *Levin v. Commerce Energy*,[42] gas consumers sued independent gas providers and the Ohio Tax Commissioner in federal court, alleging that taxes on the gas providers and consumers violated the Commerce and Equal Protection Clauses. In an opinion written by Justice Ginsburg, the Court ruled that the comity doctrine precluded federal jurisdiction over the suit. "[I]f the Ohio scheme is indeed unconstitutional," the Court held, "surely the Ohio courts are better positioned to determine—unless and until the Ohio legislature weighs in—how to comply with the mandate of equal treatment."[43] In another case validating state jurisdiction, *Vaden v. Discover Bank*,[44] Justice Ginsburg wrote for the unanimous Court that, under the well-pleaded complaint rule, a federal court lacks subject-matter jurisdiction to entertain a Federal Arbitration Act petition to compel arbitration based on the contents of a counterclaim.[45] And in *Riley v. Kennedy*—a pre–*Shelby County* case concerning whether an Alabama law providing for gubernatorial appointment to fill midterm vacancies on a county commission required preclearance under section 5 of the Voting Rights Act—Justice Ginsburg's opinion for the Court defended the role of state supreme courts in adjudicating state constitutional claims challenging state election practices.[46] "[T]he rule advocated by the dissent," the Court held, "would effectively preclude Alabama's highest court from applying to a state law a provision of the State Constitution entirely harmonious with federal law."[47] Under the facts of *Riley*, the Court rejected "that sort of interference with a state supreme court's ability to determine the content of state law."

Justice Ginsburg's deference to state court decision-making has faced challenges, particularly in the realm of punitive damages. Beginning in the mid-1990s, the Court embarked on a series of decisions imposing limits on punitive damages awards. In *BMW v. Gore*,[48] the Court held that "grossly excessive" punitive damages awards violate the Due Process Clause of the Fourteenth Amendment. The Court took a more aggressive stance several years later. In *State Farm Mutual Automobile Insurance Company v. Campbell*, it held that "few awards exceeding a single-digit ratio between punitive and compensatory damages . . . will

CIVIL PROCEDURE | 85

satisfy due process."[49] Justice Ginsburg dissented in both cases.[50] Limitations on punitive damages awards, she cautioned, are "traditionally within the States' domain."[51] While stressing that capping state damages might very well be sound legislative policy, Justice Ginsburg reiterated her view "that this Court has no warrant to reform state law governing awards of punitive damages."[52] In contrast, in *Exxon Shipping Company v. Baker*—a case involving federal maritime law rather than state law— Justice Ginsburg agreed that the Court had the authority to regulate punitive damages awards.[53] Recognizing separation of powers concerns, however, she dissented in part on the grounds that Congress was better positioned than the Court to regulate punitive damages under federal law.[54] But she carefully distinguished *Baker* as "unlike the Court's recent forays into the domain of state tort law under the banner of substantive due process."[55]

Justice Ginsburg, Procedural Pragmatist

Beneath many of Justice Ginsburg's federalism and separation-of-powers decisions lies a third axis of her procedural jurisprudence: pragmatism. Rule 1 of the FRCP decrees that the Federal Rules be construed "to secure the just, speedy, and inexpensive determination" of legal proceedings. Predictably, there are serious and sometimes irreconcilable tensions between the values of efficiency and fairness, not only in the Federal Rules but also in procedural cases more broadly. Justice Ginsburg's procedural decisions navigated this tension in two ways. First, the Justice emphasized due process and fairness to litigants; she did not privilege formal procedural compliance over the practical impact of decisions on litigants. And second, her opinions sought to bring clarity about complex procedural questions to future litigants (*Gasperini* being the possible exception).

Caterpillar v. Lewis, a case that law students love to hate, illustrates the Justice's fairness-over-technicality philosophy to a T.[56] In *Caterpillar*, the federal district court erroneously determined that removal was proper pursuant to 28 U.S.C. § 1332(a) in a product liability case that actually lacked a basis for subject-matter jurisdiction. At the time the defendant sought removal (only a day before the one-year outer deadline for removal of diversity suits),[57] there was no federal question or federal defendant, and neither was there complete diversity between the parties.[58] The plaintiff's motion to remand was denied. Six months before trial, the nondiverse party was dismissed pursuant to a settlement, which meant that, by the time the judgment for the defendant was entered following a jury verdict, there was complete diversity between the parties.[59] The court of appeals ruled that the judgment should be vacated on the separate grounds that removal had been improper and that the plaintiff's motion to remand should have been granted. The Supreme Court, in an opinion by Justice Ginsburg, reversed and sustained the judgment. Notwithstanding the errors below, and the plaintiff's diligence in preserving his objection to those errors, the Court held that "[o]nce a diversity case has been tried in federal court, with rules of decision supplied by state law under the regime of *Erie v. Tompkins*, considerations of finality, efficiency, and economy become overwhelming."[60]

Other cases similarly highlight Justice Ginsburg's prioritization of core due process values over technical compliance with procedural rules. In *Becker v. Montgomery*, her opinion for a unanimous Court held that a pro se section 1983 litigant's failure to include a handwritten signature on his notice of appeal was not a fatal jurisdictional defect.[61] The Court pushed back on the tendency to describe requirements as "jurisdictional" in a way that poses a barrier to unwary litigants.[62] Similarly, Justice Ginsburg's opinion in *Arbaugh v. Y&H Corporation*, described above, rejected an assertedly "jurisdictional" barrier in a Title VII suit.[63] Cautioning that courts—including the Supreme Court—have "sometimes been profligate in [their] use of the term" (i.e., the term "jurisdictional"), Justice Ginsburg's opinion in *Arbaugh* attempted to clarify the distinction between requirements that bear on subject-matter jurisdiction, on one hand, and requirements that go to a party's substantive claim, on the other. Noting that "this Court and others have been less than meticulous" with respect to that distinction, Justice Ginsburg's opinion sought to bring clarity to this thicket in a way that prioritized substantive law over procedural formalism. And in *Johnson v. City of Shelby*, a per curiam decision summarily reversing the Fifth Circuit, the Court held that a plaintiff's failure to expressly invoke section 1983 in a complaint does not justify dismissal for failure to state a claim.[64] This short opinion bears all the hallmarks of Justice Ginsburg's procedural pragmatism: it refused to accept the Fifth Circuit's invitation to extend the heightened pleading expectations of *Twombly* and *Iqbal*—which concern *factual* allegations—to the labeling of *legal* theories in pleadings.[65]

As the above examples illustrate, Justice Ginsburg favored due process over formal compliance, particularly where mandating strict adherence to procedural rules would predictably prejudice vulnerable litigants. That same commitment to due process, however, meant that her pragmatism had its limits. Most famously, the Justice's opinion for the Court in *Amchem Products v. Windsor* refused to approve a vast class action settlement arising out of the national asbestos litigation crisis.[66] *Amchem* is a prime example of Justice Ginsburg's quest to use Supreme Court opinions to bring clarity to the law of procedure. The first long stretch of the opinion is a primer on Rule 23. Yet *Amchem* also broke new ground, establishing important due process limits on class action settlements. Notwithstanding the obvious need for a solution to the asbestos crisis, the Court could not overlook what it found to be fatal due process problems in the proposed settlement. The Court found the settlement defective for its lack of subclasses; its failure to recognize the conflict between plaintiff-class members with current injuries and those who had been exposed to asbestos and might become injured in the future; the stringent limits on class members' ability to opt out; and the lack of any inflation adjustment for exposure-only plaintiffs who might not seek damages until their injuries became manifest.[67] *Amchem*'s message of Rule 23 moderation stresses that due process is the glue that holds classes together and calls for Congress—rather than the courts—to respond to national problems like that of asbestos.

Amchem remains the blueprint for judicial consideration of class action settlements. The Justice's opinion for a unanimous Court in *Taylor v. Sturgell* plays a similar role in an analogous context.[68] In *Taylor*, a prior plaintiff, Herrick, had sued under the Freedom of Information Act (FOIA) to obtain vintage aviation records in the possession of the Federal Aviation Administration (FAA). Herrick lost that effort. Subsequently, Taylor—a friend of Herrick, represented by the same attorney—filed a FOIA suit seeking the identical records. The FAA argued that Taylor was precluded from seeking those records because he had been "virtually represented" in the first suit by Herrick. The Court, via Justice Ginsburg, rejected such an expansive concept of virtual representation.

In a systematic opinion, Justice Ginsburg set forth six narrow exceptions that might allow a nonparty to be bound by a previous judgment: an agreement to be bound, privity, adequate representation (such as in a class action), control by the party of the prior litigation, relitigation through a proxy, and special statutory schemes.[69] The Court rejected the defendant's attempt to expand these categories on the grounds that virtual representation is inimical to due process and also that it would "likely create more headaches than it relieves."[70] Justice Ginsburg's resistance to formalism was thus embedded within a larger framework that centered due process and judicial clarity.

Importantly, this drive for clarity benefited defendants as well as plaintiffs. Justice Ginsburg's most significant procedural decisions during her last decade on the Court were in the area of personal jurisdiction. In *Goodyear Dunlop Tires Operations, S.A. v. Brown*[71] and *Daimler AG v. Bauman*,[72] the Justice led a dramatic restructuring—and retrenchment—of general personal jurisdiction over corporate defendants. Attempting to shift the nomenclature of personal jurisdiction, Justice Ginsburg in *Goodyear* referred to "case-specific" and "all-purpose" (formerly general) jurisdiction.[73] The Court then limited this "all-purpose" jurisdiction, under which a corporate defendant can be subject to a suit that bears no relationship to the forum state, to situations where defendants' "affiliations with the State are so 'continuous and systematic' as to render them essentially at home in the forum State."[74] The Court found no such connections between foreign subsidiaries of Goodyear and North Carolina.[75] In *Daimler*, Justice Ginsburg took this "at home" definition of general jurisdiction a step further, finding that a corporate defendant will typically be subject to general jurisdiction only in its state of incorporation and (if different) the state where it has its principal place of business.[76] This holding—which renders general personal jurisdiction under the Fourteenth Amendment essentially coterminous with corporate citizenship for purposes of diversity jurisdiction under section 1332—substantially narrowed the scope of general jurisdiction. In this instance, Justice Ginsburg's pursuit of clarity came at the expense of the pro se and vulnerable litigants that her other procedural opinions so often sought to protect. To be sure, Justice Ginsburg's opinions indicated that a robust case-specific jurisdiction should take up the slack, providing a ready forum for plaintiffs. But as the Court's fractured decision in

J. McIntyre Machinery, Ltd. v. Nicastro[77] underscored, the Court does not have an appetite for a more muscular specific jurisdiction jurisprudence.

Conclusion

Justice Ginsburg was an institutionalist, a federalist, a pragmatist, and a respecter of separation of powers. In essence, she was a procedural moderate. If this seems at odds with her jurisprudence in other areas, that disconnect may be more a matter of optics than reality. But if the Justice's views in procedural cases seem straightforward, even anodyne, think again. As the recent rise of the Court's shadow docket illustrates, judicial restraint is more than mere courtesy: the Court's increasing practice of resolving cases summarily without thorough briefing, oral argument, or even written reasons[78] is the antithesis of Ginsburg's dedication to cooperation, comity, and the rule of law. We can only hope that her modest approach may inspire current and future Justices to return to a less nakedly political approach to resolving cases.

NOTES

Rachel Hay, Julie Jackson, and Leila Beem Nuñez provided excellent research assistance to this chapter.

1 LINDA HIRSHMAN, SISTERS IN LAW: HOW SANDRA DAY O'CONNOR AND RUTH BADER GINSBURG WENT TO THE SUPREME COURT AND CHANGED THE WORLD 21 (2015).

2 RUTH BADER GINSBURG & ANDERS BRUZELIUS, CIVIL PROCEDURE IN SWEDEN (Hans Smit ed. 1965).

3 *See* Herma Hill Kay, *Ruth Bader Ginsburg, Professor of Law*, 104 COLUM. L. REV. 1, 10–11, 15–16 (2004).

4 *A Conversation with Justice Ruth Bader Ginsburg*, 25 Colum. J. Gender & L. 6 (2013).

5 For a glimpse into these strategies, *see* U.S. Chamber of Commerce Litig. Ctr., www.chamberlitigation.com (listing Arbitration, Class Actions, and Forum Shopping among the areas of focus for the U.S. Chamber of Commerce Litigation Center).

6 Linda Greenhouse, *Learning to Listen to Ruth Bader Ginsburg*, 7 N.Y. CITY L. REV. 213, 218 (2004) (quoting Linda Greenhouse, *The Supreme Court: A Sense of Judicial Limits*, N.Y. TIMES, July 22, 1994, at A1).

7 U.S. CONST., art. III, § 2.

8 526 U.S. 574 (1999).

9 549 U.S. 422 (2007).

10 *See id.* at 425; *Ruhrgas*, 526 U.S. at 578.

11 Steel Co. v. Citizens for a Better Environment, 523 U.S. 83, 91–93, 101 (1998).

12 This argument was made more generally in Heather Elliott, *Jurisdictional Resequencing and Restraint*, 43 NEW ENG. L. REV. 725 (2009). *But see* Kevin M. Clermont, *Sequencing the Issues for Judicial Decisionmaking: Limitations from Jurisdictional Primacy and Intrasuit Preclusion*, 63 FLA. L. REV. 301 (2011) (rejecting the argument). David Shapiro has also noted that Justice Ginsburg's approach here interferes with state judicial authority—after all, a decision on federal subject-matter jurisdiction leaves the state courts free to hear a case; a decision that a particular federal court lacks personal jurisdiction over the defendant, because that defendant lacks sufficient contacts with the relevant state, is also a decision on whether that state's courts have personal jurisdiction. David Shapiro, *Justice Ginsburg's First Decade: Some Thoughts About Her Contributions in the Fields of Procedure and Jurisdiction*, 104 COLUM. L. REV. 21, 30 (2004).

13 535 U.S. 826 (2002).

14 *Id.* at 840 (emphasis added).

15 528 U.S. 167, 174, 180 (2000).

16 *See id.* at 187 (deferring to congressional determination of what remedies would achieve congressional goals by deterring undesirable behavior and noting that choice of remedy "is a matter within the legislature's range of choice. Judgment on the deterrent effect of the various weapons in the armory of the law can lay little claim to scientific basis") (quoting Tigner v. Texas, 310 U.S. 141, 148 (1940)).

17 *Id.* at 181.

18 546 U.S. 500 (2006).

19 *Id.* at 507 (citing FRCP 12(h)(2)).

20 Justice Alito took no part in the case. *Id.* at 502.

21 *Id.* at 514.

22 *Id.* at 515.

23 545 U.S. 644 (2005).

24 28 U.S.C. § 2244(d)(1).

25 545 U.S. at 654.

26 *Id.* at 657 (internal quotation marks and citations omitted).

27 *Id.* at 650.

28 *Id.* at 662.

29 551 U.S. 308 (2007).

30 *Id.* at 313 (citing 109 Stat. 737).

31 *Id.* at 321 (citing 15 U.S.C. § 78u–4(b)(2)) (emphasis added).

32 *Id.* at 322.

33 *Id.* at 324.

34 *Id.* at 327.

35 Shady Grove Orthopedic Associates, P.A. v. Allstate Ins. Co., 559 U.S. 393, 437 (2010) (Ginsburg, J., dissenting) (quoting Roger J. Traynor, *Is This Conflict Really Necessary?* 37 TEX. L. REV. 657 (1959)).

36 Ruhrgas AG v. Marathon Oil Co., 526 U.S. 574, 586 (1999).

37 Gasperini v. Ctr. For Humanities, 518 U.S. 415 (1996).

38 *Id.* at 450 (Scalia, J., dissenting).

39 559 U.S. 393 (2010).

40 *Id.* at 399 (noting that "Rule 23 provides a one-size-fits-all formula for deciding the class action question").

41 *Id.* at 437 (Ginsburg, J., dissenting).

42 Levin v. Commerce Energy, Inc., 560 U.S. 413 (2010).

43 560 U.S. at 429.

44 556 U.S. 49 (2009).

45 *Id.* at 52.

46 553 U.S. 406 (2008).

47 *Id.* at 427.

48 BMW of N. Am., Inc. v. Gore, 517 U.S. 559 (1996).

49 State Farm Mut. Automobile Ins. Co. v. Campbell, 538 U.S. 408, 425 (2003).

50 *Campbell*, 538 U.S. at 430–39 (2003); *Gore*, 517 U.S. at 607–14.

51 *Gore*, 517 U.S. at 612; *Campbell*, 538 U.S. at 431.

52 *Campbell*, 538 U.S. at 438 (Ginsburg, J., dissenting).

53 Exxon Shipping Co. v. Baker, 554 U.S. 471, 523–25 (2008).

54 *Id.* at 523.

55 *Id.*

56 Caterpillar v. Lewis, 519 U.S. 61 (1996).

57 *Id.* at 65 (citing 28 U.S.C. § 1446(b)).

58 *Id.* at 70.

59 *Id.* at 67.

60 *Id.* at 75.

61 532 U.S. 757, 760 (2001).

62 *Id.* at 765 (finding the plaintiff's lapse curable on the ground that "his initial omission was not a 'jurisdictional' impediment to pursuit of his appeal").

63 546 U.S. 500 (2006).

64 574 U.S. 10, 11 (2014).

65 *Id.* at 11–12.

66 521 U.S. 591 (1997).

67 *Id.* at 624–28.

68 553 U.S. 880 (2008).

69 *Id.* at 893–95.

70 *Id.* at 901.

71 564 U.S. 915 (2011).

72 571 U.S. 117 (2011).

73 *Goodyear*, 564 U.S. at 927.

74 *Id.* at 919.

75 *Id.* at 921.

76 *Daimler*, 571 U.S. at 137.

77 564 U.S. 873 (2011).

78 Louisiana v. American Rivers, 142 S. Ct. 1347, 1347 (2022) (in a 5–4 decision, granting emergency stay of the district court's decision vacating and remanding Trump-era Clean Water Act rule); *id.* at 1349 (Kagan, J., joined by Roberts, C.J., and Breyer and Sotomayor, JJ., dissenting from grant of stay) ("By . . . granting relief, the Court goes astray. It provides a stay pending appeal, and thus signals its view of the merits, even though the applicants have failed to make the irreparable harm showing we have traditionally required. That renders the Court's emergency docket not for emergencies at all. The docket becomes only another place for merits determinations—except made without full briefing and argument.").

7

Copyright Law

Never Bet Against the House . . . or Senate

RYAN VACCA AND ANN BARTOW

Throughout her judicial career, Justice Ruth Bader Ginsburg was an important voice in copyright law developments. During her time as a judge on the D.C. Circuit and as a Justice on the Supreme Court, she authored sixteen opinions in copyright cases (ten majority, four concurrences, and two dissents) and joined the opinions of others in eleven cases (ten majority, five of which were unanimous, and one concurrence). Although she was best known for her progressive approach toward social justice issues, her approach in copyright cases could be fairly categorized as promoting "strong copyright" and generally favoring Goliath over David.

Justice Ginsburg's affinity for strong copyright is best illustrated by her majority opinion in *Eldred v. Ashcroft*.[1] *Eldred* addressed the question of whether the Copyright Term Extension Act (CTEA) violated the "limited times" prescription of the U.S. Constitution's Intellectual Property Clause and the First Amendment's free speech guarantee.[2] The lead plaintiff, Eldred, was a book publisher who specialized in distributing textual works that were in the public domain.[3] Eldred asserted that Congress erred by retroactively lengthening the copyright term of published works with subsisting copyrights, because the "limited time" in effect when a copyright is secured becomes the constitutional boundary for the duration of copyright protection—a clear line beyond the power of Congress to extend.[4] Eldred also argued that the CTEA was a regulation of speech that violated the First Amendment.[5] Justice Ginsburg concluded that the CTEA did not violate either provision of the Constitution and that Congress was authorized to extend protection to copyright owners, even if there might be negative consequences.[6] Her reasoning can be sardonically paraphrased: "It is not unconstitutional for Congress to make dumb policy decisions."

Though her opinions tended to be in favor of copyright holders, she joined several majority opinions in favor of accused copyright infringers. Most of these judgments were unanimous by vote, so perhaps they were easy cases. Or possibly Justice Ginsburg felt the gentle pull of peer pressure to go the way of her colleagues. In any event she was not always on the sides of copyright owners or authors.

For example, in *Fourth Estate Public Benefit Corp. v. Wall-Street.com*, the question presented was whether the copyright registration requirement was met by filing an application with the Copyright Office or only upon actual registration by the Copyright Office.[7] Justice Ginsburg wrote for the majority, which held that registration occurs when the Copyright Office registers a copyright, not upon the filing of an application.[8] In consequence, copyright holders can no longer simply apply for a copyright registration at the same time they file an infringement claim. They need to complete the registration process first. The ruling therefore inconveniences copyright owners by delaying their ability to file suit for infringement if they have not previously registered the copyright in a contested work.

Of the twenty-seven copyright cases Justice Ginsburg participated in, five were decided in favor of authors, twelve were decided in favor of copyright owners, and ten were decided in favor of accused infringers. Although it is fair to say that Justice Ginsburg generally favored copyright owners and strong copyright protection, it is inaccurate to claim that she overwhelmingly did so. But on balance, Justice Ginsburg was more conservative in her approach to copyright law than she was with respect to social justice issues.

Unlike social justice disputes, which tend to be easily sorted into liberal versus conservative terrain, the competing views sparking doctrinal flashpoints in copyright law do not predictably divide along party lines. Copyright protections have a different political valence. Neither political party has fixed positions on copyright law.

If her political leanings cannot explain Justice Ginsburg's views about copyright law, then what might? This chapter identifies three jurisprudential inclinations observable in Justice Ginsburg's copyright opinions: incrementalism, intergovernmental deference, and seeking alternatives.

Incrementalism

The first major theme we identified in Justice Ginsburg's copyright jurisprudence is incrementalism, an approach that informed her positions on many legal subjects, including copyright. Justice Ginsburg explicitly identified herself as an incrementalist at her Supreme Court confirmation hearing. In describing how she viewed the work of judging, she explained:

> I would add that the judge should carry out that function without fanfare, but with due care. She should decide the case before her without reaching out to cover cases not yet seen. She should be ever mindful, as Judge and then Justice Benjamin Nathan Cardozo said, "Justice is not to be taken by storm. She is to be wooed by slow advances."[9]

Her concern was that if judges interpreted laws too quickly or reached unnecessary issues, this would create instability and place undue stress on the judiciary.[10]

Justice Ginsburg's incrementalist tendencies are observable throughout her copyright law jurisprudence in big and small ways, reflecting her consistent cautiousness and restraint in interpreting the law. Her incrementalism manifests in two distinct ways: (1) writing narrow opinions that slowly move the law in her desired direction; and (2) writing opinions that acknowledged, but did not precipitously decide, extraneous legal issues for which she planted analytical seeds for the future.

Limited Holdings and Accretion

Justice Ginsburg's cautious incrementalism is visible in two cases involving copyright law's first sale doctrine, which is articulated in section 109 of the Copyright Act. It plays an important role in United States copyright law by limiting the rights of an intellectual property owner to control resale of products incorporating its intellectual property. Under the first sale doctrine, an individual who purchases a copy of a copyrighted work from the copyright holder receives the right to sell, display, or otherwise dispose of that particular physical copy any way they choose, notwithstanding the interests or preferences of the copyright owner. Owners of these physical objects can generally bend, fold, spindle, or mutilate their copies; they just can't copy them.

Content owners dislike the first sale doctrine because, with just a couple of exceptions, it allows purchasers to lend, rent, or resell their legally purchased copies.[11] As a result, it interferes with copyright holders' ability to prevent arbitrage. Without the first sale doctrine, a copyright owner could segment the market by charging higher prices for copies in the United States and lower prices in foreign markets without fear that the lower-priced foreign copies would make their way into the United States and directly compete with the higher-priced domestic copies. But until 2013, it was unclear whether the first sale doctrine allowed, without the copyright holder's permission, the importation of copyrighted goods that were lawfully produced abroad.

Two cases addressed this fundamental question: Do lawfully made objects suddenly become infringing when they cross national boundaries? The first, *Quality King v. L'anza*, was a dispute about the copyrighted labels on shampoo bottles.[12] The plaintiff was a company that manufactured "luxury" shampoo in the United States and sold it domestically at premium prices.[13] It also sold the shampoo abroad at much lower prices.[14] The defendant distributor noticed and began purchasing the shampoo abroad at the lower prices and bringing cases of it back to the United States to sell.[15] To try to stop this, the plaintiff sued for copyright infringement and obtained an injunction to prevent the continued importation of its shampoo by the defendant.[16] Defendants did not copy, and were not accused of copying, the shampoo bottle labels; indeed they were not accused of illicitly copying anything at all.[17] Just the act of bringing the original, unmodified shampoo bottles back into the United States from abroad without the copyright holder's permission was alleged to infringe the plaintiff's copyrights under section 602(a) of the Copyright Act. The plaintiff, L'anza, claimed that section 602(a), when properly construed, prohibited foreign distributors from reselling its products to American vendors without L'anza's permission.[18] Resolution of the case turned on how the Court resolved the conflicts between the importation restrictions of section 602(a) and the first sale doctrine. The Court decided that the relevant statutory language demonstrated that under the Copyright Act the right granted by section 602(a) was subject to section 109(a).[19]

In her concurrence, Justice Ginsburg displayed her incrementalist credentials, writing: "This case involves a 'round trip' journey, travel of the copies in question from the United States to places abroad, then back again. I join the Court's opinion recognizing that we do not today resolve cases in which the allegedly infringing imports were manufactured abroad."[20] Because L'anza had manufactured the shampoo bottles in the United States and then sent them abroad, they were "lawfully made under this title [of the United States Code]" as required by section 109(a).

In 2013, the Court was again presented with the first sale doctrine, but this time the issue arose in connection to "one way" goods manufactured abroad. The subject matter in *Kirtsaeng v. John Wiley & Sons, Inc.* was textbooks.[21] Kirtsaeng was an enterprising foreign graduate student studying in the United States.[22] After realizing that textbooks cost significantly more money in the United States than the virtually identical books did in Thailand, he encouraged his friends and family to send him lawfully made textbooks from Thailand to sell in the United States.[23] The textbooks were purchased at substantially lower prices in Thailand, and even after covering shipping costs Kirtsaeng could make substantial amounts of money reselling the books.[24] The publishers felt the impact of his actions on their domestic sales and sued him for copyright infringement.[25] No unauthorized copies had been made, but the publishers accused Kirtsaeng of violating their section 602(a) importation rights.[26] He asserted the first sale doctrine in defense, which allows the purchasers of copyrighted works to sell or otherwise dispose of their copies any way they wish, and prevailed at the Supreme Court by a 6–3 vote.[27] Justice Breyer, writing for the majority, concluded that the first sale doctrine applies to copyrighted works lawfully made abroad as well as domestically.[28]

Justice Ginsburg dissented.[29] She railed against enemies of incrementalism, and her words were blistering:

> Instead of adhering to the Legislature's design, the Court today adopts an interpretation of the Copyright Act at odds with Congress' aim to protect copyright owners against the unauthorized importation of low-priced, foreign-made copies of their copyrighted works. The Court's bold departure from Congress' design is all the more stunning, for it places

the United States at the vanguard of the movement for "international exhaustion" of copyrights—a movement the United States has steadfastly resisted on the world stage.[30]

Justice Ginsburg asserted that section 109(a) "properly read . . . afford[ed] Kirtsaeng no defense against Wiley's claim of copyright infringement."[31] The Copyright Act, she claimed, did not apply extraterritorially.[32] As an incrementalist, she saw the majority's approach as modifying copyright law too quickly, immediately moving the United States from a staunch opponent of international exhaustion for several decades[33] to "solidly in the international exhaustion camp."[34]

Sowing Analytical Seeds

Justice Ginsburg's incrementalism is also evident, though perhaps less obvious, in cases in which she acknowledged unresolved questions accompanying the specific issues being litigated but declined to resolve them. Instead, she noted the unresolved issues and expressly left them for future clarification. *Petrella v. Metro-Goldwyn-Mayer* provides one example. The primary dispute in *Petrella* was whether laches was available as a defense to damages for copyright infringement. After decisively dispatching the laches question, Justice Ginsburg explained in a footnote that "[a]lthough we have not passed on the question, nine Courts of Appeals have adopted, as an alternative to the incident of injury rule, a 'discovery rule,' which starts the limitations period when 'the plaintiff discovers, or with due diligence should have discovered, the injury that forms the basis for the claim.'"[35] By declining to decide the propriety of the discovery rule, she left the issue to percolate in the lower courts; the Supreme Court could address it later in due course.

Another case that illustrates her incrementalism is *Community for Creative Non-Violence v. Reid*,[36] written during Justice Ginsburg's time as a judge on the D.C. Circuit. The question presented was whether a sculpture commissioned by a nonprofit (CCNV) was a work made for hire within the definition of the Copyright Act. If the work was found to be a "work for hire," the nonprofit that hired the sculptor, rather than the sculptor himself, would legally be deemed the author of the sculpture and the owner of the disputed copyright.[37] Ultimately the pre-Ginsburg

Supreme Court decided that it was not a work for hire. Ginsburg's incrementalism is recognizable even while she was still an appellate judge with respect to two other issues raised by *Reid*.

One of the disputes was over access to the finished product.[38] Reid, the sculptor, was concerned that CCNV's travel plans for the sculpture might result in damage to it.[39] Because there was only one copy of the work, Judge Ginsburg expressed some concern about Reid's ability to exercise his right under section 106(1) to reproduce the work.[40] Rather than directly addressing this tricky issue, Ginsburg planted a seed for how it could be resolved upon remand. She noted that CCNV had "once invited Reid to have a 'master mold' of the sculpture made at Reid's own expense" and that the court might be able to use its equitable powers to provide this remedy.[41]

Ginsburg also used *Reid* to plant some seeds about the moral rights of human artists.[42] Although she did not declare that Reid, as copyright owner, would have a moral rights claim against CCNV, she noted in her conclusion that, if CCNV "published an excessively mutilated or altered version of [the sculpture,]" then Reid might have a claim under various statutory or common law doctrines.[43]

Intergovernmental Deference

Another pattern running through Justice Ginsburg's copyright jurisprudence is her notable deference to other government institutions. Her writings suggest a belief that the evolution and interpretation of the law optimally occurs not as a diatribe against Congress, the President, administrative agencies, or the states but as a dialogue with those other institutions.[44] Courts have institutional capacity constraints and must engage in this cooperative intergovernmental dialogue to be effective.

Intergovernmental Dialogue

In 1993 Ginsburg gave a Madison Lecture at New York University School of Law titled "Speaking in a Judicial Voice." In this speech she expressed approval for a dialogic approach to civil rights. She observed that the Court generally invalidated discriminatory laws that had become obsolete. She also noted, however, in what she called "a core set of cases" concerning social insurance benefits for the spouse or family of a worker, that the Court, rather than condemn discriminatory laws, "in effect opened a dialogue with the political branches of government." Her words articulated a belief that courts should interact with other government institutions as part of effecting changes in the law.

This affinity for intergovernmental dialogue is also evident in her copyright opinions. Her *Petrella* opinion reflects a commitment to maintaining a dialogue with Congress. Justice Ginsburg, writing for the majority, concluded that laches was unavailable as a defense to damages for particular acts of copyright infringement.[45] With respect to intergovernmental dialogue in *Petrella*, Ginsburg described the historical back-and-forth between Congress and the courts on the laches and statutes of limitation issues. She noted that "[u]ntil 1957, federal copyright law did not include a statute of limitations for civil suits. Federal courts therefore used analogous state statutes of limitations to determine the timeliness of infringement claims. . . . And they sometimes invoked laches to abridge the state-law prescription."[46] Once the statute of limitations issue shifted to the courts, they borrowed from analogous state statutes of limitation because Congress had given them nothing useful to work with.[47] But because this caused a lack of uniformity, Congress stepped back in and remedied this omission in 1957 by enacting a three-year limitations period.[48] Ginsburg cited Senate and House reports to explain what Congress's purposes were[49] and noted Congress's awareness of the policy implications of its decision.[50] She concluded that "courts are not at liberty to jettison Congress' judgment on the timeliness of suit,"[51] but if Congress was dissatisfied with the Court's interpretation or that the limitations period were causing unforeseen hardships, then it was free to carry on the conversation and to change the law.

Another example of Justice Ginsburg's desire to dialogically engage other governmental institutions is visible in her *Kirtsaeng* opinion. She grounded her dissent in the history of the copyright reform efforts that took place in the 1960s and early 1970s.[52] Reviewing the lengthy Copyright Act revision process convinced her that everyone involved in the process had considered the international exhaustion issue and come to a resolution different from the majority's conclusion.[53]

Justice Ginsburg also judicially acknowledged the executive branch's contrary position on the international trade issue[54] and noted that the government had concluded that international exhaustion "would be inconsistent with the long-term economic interests of the United States" and conflict with positions it had taken in international trade negotiations.[55] Justice Ginsburg feared that the majority's holding would harm the United States' "role as a trusted partner in multilateral endeavors."[56]

Institutional Capacity Deference

Justice Ginsburg believed that courts are limited in their power and face institutional capacity constraints, which sometimes require them to defer to other governmental institutions. She explained during a public lecture that effective judges must persuade the political branches of government to endorse their judgments:

> The judiciary, Hamilton wrote, from the very nature of its functions, will always be "the least dangerous" branch of government, for judges hold neither the sword nor the purse of the community; ultimately, they must depend upon the political branches to effectuate their judgments. Mindful of that reality, the effective judge, I believe and will explain why in these remarks, strives to persuade, and not to pontificate.[57]

Several examples of institutional capacity deference are visible in her copyright opinions. Her conclusions in the *Eldred* and *Golan* cases both accord deference to Congress with respect to the proper duration of copyright protection. During oral arguments in *Eldred*, which tested Congress's power to add twenty years to future and existing copyrights, Justice Ginsburg asked the following questions with respect to whether life plus seventy years ran afoul of the "limited times" language of the Intellectual Property Clause of the U.S. Constitution:

> But there has to be a limit, as you acknowledge. Perpetual copyright is not permitted. Who is the judge of—within that line? Who is the judge of when it becomes unlimited? Is there, in other words, judicial review and, if there is, what standard will this Court apply to determine whether something short of perpetual is still unlimited?[58]

She felt that there was nothing about judges that made them inherently superior in determining the outer limits of copyright duration, as long as those limits were outside the bounds of perpetual copyright protection, which is constitutionally prohibited.

In her majority opinion in *Eldred*, she criticized Justice Breyer's argument that the economic incentives created by the CTEA's additional twenty years of copyright protection were too insignificant to incentivize an author to create additional new works.[59] It wasn't that she believed that he was necessarily wrong in his analysis, but Justice Ginsburg thought the issue should not be a matter of the Court's concern. She explained that "[c]alibrating rational economic incentives . . . is a task primarily for Congress, not the courts."[60] She described how Congress had heard testimony from several witnesses in making its decisions about the content of the CTEA, and she stated that the Court should not "take Congress to task for crediting this evidence."[61] Similarly, she wrote that the Court was "not at liberty to second-guess congressional determination and policy judgments of this order, however debatable or arguably unwise they may be."[62] The Court, she believed, had no legitimate way of determining what the proper duration of copyright protection should be. Her concluding sentences in *Eldred* highlight her position: "[P]etitioners forcefully urge that Congress pursued very bad policy in prescribing the CTEA's long terms. The wisdom of Congress' action, however, is not within our province to second-guess. [We are s]atisfied that the legislation before us remains inside the domain the Constitution assigns to the First Branch[.]"[63]

Justice Ginsburg's jurisprudential approach to *Golan* mirrored her analysis in *Eldred*. Again writing for the majority, she explained that the decision by Congress to extend copyright protections to foreign works that had previously fallen into the public domain was not a decision the Court had "warrant to reject," because Congress had determined that doing so would further the Intellectual Property Clause's objectives.[64] In response to a question raised about orphan works, Justice Ginsburg specifically mentioned institutional capacity as a reason to leave it unaddressed. She explained that the issue was not "a matter appropriate for judicial, as opposed to legislative, resolution. Indeed, the host of policy and logistical questions identified by the dissent speak for themselves."[65]

Justice Ginsburg's majority opinion in *Fourth Estate*, a case about copyright registration, also illustrates her institutional capacity deference. Fourth Estate asserted that copyright owners might lose their ability to enforce their rights if the Copyright Office didn't act quickly enough to process a registration application and the statute of limitations expired.[66] Justice Ginsburg was not convinced by this argument, noting that the current processing time for applications was seven months, which would leave ample time to file suit.[67] She stated that, even though it was true that the registration scheme was not working as Congress envisioned (with processing times increasing from a couple weeks in 1956 to seven months), the delays were "attributable, in large measure, to staffing and budgetary shortages that Congress can alleviate, but courts cannot cure."[68]

The institutional capacity deference woven into a number of Justice Ginsburg's copyright opinions is more subtle than her incrementalism. But when combined with her commitment to intergovernmental dialogic exchanges, it powerfully elucidates Justice Ginsburg's approach to developing the law in a thoughtful, restrained, and cooperative manner.

Seeking Alternatives

Another theme running through Justice Ginsburg's copyright opinions is a willingness to seek alternative avenues of redress or relief in order to minimize the social disruptions caused by a particular outcome in a case. She explained her interest in seeking creative alternative approaches to justice during her confirmation hearings, stating: "It is much easier to criticize than to come up with an alternative. So, as a general matter, I would never tear down unless I am sure I have a better building to replace what is being torn down."[69]

Justice Ginsburg's penchant for alternative remedies was crucial to the outcome in the *Tasini* case. In *Tasini*, the Court ruled that the defendant publishers had to pay freelance authors royalties after their articles were included in electronic publishers' databases without their permission.[70] The publishers and many interested third parties worried that, if the freelancers won, the enormous quantity of articles they had written might become difficult or even impossible for the public to access, leaving a veritable hole in the nation's journalistic history.[71] Justice

Ginsburg decided that the social disruption that resulted from the free-lancers' victory in *Tasini* could be minimized if the Court declined to issue an injunction preventing inclusion of the disputed articles in data-bases and focused instead on creating a remedy that got the freelancers paid, drawing on mechanisms such as compulsory licenses and consent decrees.[72] She also pointedly reminded the parties that they had alter-native methods of advancing their interests through private negotiation and contractual arrangements.[73] After remand, the parties entered into a class action settlement,[74] which ironically made its way back to the Supreme Court.[75]

Petrella v. MGM[76] provides another example of Justice Ginsburg's en-thusiasm for seeking alternatives. Writing for the majority, she found that laches could not preclude a claim for damages brought within the three-year statute of limitations period.[77] The defendants and dissenting Justices expressed concern that a defendant, because of a long period of delay, might be harmed by its reliance on the plaintiff's silence or by the loss of potential evidence.[78] Justice Ginsburg recognized this potential for injustice and wrote that an alternative mechanism—the doctrine of estoppel—could alleviate some of these concerns.[79] She acknowledged that estoppel was not a complete replacement for laches and that estop-pel requires a more exacting test,[80] but she felt it was still a useful alter-native tool to help address some of the contrary concerns.

In *Golan v. Holder*,[81] one concern about restoring copyright protec-tion in foreign works was that entities currently using the works based on an understanding that they were in the public domain would be de-prived of their investments in these works.[82] In counterpoint, Justice Ginsburg noted that Congress under the Uruguay Round Agreements Act had created additional protections for reliance parties.[83] If users of the previously unprotected materials had exploited the work prior to restoration, then the user could continue using the work until the copy-right owner actually or constructively notified the user.[84] And even after notification, the reliance party could continue exploiting the work for an additional year.[85] Finally, reliance parties who created derivative works based on previously unprotected works could continue to exploit their derivative works upon payment of "reasonable compensation."[86]

Another case in which Justice Ginsburg listed alternatives to elimi-nate or minimize counterarguments is *Fourth Estate*.[87] The plaintiff argued that waiting until copyright registration occurred would harm plaintiffs because it delays their ability to file suit and seek relief.[88] Justice Ginsburg acknowledged the possibility but listed two alternative mechanisms that tempered its effects. First, Congress created a system of preregistration that applies to categories of works that are especially susceptible to early infringement.[89] Second, the Copyright Office permits copyright claimants to seek expedited review of their application, which was normally accomplished within five days.[90] These alternative avenues, according to Justice Ginsburg, provided some relief for copyright owners in light of the Court's interpretation of the language to require more than simply filing the application before bringing suit.

Conclusion

Ruth Bader Ginsburg's copyright decisions favored copyright owners and authors. But careful review of her writings reveals a consistent position that optimal legal changes occur in incremental steps, in collaboration with the other branches of government, and by considering alternative relief to minimize causing social disruptions.

NOTES

This chapter is based an earlier article by the authors: *Ruth Bader Ginsburg's Copyright Jurisprudence*, 22 NEV. L.J. 431 (2022).

1 Eldred v. Ashcroft, 537 U.S. 186 (2003).

2 *Id.* at 193–94.

3 *Id.* at 193.

4 *Id.*

5 *Id.* at 193–94.

6 *Id.* at 194.

7 Fourth Estate Pub. Benefit Corp. v. Wall-Street.com, LLC, 139 S. Ct. 881, 886 (2019).

8 *Id.*

9 *Nomination of Ruth Bader Ginsburg, to Be Associate Justice of the Supreme Court of the United States: Hearing Before the S. Comm. on the Judiciary*, 103rd Cong. 51 (1993) [hereinafter *Confirmation Hearing*].

10 RUTH BADER GINSBURG, WITH MARY HARTNETT & WENDY W. WILLIAMS, MY OWN WORDS 196 (2016).

11 17 U.S.C. § 109(a) (2018).

12 Quality King Distribs., Inc. v. L'anza Research Int'l, Inc., 523 U.S. 135, 138 (1998).

13 *Id.* at 138–39.

14 *Id.* at 139.
15 *Id.*
16 *Id.* at 139–40.
17 *Id.* at 140.
18 *Id.* at 143.
19 *Id.* at 143–45.
20 *Id.* at 154 (Ginsburg, J., concurring).
21 Kirtsaeng v. John Wiley & Sons, Inc., 568 U.S. 519, 525–27 (2013).
22 *Id.* at 527.
23 *Id.*
24 *Id.*
25 *Id.*
26 *Id.*
27 *Id.* at 554.
28 *Id.*
29 *Id.* at 557.
30 *Id.*
31 *Id.* at 562.
32 *Id.*
33 *Id.* at 575–76 ("[T]he United States has steadfastly 'taken the position in international trade negotiations that domestic copyright owners should . . . have the right to prevent the unauthorized importation of copies of their work sold abroad.'").
34 *Id.* at 575.
35 Petrella v. Metro-Goldwyn-Mayer, Inc., 572 U.S. 663, 670 n.4 (2014).
36 Cmty. for Creative Non-Violence v. Reid, 846 F.2d 1485 (D.C. Cir. 1988).
37 *Reid*, 846 F.2d at 1487–88.
38 *Id.* at 1498.
39 *Id.*
40 *Id.* ("But singular works of art, we recognize, do not fit comfortably into a scheme centrally concerned with reproduction of the underlying work.").
41 *Id.* (citing Baker v. Libbie, 97 N.E. 109 (Mass. 1912)).
42 *Id.* at 1498–99.
43 *Id.*
44 Ruth Bader Ginsburg, *Speaking in a Judicial Voice*, 67 N.Y.U. L. REV. 1185, 1186 (1992).
45 Petrella v. Metro-Goldwyn-Mayer, Inc., 572 U.S. 663, 668 (2014).
46 *Id.* at 669.
47 *Id.* at 669–70.
48 *Id.* at 670.
49 *Id.*
50 *Id.* at 683 ("Congress must have been aware that the passage of time and the author's death could cause a loss or dilution of evidence. Congress chose, nonetheless, to give the author's family 'a second chance to obtain fair remuneration.'").

51 *Id.* at 667.

52 Kirtsaeng v. John Wiley & Sons, Inc., 568 U.S. 519, 568–73 (2013).

53 *Id.*

54 *Id.* at 573.

55 *Id.* at 575–76.

56 *Id.* at 578. Justice Ginsburg was concerned with interrupting this dialogue in *Quality King*. During oral argument, she asked the Deputy Solicitor General if the circuit courts' different approaches was important to the government. Counsel responded: "We do think it's important because it bears on positions we've been taking in international negotiations." Quality King Distrib., Inc. v. L'anza Research Int'l, Inc., Oral Argument Transcript 40–41 (Dec. 8, 1997), www.supremecourt.gov.

57 Ginsburg, *Judicial Voice* at 1186.

58 Eldred v. Ashcroft Oral Argument Transcript 40 (Oct. 9, 2002), www.supremecourt.gov.

59 Eldred v. Ashcroft, 537 U.S. 186, 207 n.15 (2003).

60 *Id.*

61 *Id.*

62 *Id.* at 208.

63 *Id.* at 222.

64 Golan v. Holder, 565 U.S. 302, 327 (2012).

65 *Id.* at 334 (citations omitted).

66 Fourth Estate Pub. Benefit Corp. v. Wall-Street.com, LLC, 139 S. Ct. 881, 892 (2019).

67 *Id.*

68 *Id.*

69 *Confirmation Hearing* at 155.

70 New York Times Co. v. Tasini, 533 U.S.483, 492–93 (2001).

71 *Id.* at 504–05.

72 *Id.* at 505.

73 *Id.* at 502 n.11. During oral argument, Justice Ginsburg also suggested two alternatives. First, the three-year statute of limitations might reduce some of the risk for publishers. And second, authors want their works electronically published because they have an interest in exposure. New York Times Co. v. Tasini Oral Argument Transcript 9–10 (March 28, 2001), www.supremecourt.gov.

74 In re Literary Works in Electronic Databases Copyright Litigation, 509 F.3d 116 (2nd Cir. 2007), *rev'd*, Reed Elsevier, Inc. v. Muchnick, 559 U.S. 154 (2010).

75 Reed Elsevier, Inc. v. Muchnick, 559 U.S. 154 (2010).

76 Petrella v. Metro-Goldwyn-Mayer, Inc., 572 U.S. 663 (2014).

77 *Id.* at 679.

78 *Id.* at 689–90 (Breyer, J., dissenting).

79 *Id.* at 684–85.

80 *Id.* at 684.

81 Golan v. Holder, 565 U.S. 302 (2012).

82 *Id.* at 315–16.

83 *Id.* at 316.

84 *Id.* (citing 17 U.S.C. § 104A).

85 *Id.* (citing 17 U.S.C. § 104A(d)(2)(A)(ii) and (B)(ii)).

86 *Id.* (citing 17 U.S.C. § 104A(d)(3)).

87 Fourth Estate Pub. Benefit Corp. v. Wall-Street.com, LLC, 139 S. Ct. 881 (2019).

88 *Id.* at 891.

89 *Id.* at 892 (citing 17 U.S.C. § 408(f)).

90 *Id.* at 892 n.6.

8

Criminal Procedure

Honoring the Spirit of Their Rights

MELISSA L. BREGER

They have never been a 13-year-old girl. It's a very sensitive age for a girl. I didn't think that my colleagues, some of them, quite understood.
—Justice Ruth Bader Ginsburg, talking to the press about *Safford v. Redding*[1]

Justice Ruth Bader Ginsburg was a wonder in so many ways: she rose to the top of her law school class; she argued and penned compelling cases that reformed the law; she shattered glass ceilings. Yet one of her singularly remarkable strengths as a United States Supreme Court Justice was her ability to place herself in the shoes of the litigants who stood before her. Her empathy was evident in many areas of the law, and it certainly was true in many of the constitutional criminal procedure opinions in her final decades.

Justice Ginsburg tried to honor the spirit and the reality of litigants' constitutional rights, whether it was a thirteen-year-old girl accused of selling prescription drugs at her Arizona middle school,[2] a prisoner in Michigan being interrogated by the police,[3] or a Kentucky man peacefully residing in his own home when officers barged in without a warrant.[4] This chapter studies the compassion, intellectual honesty, wisdom, and humanity that was integral to Ginsburg's jurisprudential legacy. It explores how she recognized the human side of the litigants in the cases before her—whether based upon their gender, their young age, their status, or some other aspect of their identity. By examining the recent and selected cases of *Safford v. Redding*, *Kentucky v. King*, and *Howes v. Fields*, delving into *Vernonia School District 47J v. Acton* and *Board of*

Education v. Earls, and by briefly addressing *T.L.O. v. New Jersey* and *District of Columbia v. Wesby*, this chapter maps Justice Ginsburg's influence upon investigatory criminal procedure cases.

Middle and High-School Students' Rights to Privacy

Justice Ginsburg shielded the privacy rights of juveniles, in particular middle and high-school students. Her influence and her advocacy in this area are outlined below.

Safford v. Redding

The *Redding*[5] case began with a routine, ordinary search of a middle school teenager by the school administration. It had been rumored that thirteen-year-old Savana Redding was distributing prescription-strength painkillers at school, a violation of school policy.[6] The rumors had been started by another student, but it was not clear if they were grounded in truth, if they were just a case of middle school gossip, or if they fell somewhere in between.[7]

The federal case law surrounding public school searches was firmly established in *T.L.O. v. New Jersey*.[8] In that precedential case, the Supreme Court ruled upon nuanced questions of Fourth Amendment jurisprudence within the public school setting, and in doing so it devised a distinct balancing test.[9] The balancing test is different than a traditional search-and-seizure analysis because schools have an obligation to protect the entire student body's safety interests and balance those safety interests against an individual student's privacy interests.[10] Thus, in *T.L.O.*, a new "special needs" standard was born. A school search must satisfy a two-prong standard: (1) whether the search was reasonable at its inception; and (2) whether the search was justified in its scope.[11] A court must examine both prongs to determine if a school search will pass Fourth Amendment muster.

In *T.L.O.*, Terri Lyn had been smoking cigarettes in the school bathroom, which violated school rules.[12] When the school administrators searched her bags, the Court found that they did so in a fairly limited way.[13] The Supreme Court therefore concluded the physical intrusion was reasonable under both prongs, and the search of the student was upheld.[14]

When *Safford v. Redding* came before the Supreme Court in 2009, it was decided within the guidelines set out by *T.L.O.* in 1985. Yet *Safford* truly tested the boundaries of the second prong of the *T.L.O.* test. The defendant in *Safford* was summoned to the principal's office for selling prescription drugs.[15] As anyone reading this chapter will likely recall, middle school is wrought and fraught with emotion for even the most well-adjusted adolescent. When Savana entered the office, she was asked a series of questions.[16] Her bags and pockets were searched.[17] And then she was presented with the unimaginable for a thirteen-year old girl: she was instructed to go to the nurse's office and shake out her bra and underwear.[18] The search partially exposed her breasts and pelvic area.[19] It is at this point that the tenor of the room shifted. And as Justice Ginsburg notes, the tenor of the case shifted here as well.[20] For it was no longer about the first prong of *T.L.O.* and whether the search was reasonable at the outset. Now the analysis shifted to the second prong of *T.L.O.* and whether the search was justified in scope. In Justice Ginsburg's view, it was not. In her opinion, concurring in part and dissenting in part, Justice Ginsburg stated:

> Here, "the nature of the [supposed] infraction," the slim basis for suspecting Savana Redding, and her "age and sex," . . . establish beyond doubt that Assistant Principal Wilson's order cannot be reconciled with this Court's opinion in T.L.O. Wilson's treatment of Redding was abusive and it was not reasonable for him to believe that the law permitted it.[21]

Justice Ginsburg believed she needed to voice her opinion on behalf of Savana.[22] She later told the press: "They have never been a 13-year-old girl. It's a very sensitive age for a girl. I didn't think that my colleagues, some of them, quite understood."[23]

Justice Ginsburg stood in Savana's shoes and amplified her voice to the other members of the Court, who might not have fully understood the potential trauma and how pertinent the gender and age of Savana would be in these circumstances. Justice Ginsburg spoke on behalf of Savana by announcing that the treatment of her was "abusive"—particularly in accounting for Savana's "age and sex."[24] In so doing, Justice Ginsburg served as the mouthpiece for this thirteen-year-old litigant.

Vernonia and Earls

Justice Ginsburg's inclination to be protective of middle and high-school students first surfaced in the *Vernonia* and *Earls* cases, both of which addressed students' rights to privacy. These similarly situated cases were set in public schools that mandated drug testing for particular students. The students subject to this testing, along with their parents, challenged the drug testing, arguing that the tests were unconstitutional under the Fourth Amendment. In *Vernonia*, the students being tested for drugs were athletes. In *Earls*, the school district drug tested any students involved in any type of extracurricular activity.

In *Vernonia*, the Supreme Court ultimately held that, based on factors such as the decreased expectation of privacy in a school setting, the relative unobtrusiveness of the searches, and the severity of the need met by the search (overall school safety), Oregon's Vernonia School District drug-testing policy for athletes was reasonable and constitutional.[25] Seven years later, the Court in *Earls* similarly held that the drug-testing policy for students participating in extracurricular activities in a school district in Oklahoma's Pottawatomie County was also reasonable and constitutional. The majority held that the policy was an appropriate means of furthering the district's important interests to deter drug use among its schoolchildren.[26]

In *Vernonia*, Justice Ginsburg wrote a concurring opinion to Justice Scalia's majority opinion. Yet in *Earls*, Justice Ginsburg dissented fairly vigorously.[27] She believed that the *Earls* majority failed to recognize the distinctions between the students impacted in *Earls* and the students impacted in *Vernonia*, who were all athletes. Justice Ginsburg drew numerous distinctions between the two cases, and in doing so she provided a voice for a shy, young Lindsay Earls.

For example, in *Earls*, Ginsburg found not only that the particular drug-testing program of the school was unreasonable; she also stated it was "capricious, even perverse." Justice Ginsburg noted numerous differences between the context and circumstances in *Vernonia* and those present in *Earls*. Ginsburg specifically emphasized distinctions between Lindsay Earls and likeminded students in *Earls* with the athlete-students subject to drug testing in *Vernonia*. Athletes routinely undress and even shower in a group setting without so much as a partition or visual barrier of any kind to protect their privacy. In contrast, members of the choir and academic team have no such expectation when they sign up for these activities.[28] These students are more likely to be "modest and shy" (and perhaps even less likely to be involved in drugs), much like the plaintiff-respondent Lindsay Earls, as opposed to the bolder, more daring athletes of *Vernonia*.[29] Subjecting such students to invasive drug testing could deter them from accessing an invaluable opportunity of social support designed to enhance their personal growth, confidence-building, and character development.[30] Moreover, as Justice Ginsburg noted:

> If a student has a reasonable subjective expectation of privacy in the personal items she brings to school . . . surely she has a similar expectation regarding the chemical composition of her urine. Had the Vernonia Court agreed that public school attendance, in and of itself, permitted the State to test each student's blood or urine for drugs, the opinion in Vernonia could have saved many words.[31]

Justice Ginsburg amplified the voice of Lindsay Earls, again serving as a mouthpiece for a young student.

Adult Defendants' Rights to Privacy

Justice Ginsburg fiercely defended the constitutional rights not only of teenagers but also adult defendants. She was very protective of the rights enshrined in the Fourth and Fifth Amendments.

Kentucky v. King

One evening in Lexington, Kentucky, undercover police officers staged a sting operation when they observed what appeared to be a dealer selling crack cocaine.[32] After watching the transaction from an unmarked car, one of the officers radioed uniformed officers to "hurry up and get there" and apprehend the suspect, who was moving toward an apartment building.[33]

The uniformed officers entered the building and proceeded to the apartment on the left, despite instructions to go to the apartment on the right.[34] The officers smelled marijuana, banged on the door "as loud as

[they] could," and announced they were the police.[35] When they heard rustling, they immediately barged into the apartment, presumably to prevent any drugs therein from being flushed down the toilet.[36] Testimony was uncontroverted that an officer "kicked the door open."[37] Instead of seeing people moving things around, the police encountered three individuals, one in fact still seated on the couch, calmly smoking marijuana.[38] During the search of the apartment, the officers found narcotics and drug paraphernalia, and they arrested Hollis Deshaun King.[39] Eventually, upon realizing they were supposed to have searched the right-side apartment in the building, the police entered that apartment and found the actual suspect, who was the initial target of the investigation.[40]

The central issue for the courts was: Can police create their own exigency and then enter a home without a warrant based upon that police-created exigency? The Supreme Court of Kentucky held that "police may not rely on exigent circumstances, 'if it was reasonably foreseeable that the investigative tactics employed by the police would create the exigent circumstances.'"[41] Under this doctrine, police may not create an exigency by their own conduct. The validity of this police-created exigency was at the forefront of the case before the Supreme Court. Justice Ginsburg agreed with the Kentucky Supreme Court that the police could not create and then exploit their own exigent circumstances. She dissented from the majority's decision to reverse and remand the case.

In looking at the details of the underlying case, it is notable that the police invasion was at 10:00 at night[42] and described as "threatening" per King's defense attorney, Jamesa Drake, who penned a law review article about the case.[43] During oral arguments and in her law review article, Drake focused on the fact that the loud banging on the door would imply to a homeowner that the police have a warrant and are likely to rush into the home. As she noted, there is a manifest difference between "banging" on the door at ten o'clock at night and hearing a familiar voice yell out, "It's John, your next door neighbor!" versus when the unexpected visitors yell, "Police, police, police" or "This is the Police!"[44]

Hollis Deshaun King was a Black man, living in the South, when the police barged into his home that night in 2011. Attorney Drake noted:

One could easily argue that the foregoing, coupled with the Court's suggestion that "[c]itizens who are startled by an unexpected knock on the door or by the sight of unknown persons in plain clothes on their doorstep may be relieved to learn that these persons are police officers," evinces a majority of the Justices' profound misunderstanding of community-police relations in many pockets of this country.[45]

While there is no explicit indication that race played a role in Justice Ginsburg's dissent, it is certainly possible that it was one factor underlying her opinion. Justice Ginsburg vigorously voiced her concern about a man relaxing inside his own home when the police charge in without a warrant.

In *King*, Justice Ginsburg, the sole dissenter, emphasized the crucial importance of privacy in one's home, one's sanctuary.[46] In this case, the litigants were thrust into a so-called emergency setting that was in fact created by the police. The faux "emergency" was then used to justify the warrantless entry. Justice Ginsburg was understandably bothered by the failure of the police to obtain a proper warrant, which presumably would have allowed a legal and unforced entry. The fact that the police officers made a warrantless entry into the wrong home made it even more intrusive into the privacy of one's home life.

Justice Ginsburg believed that the peace and serenity of one's home shall not be infringed upon unnecessarily. As she noted:

> The Court today arms the police with a way routinely to dishonor the Fourth Amendment's warrant requirement in drug cases. In lieu of presenting their evidence to a neutral magistrate, police officers may now knock, listen, then break the door down, never mind that they had ample time to obtain a warrant. I dissent from the Court's reduction of the Fourth Amendment's force. . . . How "secure" do our homes remain if police, armed with no warrant, can pound on doors at will and, on hearing sounds indicative of things moving, forcibly enter and search for evidence of unlawful activity?[47]

Howes v. Fields

Prison, with its many rules and reduced expectations of privacy, is a setting in some ways similar to the public schools highlighted in the earlier sections. In *Howes v. Fields*, Fields was in prison for disorderly conduct when he was escorted to a conference room and questioned by two sheriff's deputies about allegations of unrelated misconduct occurring before his imprisonment.[48] Although informed that he was free to leave and return to his cell, Fields was never read his *Miranda* rights.[49] In fact, Fields told the deputies multiple times he did not want to continue speaking with them.[50] Nevertheless, the deputies proceeded to interrogate Fields for hours. In fact, the sheriffs continued their interrogation for almost seven hours, which lasted long past Fields' normal bedtime. The interrogation produced a confession that was later used to convict Fields.[51]

Fields was summoned to the prison office—not unlike Savana Redding being summoned to the school principal's office—and asked questions about an alleged crime.[52] The core question in this case boiled down to: Would a prisoner ever feel free to leave? The majority believed yes, but Justice Ginsburg disagreed. She argued:

> As the Court acknowledges, Fields did not invite or consent to the interview. He was removed from his cell in the evening, taken to a conference room in the sheriff's quarters, and questioned by two armed deputies long into the night and early morning. He was not told at the outset that he had the right to decline to speak with the deputies. Shut in with the armed officers, Fields felt "trapped." Although told he could return to his cell if he did not want to cooperate, Fields believed the deputies "would not have allowed [him] to leave the room." And with good reason. More than once, "he told the officers . . . he did not want to speak with them anymore." [Although he] was given water, [he was] not [given] his evening medications. . . . Yet the Court concludes that Fields was in "an interrogation environment in which a reasonable person would have felt free to terminate the interview and leave."[53]

As Justice Ginsburg noted in her dissent, Fields was not given his prescribed medications. More specifically, one of those drugs was an antidepressant, thereby highlighting a particular vulnerability. She evidenced empathy toward Fields that none of the other Justices articulated.

Justice Ginsburg asked aloud what many readers of the majority opinion might have wondered: "How could someone who is at the mercy of prison guards feel free to push back against law enforcement, when asked? What does voluntarily really mean in a prison setting?"[54] During oral arguments, Justice Ginsburg asked counsel for the appellant: "For one thing, he had no choice but to go with the police, right?"[55] She also asked, seemingly rhetorically: "And it doesn't make any difference that they took him from his cell; he was under compulsion to leave with them and interrogated during the hours when prisoners are ordinarily sleeping?"[56] Justice Ginsburg later inquired "is the time relevant that this was done? They took him away at 7:00 pm in the evening and kept him for 7 hours." As Justice Ginsburg's opinion noted:

> Critical to the Court's judgment is "the undisputed fact that [Fields] was told that he was free to end the questioning and to return to his cell." Never mind the facts suggesting that Fields's submission to the overnight interview was anything but voluntary.[57]

Justice Ginsburg then pointed out how the majority's ruling undermined the rights protected by the Fifth Amendment privilege. She wrote: "For the reasons stated, I would hold that the 'incommunicado interrogation [of Fields] in a police-dominated atmosphere, without informing him of his rights, dishonored the Fifth Amendment privilege *Miranda* was designed to safeguard.'"[58]

Generally speaking, *Miranda* rights protect, inter alia, one's right not to incriminate oneself and are particularly needed when the weight of the prosecution bears down on a suspect.[59] When a suspect is sealed off from the outside public and surrounded by law enforcement, that suspect may be most vulnerable to self-incrimination.[60] Thus, the prophylactic nature of *Miranda* rights is intended to safeguard a person's constitutional rights.

The key here lay within the questions the courts must ask, according to Justice Ginsburg. She stated that she would inquire

> whether Fields was subjected to "incommunicado interrogation . . . in a police-dominated atmosphere," and whether he was placed, against his will in an inherently stressful situation, and whether his "freedom of action [was] curtailed in any significant way?"[61]

Justice Ginsburg asserted that "those should be the key questions" and that to each she would answer, "Yes."[62] With regard to custodial interrogation, Ginsburg asked and answered again: "Was Fields 'held for interrogation?' Brought to, and left alone with, the gun-bearing deputies, he surely was in my judgment."[63] Justice Ginsburg placed herself in the shoes of the litigant: "Shut in with the armed officers, Fields [was] 'trapped.'" For the Justice, this was untenable and unacceptable.

Conclusion

Justice Ginsburg was fiercely protective of individual constitutional rights in the realm of criminal procedure. In fact, even in cases outside traditional criminal procedure, Justice Ginsburg raised concerns about law enforcement overreaching, such as in the 2018 case of *District of Columbia v. Wesby.*[64] *Wesby* was not a per se criminal procedure case but rather a tort action against the city and the police by partygoers who were arrested at a vacant home in Washington, D.C. Even though Justice Ginsburg concurred that the officers were protected by qualified immunity, she took the opportunity to express her consternation about police overreach and the direction of the Court. Specifically, she opined that "[t]he Court's jurisprudence, I am concerned, sets the balance too heavily in favor of police unaccountability to the detriment of Fourth Amendment protection."[65] She noted that she "question[ed] whether this Court, in assessing probable cause, should continue to ignore why police in fact acted?"[66] Justice Ginsburg's concurring opinion in *Wesby* serves as a bellwether and a harbinger for where she hoped the Court would lean.

The theme of constitutional criminal procedural rights runs strongly throughout Justice Ginsburg's decisions; she favored individual litigants' rights over unfettered rights claimed by law enforcement. This was particularly true in her later years on the Supreme Court bench, as the above selection of cases illustrates.

Justice Ginsburg magnified litigants' voices through her powerful writing and reasoning. Fittingly, the children's author Debbie Levy ends her book *I Dissent: Ruth Bader Ginsburg Makes Her Mark* as follows:

> Her voice may not carry out a tune,
> but it sings out for equality.
> Step by step, she has made a difference. . . .[67]

Justice Ruth Bader Ginsburg made sure her voice and other voices were heard. Ginsburg consistently demonstrated her ability to place herself in the shoes of the litigants who stood before her. She brought her exceptional intellect and her own life experiences to the bench and then applied them to the cases.

In the opinions detailed above (and in many others), Justice Ruth Bader Ginsburg tried to honor the spirit and the reality of the litigants. She intensely guarded their constitutional rights. Her compassion often shined through her judicial opinions.

Her criminal procedure opinions leave readers with the impression that she cared about the litigants, and she most certainly cared about their constitutional rights. She was sensitive to how gender, socioeconomic status, age, possibly race, and to some extent the potential of trauma and mental health intersected so acutely in Fourth and Fifth Amendment cases. She was able to envision the plight of similarly situated litigants and voice their concerns. For these reasons and many more, Justice Ruth Bader Ginsburg had a profound influence upon the area of constitutional criminal procedure as she had on other areas of law.

NOTES

Many thanks for the research assistance of Daniel Schmidt, Alexander Anselment, and Christina Vitolo. Thank you for editorial feedback from Professor Louis Jim and Thomas Capezza.

1 H. Darr Beiser, *Ginsburg: Court Needs Another Woman*, USA TODAY (May 5, 2009), https://usatoday30.usatoday.com (RBG speaking to *USA Today* talking about the *Safford School District v. Redding* case).

2 Safford v. Redding, 557 U.S. 364 (2009).

3 Howes v. Fields, 565 U.S. 499 (2012).

4 Kentucky v. King, 563 U.S. 452 (2011).

5 *Safford*, 557 U.S. at 368.

6 *Id.*

7 *Id.*

8 New Jersey v. T.L.O., 469 U.S. 325 (1985).

9 *Id.* at 341.

10 *Id.* at 353.

11 *Id.* at 341.

12 *Id.* at 328.

13 *Id.* at 347.

14 *Id.* at 347–48.

15 Safford v. Redding, 557 U.S. 364, 368 (2009).

16 *Id.*

17 *Id.*

18 *Id.* at 369.

19 *Id.*

20 *Id.* at 382.

21 *Id.*

22 Beiser, *Court Needs Another Woman.*

23 *Id.*

24 *Safford,* 557 U.S. at 382.

25 Vernonia v. Acton, 515 U.S. 646, 664–66 (1995).

26 Board of Ed. v. Earls, 536 U.S. 822, 838 (2002).

27 *Id.* at 842

28 *Id.* at 847 (citing Brief for American Academy of Pediatrics et al. as *Amici Curiae* 13).

29 *Id.*

30 *Id.* at 847–48, 853.

31 *Id.* at 845

32 Kentucky v. King, 563 U.S. 452, 455–58 (2011).

33 *Id.* at 456.

34 *Id.* at 456–57.

35 *Id.* at 456.

36 *Id.* at 456–57.

37 Jamesa Drake, Kentucky v. King: *A New Approach to Consent-Based Police Encounters?*, 65 ME. L. REV. 57 (2012).

38 *King,* 563 U.S. at 456–57.

39 *Id.* at 457.

40 *Id.*

41 *Id.* at 457–58; King v. Commonwealth, 302 S.W.3d 649, 651 (Ky. 2010).

42 *King,* 563 U.S. at 456–57.

43 Drake, *A New Approach* at 59–65.

44 *Id.* at 68.

45 *Id.* at 71.

46 *King,* 563 U.S. at 473 (Ginsburg, J., dissenting).

47 *Id.* at 473–75.

48 Howes v. Fields, 565 U.S. 499, 502 (2012).

49 *Id.* at 504.

50 *Id.* at 518–19.

51 *Id.* at 503–04.

52 *Id.* at 502–05.

53 *Id.* at 515.

54 *Id.*

55 Howes v. Fields Oral Argument, OYEZ, www.oyez.org.

56 *Id.*

57 *Howes*, 565 U.S. at 519.

58 *Id.* at 518.

59 Miranda v. Arizona, 384 U.S. 436, 444–45 (1966).

60 *Id.*

61 *Howes*, 565 U.S. at 519.

62 *Id.*

63 *Id.* at 519.

64 District of Columbia v. Wesby, 138 S. Ct. 577, 593–94 (2018).

65 *Id.* at 594.

66 *Id.*

67 DEBBIE LEVY, I DISSENT: RUTH BADER GINSBURG MAKES HER MARK (Simon & Schuster Books For Young Readers 2016).

9

Death Penalty

Precise Analysis but Broad Concerns

JEFFREY L. KIRCHMEIER

When Ruth Bader Ginsburg joined the United States Supreme Court in 1993, she had never ruled on a capital case as an appellate judge or sentenced a defendant accused of a capital crime. During her twenty-seven years on the nation's highest court, though, she would find herself at the center of the Court's death penalty jurisprudence, balancing her approach to the law with her concerns about capital punishment.

Justice Ginsburg authored some important decisions on capital punishment, and very often her vote on a divided Supreme Court was essential to the outcome of cases. Her written opinions covered a number of areas, although they often tended to focus on the roles of jurors and defense counsel rather than capital sentencing procedures under the Eighth Amendment.

From the start of her time on the Court, her approach to capital punishment was one of judicial restraint, so she avoided sweeping pronouncements. Although she occasionally voted to uphold death sentences, her concerns about the problems and inequities of the nation's death penalty system grew, manifesting most powerfully toward the end of her time on the Court.

The Death Penalty and Ginsburg's Appointment to the Court

When President Bill Clinton nominated Judge Ruth Bader Ginsburg to the United States Supreme Court, she had served for more than a decade as a judge for the United States Court of Appeals for the District of Columbia Circuit. Although the District of Columbia itself did not have the death penalty and Justice Ginsburg had not ruled on capital issues, some commentators viewed her record on criminal law as one of "solid conservatism."[1]

Ginsburg had not completely avoided the death penalty issue during her legal career. As a volunteer attorney for the American Civil Liberties Union (ACLU) when she was a law professor at Rutgers Law School, she co-authored an amicus brief in the capital case of *Coker v. Georgia*.[2] In that case, the ACLU took the position that capital punishment was a disproportionate punishment for the crime of rape of an adult and thus violated the Eighth Amendment,[3] a position ultimately adopted by a majority of the Court.[4]

During her Supreme Court confirmation hearings, one senator attempted to make an issue out of her work on *Coker*. In response, Ginsburg maintained that as a Supreme Court Justice she would uphold the law, adding that she would not speculate on future cases.[5] She further stressed that her *Coker* brief was not a broad attack on the death penalty but a narrower argument that capital punishment for rape violated the Eighth Amendment.[6]

She was correct that the legal arguments in the brief took a narrow approach, as amicus briefs by their nature usually do. But the brief also raised troubling aspects of the death penalty. For example, the brief explained that the use of the death penalty for rape was disproportionately applied against defendants of color.[7] Additionally, as one observer noted, the brief constituted "a powerful feminist document, linking the death penalty for rape with the patriarchal foundation of law as primarily protecting the male property interest in women's purity."[8]

During the confirmation hearings Ginsburg presented herself as a moderate judge, emphasizing her commitment to judicial restraint. And her record showed her often voting with conservative colleagues.[9] Ultimately, regarding the death penalty, Ginsburg told the senators she would be "scrupulous in applying the law on the basis of legislation and precedent."[10] Her answers satisfied the senators, who voted 96–3 to confirm her.[11]

Justice Ginsburg's Early Encounters with Capital Punishment

Justice Ginsburg joined the Court for the 1993–1994 term after she was confirmed on August 3, 1993. Although the death penalty was firmly entrenched in the United States at the time, her rise to the Court also coincided with some cracking in the foundation of cultural and political support for capital punishment. That year, Sister Helen Prejean published *Dead Man Walking*, a popular book (and later a movie) raising concerns about the death penalty.[12] In subsequent years, advocates revealed a number of innocent people on death rows, and jurisdictions began adopting moratoriums on capital punishment.[13] And during Justice Ginsburg's first term, one of her colleagues, Justice Harry Blackmun, authored a dissenting opinion concluding that the death penalty violated the Constitution.[14]

On the Court, Justice Ginsburg similarly expressed concerns about capital punishment, although she never wrote an opinion as sweeping as Justice Blackmun's critique. Instead, Ginsburg felt she would be more effective by participating in discussions about revising the legal doctrine than by taking an absolute position that the death penalty was unconstitutional.[15]

Not long after joining the Supreme Court, Justice Ginsburg encountered her first capital case in which she had to vote. On September 1, 1993, she joined two other Justices in voting for a stay of execution in *James v. Collins*.[16] Soon, she was voting on other stay requests, but not always voting for stays of execution.[17]

Justice Ginsburg's first written death penalty opinion was a dissent in *Romano v. Oklahoma*,[18] which was a 5–4 decision. In *Romano*, the capital jury had been told during the sentencing phase of the trial that the defendant already was under a death sentence from another case.[19] Justice Ginsburg reasoned that this information would affect jurors, reducing the seriousness of their decision and their personal responsibility for the defendant's life.[20] Her dissenting opinion relied upon precedent, and she emphasized the importance of a fair jury to ensure a reliable death penalty process.[21]

In June 1994, Justice Ginsburg cast her first majority vote upholding a sentence of death in *Tuilaepa v. California*,[22] joining Justice Stevens in a concurring opinion. The issue in this rape-murder case focused upon the wording of California's death penalty statute and whether several of the aggravating factors listed were unconstitutionally vague.[23] The concise, two-paragraph concurrence joined by Justice Ginsburg asserted that a prior opinion controlled the case.[24]

Thus, Justice Ginsburg's first decisions engaging with the death penalty were consistent with what she described during her confirmation hearings as a "scrupulous" approach to applying the law. She showed a willingness to come out on either side of the issue, and she did not make any sweeping calls to overrule precedent. Instead, she carefully used existing cases to support assertions that outcomes were dictated by prior opinions. Justice Ginsburg continued to use this approach to analyze legal issues in capital cases throughout her time on the Court, though her experiences clarified and broadened her reservations about the government's use of the ultimate punishment.

Justice Ginsburg's Written Opinions in Capital Cases

During her time on the Court, Justice Ginsburg voted for both petitioners and respondents in capital cases, but she most often sided with the condemned rather than with the states seeking executions. No matter her position on the issue, she fulfilled her goal of guiding the Court in death penalty cases without deviating drastically from precedent. Of course, all judges are guided by prior cases. But Justice Ginsburg's opinions hewed close to existing cases, using precise legal analysis, generally without rhetorical flourishes or impassioned pleas, even in this emotional area of law. And she provided clear support for her conclusions in a civil way that was respected by her colleagues on all sides of the issues.

Justice Ginsburg's Careful Approach Led to Opinions on Both Sides

One of Justice Ginsburg's early written opinions upholding a death sentence was a concurring opinion in *Victor v. Nebraska*.[25] Although the case did not center on issues directly related to capital punishment procedures, she concurred in the Court's judgment regarding the trial court's language for defining the "beyond a reasonable doubt" standard for finding guilt.[26]

In 2004, Justice Ginsburg wrote a majority opinion upholding the conviction of a capital defendant. But as in *Victor*, the issue regarded the finding of guilt in the case and not the constitutionality of the death sentence.[27] In *Florida v. Nixon*, her majority opinion concluded that the defendant's counsel was not automatically ineffective under the Sixth

Amendment even though the attorney failed to get the defendant's express consent to a strategy of conceding guilt.[28] The opinion was not divisive, as all participating Justices joined Justice Ginsburg's opinion and it rested on the Court's precedent in *Strickland v. Washington*, a case that made it difficult for defendants to establish Sixth Amendment violations for ineffective assistance of counsel.[29]

By contrast, in 2018 Justice Ginsburg wrote a majority opinion in *McCoy v. Louisiana*, which ruled in favor of the condemned on a Sixth Amendment issue similar to the one presented in *Nixon*.[30] In *McCoy*, the Court held that the defendant's Sixth Amendment rights were violated when counsel conceded the defendant's guilt during trial. Justice Ginsburg reasoned that the deferential *Strickland* standard was not applicable because this case involved a defendant's autonomy in making the strategic decision about whether to concede guilt.[31]

In another vote to uphold a death sentence, Justice Ginsburg wrote a concurring opinion in *Dunn v. Madison* that was joined by Justices Breyer and Sotomayor. The majority upheld a lower court's finding that the condemned was competent to be executed based upon the deferential habeas review standard of the Anti-Terrorism and Effective Death Penalty Act.[32] In a one-paragraph concurrence, Justice Ginsburg stressed that she was joining the per curiam opinion upholding the death sentence due to the review restrictions of the habeas statute. But she asserted that the underlying issue regarding the competency of a condemned inmate who cannot remember the crime was one that the Court should address in the future in a case without the procedural limitations.[33]

Justice Ginsburg's written opinions in capital cases often centered on Sixth Amendment rights regarding counsel and juries. She rarely wrote significant opinions impacting the Court's Eighth Amendment jurisprudence on capital sentencing procedures that developed following cases in the 1970s such as *Furman v. Georgia*[34] and *Gregg v. Georgia*.[35] She did, however, write important majority opinions on issues related the Court's holding in *Atkins v. Virginia* that it violates the Eighth Amendment for a state to execute an individual with an intellectual disability.[36] In *Bobby v. Bies*, a 2009 case involving an *Atkins* claim, Justice Ginsburg wrote for a unanimous Court against a capital defendant. She concluded that the state should have had an opportunity to contest the defendant's claim that he was intellectually disabled because the state was not bound by prior pre-*Atkins* statements that the defendant was intellectually disabled.[37]

In *Moore v. Texas*,[38] however, Justice Ginsburg wrote a majority opinion for the condemned in an *Atkins* case, holding that Texas was using outdated standards for determining intellectual disability and that using such standards violated the Constitution. Justice Ginsburg provided a logical and concise critique of the standards used in the Texas courts, citing previous Supreme Court cases regarding the standards while also pointing out that Texas did not use the outdated standards outside the death penalty context.[39] Even the three dissenting Justices agreed with Justice Ginsburg's constitutional conclusion, differing only on the factual question about whether the petitioner was in fact intellectually disabled.[40]

Other Important Majority Opinions

Two of Justice Ginsburg's most important majority opinions on the death penalty are *Shafer v. South Carolina* and *Ring v. Arizona*. Justice Ginsburg did not write a majority opinion in a capital case until *Shafer* in 2001, her eighth term as a Supreme Court Justice. In *Shafer*,[41] she addressed the Court's 1994 holding in *Simmons v. South Carolina*[42] that, when a capital defendant's future dangerousness was at issue and the jury was choosing between the death penalty and life imprisonment without the possibility of parole, due process required that the jury be told of the defendant's parole ineligibility if sentenced to prison. Justice Ginsburg had joined the majority in *Simmons*, and her opinion in *Shafer* reasserted its importance.

Although South Carolina altered its sentencing scheme after *Simmons* (likely as an attempt to get around the Supreme Court's opinion), Justice Ginsburg concluded that the jury's options, once an aggravating factor was found, remained comparable to the scenario in *Simmons*.[43] Thus, the judge's instruction that the jury was not to consider parole eligibility still created the same due process problem if the prosecutor argued future dangerousness.

Justice Ginsburg's most impactful majority opinion on capital punishment came the following year in *Ring v. Arizona*,[44] a 2002 opinion holding that the Sixth Amendment right to a jury trial forbids a capital sentencing judge from using any aggravating circumstance not found by a jury as a factor in sentencing.[45] The outcome drastically affected states like Arizona that relied upon judges to determine punishments in capital cases, forcing them to give jurors a more prominent role in capital sentencing.[46]

Despite the importance of the decision, Justice Ginsburg presented a nondramatic, reasoned opinion explaining that the result was dictated by the Court's 2000 decision in *Apprendi v. New Jersey*.[47] *Apprendi* was a noncapital case that held that the Sixth Amendment required jurors to make any factual findings that elevated the sentence of a noncapital defendant. Justice Ginsburg supported the holding in *Ring*, which was joined by six other Justices, by making a logical comparison to *Apprendi*: "[T]he right to trial by jury guaranteed by the Sixth Amendment would be senselessly diminished if it encompassed the fact-finding necessary to increase a defendant's sentence by two years, but not the fact-finding necessary to put him to death."[48]

Ring forced several states to change procedures and to give more power to jurors in sentencing people to death. More than a decade earlier, in 1990, the Supreme Court had upheld Arizona's judge-sentencing scheme against an Eighth Amendment challenge in *Walton v. Arizona*.[49] The state subsequently executed twenty-two condemned individuals who had been sentenced by judges before the Court in *Ring* found Arizona's sentencing scheme violated the Sixth Amendment.[50] *Ring* led to new sentencing hearings for a number of individuals on death rows around the country.[51]

Afterward, in *Shiro v. Summerlin*,[52] a majority of the Court limited the impact of *Ring* by holding that the decision would not apply retroactively to condemned inmates past their direct appeal stage. In that 5–4 decision, Justice Ginsburg joined a dissent arguing that "*Ring*'s requirement that a jury, and not a judge, must apply the death sentence aggravators announces a watershed rule of criminal procedure that should be applied retroactively in habeas proceedings."[53] Despite *Shiro*'s limitations on the application of *Ring*, the impact of Justice Ginsburg's opinion in *Ring* endures, as defendants remain entitled to jury findings of aggravating factors before they are condemned to death.

Decisions Involving Habeas Corpus Issues

A writ of habeas corpus gives prisoners access to the courts and is a vehicle for state defendants to have their constitutional issues reviewed in federal court.[54] During Justice Ginsburg's time on the Court, both the Court and Congress made it more difficult for inmates on states' death rows to obtain review of claimed constitutional violations in federal court through writs of habeas corpus. Justice Ginsburg's concern with access to the courts often led her to side with habeas petitioners. For example, her majority opinion in *Banks v. Dretke*[55] ruled in favor of a capital prisoner on a case involving prosecutor misconduct and the prisoner's ability to raise the issue on habeas corpus review. Also, in a dissenting opinion in *Gray v. Netherland*,[56] Justice Ginsburg stressed the importance of habeas review to allow a capital defendant to defend against the state's evidence.[57]

Justice Ginsburg also wrote for the majority in an important habeas corpus case involving the right to counsel. In *Maples v. Thomas*,[58] Justice Ginsburg concluded that, when the defendant's attorneys effectively abandoned his case, it constituted cause to excuse a procedural default of issues on habeas. Attorneys working on the case at a firm representing the capital defendant had left the firm, and notice of a ruling in the defendant's case did not reach the defendant's new lawyers, leading to a missed deadline in the case.[59] Justice Ginsburg's opinion gave the defendant an opportunity to be heard.

An Important Vote and an Important Voice

Justice Ginsburg's experience on the Court with capital cases led her to gradually become a stronger voice against executions. She expressed her views through her votes, public statements, and dissents. In capital cases where she did not write an opinion, Ginsburg's vote was often crucial, as she voted with the majority in every 5–4 Supreme Court decision that came out in favor of capital defendants.[60] She cast important votes striking capital punishment for people with intellectual disabilities, for juveniles, and for defendants in cases in which nobody was killed.[61]

Ginsburg also played key roles in lower-profile cases. She often voted to grant stays of executions or deny applications to vacate stays. Since the Death Penalty Information Center began keeping track of the statistic, no capital defendant received a stay of execution without her vote.[62]

Justice Ginsburg once declared: "Dissents speak to a future age. So that is the dissenter's hope: that they are writing not for today but for tomorrow."[63] She often voted against affirming death sentences, focusing on the importance of fair procedures in capital cases as well as a broader standard of review in death penalty cases. For example, in 2008 in *Baze v. Rees*,[64] the Court upheld the constitutionality of the method of lethal injection used in Kentucky (and throughout the country). In her dissenting opinion, Justice Ginsburg detailed the effects of the drugs used in lethal injection, such as one that "causes burning and intense pain as it circulates throughout the body."[65] She disagreed with the plurality's standard for determining the constitutionality of an execution method, asserting: "[I]f readily available measures can materially increase the likelihood that the protocol will cause no pain, a State fails to adhere to contemporary standards of decency [under the Eighth Amendment] if it declines to employ those measures."[66]

Ultimately, though, Justice Ginsburg did not broadly conclude that lethal injection was an unconstitutional method of execution. She explained that she would have remanded the case for the lower court to assess the state's safeguards and whether Kentucky's protocol "creates an untoward, readily avoidable risk of inflicting severe and unnecessary pain."[67]

While Justice Ginsburg continued to take a methodical approach to capital cases on the Court, she made several public statements regarding her view of capital punishment as a policy matter. For example, during a 2001 lecture in Maryland, she criticized poor legal representation of capital defendants and stated that she was "glad to see" Maryland pass an execution moratorium bill.[68] In 2011, she told law students that she hoped the Court one day would hold that "the death penalty could not be administered with an even hand."[69]

Some justices have taken such a position in their written opinions. Justices Thurgood Marshall and William Brennan rejected the return of the death penalty in the 1970s by reasoning that capital punishment violates the Eighth Amendment. Marshall and Brennan dissented in every case upholding a capital sentence throughout the rest of their careers.[70]

Other Justices later took that position near or at the end of their judicial careers. As noted earlier, in February 1994, during Ginsburg's first term on the court, Justice Harry Blackmun wrote a dissenting opinion concluding that the death penalty is unconstitutional. Around that same time, former Justice Lewis Powell revealed to his biographer that he regretted his votes upholding the death penalty.[71] Similarly, and also during Ginsburg's time on the Court, Justice John Paul Stevens concluded in a 2008 opinion that the death penalty is "'patently excessive and cruel and unusual punishment violative of the Eighth Amendment.'"[72]

Unlike those Justices, Ginsburg was not on the Supreme Court for the landmark death penalty decisions upholding the modern death penalty in the 1970s and 1980s, such as *Gregg v. Georgia* and *McCleskey v. Kemp.*[73] Her judicial experience with the death penalty largely spanned a time of declining executions, and that backdrop may have helped guide her belief in taking a gradual approach of effectively working with her colleagues and limiting the use of capital punishment rather than sweeping broadly.

Conclusion

Even though Justice Ginsburg declared to an audience in 2017, "If I were queen, there would be no death penalty," she approached the death penalty not as a monarch but as a jurist, carefully taking one case at a time. She relied on precedent to try to ensure capital sentencing followed the constitutional demands that procedures be fair and reliable, while enforcing the Court's proclamations that death sentences differ from other punishments. Her approach to capital punishment was similar to her approach to other constitutional criminal procedure cases, which has been described as illustrating a "preference for narrow rulings that adhere closely to precedent and that avoid grand pronouncements."[74]

Still, Justice Ginsburg saw broad problems with the death penalty, including limits on habeas corpus, failures to protect innocent defendants, and unequal treatment based on race and other factors. She brought to her capital punishment jurisprudence her compassion for people tossed aside by society.

Near the end of her time on the Court, Justice Ginsburg indicated that her judicial experience was leading her to a different conclusion on the constitutionality of the death penalty. Although she never wrote a sweeping opinion herself declaring the death penalty unconstitutional, her colleague Justice Stephen Breyer in 2015 wrote a dissenting opinion in *Glossip v. Gross*,[75] another case addressing the constitutionality of lethal injection. He asked that the Court request briefing on "whether the death penalty violates the Constitution."[76] The long dissent documented numerous reasons it is "highly likely that the death penalty violates the Eighth Amendment."[77] Only Justice Ginsburg joined this dissent and the call to reassess the constitutionality of the death penalty.

In July 2020, two months before Justice Ginsburg's death, she again joined Breyer in questioning the constitutionality of the death penalty.[78] The 5–4 decision in *Barr v. Lee* rejected a constitutional challenge to lethal injection, allowing Daniel L. Lee to be executed in the first federal execution in seventeen years.[79] The dissenting opinion unsuccessfully beseeched the Court to evaluate the constitutionality of the death penalty, as the resumption of federal executions provided "examples that illustrate the difficulties of administering the death penalty consistent with the Constitution." Lee's execution was followed by twelve more federal executions before the end of President Donald Trump's term in January 2021.[80]

Through Ginsburg's careful and reasoned approach to death penalty jurisprudence, she provided an important voice for moderating and challenging the American system of capital punishment. Her decisions and votes helped shape and limit the use of the modern death penalty, through decisions on issues such as the right to counsel, the right to a jury, the ban on executing those with an intellectual disability, and the ability for the most despised to have access to the courts. Her votes and analysis created an important record that remains with us as states around the country and the federal government continue to struggle with issues related to putting human beings to death.

NOTES

1 EDWARD LAZARUS, CLOSED CHAMBERS 513–14 (1998).

2 Joyce Ann Baugh et al., *Justice Ruth Bader Ginsburg: A Preliminary Assessment*, 26 U. TOL. L. REV. 1, 4 (1994).

3 Brief of Amicus Curiae in Support of Respondent in *Coker v. Georgia*, 433 U.S. 584 (1977) (No. 75–5444) [hereinafter ACLU Brief], *microformed on* U.S. Supreme Court Records and Briefs, Fiche 9–10 (Microcard Ed.).

4 Coker v. Georgia, 433 U.S. 584 (1977). The Court voted 7–2 to reverse the death sentence, although the Justices were divided on the reasoning. *See id.* at 600, 601.

5   *See* Neil A. Lewis, *Ginsburg Deflects Pressure to Talk on Death Penalty*, N.Y. TIMES at A1 (July 23, 1993).

6   *See id.*; ACLU Brief at 9.

7   ACLU Brief at 9–21.

8   Sidney Harring & Jeffrey L. Kirchmeier, *Celebrating the Jurisprudence of Justice Ruth Bader Ginsburg: Scrupulous in Applying the Law: Justice Ruth Bader Ginsburg and Capital Punishment*, 7 N.Y. CITY L. REV. 241, 246 (2004).

9   Baugh, *A Preliminary Assessment* at 4.

10 Mei-Fei Kuo & Kai Wang, *When Is an Innovation in Order? Justice Ruth Bader Ginsburg and Stare Decisis*, 20 U. HAW. L. REV. 835, 863 (1998) (quoting *Nomination of Ruth Bader Ginsburg, to be Associate Justice of the Supreme Court of the United States: Hearing Before the Comm. on the Judiciary*, U.S. Senate, 103rd Cong. 51, 53 (1993) (statement of Judge Ruth Bader Ginsburg)).

11 *Senate Confirms Ginsburg*, HOUSTON CHRONICLE at A1 (Aug. 3, 1993).

12 HELEN PREJEAN, C.S.J., DEAD MAN WALKING: AN EYEWITNESS ACCOUNT OF THE DEATH PENALTY IN THE UNITED STATES (1993).

13 *See* Jeffrey L. Kirchmeier, *Another Place Beyond Here: The Death Penalty Moratorium Movement in the United States*, 73 U. COLO. L. REV. 1, 39–43 (2002).

14 Callins v. Collins, 510 U.S. 1141, 1143 (1994) (Blackmun, J., dissenting from denial of petition for writ of certiorari).

15 JEFFREY L. KIRCHMEIER, IMPRISONED BY THE PAST: WARREN MCCLESKEY AND THE AMERICAN DEATH PENALTY 232 (2015).

16 James v. Collins, 509 U.S. 947 (1993).

17 *See, e.g.*, Campbell v. Wood, 511 U.S. 1119, 1122 (1994) (voting to grant stay of execution); Nethery v. Texas, 511 U.S. 1123 (1994) (denying stay of execution).

18 Romano v. Oklahoma, 512 U.S. 1, 15 (1994) (Ginsburg, J., dissenting).

19 *Id.* at 15–25.

20 *Id.* at 3.

21 *Id.* (discussing Caldwell v. Mississippi, 472 U.S. 320 (1985)).

22 *See* Tuilaepa v. California, 512 U.S. 967, 981 (1994).

23 *Id.* at 970.

24 *Id.* at 981.

25 Victor v. Nebraska, 511 U.S. 1 (1994).

26 *Id.*

27 Florida v. Nixon, 543 U.S. 175 (2004).

28 *Id.* at 188.

29 Similarly, in 2002 Justice Ginsburg joined the majority opinion in *Bell v. Cone*, where the Court used the standard in *Strickland v. Washington*, 466 U.S. 668 (1984), to uphold a Tennessee death sentencing involving a condemned inmate claiming ineffective assistance of counsel at his sentencing hearing. Bell v. Cone, 535 U.S. 685, 689–93 (2002).

30 McCoy v. Louisiana, 138 S. Ct. 1500 (2018).

31 *Id.* at 1504. Justice Ginsburg distinguished the case from her prior opinion in *Florida v. Nixon*, explaining that, in the prior case, the client was unresponsive and did not protest the attorney's decision to concede guilt until after the trial. *Id.*

32 Dunn v. Madison, 138 S. Ct. 9 (2017).

33 *Id.* at 12.

34 408 U.S. 902 (1972).

35 428 U.S. 153 (1976).

36 Atkins v. Virginia, 536 U.S. 304 (2002).

37 Bobby v. Bies, 556 U.S. 825 (2009).

38 Moore v. Texas, 137 S. Ct. 1039 (2017).

39 *Id.* at 1051 (quoting Hall v. Florida, 572 U.S. 701, 704 (2014)).

40 *Id.* at 1053 (Roberts, C.J., dissenting).

41 532 U.S. 36 (2001).

42 Simmons v. South Carolina, 512 U.S. 154 (1994).

43 *Shafer*, 532 U.S. at 51.

44 Ring v. Arizona, 536 U.S. 584 (2002).

45 *Id.* at 609.

46 Jason E. Barsanti, Ring v. Arizona, *The Sixth and Eighth Amendments Collide, Out of the Wreckage Emerges a Constitutional Safeguard for Capital Defendants*, 31 PEPP. L. REV. 519, 573 (2004).

47 Apprendi v. New Jersey, 530 U.S. 466 (2000). *Apprendi* "held that the Sixth Amendment does not permit a defendant to be exposed . . . to a penalty exceeding the maximum he would receive if punished according to the facts reflected in the jury verdict alone." *Ring*, 536 U.S. at 588–89 (citing *Apprendi*, 530 U.S. at 483) (emphasis in original omitted).

48 *Ring*, 536 U.S. at 609.

49 Walton v. Arizona, 497 U.S. 639 (1990).

50 *See* David G. Savage, *Executions Becoming Province of the South, Report Finds*, L.A. TIMES at 10 (Jan. 2, 2003).

51 At the time of *Ring*, eleven states used a capital sentencing procedure that relied, at least to some extent, upon judicial findings of fact. *See* Barsanti, *The Sixth and Eighth Amendments Collide* at 555; Jeffrey L. Kirchmeier, *Aggravating and Mitigating Factors: The Paradox of Today's Arbitrary and Mandatory Capital Punishment Scheme*, 6 WM. & MARY BILL RTS. J. 345, 346 n. 6 (1998).

52 Schiro v. Summerlin, 542 U.S. 348 (2004).

53 *Id.* at 366 (Breyer, J., dissenting).

54 *See, e.g.,* JAMES S. LIEBMAN & RANDY HERTZ, FEDERAL HABEAS CORPUS PRACTICE AND PROCEDURE § 2.3 (3rd ed. 2001).

55 Banks v. Dretke, 124 S. Ct. 1236 (2004).

56 Gray v. Netherland, 518 U.S. 152 (1996).

57 *Id.* at 180–86.

58 Maples v. Thomas, 565 U.S. 266 (2012).

59 *Id.* at 270–71.

60 *U.S. Supreme Court Justice Ruth Bader Ginsburg, Death Penalty Skeptic, Has Died,* DEATH PENALTY INFORMATION CENTER, Sept. 19, 2020, https://deathpenaltyinfo.org [hereinafter *Death Penalty Skeptic*].

61 *See, e.g.,* Atkins v. Virginia, 536 U.S. 304 (2002) (6–3 decision finding it unconstitutional to execute an intellectually disabled individual); Roper v. Simmons, 543 U.S. 551 (2005) (a 5–4 decision finding unconstitutional the use of the death penalty on juvenile offenders); Kennedy v. Louisiana, 554 U.S. 407 (2008) (5–4 decision finding unconstitutional to sentence a defendant to death for the rape of a child where the crime did not result in the death of the victim).

62 *Death Penalty Skeptic.*

63 Thomas Adcock, *CUNY Law School Hosts Justice Ginsburg,* N.Y. LAWYER at 16 (Mar. 19, 2004).

64 Baze v. Rees, 553 U.S. 35 (2008).

65 *Id.* at 114.

66 *Id.* at 117.

67 *Id.* at 123.

68 Kirchmeier, *Imprisoned by the Past* at 232.

69 *Id.*

70 *See, e.g.,* Alan I. Bigel, *Justice William J. Brennan, Jr. and Thurgood Marshall on Capital Punishment: Its Constitutionality, Morality, Deterrent Effect, and Interpretation by the Court,* 8 NOTRE DAME J. L. ETHICS & PUB. POL'Y 12 (2012).

71 JOHN C. JEFFRIES JR., JUSTICE LEWIS F. POWELL, JR.: A BIOGRAPHY 451 (New York: Fordham University Press, 1994).

72 Baze v. Rees, 553 U.S. 35, 87 (2008) (Stevens, J., concurring) (quoting Furman, 408 U.S. at 312 (White, J., concurring)).

73 481 U.S. 279 (1987).

74 Christopher Slobogin, *Justice Ginsburg's Gradualism in Criminal Procedure,* 70 OHIO ST. L.J. 867, 867 (2009).

75 Glossip v. Gross, 576 U.S. 863 (2015).

76 *Id.* at 908 (Breyer, J., dissenting).

77 *Id.* at 946 (Breyer, J., dissenting).

78 Barr v. Lee, 140 S. Ct. 2590 (2020).

79 Ariane de Vogue, Chandelis Duster & David Shortell, *Daniel Lewis Lee Executed After Supreme Court Clears the Way for First Federal Execution in 17 years,* CNN (July 14, 2020), www.cnn.com.

80 Holly Honderich, *In Trump's Final Days, a Rush of Federal Executions,* BBC NEWS (Jan. 16, 2021), www.bbc.com.

10

Employee Retirement Income Security Act (ERISA)

Toward a Reasonable and Coherent Framework

MARIA C. O'BRIEN

Few federal statutes have as direct an impact on the lives of average Americans as the Employee Retirement Income Security Act (ERISA).[1] The obscure but complicated 1974 statute regulates nearly every employee's health insurance, group life insurance, pension, long- and short-term disability coverage, and numerous other work-based benefits. It created a regulatory regime that has not been fully effective at protecting employees by ensuring that employers keep retirement-related promises. Ruth Bader Ginsburg's principal contribution to ERISA jurisprudence was a pragmatic sensibility consistently grounded in basic fairness for plan participants (employees and their dependents), with a strong distaste for unpredictable, distorted, or peculiar outcomes.

When Ginsburg ascended to the Supreme Court in 1993, the Court was grappling with myriad issues presented by this poorly drafted statute. Health care was relatively affordable in 1974,[2] but by 1993 health care costs in the United States were rising rapidly.[3] By the mid 1990s, employer-sponsored health insurance litigation was accelerating in both federal and state courts. And ERISA, which was crafted primarily to address defects in the pre-1974 world of defined benefit pension plans,[4] was repeatedly scrutinized during efforts to resolve the battles that ensued when plan sponsors simultaneously confronted longer lifespans and dramatic increases in health care costs and life-saving technology.[5] Plan participants wanted and needed more, while employers scrambled to reduce, offload, and/or exclude costs. This dynamic environment triggered important cases before the Court.

Ginsburg's consistent approach to this important area of the law was unwavering faithfulness to the text of the 1974 statute,[6] tempered by concerns for practicality and workability. Her opinions were always infused with a desire to heed the legislative history of the statute and its ambitious goals. This may have been a reaction to the foundational cases during her time on the Court, which featured plan administrators who were eager for broad powers to interpret plan documents and to make decisions largely insulated from review or challenge.

This chapter is divided into five sections, each focused on a group of cases in which Ginsburg played a major role in shaping the development of ERISA doctrine. These are: preemption;[7] health plan reimbursement provisions;[8] conflicted decision-making (which has proved to be especially critical in the disability insurance area);[9] "lifetime" health benefits for retirees; and the parameters of fiduciary duty.[10] Justice Ginsburg's contributions to this often ignored but critical area of American law are identified and explained. Despite the relatively few opinions she authored on this topic, she wielded an outsized influence on this area of the law.

Preemption Doctrine

ERISA's poorly drafted preemption language[11] provided little helpful guidance about what employee benefits matters states could regulate after 1974. The Court has famously referred to ERISA's preemption provisions as an "unhelpful text" and "not a model of legislative drafting."[12] Ginsburg arrived just as the Court was rethinking its early, broad field preemption approach. She embraced what Professor Colleen Medill has called the "modern" view, with a rebuttable presumption that Congress did not intend to preempt "traditional areas of state law regulation."[13]

In 1999, Justice Ginsburg penned the majority opinion in *Unum Life Insurance Co. v. Ward.*[14] The plaintiff-respondent in this case, Ward, became permanently disabled on May 5, 1992. In late February or early March 1993, he qualified for state disability benefits in California, and in April 1994 Ward submitted an application to his employer's long-term disability plan. Because this notice was late under the policy terms, it was denied as untimely, and litigation followed. Ultimately, a unanimous Supreme Court concluded that the notice-prejudice rule "regulates insurance" as a matter of common sense. Justice Ginsburg observed that the Court does not normally disturb an appellate court's judgment on an issue so heavily dependent on analysis of state law, and that there was no cause to do so here.

A few years later, she concurred in the *Aetna v. Davila* case, in which the Court preempted a Texas statute that purported to create state law causes of action that impermissibly duplicated, supplemented, or supplanted ERISA's civil enforcement remedies.[15] Ginsburg noted that this direct attempt by the Texas legislature to craft its own remedies for Texans who were unhappy with health care provided by an ERISA plan was unquestionably and "totally preempted" under the Court's modern preemption approach.[16]

However, the bulk of her concurrence, in which Justice Breyer joined, focused not on the obvious defects of the Texas approach (which Justice Thomas's majority opinion described in detail), but rather on the alarming problem of robust ERISA preemption combined with what she described as the "cramped construction" of remedial options.[17] This combination, she argued forcefully, created a "regulatory vacuum" in which "virtually all state law remedies are preempted but very few federal substitutes are provided."[18] Though the Texas approach was fatally flawed, she argued that states should have some ability to regulate in this area.

Ginsburg's insistence on the need for the Court and/or Congress to address the crisis created by the twin forces of preemption and a narrow view of ERISA's remedial options was perhaps her most important contribution to the ERISA dialogue during her tenure on the Court. Her insistence on the profound injustice "in which persons adversely affected by ERISA-proscribed wrongdoing cannot gain make-whole relief"[19] put her at odds with her good friend and colleague Justice Antonin Scalia, who expressed concerns about the technical construction of the statute but seemed less interested in its practical consequences for plan participants and their dependents.[20]

In 2016, when it was probably becoming obvious to Ginsburg that her calls for reform of ERISA's preemption and remedial schemes was not something she was likely to live to see, she authored a dissent in a case involving the Vermont legislature's attempt to gather health claims data from insurers doing business in the state.[21] In *Gobeille v. Liberty Mutual Insurance Co.*, Ginsburg's lengthy and detailed dissent conveyed deep frustration with the majority's strategy of waiting for Congress to act productively in the future. Ginsburg noted that the data Vermont sought was central neither to plan administration nor to regulating the management or solvency of ERISA plans. She criticized Justice Breyer's conjecture that the federal government might decide to collect this data and might then also decide "to pass this data on to the States." This scenario, she concluded, was "unsettling . . . [and left] the States dependent on a federal agency's grace—i.e. the Department of Labor's willingness to take on a chore divorced from ERISA's objectives."[22] The majority opinion in *Gobeille*, she asserted, amounted to a "retrieval of preemption doctrine that belongs in the discard bin."[23] Ginsburg seemed worried that, after several years of post-*Travelers* preemption jurisprudence that allowed for a degree of state regulation, the Court was prepared to return to a broad preemption approach that left few opportunities for states to promulgate regulations.

Health Plan Reimbursement Provisions

Ginsburg's singular alarm about the absence of protections for ERISA plan participants can be fully appreciated only in light of her sarcastic and perceptive dissent in the 2002 case *Great-West Life & Annuity Insurance Company v. Knudson.*[24] In *Great-West*, an ERISA plan administration sought reimbursement from a seriously injured beneficiary who had recovered monetary damages from a tortfeasor. Much of the tort recovery went into a trust established for future medical care, with a small portion set aside to satisfy Great-West's reimbursement claim. Unhappy with the amount designated for reimbursement, Great-West sued to enforce its reimbursement clause under a section of the statute providing for a civil action to "obtain appropriate equitable relief."[25]

Justice Scalia, writing for a narrow majority of five, concluded that a line of cases beginning with *Massachusetts Mutual Life v. Russell*[26] and *Mertens v. Hewitt Associates*[27] had already made clear that "'equitable' relief must mean *something* less than *all* relief."[28] In emphasizing the unique characteristics of relief typically available in courts of equity, Scalia concluded that the reimbursement money sought by Great-West was a form of legal (rather than equitable) relief and therefore not available. He declined to tinker judicially with the "carefully crafted and detailed enforcement scheme" Congress laid out in ERISA.[29] Instead, he characterized ERISA as "'a comprehensive and reticulated statute,' the product of a decade of congressional study of the Nation's private employee benefit system" with a "carefully crafted and detailed enforcement scheme."[30]

Ginsburg was not having it. She rejected this approach entirely, describing it as a project to "exhume the 'fine distinction[s]' borne of the 'days of the divided bench,'" which was intent on using an "ancient classification . . . to obstruct the general goals of ERISA."[31] Noting that ERISA is a "distinctly modern statute" (whereas the Judiciary Act of 1789, which Scalia relied on, was not), Ginsburg disdained the majority's "antiquarian inquiry" because it "needlessly obscures the meaning and complicates the application of § 502(a)(3)."[32]

Limited options for recovery make it hard—if not impossible—for plaintiffs to pursue claims under virtually all circumstances.[33] Ginsburg understood that the hyper-narrow interpretation of ERISA provisions reflected in Scalia's Great-West opinion not only complicated and reduced access to those with legitimate claims against a plan but also would leave many without any effective remedy at all. Taken in combination with ERISA's broad preemption scheme, it meant that parallel state remedies were often unavailable as well.

Ginsburg dissented again in another major recoupment case, Montanile,[34] fourteen years later. By this time, she was clearly tiring of making the same point over and over again: that the Court's jurisprudence in this area was illogical and led to "bizarre conclusions."[35] In contrast with her long and carefully crafted dissenting opinion in Great-West, Ginsburg's Montanile dissent was short and crackled with frustration at the Court's persistent refusal to change course in a manner that would lead to fairer, more equitable, and more predictable results for litigants. Ginsburg expressed certainty that the twin formula of broad preemption and narrow remedies could not possibly be what Congress had in mind when it promised greater security to millions of plan participants.

Glenn, Firestone, and Conflicted Decision-making

One of the most important ERISA cases decided during Ginsburg's tenure on the Court, Metropolitan Life Insurance Co. v. Glenn,[36] presented an opportunity to correct the problem created by the Court nearly twenty years earlier in the lamentable *Firestone* decision.[37] In *Firestone,* the Court sanctioned the ability of a plan administrator to insulate itself from de novo review of a denial of a claim in federal court, simply by including language granting the administrator discretionary authority in the plan documents. This meant that a plan administrator's denials could only be reviewed under an "arbitrary and capricious" standard.

The problem this created was particularly acute in cases where the plan administrator both determined eligibility for benefits and paid those benefits. Under *Firestone,* "conflicted" administrators understood that the likelihood of an adverse result in a federal forum was remote indeed. The holding in *Glenn,* written by Justice Breyer and joined by Justice Ginsburg, made the existence of a conflict of interest a factor to consider when deciding whether a plan administrator abused its discretion when denying benefits. This was important because most ERISA plans operate in the conflicted manner protected by *Firestone* and acknowledged as problematic in *Glenn.*

The significance of *Glenn* is hard to overstate for people with disabilities and especially for those who are dependent on their disability income. As James Goodley, a prominent workers' rights attorney, noted in an analysis of post-*Glenn* circuit decisions: "It seems that plaintiffs in this area do not really win cases. Rather plan administrators lose cases through procedural mishaps. This is an unjust result for plaintiffs who seek ERISA's protection."[38]

Retiree Health Benefits All but Disappear

In a somewhat obscure case decided in 1998, *Eastern Enterprises v. Apfel,*[39] a majority of Supreme Court Justices concluded that the imposition of liability upon a former coal operator to fund health benefits for retired miners was an unconstitutional taking. Even though the employer left the coal industry in 1965, it convinced a majority of Justices that the "reachback" liability it complained of frustrated its settled expectations so much as to be unconstitutional. In dissent, Justice Breyer opined:

> For many years Eastern benefited from the labor of those miners. Eastern helped to create conditions that led the miners to expect continued

health care benefits for themselves and their families after they retired. And Eastern, until 1987, continued to draw sizable profits from the coal industry through a wholly owned subsidiary. For these reasons, I believe that Congress did not act unreasonably or otherwise unjustly in imposing these health care costs upon Eastern. Consequently, in my view, the statute before us is constitutional.[40]

Breyer rejected the notion that the Takings Clause of the U.S. Constitution even applied to ordinary liability to pay money to third parties. Liability, after all, extended only to miners who were actually employed by the employer and whose "labor benefited Eastern when they were younger and healthier. In so far as working conditions created a risk of future health problems for those miners, Eastern created those conditions."[41] Explaining that "health care costs inevitably arise in old age,"[42] the dissenters emphasized that miners "went to work each day under the assumption that their health benefits would be there when they retired."[43] The dissenters argued it was important that promises "made to them during their working years are not now . . . reneged upon."[44] That non-ERISA case, in which Ginsburg joined Breyer's dissent, anticipated some of the same arguments the Court would confront in its well-known ERISA retiree health benefits case, *M&G Polymers v. Tackett*,[45] seventeen years later.

Tackett required the Court to consider whether inferences arising from negotiations for a collective bargaining agreement were sufficient to create a vested right to lifetime health care benefits. Noting that employers have "large leeway to design disability and other welfare plans as they see fit,"[46] Justice Thomas concluded that basic contract law principles were inconsistent with the Sixth Circuit's long-standing view of the significance of labor contract negotiations as described in its famous opinion in *UAW v. Yard-Man*.[47] Thomas dismantled *Yard-Man*'s foundational inference—that parties would never have left retiree health benefits open to future negotiation and must have intended them to vest for the life of each retiree. Ginsburg and others concurred, agreeing that ordinary contract principles applied, but they urged the court of appeals on remand to consider "the entire agreement to determine whether the parties intended retiree health-care benefits to vest." As Justice Ginsburg explained:

Because the retirees have a vested, lifetime right to a monthly pension, a provision stating that retirees "will receive" health care benefits if they are "receiving a monthly pension" is relevant to this examination. . . . [And if] the Court of Appeals concludes that the contract is ambiguous, it may turn to extrinsic evidence—for example, the parties' bargaining history.[48]

Her concurrence reads like a road map, suggesting a path forward to salvage retiree health care benefits for the retired union members in *Tackett*, whose increasingly expensive coverage made health care promises, if indeed they were made, costly and untenable.

Fiduciaries and Remedies for Breach of Their Duties

No discussion of Justice Ginsburg's participation in ERISA decisions would be complete without recounting her support for Justice Breyer's opinion in *Varity Corp. v. Howe*.[49] *Varity* forced the Court to consider whether an employer and owner also functions as an ERISA fiduciary when speaking about ERISA-regulated benefits and whether ERISA authorized a suit for individualized equitable relief for employees who were deliberately misled. Justice Breyer's opinion recounts in some detail the strenuous efforts of Varity to "sell" the transfer of its nonpension (and other) assets to employees via a program it dubbed "Project Sunshine." Employees were required to listen to presentations designed to persuade them to agree to change both their employer and benefit plans. "The thrust . . . was that the employees' benefits would remain secure if they voluntarily transferred to" the new entity.[50]

Given the outrageous conduct of the employer/fiduciary here, it is not surprising that Ginsburg joined Breyer's opinion, which contained an exhaustive review of Varity's extensive efforts to *knowingly mislead* its own plan participants about the security of their benefits. The majority noted that "[l]ying is inconsistent with the duty of loyalty owed by all fiduciaries."[51] The Court concluded that a remedy under section 502(a)(3) must be available, because otherwise "they have no remedy at all."[52] And the majority, unable to ascertain what ERISA purpose is served by the denial of any remedy, insisted it must exist in this section.

Conclusion

In analyzing Ginsburg's participation in ERISA cases while she was on the Supreme Court, one cannot claim that she was radical or even pioneering in her approach to ERISA litigation. On the contrary, her approach to each problem was workerlike and generally faithful to liberal-identified precedent. Her most pronounced contribution was her consistent emphasis on a methodology that yielded fair and predictable outcomes and that hewed closely to the original goals of the statute—to increase retirement and welfare benefits security for employees and retirees. She cared deeply about the promises that were made to plan participants and consistently fashioned decisions that honored their expectations to the greatest degree possible. Neither the Court nor Congress has yet to take up the calls for reform she articulated so clearly and passionately in her well-known dissent in *Great-West*. Maybe the Court will one day have a majority that eschews theoretically clever, historical, and intensely technical details of ERISA in favor of an approach promoting financial security for every plan participant.

NOTES

1 *See generally* Employee Retirement Income Security Act of 1974, Pub. L. No. 93–406, 88 Stat. 829 (1974) (codified in sections of 29 U.S.C.).

2 For a thorough and entertaining account of the genesis of ERISA, see James Wooten, *The Most Glorious Story of Failure in the Business: The Studebaker-Packard Corporation and the Origins of ERISA*, 49 BUFF. L. REV. 683 (2001).

3 By 1993 the United States was experiencing significant year-over-year increases in the cost of health care. *See* Rabah Kamal et. al., *Peterson-KFF Health System Tracker, How Has U.S. Spending on Healthcare Changed Over Time?* (2020), www.healthsystemtracker.org. In 1970, for example, $353 per person was the average cost. By 2019 that number had increased by more than thirty times, to $11,582 per person. Overall spending in 1993 was about $1.4 trillion in constant 2019 dollars; by 2019 that number had risen to approximately $3.8 trillion. *Id.* Interestingly, personal consumption expenditures for health care dropped dramatically in 2020 as a consequence of the COVID-19 pandemic, with millions of people delaying or foregoing care. Cynthia Cox et. al., *Peterson-KFF Health System Tracker, How Have Health Spending and Utilization Changed During the Coronavirus Pandemic?* (2021), www.healthsystemtracker.org.

4 For a discussion of employers' widespread shift from defined benefit plans to defined contribution plans, and its effects, see Maria O'Brien Hylton, *Insecure Retirement Income, Wrongful Plan Administration and Other Employee Ben-*

efits Woes—Evaluating ERISA at Age Thirty, 53 BUFF. L. REV. 1193, 1202–06 (2005).

5 Many papers attempt to explain the unrelenting increase in health care costs in the United States. *See, e.g.*, Gary Branning & Martha Vater, *Healthcare Spending: Plenty of Blame to go Around*, 9 AM. HEALTH & DRUG BENEFITS 445, 445 ("The United States is the only profit-motivated healthcare system in the world, and perhaps it is no coincidence that this country also has the most expensive healthcare of any nation. . . . The central challenge facing the US healthcare system is not the motivation of stakeholders to earn a profit, but rather the misaligned incentives among healthcare stakeholders."); PRICEWATERHOUSECOOPERS, MEDICAL COST TREND: BEHIND THE NUMBERS 2017 (June 2016), www.pwccn.com (explaining factors affecting past and current health care costs). Few federal statutes have as direct an impact on the lives of average Americans as ERISA. Yet most would certainly assert the importance of various constitutional rights—free speech, freedom of religion, or the right to bear arms—long before they thought to consider the significance of an obscure 1974 statute that regulates their health insurance, group life insurance, pension, long- and short-term disability coverage, and numerous other work-based benefits. For employees at virtually every level of compensation and skill, ERISA is almost always more impactful than virtually any other federal law.

6 *See generally* Employee Retirement Income Security Act of 1974, Pub. L. No. 93–406, 88 Stat. 829 (1974) (codified in sections of 29 U.S.C.).

7 *See* Unum Life Ins. Co. of America v. Ward, 526 U.S. 358, 363–79 (1999). Much has been written about the Court's struggle to develop a coherent approach to ERISA preemption. *See, e.g.*, James E. Holloway, *ERISA, Preemption and Comprehensive Federal Health Care: A Call for "Cooperative Federalism" to Preserve the States' Role in Formulating Health Care Policy*, 16 CAMPBELL L. REV. 405 (1994); Leon E. Irish & Harrison J. Cohen, *ERISA Preemption: Judicial Flexibility and Statutory Rigidity*, 19 U. MICH. J. L. REFORM 109 (1985).

8 Great West Life & Annuity Ins. Co. v. Knudson, 534 U.S. 204, 224 (2002) (Ginsburg, J., dissenting).

9 Firestone Tire & Rubber Co. v. Bruch, 489 U.S. 101 (1989). Professor John Langbein has pointed out that *Firestone* "all but invited" plan administrators to simply provide for administrator discretion in order to completely insulate themselves from subsequent, meaningful review. John Langbein, *Trust Law as Regulatory Law: The Unum/Provident Scandal and Judicial Review of Benefit Denials Under ERISA*, 101 NW. U. L. REV. 1315, 1316 (2007). *See also* John H. Langbein, *What ERISA Means By "Equitable": The Supreme Court's Trail of Error in Russell, Mertens and Great West*, 103 COLUM. L. REV. 1317 (2003); Aetna Health Inc. v. Davila, 542 US 200, 222 (2004) (Ginsburg, J., concurring).

10 Varity Corp. v. Howe, 516 U.S. 489 (1996).

11 Volumes have been written about preemption. *See, e.g.*, James A. Wooten, *A Legislative and Political History of ERISA Preemption, Part 1*, 14(1) J. PENSION

BENEFITS 31 (2006); James A. Wooten, *A Legislative and Political History of ERISA Preemption, Part 2*, 14(3) J. PENSION BENEFITS 5 (2007); James A. Wooten, *A Legislative and Political History of ERISA Preemption, Part 3*, 15(3) J. PENSION BENEFITS 15 (2008); James A. Wooten, *A Legislative and Political History of ERISA Preemption, Part 4, The Deemer Clause*, 22(1) J. PENSION BENEFITS 3 (2014).

12 New York State Conf. of Blue Cross & Blue Shield Plans v. Travelers Ins. Co., 514 U.S. 645, 656 (1995) ("We simply must go beyond the unhelpful text."); Metro. Life Ins. Co. v. Massachusetts, 471 U.S. 724, 739 (1985) ("The two pre-emption sections, while clear enough on their faces, perhaps are not a model of legislative drafting.").

13 COLLEEN MEDILL, INTRODUCTION TO EMPLOYEE BENEFITS LAW: POLICY AND PRACTICE 730 (5th ed. 2018). ERISA preemption has proved to be fertile ground for academic commentary, particularly with respect to its impact on the ability of states to promote reforms designed to expand access to health insurance and substantive health care benefits. *See, e.g.*, Elizabeth Y. McCuskey, *ERISA Reform as Health Reform: The Case for an ERISA Preemption Waiver*, 48 J. L. MED. & ETHICS 450 (2021); Alexandra M. Stecker, *The Great Divide: ERISA Integrity versus State Desire to Hold Pharmacy Benefit Managers Accountable for Pharmaceutical Drug Pricing*, 44 U. IOWA J. CORP. L. 171 (2018).

14 526 U.S. 358 (1999).

15 Aetna Health Inc. v. Davila, 542 U.S. 200 (2004).

16 *Id.* at 222 (Ginsburg, J., concurring).

17 *Id.*

18 *Id.*

19 *Id.*

20 Ginsburg argued that Congress could not have intended to limit relief to equitable relief, despite the placement of the word "equitable" in section 502(a)(3). Great-West Life & Annuity Ins. Co. v. Knudson, 534 U.S. 204, 227 (2002) (Ginsburg, J., dissenting). "[W]hen Congress' clearly stated purpose so starkly conflicts with questionable inferences drawn from a single word in the statute, it is the latter, and not the former, that must give way." *Id.* Scalia criticized Ginsburg's "antiquarian inquiry" of the term and thought that the Court should respect Congress's choice to use the term. "If, as Justice GINSBURG surmises . . . Congress meant to rule out nothing more than 'compensatory and punitive damages,' it could simply have said that. That Congress sought to achieve this result by subtle reliance upon the dissenters' novel and expansive view of equity is most implausible. Respecting Congress's choice to limit the relief available under § 502(a)(3) to 'equitable relief' requires us to recognize the difference between legal and equitable forms of restitution." *Id.* at 217–18.

21 Gobeille. v. Liberty Mut. Ins. Co., 577 U.S. 312, 332 (2016) (Ginsburg, J., dissenting).

22 *Id.* at 345.

23 *Id.* at 346.

24 *Great-West*, 534 U.S. at 224 (Ginsburg, J., dissenting).

25 29 U.S.C. § 1132 ("A civil action may be brought . . . to obtain appropriate equitable relief.").

26 473 U.S. 134 (1985).

27 508 U.S. 248 (1993).

28 *Great-West*, 534 U.S. at 209 (quoting *Mertens*, 508 U.S. at 258).

29 *Id.* at 221.

30 *Id.* at 209.

31 *Id.* at 224 (Ginsburg, J., dissenting).

32 *Id.* at 234 (Ginsburg, J., dissenting).

33 *See, e.g.*, John Langbein, *Trust Law as Regulatory Law* at 1316; Larry Magarik, *Plan Reimbursement and Subrogation of Third-Party Recovery*, 24 BENEFITS L.J. 40 (2011); Peter A. Meyers, *Discretionary Language, Conflicts of Interest, and Standard of Review for ERISA Disability Plans*, 28 SEATTLE U. L. REV. 925 (2005).

34 Montanile v. Bd. Tr. of Nat'l Elevator Indus. Health Benefit Plan, 577 U.S. 136 (2016).

35 *Id.* at 151 (Ginsburg, J., dissenting).

36 Metropolitan Life Ins. Co. v. Glenn, 554 U.S. 105 (2008).

37 Firestone Tire & Rubber v. Bruch, 489 U.S. 101 (1989).

38 James Goodley, *The Effect of* Metropolitan Life v. Glenn *on ERISA Benefit Denials: Time for the "Treating Physician Rule,"* 26 J. OF CONTEMP. HEALTH L. & POL'Y 403, 421 (2010); *see also* Beverly Cohen, *Divided Loyalties: How the* Metlife v. Glenn *Standard Discounts ERISA Fiduciaries' Conflicts of Interest*, 2009 UTAH L. REV. 955 (2009).

39 Eastern Enterprises v. Apfel, 524 U.S. 498 (1998).

40 *Id.* at 553–54 (1998) (Breyer, J., dissenting).

41 *Id.* at 560 (Breyer, J., dissenting).

42 *Id.*

43 *Id.* at 564 (citation omitted).

44 *Id.*

45 M & G Polymers USA, LLC v. Tackett, 574 U.S. 427 (2015).

46 *Id.* at 427 (quoting Black & Decker Disability Plan v. Nord, 538 U.S. 822, 833 (2003)).

47 Int'l Union, United Auto., Aerospace and Agric. Implement Workers of Am. v. Yard–Man, Inc., 716 F.2d 1476 (6th Cir. 1983).

48 *Tackett*, 574 U.S. at 443–44.

49 Varity Corp. v. Howe, 516 U.S. 489 (1996).

50 *Id.* at 494.

51 *Id.*

52 *Id.* at 515.

11

Employment Discrimination

Justice Ginsburg Dissents

SANDRA F. SPERINO

Justice Ruth Bader Ginsburg is known for dissenting. The Justice's face, together with the phrase "I dissent" and her iconic initials, R.B.G., decorate coffee mugs, T-shirts, and a children's book. There is good reason that her dissenting opinions have captured the public imagination. They exhibit a striking ability to frame seemingly esoteric legal issues in ways that are accessible to the lay reader and show that reader how the choices made by the Court affect the reach of federal discrimination law.

This chapter explores Justice Ginsburg's dissenting opinions in three employment discrimination cases: *University of Texas Southwestern Medical Center v. Nassar,*[1] *Vance v. Ball State University,*[2] and *Ledbetter v. Goodyear Tire & Rubber Co., Inc.*[3] Justice Ginsburg penned these dissents at a particularly interesting time in employment discrimination jurisprudence. While the Supreme Court ruled in favor of workers in a few high-profile cases,[4] the Court also eroded employment law protections in cases that garnered less public attention. The stakes of these cases were often difficult to see because the Court framed the cases as procedural or as involving arcane legal issues. Justice Ginsburg understood how important these cases were, and her dissenting opinions highlighted how the Court's rulings on issues such as agency and causation would affect workers.

Three themes emerge from Justice Ginsburg's dissents in the three named cases.

First, Justice Ginsburg focused on the facts of the cases, highlighting facts ignored or undervalued by the majority. The majority's opinions framed the cases as involving narrow, esoteric legal issues and avoided discussing whether the outcomes would prevent discrimination in actual workplaces. In each of these cases, the majority opinion recounted a selectively edited version of the facts that ignored or undercut the workers' claims and evidence. The bare-bones facts presented in these opinions are often so muted or weighted toward the employer that it is difficult to understand why the plaintiff might have a valid claim.

A reader of employment discrimination cases could be forgiven for feeling a little uneasy about dissenting opinions penned by Justice Ginsburg because she filled in vital facts omitted from the majority opinion. She provided detailed evidence presented at the trial court levels that supported the workers' cases. By describing the workers' evidence, Justice Ginsburg's dissents highlighted how the majority's narrow views of discrimination law were aimed at making litigation easier as opposed to preventing discrimination.

Second, Justice Ginsburg's dissents often explained that the broad text of the discrimination statutes did not require the cramped reading claimed by the majority. In each of the cases discussed in this chapter, the majority opinion failed to discuss the legal ambiguity in the question presented to it and pretended that the answer was clear and that only one answer was legally permissible. Justice Ginsburg's dissents criticized them for taking narrow, litigation-centric views of discrimination law rather than choosing other options that would effectuate both the language and the underlying purposes of discrimination law outside litigation.

Finally, Justice Ginsburg's dissents exhibited a respect for the Equal Employment Opportunity Commission (EEOC), unlike the majority opinions. The EEOC is the federal administrative agency tasked with enforcing many federal discrimination laws and is a source of deep expertise about those statutes. In *Nassar*, *Vance*, and *Ledbetter*, the majority either ignored or outright rejected the views of this agency. Even though there are judicial doctrines that encourage the Supreme Court to defer to agencies with expertise,[5] during the 2000s the Supreme Court was often hostile to the EEOC, rejecting the agency's interpretation of discrimination law. The majority opinions claimed that the complex phenomenon of employment discrimination can best be understood by picking out a couple of words in a discrimination statute and looking up those words in a dictionary. In her dissenting opinions Justice Ginsburg advocated for the positions advanced by the EEOC, which addressed ways that workers actually experience discrimination.

University of Texas Southwestern Medical Center v. Nassar

Justice Ginsburg's dissent in *University of Texas Southwestern Medical Center v. Nassar* is illustrative. In that case, Dr. Naiel Nassar alleged he was discriminated against and retaliated against because of his national origin and religion.[6] A jury found in favor of Dr. Nassar on both claims, finding that the facts warranted an award of $400,000 in back pay and $3 million in compensatory damages.[7]

Nassar brought his claims under Title VII, a federal civil rights statute that prohibits discrimination based on race, sex, religion, color, and national origin. It also prohibits employers from retaliating against workers for complaining about discriminatory treatment. When the jury was asked whether Nassar faced discrimination because of his protected traits and retaliation after complaining about discrimination, the jury reached an answer: yes, he did.

Despite Nassar's resounding victory at the trial court, the majority opinion written by Justice Kennedy contained only a couple of sentences describing the evidence that supported the jury's decision. In the paragraph that provided the most facts, Justice Kennedy emphasized evidence that favored the employer.[8] When an appellate court hears a case on appeal from a jury verdict, the appellate court is required to read the facts in the light most favorable to the jury's verdict. Yet the brief facts that Justice Kennedy provided do not describe the evidence in the light most favorable to the jury's verdict.

By the time Nassar's case reached the Supreme Court, there was only one legal issue remaining: the appropriate causal standard for Title VII retaliation claims. The retaliation provision of Title VII is broad, prohibiting an employer from discriminating against employees because they complained about unlawful employment practices.[9] Justice Kennedy's opinion did not evaluate the facts of the case and determine whether a reasonable jury could determine that the employer retaliated "because of" Dr. Nassar's complaint. Instead, Justice Kennedy's opinion focused on defining the causal standard courts should apply to Title VII claims in a hyper-technical, litigation-specific way.

Causation may seem like an esoteric and relatively unimportant legal issue, but in some cases it can determine who wins the lawsuit. In fact, causation is so important in discrimination law that the Supreme Court has returned to it multiple times.[10]

Causation is comprised of two separate inquiries: (1) ascertaining which party is required to prove it; and (2) determining how high the legal standard for proving it will be. In litigation, courts often define causation in a specific way, requiring the plaintiff to establish what is called "but for" cause. While this construct often works to adjudicate cases, it is different than how typical people think of causation—and it also has well-known flaws. Thus, lawyers know that the "but for" cause standard needs to be modified in certain kinds of cases or else it will produce unfair results.

One famous case illustrating the stakes of causation is *Summers v. Tice*.[11] In that case, three people were hunting together. Two of the hunters negligently shot toward the third hunter. Shot from one of the hunter's guns hit the plaintiff near the eye. If the plaintiff was required to prove which of the two hunters shot him, he would lose his case because, although both hunters shot in a negligent way, the plaintiff could not prove which one actually shot him. The court believed this outcome would be unfair and instead chose a causal standard that would place some of the causal burden on the two negligent hunters. The *Summers* case is one example of a situation in which requiring the plaintiff to establish "but for" cause can lead to an unfair outcome. The case is regularly taught in law schools and is widely known by lawyers. Thus, when lawyers approach the concept of causation, they know that there are recognized exceptions to the default standard and that some of the exceptions arise when the plaintiff lacks complete information about how events lead to an end result.

Indeed, when the Supreme Court addressed causation in the 1989 case *Price Waterhouse v. Hopkins*, the Supreme Court adopted a causation standard that recognized that an information asymmetry exists in many employment discrimination cases.[12] The employer possesses better information about why it made an employment decision than the worker possesses. Additionally, in some cases, like those involving group decision-making, a plaintiff may be able to show only that a protected trait played some role in an outcome, without being able to pinpoint exactly what role it played. In *Price Waterhouse*, the Supreme Court held that to prevail on a Title VII claim a plaintiff is required only to show that her protected trait was a motivating factor in an employment decision.[13]

When the Supreme Court decided *Nassar*, it was clear that causation law permitted choices. In other words, cases like *Summers*, *Price Waterhouse*, and others had held that a plaintiff is not always required to establish "but for" cause to prevail. Yet in *Nassar*, the majority opinion acted as if only one causal choice were possible: the plaintiff is required to establish "but for" cause. Although there are significant problems with the majority's reasoning through the *Nassar* opinion, one of its most striking features is its decision to hide the menu of choices that the law has long recognized about causation. Indeed, for causal inquiries, the law often requires the plaintiff to establish "but for" cause in most cases but then alters the standard in cases where "but for" cause leads to an unjust result. In other words, the concept of factual cause not only includes the "but for" cause standard but also includes all of the exceptions to that standard.

Justice Kennedy's majority opinion in *Nassar* argued that Title VII's retaliation provision must embrace a "but for" cause standard because of the demands of the judicial and litigation system.[14] He posited that an employee might try to avoid termination by filing a fake retaliation claim against his employer.[15] He also expressed fears about courts, administrative agencies, and employers being subjected to "floodgates" of litigation if the Court chose a different causal outcome.[16] He then explicitly used these concerns about fakers and floodgates to justify the "but for" cause standard. Yet Justice Kennedy provided no empirical support for his position that agencies or courts were being flooded with fake claims or that changing the causal standard would deter plaintiffs from filing claims.

Even more surprisingly, Justice Kennedy expressed concern for the workload of the EEOC and used that concern to justify the outcome. He argued that, if the Court did not require the plaintiff to establish "but for" cause, the administrative agency would be overwhelmed with frivolous claims. This was a strange argument to make because the EEOC advocated for a less onerous causal standard. Justice Kennedy's opinion explicitly rejected the standard advocated by the EEOC, a standard that the EEOC thought would better remedy retaliation in American workplaces.[17]

What is especially noteworthy about the majority opinion is that it centered the needs of judges and the litigation system. While one purpose of Title VII is to provide a remedy once a worker experiences discrimination or retaliation, its broader impact arises outside of litigation. The statute is not aimed primarily at litigation but at trying to prohibit discrimination and retaliation before it occurs. A litigation-centric interpretation of the statute may not effectuate the broader nonlitigation goals of the discrimination statutes. Nowhere in *Nassar* does Justice Kennedy consider which interpretation of Title VII would best meet the needs of employers and workers outside of litigation. This is a huge omission both in this case and in the broader context of discrimination jurisprudence. By focusing on the needs of judges and litigators, the Supreme Court ignored the transactional, nonlitigation contexts in which antidiscrimination law is most frequently and meaningfully applied. Instead of asking what standards would make litigation easier, the Justices should be most concerned with which standards will reduce discrimination and retaliation in the workplace and best remedy it after it occurs.

Justice Ginsburg authored a dissenting opinion in *Nassar*, joined by Justices Breyer, Sotomayor, and Kagan.[18] The dissent examined the statutory words "because of" and noted that the Court should be trying to effectuate a meaning that enforces the purposes of Title VII outside the litigation context. In the first paragraph of her dissent, Justice Ginsburg recognized that retaliation law "is essential to securing a workplace where individuals are not discriminated against because of their racial, ethnic, religious, or gender-based status."[19]

Justice Ginsburg spent a considerable portion of the dissent explaining the potential causal standard options from both Title VII jurisprudence and tort law.[20] She explained why the Supreme Court rejected the "but for" causal standard in *Price Waterhouse* and also why tort law often seeks an alternative standard.

In multiple paragraphs, Justice Ginsburg's dissent described the evidence related to Dr. Nassar's discrimination and retaliation claims.[21] She focused on the evidence that supported the plaintiff, which was appropriate given the fact that the Supreme Court was considering an appeal from a jury verdict. By telling the worker's story, Justice Ginsburg made it easier for a lay reader to understand how Dr. Nassar's complaints connected to the negative action taken against him.

Justice Ginsburg recognized that reciting the facts would power-fully highlight the stakes of choosing one causal standard over another. Her use of the facts also showed her commitment to viewing the dis-crimination statutes as having their central focus within workplaces, not in litigation. Justice Ginsburg recognized that focusing too heavily on litigation efficiency would often mean that other important values were being lost. She also pushed back against the majority's claim that its standard would be easy to administer, pointing out that the Court's choice meant that one causal standard applied to Title VII discrimina-tion claims and a separate standard applied to retaliation claims brought under the same statute.

Justice Ginsburg also relied on EEOC guidance to answer the ques-tion before the Court. Although the EEOC does not possess the author-ity to issue regulations on the substantive provisions of Title VII, Justice Ginsburg argued that the EEOC's long-standing guidance that a plaintiff could prevail on a retaliation claim without establishing "but for" cause merited respect.[22]

The dissenting opinion in *Nassar* illustrates key themes in Justice Ginsburg's employment discrimination jurisprudence: a deep respect for the facts of actual cases, a rejection of a narrow, litigation-centric view of discrimination law, and deference to the EEOC, the government agency with the most expertise in discrimination law.

Vance v. Ball State University

Agency law plays an important role in discrimination cases. The Supreme Court has interpreted the federal discrimination statutes in a way that allows employers to escape liability for workplace harassment in certain cases. The Supreme Court added an agency analysis to harass-ment cases in two opinions issued on the same day in 1998: *Faragher v. City of Boca Raton*[23] and *Burlington Industries, Inc. v. Ellerth*.[24] Jus-tice Ginsburg joined the majority opinion in both cases, which together created a complicated framework for evaluating employer liability.[25] In deciding when the employer could be liable for harassment, the Court drew a dividing line between coworkers and supervisors. The Court held that an employer is liable for harassment if it is negligent in that it knew or should have known about the conduct and failed to stop it.[26]

However, the Court held that an employer would be automatically liable for a supervisor's harassment in certain instances. Thus, who counted as a supervisor became critically important to harassment cases.

In *Vance v. Ball State University*, the Supreme Court resolved a circuit split and defined the term "supervisor" for purposes of harassment liability.[27] Over a robust dissent by Justice Ginsburg, the Court held that the only employees who qualify as "supervisors" are those who have the power to take tangible employment actions against the complaining employee.[28] The Court noted that a tangible employment action is a "significant change in employment status, such as hiring, firing, failing to promote, reassignment with significantly different responsibilities, or a decision causing a significant change in benefits."[29]

The *Vance* case could easily appear to be about an esoteric or unimportant legal question. However, the issue of whether employers are automatically liable for a particular person's harassment is vitally important to federal discrimination law because employers are the only entity that can potentially be liable under Title VII, the Age Discrimination in Employment Act (ADEA), and the Americans with Disabilities Act (ADA). If the Court rules that an employer is not automatically liable for harassment by certain employees, it is essentially making it more difficult or impossible for plaintiffs to obtain a remedy for workplace harassment.

To reach this outcome, the Supreme Court could not rely on the dictionary definition of "supervisor," because, as the Court noted, the word often has different meanings both in colloquial and legal usages. Instead, the Court reasoned that *Faragher* and *Ellerth* contemplated a sharp division between who was a supervisor and who was not, given that the test enunciated in those opinions relied heavily on the distinction.

While the *Vance* majority recognized the ambiguity in the term "supervisor," its choice among those options was based heavily on which option would be easier for courts to use during litigation. In other words, the majority Justices were more concerned about whether trial court judges could easily use the standard in litigation rather than whether the standard would discourage retaliation in the workplace and provide a remedy for it if it occurred. Indeed, the majority opinion spent more paragraphs discussing the need for a litigation-friendly standard than it did discussing the facts of the case.[30]

Just like in *Nassar*, the Court explicitly rejected the EEOC's proposed definition for the term "supervisor,"[31] asserting that the EEOC's definition did not provide enough certainty for litigation.[32] The majority adopted a different version of the term "supervisor" because it believed its definition would allow the parties to the litigation to more easily discern who fell within the definition and would allow judges to determine whether summary judgment was appropriate.[33] It also believed the EEOC definition would "frustrate judges and confound jurors."[34] The majority expressed no concerns about whether its chosen definition should try to advance the underlying goals of Title VII to prevent and remedy workplace discrimination. This is in stark contrast to how Justice Ginsburg viewed the term "supervisor."

Justice Ginsburg's dissent in *Vance* was joined by Justices Breyer, Kagan, and Sotomayor.[35] Justice Ginsburg argued that "supervisor" should include not only people who could hire and fire employees but also individuals who controlled the day-to-day work of employees. As in *Nassar*, Justice Ginsburg advocated for an outcome based on the EEOC's guidance and one she believed would align with the realities of the workplace and better fulfill Title VII's objectives, both inside and outside litigation. She wrote: "The limitation the Court decrees . . . ignores the conditions under which members of the work force labor[] and disserves the objective of Title VII to prevent discrimination from infecting the Nation's workplaces."[36]

Justice Ginsburg devoted an entire section of her opinion to the facts of the *Vance* case itself.[37] She spent a significant portion of the rest of the dissent discussing the cases of real workers and how the Court's narrow standard would affect their cases.[38] She advocated for a standard that she thought would best address discrimination as it happened in the workplace rather than choosing a standard that primarily focused on making litigation easier.

Justice Ginsburg also devoted an entire section of the dissent to the EEOC's long-standing guidance, arguing that EEOC's definition "reflects the agency's informed judgment and body of experience in enforcing Title VII."[39] Justice Ginsburg chided the majority for ignoring "workplace realities," as well as the EEOC's guidance.[40]

She argued that the majority "embraces a position that relieves scores of employers of responsibility for the behavior of the supervisors they employ" for the sake of adopting a definition that is simple and administrable.[41] She also pointed out that the majority's definition was not as simple or as administrable as the majority claimed.[42] Indeed, Justice Ginsburg rejected the idea that a simple standard could ever work given the myriad ways American employers choose to organize their workforces. She stated:

> Supervisors, like the workplaces they manage, come in all shapes and sizes. Whether a pitching coach supervises his pitchers (can he demote them?), or an artistic director supervises her opera star (can she impose significantly different responsibilities?), or a law firm associate supervises the firm's paralegals (can she fire them?) are matters not susceptible to mechanical rules and on-off switches. One cannot know whether an employer has vested supervisory authority in an employee, and whether harassment is aided by that authority, without looking to the particular working relationship between the harasser and the victim.[43]

Justice Ginsburg's dissent in *Vance* has the same characteristics as her dissent in *Nassar*. She relied on the facts of actual cases to describe the real-world effect of the Court's choice. She rejected a simplistic, formalistic view of discrimination law and described how a narrow, litigation-focused standard ignored the realities of the workplace and would not be as simple to administer at the majority claimed. Justice Ginsburg again argued that the EEOC's chosen standard better balanced all of the competing issues and would discourage employers from retaliating against workers.

Ledbetter v. Goodyear Tire Rubber Co., Inc.

These same themes resonate in *Ledbetter v. Goodyear Tire Rubber Co., Inc.*[44] Like *Nassar* and *Vance*, the *Ledbetter* case appears to be about a mundane topic—a statute of limitations question about how long people who faced pay discrimination could wait before presenting their claims to an administrative agency.

The employment discrimination statutes require victims of discrimination to first present their allegations to either the EEOC or to a state administrative agency. This must be done within either 180 or 300 days from the date of the discrimination.[45] If the worker misses the required deadline, she will likely be barred from raising her claim later in court. This means a worker will never receive a remedy, even if she faced discrimination.

In the *Ledbetter* case, the Court considered whether pay discrimination arose at the time the initial discriminatory pay rate was decided or whether the discrimination occurred each time the worker received a paycheck at the discriminatory wage.[46] The Supreme Court held that the worker must file her pay discrimination claim within 180 days or 300 days of when the employer set the discriminatory pay and not the later paychecks. The majority claimed that the text of the statute demanded this outcome.[47]

Justice Ginsburg wrote a dissenting opinion in the case, joined by Justices Stevens, Souter, and Breyer. As in *Nassar* and *Vance*, Justice Ginsburg focused on the facts of the case. She told plaintiff Lilly Ledbetter's story. Ledbetter was a supervisor at a Goodyear Tire & Rubber plant in Alabama, working in a position mostly occupied by men. Over time, her salary became out of alignment with male managers with the same or less seniority. In 1997, as Justice Ginsburg recounted, Ledbetter was the only woman working as an area manager, and "the pay discrepancy between Ledbetter and her 15 male counterparts was stark: Ledbetter was paid $3,727 per month; the lowest paid male area manager received $4,286 per month, the highest paid $5,236."[48]

In 1998, Ledbetter filed a charge of discrimination with the EEOC and then later filed a claim in court. A jury heard Ledbetter's discrimination claim and found in her favor.[49]

After reciting the facts, Justice Ginsburg described why the majority's choice ignored the realities of pay discrimination in actual workplaces. Justice Ginsburg noted that pay discrimination often occurs incrementally over time and that workers often do not have access to information about how much their employer pays similar workers.[50] Justice Ginsburg recognized that workers are likely to complain about pay disparities (especially to an administrative agency or a court) only when the pay differential is significant.

Justice Ginsburg understood that the text of the discrimination statutes did not explicitly answer the question raised in *Ledbetter*. Justice Ginsburg would interpret the text of the discrimination statutes and the Supreme Court precedents related to statute of limitations issues in a way that honored the reality of how workers experience and respond to pay discrimination. She viewed pay discrimination as a continuing violation that occurred not only when the wage was set but also when the employer continued to pay the discriminatory wage over time.

Justice Ginsburg also noted that her reading of the statute aligned with the EEOC's position. In doing so, she cited EEOC administrative decisions in which the agency had held that discriminatory pay occurs with each unequal paycheck if the reason for the disparity is a person's sex or other protected trait.[51]

Justice Ginsburg expressed disapproval of the majority's claim that its interpretation was necessary to prevent employers from facing lawsuits for employment decisions that are long past. Justice Ginsburg found two problems with this assertion. First, to the victim of pay discrimination the effect of the discrimination was not long past. It happened each time she was paid less than similarly situated male workers. Second, Justice Ginsburg found the majority's description of the law incomplete and described a series of legal defenses an employer might raise in cases where the plaintiff unreasonably delays presenting her claim.

Near the end of the dissent, Justice Ginsburg provided more details about Lilly Ledbetter's specific case, summing up the critical differences between her approach to discrimination law and the majority's. She noted that the majority's chosen standard was "totally at odds with the robust protection against workplace discrimination Congress intended Title VII to secure."[52] She also chided the Court for its history of "cramped interpretations" of Title VII that were "incompatible with the statute's broad, remedial purpose."[53]

Justice Ginsburg implored Congress to intervene—and it did. Congress passed and President Barack Obama signed the Lilly Ledbetter Fair Pay Act of 2009. The statute amends Title VII, the ADEA, the ADA, and the Rehabilitation Act. It defines when discrimination occurs in compensation. It does so "when an individual becomes subject to a discriminatory compensation decision or other practice, or when an individual is affected by application of a discriminatory compensation decision or other practice."[54]

Conclusion

Three themes emerge from Justice Ginsburg's dissents in employment discrimination cases. First, Justice Ginsburg respected the facts of cases and the realities of what happens in workplaces. She often explained the stakes of cases and interpreted the statutory language through the lens of these facts.

Justice Ginsburg also understood how seemingly esoteric topics affected the potential reach of discrimination law, and she resisted the majority's attempts to frame these issues as only technical issues that demanded a single narrow answer. Justice Ginsburg argued that it was inappropriate to interpret the federal discrimination statutes in ways that created an easy solution for litigation but did not consider the discrimination statutes' broader goal of eliminating or reducing workplace discrimination and retaliation.

Finally, Justice Ginsburg often advocated relying on the expertise of the EEOC. She argued that the EEOC's views were often best aligned with the statutes' texts and their underlying goals.

Justice Ginsburg's dissents in *Nassar, Vance,* and *Ledbetter* highlight how the discrimination statutes are written in broad language with very little guidance from Congress about how to define that language. In interpreting the words of these statutes, the Supreme Court often faces choices. Justice Ginsburg recognized that the Court should acknowledge both the ambiguity and the choices it is making, instead of claiming that the statutes demand one, narrow, litigation-focused answer.

NOTES

I would like to thank Mallory Perazzo for her help in researching Justice Ginsburg's dissenting opinions.

1   570 U.S. 338 (2013).
2   570 U.S. 421 (2013).
3   550 U.S. 618 (2007). Justice Ginsburg also wrote dissenting opinions in other employment discrimination cases. *See* Ricci v. DeStefano, 557 U.S. 557 (2009); AT & T Corp. v. Hulteen, 556 U.S. 701(2009); Wal-Mart Stores, Inc. v. Dukes, 564 U.S. 338 (2011); Clackamas Gastroenterology Associates, P. C. v. Wells, 538 U.S. 440 (2003); Buckhannon Bd. and Care Home, Inc. v. West Virginia Dept. of Health and Human Resources, 532 U.S. 598 (2001).
4   *See, e.g.,* Bostock v. Clayton Cnty., 140 S. Ct. 1731 (2020); Young v. UPS, Inc., 575 U.S. 206 (2015).

5 Chevron U.S.A. Inc. v. Natural Res. Def. Council, Inc., 467 U.S. 837 (1984); Skidmore v. Swift & Co., 323 U.S. 134 (1944).

6 570 U.S. 338.

7 *Id.* at 345. The trial court judge reduced the compensatory damages award to $300,000, consistent with Title VII's cap on certain types of damages.

8 *Id.* at 344–45.

9 42 U.S.C. § 2000e-3(a).

10 *See, e.g.*, Babb v. Wilkie, 140 S. Ct. 1168 (2020); Comcast v. National Association of African-American Owned Media, 140 S. Ct. 1009 (2020).

11 199 P.2d 1, 3 (Cal. 1948).

12 490 U.S. 228, 230 (1989) (plurality).

13 *Id.* at 250.

14 *Nassar*, 570 U.S. at 358.

15 *Id.*

16 *Id.*

17 *Id.* at 360–61.

18 *Id.* at 363 (Ginsburg, J., dissenting).

19 *Id.*

20 *Id.* at 370–71, 383–84.

21 *Id.* at 364–66.

22 *Id.* at 372–74.

23 524 U.S. 775 (1998).

24 524 U.S. 742 (1998).

25 *See generally* 524 U.S. 775; 524 U.S. 742.

26 524 U.S. at 759.

27 570 U.S. 421, 431 (2013).

28 *Id.*

29 *Id.*

30 *Id.* at 431–32, 441–45.

31 *Id.* at 431–32.

32 *Id.* at 441.

33 *Id.*

34 *Id.* at 432.

35 *Id.* at 451.

36 *Id.* (Ginsburg, J., dissenting).

37 *Id.* at 468.

38 *Id.* at 458–62.

39 *Id.* at 462 (internal citation omitted).

40 *Id.* at 463.

41 *Id.*

42 *Id.* at 464–65.

43 *Id.* at 465.

44 550 U.S. 618 (2007).

45 *Id.* at 623.
46 *Id.* at 624–25.
47 *Id.* at 642–43.
48 *Id.* at 643 (Ginsburg, J., dissenting).
49 *Id.* at 644.
50 *Id.* at 645.
51 *Id.* at 656.
52 *Id.* at 660.
53 *Id.* at 661.
54 42 U.S.C. § 2000e-5(e)(3)(A); 29 U.S.C. § 626(d)(3); 42 U.S.C. § 12117(a); 29 U.S.C. § 791(g).

12

Environmental Law

Justice Ruth Bader Ginsburg's Principled Legacy

UMA OUTKA

Following Justice Ruth Bader Ginsburg's death in 2020, Professor Richard Lazarus, who has written extensively on the Supreme Court and environmental law, described the Justice as first and foremost "an outstanding lawyer" and a person "who did not come to the cases predisposed to necessarily rule in favor environmentalists" but "with an open mind . . . willing . . . to be persuaded by legal arguments."[1] The characterization captures well Justice Ginsburg's thoughtful and practical perspective on the environmental law cases she reviewed during her time on the Supreme Court. She stands out as a Justice with a legacy of principled environmental protection, consistent in her analytical approach and grounded by the real-world contexts that shaped the cases that came before the Court.

This chapter details Justice Ginsburg's impact on the field of environmental law. It highlights the environmental issues her opinions addressed, key cases for which her decision to join the majority or dissent was important, and her characteristically incisive dissents. Focusing primarily on the environmental statutes she considered in the most depth, the Clean Water Act and Clean Air Act, the chapter conveys Justice Ginsburg's impact on vital and long-standing statutory frameworks and the communities and natural environments they were designed to protect.

The Clean Water Act

The Clean Water Act is the centerpiece of federal protection for U.S. surface waters and wetlands.[2] During Justice Ginsburg's years of service, the statute and its implementing regulations were the subject of significant Supreme Court attention—and often discord. This section considers her most memorable Clean Water Act cases.

Friends of the Earth v. Laidlaw Environmental Services

In perhaps her best-known opinion on environmental law, *Friends of the Earth v. Laidlaw Environmental Services*, Justice Ginsburg had occasion to validate a critical feature of the Clean Water Act: its citizen suit provision.[3] In *Laidlaw*, she wrote for the majority to confirm the viability of citizen enforcement of the Clean Water Act and blunt a series of cases authored by Justice Antonin Scalia that threatened to undercut citizen standing more broadly.[4] Among environmental law attorneys, *Laidlaw* has been considered one of the Supreme Court's most significant environmental law cases, and it has been called Justice Ginsburg's "greatest achievement on behalf of the environment."[5]

Laidlaw operated a large hazardous waste incinerator in South Carolina and had a Clean Water Act permit, issued by the state, to discharge treated wastewater into the North Tyger River. The permit authorized Laidlaw's wastewater to contain limited amounts of pollutants including mercury. The company was in chronic violation, however; between 1987 and 1995, Laidlaw exceeded the mercury limits nearly five hundred times.[6] According to the U.S. Environmental Protection Agency (EPA), mercury is a toxic pollutant that harms "the brain, heart, kidneys, lungs, and immune system of people of all ages" and impairs nervous system development.[7]

After discovering Laidlaw's permit violations, Friends of the Earth (FOE) filed a citizen suit, a key public function within the statute's enforcement structure, seeking injunctive relief and civil penalties. The district court imposed a $400,000 penalty but denied injunctive relief on the ground that Laidlaw was by then in substantial compliance with its permit.

FOE appealed. The Fourth Circuit assumed standing but stated the case was moot because, in part, civil penalties paid to the government would not redress the injury alleged. This reasoning gravely concerned environmental groups. As Professor Bill Buzbee explained in an excellent account of this litigation, they feared that if the opinion was allowed to stand "virtually any sloppy polluter could potentially escape liability and payment of fees merely by belatedly improving compliance efforts."[8]

Laidlaw also made a standing argument that threatened public enforcement of the Clean Water Act, claiming there could be no standing, even for injunctive relief, if FOE had not affirmatively proved the mercury-laden discharges harmed the environment. As the case made its way to the Supreme Court, the stakes were exceedingly high: a ruling in Laidlaw's favor could have ramifications well beyond the Clean Water Act.

In the closely watched ruling, Justice Ginsburg's majority opinion maintained the viability of citizen suits. She clarified that "the relevant showing for purposes of Article III standing . . . is not injury to the environment but injury to the plaintiff."[9] Plaintiffs need not be in a position to prove the effect of mercury discharges on the environment simply to advance their case. Moreover, "[a] defendant's voluntary cessation of allegedly unlawful conduct ordinarily does not suffice to moot a case."[10] To the extent civil penalties "encourage defendants to discontinue current violations and deter them from committing future ones," Justice Ginsburg explained, "they afford redress to citizen plaintiffs who are injured or threatened with injury as a consequence of ongoing unlawful conduct."[11] She reasoned: "A would-be polluter may or may not be dissuaded by the existence of a remedy on the books, but a defendant once hit in its pocketbook will surely think twice before polluting again."[12]

This opinion was key to allowing citizens to continue actively and effectively protecting water resources through the Clean Water Act. *Laidlaw* also marked a shift at the time in the Court's jurisprudential trajectory—real, if not dramatic—toward, as Professor Jonathan Cannon has put it, a "greater receptivity to public interest plaintiffs in environmental cases."[13]

Noteworthy Clean Water Act Dissents

Justice Ginsburg's Clean Water Act legacy also includes important dissents. As she explained in a published lecture titled "The Role of Dissenting Opinions," any Justice, when contemplating whether to write separately, "should always ask herself: Is this dissent or concurrence really necessary?"[14] In other words, she did not make such decisions lightly or shy away from them—indeed, she felt an obligation "to speak in dissent when important matters are at stake."[15] She authored a dissent in the 2009 case *Coeur Alaska, Inc. v. Southeast Alaska Conservation Council*[16] and joined dissents in two closely watched cases addressing the Clean Water Act's jurisdictional reach.

Coeur Alaska, Inc. v. Southeast Alaska Conservation Council

This litigation stemmed from a gold mining company's proposal to use a wilderness lake in Alaska's Tongass National Forest as a dump site for millions of tons of mine tailings and wastewater. The Southeast Alaska Conservation Council strongly opposed the plan and, when the Army Corps of Engineers issued a permit under Clean Water Act section 404 (required for dredged and fill material), the group sued, arguing the wrong permit "was issued by the wrong agency—Coeur Alaska should have sought a section 402 permit from EPA" (required for point source discharges of a pollutant).[17] The EPA and the Army Corps share responsibility under the statute.

The legal distinction mattered because the type of permit required dictated whether a highly stringent section 306 "new source performance standard" applied to the mine.[18] The EPA had developed a standard for all new froth-flotation gold mines that allowed for "*no* discharge of process wastewater" from these mines.[19] If the mine needed a section 402 permit, the standard would be incorporated, barring the fill. In contrast, "the CWA [was] ambiguous" on whether the standard would obtain in a section 404 permit.[20]

The Court held a permit under section 404 was appropriate because the planned discharges into the lake were "fill."[21] Thus, the Court reasoned, section 306 standards did not apply to tailings added to the wilderness lake.

Justice Ginsburg's dissent advanced an alternative interpretation more closely aligned with the statute's protective goals. Instead of focusing on divisions of permitting authority, she reframed the litigation as presenting "a single question: Is a pollutant discharge prohibited under § 306 of the Act eligible for a § 404 permit as a discharge of fill material?"[22] In her view, the answer was no, yielding a "simple rule" treating any discharges subject to EPA performance standards as also governed by EPA for permitting.[23] Compared with this approach, she wrote, the majority's reading "strains credulity"—"[p]roviding an escape hatch for polluters whose discharges contain solid matter . . . is particularly perverse [given that] the Act specifically focuses on solids as harmful pollutants."[24] It is only in her dissent that there is any mention of the "concentrations of aluminum, copper, lead, and mercury" in the discharge and the undisputed fact that it "would kill all of the lake's fish and nearly all of its other aquatic life."[25]

The "Waters of the United States" Trilogy of Cases

Among the most contested statutory terms in federal environmental law is "navigable waters"—defined in the Clean Water Act, ambiguously, as "waters of the United States."[26] This ambiguity has prompted significant litigation over the contours of Clean Water Act jurisdiction, particularly the extent and limits of federal authority over intrastate wetlands. A trilogy of cases has addressed this question through the lens of a series of implementing regulations, beginning with the unanimous *United States v. Riverside Bayview Homes*, followed by the divided *Solid Waste Agency of Northern Cook County v. Army Corps of Engineers (SWANCC)* (5–4), and the even more divided *Rapanos v. United States*, which yielded only a plurality opinion (4–1–4) and did less to clarify than to confuse lower courts, agencies, and property owners.[27] In the latter two highly watched cases, Justice Ginsburg joined Justice Stevens' dissenting opinions.

In *SWANCC*, the majority rejected an Army Corps regulation that applied the Clean Water Act to an intrastate isolated wetland based on its importance as habitat for migratory birds. Justice Ginsburg disagreed and joined Justice Stevens in centering jurisdictional reach on two principles: Congress's goal "to establish a *comprehensive* long-range policy for the elimination of water pollution,"[28] and the federal government's authority to regulate activities that harm the environment, as well as "individual actions that, in the aggregate, would have the same effect."[29]

In *Rapanos*, also a wetlands case, Justice Ginsburg joined the dissenters in a "straightforward" analysis deferring to the regulatory judgment of the Army Corps that "wetlands adjacent to tributaries generally have a significant nexus to the watershed's water quality" and their protection serves the Clean Water Act's purpose: "[T]o restore and maintain the chemical, physical, and biological integrity of the Nation's waters.[30] Against the backdrop of uncertainty created by this line of cases, Justice Ginsburg will be remembered for validating heightened protections for wetlands as constitutional and consistent with the Clean Water Act.

Final Clean Water Act Case: County of Maui v. Hawaii Wildlife Fund

In her final months on the Court, Justice Ginsburg participated in her last Clean Water Act case, *County of Maui v. Hawaii Wildlife Fund*,[31] which raised the long-unaddressed question of whether the Clean Water Act requires a permit when pollutants originate from a point source but are conveyed to navigable waters indirectly via groundwater. Justice Ginsburg joined the 6–3 majority to answer that question affirmatively, holding a permit *is* required "if the addition of the pollutants through groundwater is the functional equivalent of a direct discharge from the point source into navigable waters."[32] Consistent with her position in the "waters of the United States" cases, Justice Ginsburg agreed with an interpretation of the statute grounded in a realistic assessment of how polluting activity actually affects the health of the nation's waters.

The Clean Air Act

Justice Ginsburg authored several important Clean Air Act cases, though she may be most widely remembered for her role in the 2007 landmark decision in *Massachusetts v. EPA*.[33] It was significant at that time and remains significant to this day because the Court, even if by a 5–4 margin, explicitly recognized the "well-documented rise in global temperatures" associated with carbon dioxide emissions and acknowledged that the risk of catastrophic harm from climate change is real.[34] At a point when the EPA was disclaiming authority to regulate carbon dioxide and other greenhouse gases (GHGs) under the Clean Air Act, the Court confirmed the agency *does* have that authority (under section 202, relating to new motor vehicles, or "mobile sources" of air pollution) if the EPA determines GHGs "cause or contribute" to climate change because they are "air pollutants" under the Clean Air Act.[35]

Justice Stevens wrote the majority opinion, but as Professor Lazarus details in his book on the litigation strategy and judicial decision-making in *Massachusetts v. EPA*, Justice Ginsburg played an important role at numerous points in the process beyond simply being one of the five-Justice majority. At oral argument, for example, it was she who explained from the bench "that if EPA were correct about the meaning of the Clean Air Act, the EPA would lack authority to reduce GHG emissions of all sources, including carbon dioxide from power plants."[36] He recounts how, in the case conference following oral argument, after Justice Thomas expressed his agreement with Justice Scalia, "Justice Ginsburg then announced that she shared Stevens's view. Her voice was so quiet," Lazarus writes, "and at times even halting that the other Justices often had to strain to hear her words. But there was no denying the force of her views."[37] The holding in *Massachusetts v. EPA* set in motion EPA's regulation of GHGs, first from mobile sources and later from major stationary sources including power plants.[38]

American Electric Power v. Connecticut

Four years later, in 2011, Justice Ginsburg authored a unanimous opinion also related to climate change, *American Electric Power v. Connecticut*.[39] The plaintiffs were several states, the City of New York, and private land trusts that, prior to the ruling in *Massachusetts v. EPA*, had sued major carbon dioxide–emitting electric power utilities, arguing the emissions "created 'a substantial and unreasonable interference with public rights,' in violation of the federal common law of interstate nuisance, or in the alternative, of state tort law."[40] They sought a "decree setting carbon-dioxide emissions for each defendant at an initial cap, to be further reduced annually."[41]

Leaving the question of state tort claims to another day, Justice Ginsburg wrote for the Court that the "Clean Air Act and the Environmental Protection Agency action the Act authorizes" (referring to EPA's authority to regulate greenhouse gases confirmed in *Massachusetts v. EPA*) displaced the federal common law public nuisance claims.[42] She rejected the claims even though they were filed before *Massachusetts v. EPA* was decided and even though EPA had not yet begun regulating GHGs in earnest. Connecticut argued any displacement should depend on, and not precede, EPA *actually* exercising its regulatory authority, but in rejecting that argument Justice Ginsburg explained: "The Act provides a means to seek limits on emissions of carbon dioxide from domestic power plants—the same relief the plaintiffs seek by invoking federal common law. We see no room for a parallel track."[43]

Ultimately, she wrote, the "judgments the plaintiffs would commit to federal judges, in suits that could be filed in any federal district court, cannot be reconciled with the decision-making scheme Congress enacted."[44] Rather, the "expert agency is surely better equipped to do the job than individual district judges issuing ad hoc, case by case injunctions."[45] If the EPA decided not to regulate, she reminded the parties, that decision would be subject to judicial review.[46] The opinion reflected the Court's unified view (on these facts, at least) of the limitations of the role of federal judges. The effect of the opinion was to reorient advocates toward the EPA and Congress, as well as toward state law for climate tort claims.

Alaska Department of Environmental Conservation v. EPA

In this case, Justice Ginsburg clarified the state-federal relationship in air permitting decisions under the Clean Air Act. Tech Cominco Alaska, Inc., the region's largest private employer, operated the Red Dog Mine, twenty-four hours per day, 365 days per year, using on-site diesel generators and sought an air permit from the Alaska Department of Environmental Conservation (ADEC) to expand production by 40 percent.[47] Due to the mine's location in remote northwest Alaska, an area designated for "prevention of significant deterioration," the permit required "best available control technology" (BACT) to control emissions at the facility.[48] The agency defined BACT as Cominco requested, employing cheaper, less-effective measures than others that were readily available and recommended by department staff.[49] EPA objected to the permit on this basis, but ADEC approved it anyway. EPA issued an order prohibiting Cominco from acting on the permit. ADEC and Cominco petitioned for review.

The issue at the heart of the case was the proper scope of EPA's oversight authority. ADEC argued that the EPA's role was limited to checking that a permit *contains* a BACT limitation and that it may *not* question the state's judgment in selecting BACT for a particular facility.[50]

Justice Ginsburg wrote for the 5–4 majority, reinforcing that EPA oversight under the Clean Air Act is *substantive*, not merely procedural. She wrote that "[w]e fail to see why the Congress, having expressly endorsed an expansive surveillance role for EPA in two independent provisions, would then implicitly preclude the Agency from verifying substantive compliance with the BACT provisions, and instead limit the EPA's superintendence to the insubstantial question whether the state permitting authority had uttered the words 'BACT.'"[51]

Justice Ginsburg emphasized states still have "considerable leeway" in issuing air permits and EPA "may only step in to ensure that the statutory requirements are honored" if a state "determination is not based on a reasoned analysis."[52] With this ruling, Justice Ginsburg led the Court in declining to weaken Clean Air Act protections and preserving a federal check against undue industry influence at the state level.

EPA v. EME Homer City Generation LP

In 2014, Justice Ginsburg delivered the opinion of the Court in *EPA v. EME Homer City Generation LP*, upholding the EPA's Cross-State Air Pollution Rule.[53] The rule implemented the Clean Air Act's so-called Good Neighbor Provision, which requires states to ensure that air pollutants emitted from in-state sources do not "contribute significantly" to a downwind state's ability to attain and maintain air quality standards.[54] The ruling reversed a D.C. Circuit Court of Appeals opinion (authored by then–Circuit Judge Brett Kavanaugh), which rejected the rule.[55]

Justice Ginsburg's unique voice came through in this case. In acknowledging the immense complexity of tracking and regulating interstate air pollution, she quoted the Bible—"The wind bloweth where it listeth, and thou hearest the sound thereof, but canst not tell whence it cometh and whither it goeth"—to explain that "air pollution is transient, heedless of state boundaries" and to convey the challenge regulators face in accounting for "the vagaries of the wind."[56] The opinion opened by acknowledging the environmental harm that air pollution in one state can cause in another. Congress recognized that "[p]ollutants generated by upwind sources are often transported by air currents, sometimes over hundreds of miles, to downwind states," and if "[l]eft unregulated, the emitting or upwind State reaps the benefits of the economic activity causing the pollution without bearing all the costs."[57]

The opinion was important in at least two key respects. First, and specific to implementation of the Good Neighbor Provision, the opinion put an end to more than a decade of delay tactics by upwind states and industry seeking to avoid more stringent controls on air-polluting facilities affecting downwind states. The rule under review was an in-depth revision of an earlier attempt to regulate interstate air pollution, which had also been rejected by the D.C. Circuit. In that case, *North Carolina v. EPA*, as in *EME Homer City*, the plaintiffs' strategy was, effectively, to question the validity of myriad structural features contained in intricate and complicated rules.[58] Justice Ginsburg's opinion addressed each objection in detail, amply demonstrating her deep Clean Air Act conversance, finding "EPA's cost-effective allocation of emission reductions among upwind States . . . a permissible, workable, and equitable interpretation of the Good Neighbor Provision."[59] The problem of interstate air pollution had come before Justice Ginsburg before, at least as far back as 1988, when as an appellate judge on the D.C. Circuit she joined a panel decision finding that the EPA's denial of state petitions under Clean Air Act section 126 seeking enforcement against upwind state sources of air pollution was "based on a reasonable interpretation of the relevant statutes and [] not arbitrary and capricious."[60] Yet she wrote a concurring opinion that made clear the holding gave her no joy, writing "separately only to spotlight a reality that the language of the Clean Air Act condones."[61] The concurrence was critical of the agency, noting that, as "counsel for the EPA acknowledge at oral argument, the EPA has taken no action against sources of interstate air pollution under either [available statutory authority, section 126 and section 110] in the decade-plus since those provisions were enacted."[62] Justice Ginsburg was also critical of Congress for failing to supply needed "direction" to the agency and leaving "unchecked" this inadequate "approach to interstate air pollution."[63] In *EME Homer City*, she finally had the chance to review and approve a substantive regulatory response to interstate air pollution.

Second, the opinion reinforced and drew extensively from *Chevron U.S.A. Inc. v. Natural Resources Defense Council, Inc.* The *Chevron* case, also interpreting the Clean Air Act, has become shorthand for judicial deference to agency expertise in reasonably interpreting ambiguous language in a statute the agency administers.[64] Although the durability of *Chevron* deference is now in question given the current composition of the Court,[65] Justice Ginsburg's discussion of *Chevron* in *EME Homer City* demonstrates the respect *she* had for *Chevron*'s key principle, carrying it forward in another major Clean Air Act opinion.

Other Noteworthy Environmental Law Dissents

Two additional Ginsburg opinions deserve mention: her dissent in *Winter v. Natural Resources Defense Council, Inc.*, a National Environmental Policy Act (NEPA) case; and her dissent in *Burlington Northern & Santa Fe Railway Co. v. United States*, interpreting the Comprehensive Environmental Response, Compensation, and Liability Act (CERCLA).

Winter v. Natural Resources Defense Council, Inc.

In *Winter*, the Natural Resources Defense Council sought a preliminary injunction against the United States Navy to stop undersea sonar training exercises harmful to whales and other marine mammals until an environmental impact assessment required by the National Environmental Policy Act was performed.[66] The Court reversed a grant of the preliminary injunction, holding that the Navy's need to conduct its trainings "plainly outweighed" the danger to marine mammals.[67]

Justice Ginsburg's dissent in *Winter* appears to be her only dissent in a NEPA case. Whereas the majority focused on the framework for preliminary injunctions, she centered her analysis on the purpose of NEPA and, importantly, how that purpose could and should have been served in this case without hindering the Navy's military objectives. She outlined in detail how, instead, the Navy took "extraordinary" measures to avoid meeting its NEPA obligations, underscoring her dedication to process and procedure.[68] She sharply criticized how the Navy, rather than pursuing a legislative exemption from Congress, sought "rapid, self-serving resort to an office in the White House [the Council on Environmental Quality]" that "lacks authority to countermand or revise NEPA's requirements"—"surely not what Congress had in mind when it instructed agencies to comply with NEPA to the fullest extent possible."[69] Justice Ginsburg rejected the suggestion, seemingly accepted by the majority, that marine mammal protection necessarily had to yield without compromise in the face of military training needs.

Burlington Northern & Santa Fe Railway Co. v. United States

In *Burlington Northern & Santa Fe Railway Co. v. United States*,[70] the Supreme Court considered a key question related to how CERCLA holds certain parties accountable for environmental contamination and financially responsible for the costs of remediation.[71] The statute identifies as "potentially responsible parties" those who currently own or operate a contaminated facility, those who owned or operated a facility whenever contamination occurred, certain transporters of hazardous substances that became the source of contamination at a facility, and those who arranged for the disposal of hazardous substances.[72]

This case zeroed in on so-called arranger liability. Shell Oil Company sent hazardous chemicals to an agricultural chemical distributor for many years, during which time chemical spills and leaks during transfers and deliveries caused severe contamination of soil and groundwater. The EPA and the state of California remediated the site and sought $8 million in costs from Shell (and other parties).[73] The courts below held Shell liable as an "arranger" under CERCLA, but the Supreme Court disagreed. Although Shell was well aware of the spills, the Court held that "mere knowledge that spills and leaks continued to occur [was] insufficient grounds for concluding that Shell 'arranged for' the disposal."[74]

Justice Ginsburg was the lone dissenter. Although she believed "the question is close," she would have affirmed Shell's arranger status based on its knowledge that spills were inevitable and occurring, for over twenty years, using storage and delivery methods it dictated because they were "economically advantageous."[75] She highlighted how Shell had, in the words of the district court, "pursued a scorched earth, all-or-nothing approach to liability" without acknowledging "an iota of responsibility."[76] Her analysis returned to the purpose of CERCLA and the effect of the Court's decision: "Relieving Shell of any obligation to pay for the cleanup undertaken by the United States and California is hardly commanded by CERCLA's text[] and is surely at odds with CERCLA's objective to place the cost of remediation on persons whose activities contributed to the contamination rather than on the taxpaying public."[77] Not holding Shell accountable, she emphasized, did not mean no one had to pay; instead, the public would be forced to clean up contamination it in no way caused.

Conclusion

Justice Ginsburg's authored opinions and dissents, as well as those she joined, convey a sense of care and realism as she endeavored to understand the context for the environmental law cases she reviewed. She was a proceduralist—but not one to lose sight of the forest for the trees. She did not side with environmental plaintiffs in every case, and she is not generally regarded as a Justice with an environmental agenda. In assessing her legacy in environmental law, however, Justice Ginsburg could be relied upon to take seriously what was at stake not only for environmental plaintiffs but also for what they sought to protect. In comparing Justice Ginsburg's environmental record with other Justices, Professor Cannon found that she "voted with environmentalists in a higher percentage of cases—and has arguably registered deeper sympathy with the environmental cause—than any recent justice, despite a voice of restraint."[78] It is difficult to predict the longevity of a Justice's impact on the law she reviewed during her time on the Court, as Congress amends statutes, agencies revise regulations, and Supreme Court jurisprudence evolves. Yet Justice Ginsburg's legacy in environmental law will always be tied to preserving citizen enforcement of environmental protection laws; expanding wetlands protection; holding polluters accountable for the cost of cleaning up contamination they caused; acknowledging the necessity of clean air; and preserving flexibility for agencies working to apply their statutory authority to the complexities of environmental problems, including the urgent threat of climate change.

NOTES

Thanks is due to Professors Richard Levy and Steve McAllister for their thoughtful comments and to Alexandra Finley (KU Law Class of 2023) for excellent research assistance.

1   Adam Wernick, *Ruth Bader Ginsburg Left Behind a Powerful Environmental Legacy*, THE WORLD (Oct. 9, 2020), https://theworld.org.

2 33 U.S.C. § 1251 *et seq.*

3 Friends of the Earth v. Laidlaw Envt'l Serv., 528 U.S. 167 (2000).

4 For discussion of relevant case law leading up to *Laidlaw, see* William W. Buzbee, *The Story of* Laidlaw: *Standing and Citizen Enforcement, in* ENVIRONMENTAL LAW STORIES 201 (Richard Lazarus & Oliver Houck eds. 2005).

5 *See* J. B. Ruhl and James E. Salzman, *American Idols,* ENVTL. F. (May–June 2019); Robert Percival, *Remembering Justice Ginsburg, An Environmental Champion* (Oct. 13, 2020), www.eli.org.

6 *Laidlaw,* 528 U.S. at 176.

7 *See* U.S. EPA, *Basic Information About Mercury: Health Effects Associated with Exposures to Mercury,* www.epa.gov.

8 Buzbee, *The Story of* Laidlaw at 213.

9 *Laidlaw,* 528 U.S. at 181.

10 *Id.* at 189.

11 *Id.* at 186.

12 *Id.*

13 JONATHAN Z. CANNON, ENVIRONMENT IN THE BALANCE: THE GREEN MOVEMENT AND THE SUPREME COURT 159 (2015). For discussion of *Laidlaw*'s intervention in environmental cases, see *id.* at 141–69.

14 Ruth Bader Ginsburg, *Lecture: The Role of Dissenting Opinions,* 95 MINN. L. REV. 1, 1 (2010).

15 *Id.* at 7.

16 Coeur Alaska, Inc. v. Se. Alaska Conservation Council, 557 U.S. 261 (2009).

17 *Id.* at 271.

18 A new source performance standard under section 306 (42 U.S.C. § 1316) is a technology-based standard developed for a defined category of dischargers and applicable to all new sources within that category after the standard is finalized.

19 *Coeur Alaska,* 557 U.S. at 271 (citing 40 C.F.R. § 440.104(b)(1)).

20 *Id.* at 281.

21 *Id.* at 274.

22 *Id.* at 277.

23 *Id.* at 301.

24 *Id.* at 302–03.

25 *Id.* at 297.

26 Clean Water Act § 502(7), 42 U.S.C. § 1367(7).

27 United States v. Riverside Bayview Homes, 474 U.S. 121 (1985); Solid Waste Agency of No. Cook Cty. v. U.S. Army Corps of Eng'rs, 531 U.S. 159, 179 (2001); Rapanos v. United States, 547 U.S. 715 (2006).

28 *Solid Waste,* 531 U.S. at 179 (dissenting) (citing legislative documents).

29 *Id.* at 196.

30 *Rapanos,* 547 U.S. at 788 (dissenting).

31 Cty. of Maui v. Hawaii Wildlife Fund, 140 S. Ct. 1462 (2020).

32 *Id.* at 1476.

33 Massachusetts v. EPA, 549 US. 497 (2007).

34 *Id.* at 504.

35 *Id.* at 532–35.

36 RICHARD LAZARUS, THE RULE OF FIVE: MAKING CLIMATE HISTORY AT THE SUPREME COURT 196 (2020).

37 *Id.* at 231.

38 *See* Utility Air Reg. Group v. EPA, 572 U.S. 302, 308–10 (2014).

39 Am. Elec. Power Co. v. Connecticut, 564 U.S. 410 (2011).

40 *Id.* at 418.

41 *Id.* at 415.

42 *Id.* at 424.

43 *Id.* at 425.

44 *Id.* at 429.

45 *Id.* at 428.

46 *Id.* at 427.

47 Alaska Dep't of Envtl. Conserv. v. EPA, 540 U.S. 461 (2004). *See also* Alaska Dep't of Nat. Res., *Red Dog Mine: Project Description*, https://dnr.alaska.gov.

48 Clean Air Act §§ 165(a)(4), 169(3); 42 U.S.C. 7475(a)(4) & 7479(3).

49 *Alaska Dep't of Envtl. Conserv.*, 540 U.S. at 474–75.

50 *Id.* at 488.

51 *Id.* at 490.

52 *Id.*

53 EPA v. EME Homer City Generation LP, 572 U.S. 489 (2014).

54 Clean Air Act § 110(a)(2)(D), 42 U. S. C. § 7410(a)(2)(D).

55 EPA v. EME Homer City Generation LP, 696 F.3d 7 (D.C. Cir. 2013).

56 *EME Homer City*, 572 U.S. at 497.

57 *Id.* at 495.

58 North Carolina v. EPA, 531 F.3d 896 (D.C. Cir. 2008) (per curiam). On rehearing, the court left the Clean Air Interstate Rule in place, directing EPA to quickly address the problems identified. *See* North Carolina v. EPA, 550 F.3d 1176, 1178 (D.C. Cir. 2008) (per curiam).

59 *EME Homer City*, 572 U.S. at 524.

60 New York v. EPA, 852 F.2d 574, 576 (D.C. Cir. 1988).

61 *Id.* at 581 (concurrence).

62 *Id.*

63 As the D.C. Circuit later observed, 1990 amendments strengthened protection of downwind states with changes to section 110. *See* Michigan v. EPA, 213 F.3d 663, 674 (D.C. Cir. 2000).

64 Chevron U.S.A. Inc. v. Natural Res. Def. Council, Inc., 467 U.S. 837, 842–43 (1984).

65 *See* the *Duke Law Journal's* 2021 symposium publication on the future of *Chevron* deference, https://dlj.law.duke.edu.

66 Winter v. Natural Res. Def. Council, Inc., 555 U.S. 7 (2008).

67 *Id.* at 33.

68 *Id.* at 46–47.
69 *Id.* at 44, 51.
70 Burlington No. & Santa Fe Ry. Co. v. United States, 556 U.S. 599 (2009).
71 CERCLA § 107(a)(3), 42. U.S.C. § 9607(a)(3).
72 CERCLA § 107(a), 42 U.S.C. § 9607(a).
73 *Burlington No.*, 556 U.S. at 605.
74 *Id.* at 613.
75 *Id.* at 621 (dissenting).
76 *Id.* at 622.
77 *Id.*
78 CANNON, ENVIRONMENT IN THE BALANCE at 229.

13

Family Law

The Egalitarian Family

JOANNA L. GROSSMAN

Justice Ruth Bader Ginsburg was perhaps best known for her contributions as an advocate for and a jurist of gender law. As a lawyer, she was the architect of the constitutional right of sex equality; as a Supreme Court Justice, she demanded that the government prove sex-based classifications were rooted in real differences rather than generalizations. The consistent thread was her belief that all people ought to have an equal opportunity to capitalize on their natural talents and abilities, without being relegated to a kind of second-class citizenship by laws and practices based on stereotypes. She took this approach not only in antidiscrimination cases where women's equality was squarely at stake but also in her family law opinions and dissents. In a line of cases involving the rights of unwed fathers, Justice Ginsburg grappled with the challenges of defining equality between mothers and fathers given their unique biological roles in reproduction. She embraced a vision of equality that promoted men's opportunity to assume the obligations of parenthood—a shift that enhanced women's opportunity to participate in economic life by sparing them some of the grossly disproportionate burdens of parenting. In the same vein, she wrote strong opinions and vigorous dissents that sought broad protection for women's control over reproduction. She never wrote about the family or family law without tying it to the broader gender context in which the family operates. This is an important yet somewhat unappreciated aspect of her legacy.

The Connection Between Family, Parenting, and Equality

Ruth Bader Ginsburg began her legal studies at Harvard Law School, where she was one of only nine women in a class of 561. She stood out not only because of her gender (and diminutive stature) but also because she was married and the mother of a toddler. She excelled and became the first woman to make the *Harvard Law Review*. During her second year, her husband, also a law student, was diagnosed with cancer. She nursed him through his illness—while taking care of their daughter, maintaining her studies, and making sure her husband was able to keep up with his studies. She typed up class notes and took dictation of papers at his bedside, often past midnight when the effects of his radiation had worn off. She hardly slept, but he survived, and their family thrived. She finished her law degree at Columbia because her husband graduated and joined a law firm in New York City. Then, despite having done it all and then some, she was unable to find work as a lawyer for no reason other than her sex. The doors were slammed shut.

Throughout her career, Ginsburg wrote like someone who had a deep personal understanding of the relationship between work and family and the relevance of both to equality. She came of age when there were no formal rights for women. Although women gained the right to vote in 1920 through the Nineteenth Amendment, courts were quick to cabin that right against the claims of advocates that it should be interpreted to protect a broad spectrum of civil and political rights.[1] At the start of her legal career in 1959, there were no federal laws promising sex equality in any context, and the Equal Protection Clause had never been applied to invalidate a law that discriminated on the basis of sex.

The Architect of Equality: Ginsburg the Advocate

As an advocate, Ginsburg was the architect of the idea that the Constitution guarantees all people—including women—the equal right to capitalize on their innate abilities, unimpeded by formal or other barriers to equal participation. Women in the United States at that time were not even within spitting distance of equality. In addition to the vast number of gender-based laws that went unchallenged—laws that together reflected a society not only with clear gender stratification but also with an unmistakable gender hierarchy—the Supreme Court relied on separate spheres ideology as the defining natural order. It was used to explain (and uphold) prohibitions on women's serving on juries, practicing law, working long hours, and working in certain jobs.[2] The law embraced the idea of women as a monolithic group and empowered states to treat all women as mothers whose primary devotion was to home and hearth.

Ginsburg challenged the pervasive legal prejudices against women. She worked first with the New Jersey ACLU to challenge wage discrimination against women. She also began teaching at Rutgers Law School, where she taught a class on gender law that was mostly aspirational— there was no doctrine to teach. The high point of her legal life came in the 1970s when a lawyer from Idaho asked the ACLU for help challenging a state law that arbitrarily preferred men over women as administrators of intestate estates on the assumption that they were better suited to deal with legal and financial matters. Ginsburg argued that the Equal Protection Clause of the Fourteenth Amendment did not permit states to discriminate against women in such an arbitrary way. The Supreme Court agreed, holding in *Reed v. Reed* that the law was unconstitutional because there was not a close enough connection between the discriminatory means and the goals of the statute.[3] Representing the first time the Supreme Court had invalidated a state law on sex equality grounds, *Reed* ushered in a new jurisprudential era in which states were forced to justify their legislative choices rather than being permitted to reflexively organize society by gender based on overbroad generalizations about the differences between the sexes.

Ginsburg built on this success after founding the Women's Rights Project at the ACLU. There, she began the project of dismantling the legal infrastructure that operated to the systematic disadvantage of women. She would argue five sex equality cases before the Supreme Court during the 1970s—and would win four of them.[4] Her handiwork was reflected in briefs written for eleven other cases. The existence of a constitutional right of sex equality is largely due to the brilliant strategy and advocacy skills of Ruth Bader Ginsburg.

Justice Ginsburg: A Jurist for Home, Hearth, and the Office

As Ginsburg shifted from advocate to jurist, her ideas about equality, autonomy, and the limits of state power would reach other areas, including family law. As a Supreme Court Justice, she had the opportunity to consider enormous questions about the relationship of the family to the government and broader society, as well as about the relationship of individuals within a family to one another.

Justice Ginsburg remarked that an early case, *M.L.B. v. S.L.J.*, was a favorite.[5] A woman whose parental rights had been terminated could not appeal because she couldn't afford the trial transcript, a prerequisite to filing an appeal. Justice Ginsburg, writing for a 6–3 majority, held that this constituted a denial of substantive due process given the importance of the right at stake—her fundamental right to the care, custody, and control of her children. "Choices about marriage, family life, and the upbringing of children," she stated, "are among associational rights this Court has ranked as 'of basic importance in our society,' rights sheltered by the Fourteenth Amendment against the State's unwarranted usurpation, disregard, or disrespect."[6] This was not a fight over who pays for a transcript but rather a mother's efforts to "defend against the State's destruction of her family bonds, and to resist the brand associated with a parental unfitness adjudication."[7] The mother was seeking only "to be spared from the State's devastatingly adverse action."[8] Throughout her time on the high court, Justice Ginsburg grappled with the human cost of unfair laws. By centering the ordinary individuals and families affected by governmental overreach in her opinions, she was a steady voice for law's humanity—or lack of it.

By the time Ginsburg ascended to the Supreme Court, the Constitution's commitment to sex equality had been firmly cemented. She applied that rule in only one major case, *U.S. v. Virginia*, invalidating the long-standing male-only admissions requirement of the Virginia Military Institute.[9] In the majority opinion, Justice Ginsburg wrote that "[n]either federal nor state government acts compatibly with equal protection when a law or official policy denies to women, simply because they are women, full citizenship stature—equal opportunity to aspire, achieve, participate in and contribute to society based on their individual talents and capacities."[10]

She invoked this notion of equal citizenship again in her dissent in *AT&T Corp. v. Hulteen*, denouncing the majority's decision to allow the company to maintain a retirement system that penalized workers who took pregnancy-related disability leaves before passage of the Pregnancy Discrimination Act.[11] She linked the company's discrimination to a broader history of inequality for women, in which "[c]ertain attitudes about pregnancy and childbirth, throughout human history, have sustained pervasive, often law-sanctioned, restrictions on a woman's place among paid workers and active citizens."[12] Ginsburg sounded an alarm about the delicate relationship between work and family, as well as the way government regulation in both arenas has the potential to impede equality and human flourishing.

As an advocate, Ginsburg was deprived of the opportunity to press this theory before the Supreme Court when a case she was litigating, *Struck v. Secretary of Defense*, was dismissed for mootness.[13] The case involved a challenge to an Air Force rule that required pregnant service members to get an abortion or be ousted from the military. Ginsburg wrote later that she had hoped to use this case to introduce the concept of reproductive choice—that no woman should have to choose between pregnancy and a job. It would have, in Ginsburg's words, been an ideal case to argue the "sex equality dimensions of laws and regulations governing pregnancy and childbirth."[14]

For Justice Ginsburg, women's equality depended just as much on what happens in the home as what happens at work. Two subthemes emerge from her opinions and dissents that touch on the family. First, women's full participation in society depends on their ability to control reproduction. Second, men must be given the room to develop their capacity as fathers to promote equality for both men and women.

Reproductive Rights and the Importance of Autonomy for Women

Two years before Ginsburg was confirmed to her position on the Supreme Court, the Court decided *Planned Parenthood v. Casey*.[15] The Court considered the constitutionality of a Pennsylvania abortion law designed to test the limits and vitality of *Roe*. The Court reaffirmed *Roe*'s basic premise that the right of privacy under the Due Process

Clause protects a person's right to terminate a pregnancy up to a certain point but revised the framework for balancing the woman's right to bodily and decision-making autonomy against the state's interest in protecting potential life. In a joint opinion, three justices wrote that a pregnant woman has the right to terminate a pregnancy before viability without undue burden from the government. This standard, supported by a majority of the justices, gave the state more flexibility to express its preference for childbirth over abortion through onerous "informed consent" requirements like waiting periods, mandatory ultrasounds, and scripted counseling. The Court could have overruled *Roe* given a rightward shift in composition (which it eventually did in *Dobbs*, two years after Ginsburg's death). But the Court chose instead to recalibrate the right in favor of greater state control. Although stare decisis was an important factor, the plurality noted the relationship between reproductive autonomy and women's equality. The "ability of women to participate equally in the economic and social life of the Nation has been facilitated by their ability to control their reproductive lives."[16]

Justice Ginsburg was often alone in elucidating the ties between reproductive autonomy and sex equality once she joined the Court, despite the recognition in *Casey* of the inextricable connection. Consider the premise of her dissent in *Gonzales v. Carhart*, a case in which the Supreme Court upheld the federal Partial Birth Abortion Ban Act against a constitutional challenge.[17] Although the Court recognized that states cannot ban abortion before viability, it permitted Congress to take one safe method off the table on the unproven theory that no amount of informed consent could spare women the potential regret after learning the "precise details" of how an intact dilation and evacuation abortion is performed.[18] Justice Kennedy, writing for the majority, assumed that a woman who underwent this type of abortion would "struggle with grief more anguished and sorrow more profound" when she later learned "that she allowed a doctor to pierce the skull and vacuum the fast-developing brain of her unborn child, a child assuming the human form."[19]

In dissent, Justice Ginsburg rebuked the majority's logic, arguing persuasively that the notion of informed consent could not be pushed to the point that it encompassed a ban, but she also broadened the lens through which to view the prohibition. She focused not on the potential emotional reaction of a woman in an abortion provider's office, about which no evidence had been entered in the record, but rather on the catastrophic consequences for women denied the ability to control reproduction. Ginsburg dismissed the majority's feigned concern with regret as "antiabortion shibboleth," a use of Yiddish that was as catchy as it was apt. But her dissent was much more than a tagline. She criticized the majority for departing from the Court's prior recognition of the important role that reproductive rights play in securing women's equal participation in society. The *Carhart* majority opinion was dripping with conservative ideals about women's role in society, motherhood, and the capacity of women to make good decisions. Inherent in this view is a deep skepticism about women's capabilities and a retreat from the establishment of women's hard-fought freedom to avoid the constraints of state-enforced gender roles. It is no surprise that Justice Ginsburg, having crafted the jurisprudence that revolved around evaluating every person as an individual rather the member of an identity group, found the decision "alarming."[20] The majority made unfounded assumptions about the emotions of pregnant women—and used them to curtail their liberty. As Justice Ginsburg noted: "This way of thinking reflects ancient notions about women's place in the family and under the Constitution— ideas that have long since been discredited."[21] She implored her colleagues to remember that the fight over restrictive abortion laws is not "to vindicate some generalized notion of privacy" but rather to secure "a woman's autonomy to determine her life's course, and thus to enjoy equal citizenship stature."[22]

As she did with the mother in *M.L.B.*, Justice Ginsburg recognized the dire human cost of antiabortion laws. The ban does not "save any fetus from destruction"; neither does it "seek to protect the lives or health of pregnant women."[23] It simply burdens access to abortion. She made the same point in *Whole Woman's Health v. Hellerstedt*, a 2016 case in which the Supreme Court invalidated two Texas laws designed to regulate abortion clinics out of existence. Concurring, Justice Ginsburg wrote separately to emphasize that childbirth is vastly more dangerous than abortion and yet subject to fewer regulations—and that Texas, by reducing the number of abortion clinics, was likely to have driven patients to "unlicensed rogue practitioners, *faute de mieux*, at great risk to their health and safety." As she often did, she interjected fact to refute stereotypes and imagined realities.

Justice Ginsburg emphasized the importance of reproductive autonomy outside the abortion context as well. In *Burwell v. Hobby Lobby
Stores, Inc.*, the Court ruled that a closely held, for-profit company could
demand an exemption from the contraceptive mandate under the Affordable Care Act.[24] Even though prescription contraceptives are used
only by women, the majority did not even acknowledge the consequences for equality of protecting a corporation's "religious freedom" at
the expense of women's reproductive control. Justice Ginsburg, in dissent, began by quoting the language from *Casey* about the connection
between women's reproductive control and their participation in "the
economic and social life of the Nation."[25] She then recounted the history of the contraceptive mandate, which was based on a finding that
access to contraception is essential to women's health—and that cost is
the major barrier to access.[26] She criticized the majority for ignoring
the government's interest in promoting public health and women's well-
being, both compelling enough to justify an incursion (if there was one)
into the plaintiffs' religious freedom. She made a similar point in a later
case about the contraceptive mandate. In *Little Sisters of the Poor Saints
Peter and Paul Home v. Pennsylvania*, she castigated the majority for
casting "totally aside countervailing rights and interests in its zeal to
secure religious rights to the nth degree"; and the countervailing rights
were those designed by Congress "to afford gainfully employed women
comprehensive, seamless, no-cost insurance coverage for preventive care
protective of their health and well-being."[27] She noted that the expansive
religious exemption at issue would result in as many as 125,000 women
of childbearing age losing contraceptive coverage previously available
to them; and the majority was quite willing to "jettison an arrangement
that promotes women workers' well-being" in order to accommodate
"employers' religious tenets."[28]

A Voice for Fathers Too

As a lawyer, Ginsburg was very intentional about the cases she pursued. One of her strategies was to argue cases with male plaintiffs (often
married ones) to make the point that everyone is harmed by discrimination.[29] All law students are taught the case of *Craig v. Boren*, in which the
Supreme Court invalidated a law that permitted girls to buy low-alcohol

beer at a younger age than boys.[30] The Court settled on an "intermediate scrutiny" standard of review for sex-based classifications and modeled how to determine whether a "sex-centered generalization actually comported with fact" or was simply premised on "outdated misconceptions concerning the role of females in the home rather than in the 'marketplace and the world of ideas.'"[31] Ginsburg highlighted the pervasive reliance on sex stereotypes by "representing non-traditional men—men who were primary caretakers of their children and their elderly mothers, men who were not the primary breadwinners in their family, and men who defied traditional norms of masculinity in the 1970s."[32] Although she believed this would make the claims more palatable to male jurists, she also believed that men's equality was a necessary component of women's equality. She wrote in a 1975 article: "Solutions to the homework problem are as easily stated as they are hard to realize; man must join woman at the center of family life, and government must step in to assist both of them during the years when they have small children."[33]

Once on the bench, Ginsburg applied this idea beyond the Equal Protection Clause in cases involving discrimination against fathers. In *Coleman v. Court of Appeals*, she dissented from the Court's ruling that the self-care provision of the Family and Medical Leave Act (FMLA) could not be enforced against the states on sovereign immunity grounds and thereby deny the male plaintiff any remedy for his public employer's refusal to grant him leave when he was seriously ill.[34] Justice Ginsburg showed that the entire statute was predicated on the state-sponsored history of discrimination against women and mothers and that providing gender-neutral leave not only for parenting but also to tend to an employee's own serious health conditions was designed to "counter employers' impressions" that only female employees take leave for caretaking.[35] Moreover, she observed, the majority "pays scant attention to the overarching aim of the FMLA: to make it feasible for women to work while sustaining family life."[36] By design, Congress "reduced employers' incentives to prefer men over women, advanced women's economic opportunities, and laid the foundation for a more egalitarian relationship at home and at work."[37] Ginsburg understood that only by bringing men more into the home can women venture farther from it.

Justice Ginsburg took steps in the immigration context to reduce the differential treatment of unwed mothers and unwed fathers. In the

United States, citizenship can be acquired by place of birth or by descent. The federal statute on citizenship by descent gave citizen mothers whose babies were born outside of the United States a greater ability to pass on citizenship than citizen fathers in the same situation. In several cases, citizen fathers challenged these differential schemes but generally lost. The Supreme Court upheld the double standard on the ground that the differing roles in reproduction are relevant to citizenship by descent. These opinions are not convincing and reek more of sexism than anything else.[38] In *Miller v. Albright*, the Court upheld rules making it more onerous for children of a citizen father to document paternity than for children of a citizen mother to document maternity.[39] Justice Ginsburg criticized the majority for allowing Congress to base important rules on stereotypes about unwed fathers. She wrote:

> This section rests on familiar generalizations: mothers, as a rule, are responsible for a child born out of wedlock; fathers unmarried to the child's mother, ordinarily, are not. The law at issue might have made custody or support the relevant criterion. Instead, it treats mothers one way, fathers another, shaping Government policy to fit and reinforce the stereotypes of historic pattern.[40]

The Court again upheld a differential rule for mothers and fathers in this context in *Nguyen v. INS*, resulting in the deportation of a young man who was born to a Vietnamese mother and American father during the Vietnam War and who came to the United States as a young child after his mother abandoned him.[41] But the Court was convinced that Congress could demand greater proof of a parent-child tie from fathers than from mothers, despite its equal protection cases that permit disparate treatment only in the case of real gender difference. The majority decided that Congress's asserted interests—preventing fraudulent citizenship claims and ensuring the establishment of ties between the child and the United States—justified the disparate treatment. These may be valid interests, but the means were not related closely enough to justify the discrimination. The first could be met by a requirement that paternity be established at any time, rather than only before the child turns eighteen. And the second justifies a different rule for mothers and fathers only if you assume that mothers are substantially more likely to have a relationship with their children than are fathers. That is no more than an overbroad generalization of the type that usually is rejected in equal protection cases. The mother's presence at birth is not a guarantee of a meaningful parent-child relationship (and thus ties between the child and U.S. national ideals or culture), and the father's potential absence at birth does not preclude such a relationship. Fathers who do not fit the stereotype of the American G.I. carelessly fathering children abroad and abandoning them should, at the bare minimum, be permitted to prove they deserve the same treatment as mothers.

But in the most recent ruling on this set of issues, Justice Ginsburg, writing for the Court, invalidated a provision that expressly made it more difficult for citizen fathers to pass on citizenship than for citizen mothers. In that case, *Sessions v. Morales-Santana*, the plaintiff challenged a provision requiring citizen fathers to have five years of continuous physical presence in the country to pass on citizenship but required citizen mothers to have only one year.[42] The majority held that the different requirements for men and women constituted unconstitutional sex discrimination. It did so without revisiting *Nguyen*, concluding only that the physical presence requirement was not justified by any real difference between mothers and fathers. No biological difference could explain the disparate number of years required in the United States prior to the child's birth. Justice Ginsburg wrote that "a man needs no more time in the United States than a woman 'in order to have assimilated citizenship-related values to transmit to [his] child.'"[43] Rather, the distinction flew in the face of decades of rulings designed to eliminate archaic generalizations and stereotypes from American law. Justice Ginsburg concluded that the disparate rules were animated by the assumption that mothers play a different role in children's lives than fathers.[44] Mothers were the natural guardians of illegitimate children—indeed, for most of American history, nonmarital children were deemed fatherless by law. Citizenship law was rife with rules that reinforced the notion that children of a marriage belonged to the father whereas children born out of wedlock belonged to the mother. The shorter physical presence requirement made sense only if one assumed that children would be naturally bonded to their mothers—and thus not likely to fall prey to the competing national commitments of the alien father even if the mother's ties to the United States were relatively weak. The presumed weak ties to the father had to be offset by the father's strong ties to the United States. The only reason to apply different rules here was if one indulged the stereotyped assumptions about the ties between children and mothers versus fathers.[45]

Conclusion

It is impossible to capture the many contributions of one person who devoted such a long life to the study, practice, and interpretation of law. But in the realm of the family, Justice Ruth Bader Ginsburg was weaving a beautiful tapestry in which individuals would care for themselves and for one another while pursuing their dreams outside the home. Yet so much work remains. It is an unfinished tapestry. As she said in an interview with Linda Greenhouse, the "overt lines" of gender are largely gone, but challenges remain, perhaps the most significant of which is "mak[ing] it possible for people to thrive in both a work life and a family life."[46] Although women now compose about half of the American labor force, their experiences are anything but equal. The inequality is tied to the persistence of traditional family norms that mean women continue to perform the bulk of the child-rearing tasks even when they work the same hours as their male partners. Pregnancy and motherhood still befuddle employers, and the law has been slow to provide accommodations that would make it easier for women to maintain workforce attachments through the demanding years of childbearing. State legislatures, meanwhile, have waged an all-out war on women's sexual and reproductive health. And these private realities are exacerbated by the fact that the United States ranks last among industrialized countries in the provision of paid leave and other support for working parents and families.

Ginsburg recognized the limits of her position as a jurist. "Devising means to facilitate a balanced work and personal life," she wrote, "is First branch work; such arrangements are beyond the province of the judiciary to shape and decree."[47] But her contributions as an advocate and jurist to our understanding of gender and the family were mighty.

NOTES

Stephanie Mills ably assisted with the research for this chapter.

1 Reva Siegel, *She the People: The Nineteenth Amendment, Sex Equality, Federalism, and the Family*, 115 HARV. L. REV. 947, 1012 (2002).

2 *See, e.g.*, Hoyt v. Florida, 368 U.S. 57 (1961) (automatic exemption for women from jury service); Goesart v. Cleary, 335 U.S. 464 (1948) (restrictions on women as bartenders); Muller v. Oregon, 208 U.S. 412 (1908) (restriction on hours per day worked in factory or laundry); Bradwell v. Illinois U.S. (16 Wall.) 130 (1872) (refusal to permit women to practice law).

3 404 U.S. 71 (1971).

4 *See* Frontiero v. Richardson, 411 U.S. 677 (1973); Kahn v. Shevin, 416 U.S. 351 (1974); Edwards v. Healy, 421 U.S. 722 (1975); Weinberger v. Wiesenfeld, 420 U.S. 626 (1975); Califano v. Goldfarb, 430 U.S. 199 (1977).

5 519 U.S. 102 (1996); *see* Ruth Bader Ginsburg, *A Conservation with Justice Ruth Bader Ginsburg* (Oct. 19, 2012), 122 YALE L.J. ONLINE 283 (Mar. 1, 2013).

6 M.L.B., 519 U.S. at 116.

7 *Id.* at 125.

8 *Id.*

9 518 U.S. 515, 519 (1996).

10 *Id.* at 532.

11 556 U.S. 701, 717 (2009) (2009) (Ginsburg, J., dissenting).

12 *Id.* at 724. On her "pregnancy jurisprudence" more broadly, see Reva B. Siegel, *The Pregnant Citizen, from Suffrage to the Present*, 108 GEO. L.J. 167, 181–85 (2020).

13 460 F.2d 1372 (9th Cir. 1971), *cert. granted*, 409 U.S. 947, *vacated*, 409 U.S. 1071 (1972).

14 Ruth Bader Ginsburg, *A Postscript to Struck by Stereotype*, 59 DUKE L.J. 799, 799 (2010); Reva B. Siegel, *Equality and Choice: Sex Equality Perspectives on Reproductive Rights in the Work of Ruth Bader Ginsburg*, 25 COLUM. J. GENDER & L. 63 (2013); Neil S. Siegel & Reva B. Siegel, *Struck by Stereotype: Ruth Bader Ginsburg on Pregnancy Discrimination as Sex Discrimination*, 59 DUKE L.J. 771 (2010).

15 505 U.S. 833 (1992).

16 *Id.* at 856.

17 550 U.S. 124 (2007).

18 *Id.* at 159.

19 *Id.* at 159–60.

20 *Id.* at 170.

21 *Id.* at 185.

22 *Id.* at 172.

23 Stenberg v. Carhart, 530 U.S. 914, 952 (2000) (Ginsburg, J., concurring).

24 573 U.S. 682 (2014).

25 *Id.* at 741.

26 *Id.* at 741–44 (Ginsburg, J., dissenting).

27 140 S. Ct. 2367, 2400 (2020).

28 *Id.* at 2403–04.

29 *See* David Cole, *Strategies of Difference: Litigating for Women's Rights in a Man's World*, 2 LAW & INEQ. 33, 94 (1984); Cary Franklin, *The Anti-Stereotyping*

Principle in Constitutional Sex Discrimination Law, 85 N.Y.U. L. REV. 83, 84 (2010).

30 429 U.S. 190 (1976).

31 *Id.* at 198–99. Ginsburg authored the ACLU's amicus brief in *Craig*, in which she advocated for the adoption of heightened scrutiny, and sat at counsel table with the lawyer who argued the case for the plaintiff. *See* Wendy Webster Williams, *Ruth Bader Ginsburg's Equal Protection Clause: 1970–80*, 25 COLUM. J. GENDER & L. 41, 43 (2013).

32 Katherine Franke, *Introduction: Symposium Honoring the Advocacy, Scholarship, and Jurisprudence of Justice Ruth Bader Ginsburg*, 25 COLUM. J. GENDER & L. 1, 3 (2013).

33 Ruth Bader Ginsburg, *Gender and the Constitution*, 44 U. CIN. L. REV. 1, 34 (1975).

34 566 U.S. 30 (2012).

35 *Id.* at 62 (Ginsburg, J., dissenting).

36 *Id.* at 65.

37 *Id.*

38 *See* Miller v. Albright, 523 U.S. 420 (1998) (upholding provision requiring unwed fathers but not unwed mothers to acknowledge children before the age of eighteen in order to transmit citizenship).

39 *Id.*

40 *Id.* at 460 (Ginsburg, J., dissenting).

41 533 U.S. 53 (2001) (upholding disparate burdens imposed on unwed fathers versus unwed mothers to establish paternity before passing on citizenship).

42 137 S. Ct. 1678 (2017).

43 *Id.* at 1694.

44 *Id.* at 1695.

45 Justice Ginsburg remedied the unconstitutionality, though, by "leveling down." She held that Congress would have to extend the one-year exception to unwed fathers; the Court would deny it to mothers only in the name of equality. *Id.* at 1698–99.

46 Ruth Bader Ginsburg & Linda Greenhouse, *A Conversation with Justice Ginsburg*, 122 YALE L.J. ONLINE 283, 297 (2013).

47 Ruth Bader Ginsburg, Muller v. Oregon, *One Hundred Years Later*, 45 WILLAMETTE L. REV. 359, 379–80 (2009).

14

Freedom of Expression

A Practical Evolution

DR. JOANNE SWEENY

Justice Ginsburg's freedom of expression opinions, both as a Supreme Court Justice and D.C. Circuit appellate judge, reflect an ardent belief in the importance of freedom of speech as well as its ability to evolve. Moreover, these opinions showcase her most defining traits as a writer and jurist. Her focus on history and context, and her incrementalism, are evident throughout her opinions. This chapter analyzes Justice Ginsburg's freedom of expression opinions, extrajudicial writings, and speeches to show her evolving views toward freedom of expression and the masterful way she disentangled the complex web of First Amendment jurisprudence to craft thoughtful, fact-sensitive judicial opinions.

Like many jurists, Justice Ruth Bader Ginsburg emphasized the importance of freedom of speech. Her views on freedom of speech had their foundation in the Founders' idea of the right to speech already existing with the people, which the Bill of Rights merely preserved.[1] Justice Ginsburg's veneration for the First Amendment's protection of speech was rooted in her memories of the McCarthy hearings while she was in college.[2] She described the McCarthy hearings as including statements from "brave lawyers" who were "reminding our Senate, 'Look at the Constitution, look at the very First Amendment. What does it say? It says we prize, above all else, the right to think, speak, to write, as we will, without Big Brother over our shoulders.'"[3] Justice Ginsburg has credited the harms of McCarthyism for its role in making her politically active.[4] The hearings also made her want to be a lawyer because, as she put it, "if lawyers can be helping us get back in touch with our most basic values, that's what I want to be."[5]

Justice Ginsburg was perhaps most eloquent in her defense of the First Amendment in her dissent in *Beard v. Banks*,[6] a case where a Pennsylvania prison official promulgated a rule that prohibited maximum security prisoners from "possessing any secular, nonlegal newspaper, newsletter, or magazine during the indefinite duration of their solitary confinement." In her many objections to this rule, Justice Ginsburg noted that "the right of freedom of speech and press includes not only the right to utter or to print, but the right to distribute, the right to receive, the right to read and freedom of inquiry, freedom of thought."

The rule restricting these prisoners' reading materials, Justice Ginsburg noted, "comes perilously close to a state-sponsored effort at mind control." The media restriction, she remarked, "prevents prisoners from receiving suitable access to social, political, esthetic, moral, and other ideas, which are central to the development and preservation of individual identity, and are clearly protected by the First Amendment."[7] These effects were exacerbated by the enforced solitude these prisoners faced. Her concerns for these prisoners was manifest in this dissent, particularly when she implied that these prisoners may not have been treated in accordance with "the ethical tradition that accords respect to the dignity and intrinsic worth of every individual."[8]

Justice Ginsburg was outspoken in her belief that "the message of the first amendment is tolerance of speech, not the speech we agree with, but the speech we hate."[9] In her confirmation hearings, she used the example of incitement as articulated in *Brandenburg v. Ohio*[10] to argue that our vision of what is protected under the First Amendment has evolved significantly over time and will continue to do so.[11]

With regard to offensive speech, Justice Ginsburg was not speaking hypothetically. In her Senate Confirmation hearings, she detailed multiple instances of offensive and discriminatory speech that she willingly endured because of her belief that people have the right to speak their minds.[12] Justice Ginsburg demonstrated tolerance for hate speech in her concurring opinion in *Capitol Square Review and Advisory Board v. Pinette*, where she wrote that the state did not have a compelling justification for denying a permit to display the Ku Klux Klan cross along with a disclaimer.[13]

However, Justice Ginsburg was not an originalist by any means. She believed in the principles articulated in the Constitution and other founding documents but also recognized that the Founders were limited by their own experiences. As Ginsburg observed in her Senate confirmation hearings, although the text of the First Amendment has not changed since it was adopted in 1791, our understanding of it has.[14] In 1798, President John Adams signed into law the Alien and Sedition Act, which made it a crime to "write, print, utter, or publish . . . any false, scandalous and malicious writing" against the government, and that law has never been ruled unconstitutional.[15] And yet, as Justice Ginsburg explained, it would certainly be overturned today.

Justice Ginsburg did not support an unbounded First Amendment. In an interview in 2014, she pointed out that, despite the First Amendment's broad language ("Congress shall make no law"), it is not absolute.[16] Her dissent in *Burwell v. Hobby Lobby Stores, Inc.* stated that "with respect to free exercise claims no less than free speech claims, your right to swing your arms ends just where the other man's nose begins."[17] It was this tension between different rights that informed much of Justice Ginsburg's First Amendment jurisprudence. As a result of this tension, Justice Ginsburg saw freedom of expression on a continuum where some speech is not protected at all, such as obscenity, and other speech deserves the highest protection, such as political speech.[18] In the middle of those two extremes is a wide variety of speech such as commercial speech and indecent speech.[19] Justice Ginsburg also believed that some restrictions on speech are entirely unconstitutional, such as viewpoint discrimination.[20]

Justice Ginsburg was also a pragmatic incrementalist and situated her First Amendment jurisprudence within existing cases. In *United States v. Sineneng-Smith*, Justice Ginsburg wrote that the Ninth Circuit should not have gone beyond the claims presented by the parties to request amicus briefing to determine whether the challenged statute was overbroad.[21] The appellant had raised other First Amendment claims, but according to Justice Ginsburg the Ninth Circuit had improperly inserted its own theory of the case and should have restricted itself to the issues framed by the parties.

Fact-Sensitive Analysis

Justice Ginsburg used three primary analytical techniques in First Amendment cases: fact-sensitive analysis, historical references, and focus on real-world impact. When she was an appellate judge on the D.C. Circuit, her concurring opinion in *Community for Creative Non-Violence v. Watt* focused heavily on the facts of the case to fully explain her reasoning. The issue in *Community for Creative Non-Violence* was tricky: protestors wanted to sleep in the National Mall and Lafayette Park in Washington, D.C., as part of their multiday protest of the Reagan administration's treatment of the poor and homeless.[22] Although the protestors were given permission to set up "symbolic camps," they were prohibited from actually sleeping in them under a regulation that prohibited camping in national parks. The protestors' lawsuit focused on whether the First Amendment prohibited such a restriction since, according to the protestors, sleeping was an essential and symbolic part of their message. Judge Ginsburg was skeptical of that claim, arguing that sleeping also was essential to allow the protestors to regain energy to continue their protests (which the First Amendment does not protect), and she argued for "rules that are sensible, coherent, and sensitive to the speech interest involved."[23] Ultimately, Ginsburg's analysis rested on a careful examination of what the expressive value of the behavior actually was, and unlike her colleagues on both sides, she refused to draw any sharp categorical distinctions.[24] Instead, Judge Ginsburg argued that "courts should draw no bright line between verbal speech and other comprehensible symbols of expression, or between 'traditional communicative activity' and non-traditional modes of expression" and ultimately found that the National Park Service's regulation was not rational because it forbade "sleeping while permitting tenting, lying down, and maintaining a twenty-four hour presence."

In *Christian Legal Society v. Martinez*, Justice Ginsburg relied upon a close reading of the facts to decide that the University of Hastings College of Law could have a policy requiring official student organizations to accept anyone who wanted to join.[25] The Christian Legal Society's application to become a registered student organization was rejected because it excluded students based on religion and sexual orientation. The Christian Legal Society sued, arguing viewpoint discrimination. Justice Ginsburg's opinion noted Supreme Court precedent prohibiting universities from discriminating against student groups on the basis of their viewpoint but found that the Hastings policy did not do that. Because it focused on "the *act* of rejecting would-be group members without reference to the reasons motivating that behavior," Justice Ginsburg concluded that the policy was viewpoint-neutral despite the disparate impact it would have on organizations seeking to restrict membership based on their own, in Justice Ginsburg's words, "viewpoint discrimination."

Justice Ginsburg was likewise concerned with the unique facts of the case in *Thompson v. Hebdon*, a case where Alaska's limits on individual campaign contributions were challenged under the First Amendment.[26] Justice Ginsburg concurred with the decision to remand the case but also noted the unique features of Alaska: "[I]t has the second smallest legislature in the country and derives approximately 90 percent of its revenues from one economic sector—the oil and gas industry." These features, she explained, make it "highly, if not uniquely, vulnerable to corruption in politics and government."[27] With these unique characteristics, Justice Ginsburg noted that there may be a "special justification" for the low individual contribution limit.

Justice Ginsburg's dissent in *Masterpiece Cakeshop, Ltd. v. Colorado Civil Rights Commission* is similarly grounded in the practical realities of the case. She noted that that the bakery in question, which refused to make a traditional cake for two men getting married, stood in stark contrast to the customer who asked different bakeries to prepare cakes with messages disapproving same-sex marriage on religious grounds.[28] Justice Ginsburg approved of the Colorado Court of Appeals treating those two cases differently because one couple was "denied service based on an aspect of their identity" whereas the other customer was denied "because of the offensive nature of the requested message."[29] This distinction, according to Justice Ginsburg, was critical because only the latter implicated the speech rights of the bakery.

Justice Ginsburg also scrutinized evidence presented by government actors when they attempted to justify First Amendment restrictions. For example, Justice Ginsburg emphasized the value of truthful, relevant commercial speech and struck down the Florida Department of Business and Professional Regulation's sanctions against an attorney who had truthfully advertised herself as a licensed CPA.[30] For Justice Ginsburg, the real-world impact and the individual facts of the case were of paramount importance. To justify a restriction, even on commercial speech, she required evidence of actual harm.[31]

Justice Ginsburg focused on the facts of the case to thoroughly debunk the government's rationale for prohibiting maximum security prisoners in solitary confinement from accessing secular newspapers, magazines, and personal photos. She did this by persuasively noting that secular reading materials did not present any more of a security risk than religious written materials or the other items furnished to these prisoners such as clothing, writing materials, and bedding, which could also be used to start a fire, hide contraband, or catapult feces.[32] Justice Ginsburg noted that the deputy superintendent's own deposition testimony undermined that justification when he admitted that "inmates could engage in any of the behaviors that worried prison officials without using banned materials."

Historical References

In addition to scrutinizing the facts, Justice Ginsburg also relied on historical references to analyze First Amendment issues. Justice Ginsburg was an accomplished scholar as well as a judge, and her knowledge of American history, both political and judicial, gave her a long view of the progress of the nation with regard to freedom of expression. Her knowledge of history allowed her to put the First Amendment into a historical context, which was evident in her decisions and speeches.

She also used historical examples in her written opinions as powerful illustrations of the founding principles of the country. In *Community for Creative Non-Violence v. Watt*, a D.C. Circuit case, Judge Ginsburg referred to the Boston Tea Party as the epitome of symbolic speech; that night, though no words were spoken, a statement was certainly made.[33] In her confirmation hearings, Ginsburg used another example when discussing the importance of symbolic speech: the king of Denmark was seen in public in Copenhagen wearing a yellow armband during World War II to support the Jewish people living there, which, according to Ginsburg, "expressed the idea more forcefully than words could."[34] In her dissent in *DKT Memorial Fund Ltd. v. Agency for International Development*, another D.C. Circuit case, Judge Ginsburg used the historical example of the "first federal law the Supreme Court ever held violative of the first amendment," which involved "a restraint on delivery of mail from abroad" due to fears of communist propaganda to argue that the

First Amendment must apply to the United States' laws that affect other nations as well as our own.[35]

Real-Life Impact of Laws

Justice Ginsburg's First Amendment jurisprudence was quite practical, and she often used real-life examples or hypotheticals to explain her position or to tease out the problems inherent in her colleagues' reasoning. Ginsburg's dissenting opinion in *Beard v. Banks*, mentioned at the beginning of this chapter for its eloquent defense of the First Amendment, epitomizes this technique. In that case, she stated she would overturn the prison's ban on secular reading materials in solitary confinement in part because the government produced no studies showing that the rehabilitation interests allegedly served by the restrictions had any basis in known psychological research or even data gathered by the prison itself.[36] Justice Ginsburg also criticized the prison's use of a deprivation theory of rehabilitation by arguing that such a theory can have no limit; anything can be restricted if the prison can simply argue that the prisoner could earn that privilege back with good behavior. She ultimately found this justification to be exaggerated and unnecessary, partially because the other conditions of solitary confinement were so unpleasant, and partially because several other prisons did not have such restrictions and still served their penological interests.

In *Community for Creative Non-Violence* (D.C. Circuit), Judge Ginsburg used detailed hypotheticals to show the "untenable" nature of Judge Antonin Scalia's proposal that the First Amendment protected only "spoken and written thought." In her concurring opinion, Ginsburg highlighted Scalia's proposal's unintended consequences: that someone waving a flag or wearing a ribbon would receive no First Amendment protection, but if they printed any word or phrase on the flag or ribbon, then the First Amendment would suddenly protect them.[37]

Similarly, Justice Ginsburg focused on the practical effects of a regulation that required ballot circulators to be registered voters. Such a restriction, she reasoned, necessarily lowered the number of potential circulators, thereby decreasing the "number of voices who will convey the initiative proponents' message and, consequently, cut down the size of audience proponents can reach."[38]

Even when writing a concurring opinion that favored the police in a case alleging suppression of speech, Justice Ginsburg noted several examples of the police abusing their arrest authority "to disrupt the exercise of First Amendment speech and press rights," including a case involving the arrest of photographers documenting a Black Lives Matter protest, ostensibly for failing to use a crosswalk the police had blocked.[39] These examples concerned Justice Ginsburg enough to disagree with the majority, which held that any arrest supported by probable cause could not form the basis of a section 1983 action. Because of the myriad tools the police have to proscribe speech, such as disorderly conduct or breach of the peace, Justice Ginsburg believed that it would be far too easy for the police to "justify an arrest as based on probable cause when the arrest was in fact prompted by a retaliatory motive."

Justice Ginsburg also focused on the practical effects a restriction would have on the freedom to communicate, because funding restrictions logically impacted the availability of speech. In her dissent in *DKT Memorial Fund Ltd. v. Agency for International Development*, she argued that a law that denied funding to foreign governments who gave abortion counseling would necessarily reduce that kind of speech, even though it was protected by the First Amendment.[40] She noted that lack of funding can impermissibly reduce the impact of speech in various ways, such as requiring licenses for professional fundraisers for charities or prohibiting paying circulators of initiative petitions.

Limitations on charities' ability to use professional fundraisers came up in *Illinois, ex rel. Madigan v. Telemarketing Associates, Inc.*[41] Justice Ginsburg's majority opinion made a careful distinction between laws that prohibit fund-raising where a certain percentage did not go to charitable work itself, versus individual cases alleging fraudulent practices by fundraisers. Although solicitation of funds for charities is protected by the First Amendment, according to Justice Ginsburg, states may bring "a properly tailored fraud action [where] the State bears the full burden of proof," and a properly tailored fraud action leaves ample First Amendment protection because it requires not just a misstatement but an intent to deceive for material gain.

Even when upholding a viewpoint-neutral regulation on solicitation, Ginsburg explicitly warned the government that its "taxing and spending" decisions, even those that appear to give citizens a choice, "*can* seriously interfere with the exercise of constitutional freedoms."[42] Justice Ginsburg's focus on the inseparable connection between speech and money is also evident in her dissent in *Citizens United v. FEC*,[43] which she hoped (though was not very hopeful) would someday be overturned.[44]

Judicial Speech

Justice Ginsburg believed that states should have considerable latitude in regulating judicial elections despite freedom of speech concerns because of her strong belief that judges are different from other political actors. In her dissenting opinion in *Republican Party v. White* and her concurring opinion in *Williams-Yulee v. Florida Board*, for example, Justice Ginsburg drew a sharp distinction in how the First Amendment should apply to judicial elections compared to elected officials in the other two branches of government.[45]

According to Justice Ginsburg, "judges represent the law"[46] and have to stand "up to what is generally supreme in a democracy: the popular will."[47] To Justice Ginsburg, the role of the judiciary required judges "to be indifferent to popularity."[48] In her dissent, she drew upon multiple Supreme Court cases, scholarly articles, and even the *Federalist Papers* to argue that judicial independence is of paramount importance to the efficacy of the U.S. government. Justice Ginsburg focused on the role judicial elections play in ensuring that judges remain impartial and independent and also indicated her willingness to allow states to restrict judicial campaign speech in a way that would be improper for elected representatives.

In *White*, Justice Ginsburg approved of a law that prohibited judges from "publicly making known how they would decide issues likely to come before them as judges" because she believed that it was "precisely targeted."[49] Justice Ginsburg highlighted a critical aspect of the Minnesota law: "The provision does not bar a candidate from generally 'stating her views' on legal questions; it prevents her from 'publicly making known how she would *decide*' disputed issues."[50] Justice Ginsburg noted that judges could still discuss legal issues generally or criticize past decisions, which was sufficient for her to believe that the law did not run afoul of the First Amendment. Finally, Justice Ginsburg used historical examples of the law in question being applied fairly to a judicial candidate and not chilling his speech, as well as a hypothetical to dispute a distinction made by the majority between statements promising to rule a certain way and statements approving of such a ruling.[51]

Years later, she reiterated these arguments in *Williams-Yulee*, arguing that the holding of *Citizens United* (which she bitterly dissented from) should not apply to judicial elections.[52] Noting the interplay of money and speech, influence, and access, Justice Ginsburg argued that such favoritism is "disqualifying" for judges. She observed that "campaign contributors 'mean to be buying a vote.'"[53] To emphasize her point, Justice Ginsburg used the example of the massive fund-raising reaction to the Iowa Supreme Court's invalidation of the state's same-sex marriage ban. Justice Ginsburg referenced studies showing not only that money spent on campaigns actually does impact judicial decision-making but also that it erodes public confidence in the impartiality of the judiciary. Due to these negative impacts, Justice Ginsburg opined that the importance of judicial impartiality and integrity required a unique kind of balancing against freedom of expression and argued that states should be given the leeway to do that balancing.[54]

Despite her clearly stated convictions, Justice Ginsburg's stance on the propriety of unfettered judicial campaign speech was perceived to be in conflict with her behavior as a Supreme Court Justice, and she was criticized for public statements she made on a variety of political issues. In a speech she gave in 2012, Justice Ginsburg refrained from indicating which way the Supreme Court would decide cases it was currently considering, but she did indicate that the cases were controversial and might result in a close vote.[55] In 2013, she noted that the Supreme Court, though more conservative, was more "activist" in its willingness to overturn its prior decisions.[56] In 2015, in the wake of the Supreme Court's decision on *Obergefell v. Hodges*,[57] she stated said she believed that people would come to accept same-sex marriage, though she did not predict how the Court would rule on the issue.[58] Justice Ginsburg's impression of the Supreme Court's activist nature was exemplified in the 2022 decision *Dobbs v. Jackson Women's Health Organization*,[59] which overturned *Roe v. Wade*.[60]

The election of Donald Trump seemed to have tested her stance on the importance of judicial silence on upcoming cases or controversial political issues. In 2016 Justice Ginsburg repeatedly criticized then-candidate Donald Trump, calling him "bad for the country" and a "faker."[61] In response, Trump stated that Ginsburg should step down, and Ginsburg later apologized, stating that judges "should avoid commenting on a candidate for public office" and that "[i]n the future [she] will be more circumspect."[62] She nevertheless made controversial statements regarding what she believed to be the "sexist" results of the 2016 presidential election,[63] and she criticized professional football player Colin Kaepernick's decision to kneel during the national anthem.[64] Justice Ginsburg later wrote an apology for her statements about Kaepernick, stating that, when asked about it, she "should have declined to respond." After this apology, there were no more reported controversial statements before her death.

Conclusion

Though Justice Ginsburg is not primarily known for her First Amendment decisions, her work in this area highlights her belief in the ability of the Constitution to evolve, as well as her tremendous skills as a jurist and writer. Freedom of expression is an exceedingly complex area of law that has significant and sometimes nonobvious real-world impacts, and it typically involves conflict with other important rights and state interests. Justice Ginsburg's ability to navigate these conflicts and explain her reasoning in clear and compelling prose is a testament to her phenomenal intellect and sense of justice. That she struggled with where to draw these lines with her own speech as a judge does not diminish her achievements and instead showcases her own humility and willingness to admit her mistakes.

NOTES

1 Ruth Bader Ginsburg, *An Overview of Court Review for Constitutionality in the United States*, 57 LA. L. REV. 1019, 1025 (1997).

2 *Nomination of Ruth Bader Ginsburg, to Be Associate Justice of the Supreme Court of the United States: Hearing Before the S. Comm. on the Judiciary*, 103rd Cong. 51 (1993) (hereinafter "Nomination") at 314, available at www.govinfo.gov; Justice Ruth Bader Ginsburg & Robert A. Stein, *The Stein Lecture: A Conversation Between Justice Ruth Bader Ginsburg and Professor Robert A. Stein*, 99 MINN. L. REV. 1, 20 (2014).

3 Jessica Ní Mhainín, *Choose Your Moment: The Inspirational Ruth Bader Ginsburg*, INDEX ON CENSORSHIP (Sep. 24, 2020), www.indexoncensorship.org.

4 Nomination at 313–14.

5 *Supreme Court Justice Continues Equality Fight*, VOA NEWS, Dec. 12, 2011 7:00 PM, www.voanews.com.

6 548 U.S. 521, 542–53 (2006) (Ginsburg, J., dissenting).

7 *Id.* (internal quotation marks and citation omitted).

8 *Id.*

9 Nomination at 185.

10 395 U.S. 444 (1969).

11 Nomination at 313.

12 *Id.* at 358–59.

13 Capitol Square Rev. and Advisory Bd. v. Pinette, 515 U.S. 753, 783 (1995) (Ginsburg, J., concurring).

14 Nomination at 313.

15 Erwin Chemerinsky, *False Speech and the First Amendment*, 71 OKLA. L. REV. 71 1, 1 (2018).

16 *User Clip: Justice Ruth Bader Ginsburg on the First Amendment*, C-SPAN (Apr. 21, 2014), www.c-span.org, at 00:05:09.

17 Burwell v. Hobby Lobby Stores, Inc., 573 U.S. 682, 746 (2014) (quoting Zechariah Chafee, *Freedom of Speech in War Time*, 32 HARV. L. REV. 932, 957 (1919) (internal quotation marks omitted)).

18 Nomination at 315.

19 *Id.*

20 *Id.* at 183–84.

21 140 S. Ct. 1575, 1581–82 (2020).

22 Community for Creative Non-Violence v. Watt, 703 F.2d 586, 608 (D.C. Cir. 1983) (Ginsburg, J., concurring), *rev'd sub nom.* Clark v. Community for Creative Non-Violence, 468 U.S. 288 (1984).

23 *Id.*

24 On appeal, the Supreme Court reversed the D.C. Circuit, finding the regulation a proper time, place, or manner restriction. In his dissent, Justice Marshall explicitly agreed with Judge Ginsburg's nuanced approach. Clark v. Community for Creative Non-Violence, 468 U.S. 288, 310 n.7 (1984) (Marshall, J., dissenting).

25 Christian Leg. Soc. Chapter of the U. of California, Hastings College of the Law v. Martinez, 561 U.S. 661, 696 (2010).

26 Thompson v. Hebdon, 140 S. Ct. 348, 351–52 (2019).

27 *Id.* (internal quotation marks and citation omitted).

28 Masterpiece Cakeshop, Ltd. v. Colorado Civ. Rights Comm'n., 138 S. Ct. 1719, 1750–51 (2018) (Ginsburg, J., dissenting).

29 *Id.* (internal quotation marks and citation omitted).

30 Ibanez v. Fla. Dept. of Bus. and Prof. Reg., Bd. of Accountancy, 512 U.S. 136, 142–43 (1994).

31 *Id.* at 148–49.
32 *Beard,* 548 U.S. at 542–53 (Ginsburg, J., dissenting).
33 *Community for Creative Non-Violence,* 703 F.2d at 608 (Ginsburg, J., concurring).
34 Nomination at 226. This story has been debunked several times but remains a powerful and popular story that emphasizes King Christian X's support of Danish Jews. Vilhjálmur Örn Vilhjálmsson, *The King and the Star,* in DENMARK AND THE HOLOCAUST 102 (Mette Bastholm Jensen & Steven L. B. Jensen eds. 2003).
35 887 F.2d 275, 303–04 (D.C. Cir. 1989) (citing Lamont v. Postmaster General, 381 U.S. 301 (1965)).
36 *Id.*
37 *Community for Creative Non-Violence,* 703 F.2d at 608 (Ginsburg, J., concurring). She was similarly skeptical of Judge Wilkey's approach, which would protect "traditional" symbolic speech (such as marching or picketing) but not other types (such as flag-waving) that could equally convey a message. *Id.*
38 Buckley v. Am. Constitutional L. Found., Inc., 525 U.S. 182, 194–95 (1999) (internal quotation marks and citation omitted).
39 Nieves v. Bartlett, 139 S. Ct. 1715, 1734 (2019) (Ginsburg, J., dissenting).
40 887 F.2d 275, 303–04 (D.C. Cir. 1989). Justice Ginsburg also emphasized that there should be no distinction between U.S. laws that impact speech in foreign countries or on domestic soil. If something is protected by the Constitution, it must be protected everywhere. Ruth Bader Ginsburg, *The Value of a Comparative Perspective in Judicial Decisionmaking: Imparting Experiences to, and Learning from, Other Adherents to the Rule of Law,* 74 REV. JURIDICA U.P.R. 213, 225–26 (2005).
41 538 U.S. 600, 617 (2003).
42 Fed. Election Comm'n. v. Intl. Funding Inst., Inc., 969 F.2d 1110, 1118 (D.C. Cir. 1992) (Ginsburg, J., concurring).
43 Citizens United v. Federal Election Commission, 558 U.S. 310 (2010).
44 Tara Golshan, *Ruth Bader Ginsburg Says Her "Impossible Dream" Is for* Citizens United *to Be Overturned,* VOX (Jul. 11, 2016), www.vox.com.
45 Republican Party of Minn. v. White, 536 U.S. 765, 803–21 (2002) (Ginsburg, J., dissenting); Williams-Yulee v. Fla. B., 575 U.S. 433, 457–62 (2015) (Ginsburg, J., concurring).
46 *Republican Party of Minn.,* 536 U.S. at 803 (Ginsburg, J., dissenting) (quoting Chisom v. Roemer, 501 U.S. 380, 411 (1991) (Scalia, J., dissenting)) (internal quotation marks omitted).
47 *Id.* (quoting Scalia, *The Rule of Law as a Law of Rules,* 56 U. CHI. L. REV. 1175, 1180 (1989)).
48 *Williams-Yulee,* 575 U.S. at 457 (Ginsburg, J., concurring) (quoting *Chisom,* 501 U.S. at 401 n.29).
49 *Republican Party of Minn.,* 536 U.S. at 805 (Ginsburg, J., dissenting)
50 *Id.* (internal quotation marks and citation omitted).
51 *Id.* at 820.

52 *Williams-Yulee*, 575 U.S. at 457–62 (Ginsburg, J., concurring).

53 *Id.* (quoting Liptak & Roberts, *Campaign Cash Mirrors a High Court's Rulings*, N.Y. TIMES A1, A22 (Oct. 1, 2006)).

54 Justice Ginsburg's literary flair was particularly evident in the conclusion of her concurrence. She quoted both *Anna Karenina* ("All happy families are alike") and Gertrude Stein's *Geography and Plays* ("Rose is a rose is a rose"). *Williams-Yulee*, 575 U.S. at 462 (Ginsburg, J., concurring).

55 Kyle Cheney, *Ginsburg: "Disagreement" Ahead*, POLITICO (June 15, 2012), www.politico.com.

56 Adam Liptak, *How Activist Is the Supreme Court?* N.Y. TIMES (Oct. 12, 2013), www.nytimes.com.

57 576 U.S. 644 (2015).

58 Inae Oh, *Ruth Bader Ginsburg: America Is Ready to Accept a Pro-Gay-Marriage SCOTUS Ruling*, MOTHER JONES (Feb. 12, 2015), www.motherjones.com.

59 142 S. Ct. 2228 (2022).

60 410 U.S. 113 (1973).

61 Richard L. Hasen, *Commentary: Ruth Bader Ginsburg's Slam of Trump Does the Nation No Favors*, REUTERS (July 13, 2016), www.reuters.com.

62 *Id.*

63 Sally Persons, *Ruth Bader Ginsberg: Sexism Played 'Prominent' Role in Hillary Clinton Loss*, WASH. TIMES (Feb. 12, 2018), www.washingtontimes.com.

64 Adam Kilgore, *Justice Ruth Bader Ginsburg Apologizes for Criticism of Colin Kaepernick*, WASH. POST (Oct. 14, 2016), www.washingtonpost.com. Katie Couric later revealed that Justice Ginsburg's negative statements toward Kaepernick and other Black athletes were much harsher than she originally reported and that she (Couric) concealed the full statements in an effort to protect Justice Ginsburg. Aaron Blake, *Katie Couric's Self-defeating Effort to "Protect" Ruth Bader Ginsburg*, WASH. POST (Oct. 14, 2021, 4:58 p.m. EDT), www.washingtonpost.com.

15

Health Law

Equity Is Inextricably Linked to Health Care

TARA SKLAR AND KIRIN GOFF

Throughout her sixty-year legal career as a lawyer, law professor, circuit judge, and Supreme Court Justice, Ruth Bader Ginsburg made many contributions to the evolution of health law jurisprudence. Most notable are her decisions around access to health care services, which carried substantial weight during the landmark Affordable Care Act cases.[1] Specifically, Justice Ginsburg consistently supported Congress's attempts to expand health insurance coverage options and recognize reproductive health needs, including insurance coverage for contraception. Her frequently cited opinions continue to influence her colleagues, the courts, and public opinion in the health law field.

Always a pragmatist, Justice Ginsburg articulated the economic, social, and health consequences that disproportionately impact those with lower socioeconomic status when access to health care is limited, especially among women.[2] Her opinions often addressed how some legal interpretations are grounded in stereotypes about women's physical and mental vulnerabilities, which discriminate against women under the guise of ensuring their protection and safety. She countered these arguments by citing current scientific and economic evidence that demonstrated the opposite—that is, the financial harm and adverse health consequences women face when there are restrictions and cost-related barriers to accessing health care.[3]

Relatedly, Justice Ginsburg was a "living constitutionalist," meaning that, like many liberal judges, she believed that the Constitution should be interpreted within the context of the current era, given that the needs, norms, and values of a society shift dramatically over time. Her writing reflects the view that the text of the Constitution is intentionally broad because the drafters could not conceive of the types of situations that might arise or the way society would be structured in the future. This judicial interpretation aligns with Justice Ginsburg's statements that the Supreme Court of the United States should not drive social change but rather respond to legal and cultural shifts that have already occurred in the broader society.[4] Many of her decisions illustrate a continuous effort to uphold the institutional legitimacy of the Court by both incorporating the realities of the law on people's lives and by prioritizing targeted, incremental change in lieu of sweeping reforms. While she regularly dissented, especially in her later years on the Court, she was conscientious about doing so. Justice Ginsburg knew a unanimous or near-unanimous decision by the Court would carry more authority, but she viewed her dissents as necessary to protect the disenfranchised in future legislation or legal decisions.[5]

While Justice Ginsburg's influence on health law jurisprudence began before she was appointed to the Court, this chapter focuses solely on her tenure as a Supreme Court Justice and proceeds as follows. The first section examines Justice Ginsburg's judicial decisions that highlight how access to health care and affordable health insurance coverage is fundamental to full participation in a democratic society. The second section expands on this concept with two examples in reproductive health—contraception and abortion—as essential health care services for women to exercise control over their reproduction and, ultimately, their destiny. The chapter concludes by recognizing Justice Ginsburg's legacy to health law jurisprudence through her judicial decisions, which continue to shape the inextricable link between access to health care and achieving a more humane and equitable society.

Equity and Access to Health Care

In Justice Ginsburg's view, access to health care is a key determinant of one's ability to live autonomously in society. Therefore, the cases challenging the Patient Protection and Affordable Care Act[6] (ACA) were perhaps the most consequential of her tenure.

The first lawsuits were filed the same day the ACA was signed into law, March 23, 2010,[7] and more lawsuits have been filed challenging the ACA than any other statute in American history.[8] By June 2021, there were nearly 2,000 attempted lawsuits, with six reaching the U.S. Supreme Court.[9] The ACA survives, but together those six cases led to significant alterations of the law.

Justice Ginsburg's participated in three landmark ACA cases: *National Federation of Independent Business v. Sebelius (NFIB)*, which challenged the federal government's mechanism for incentivizing states to expand their Medicaid programs; and *Burwell v. Hobby Lobby* and *Little Sisters of the Poor v. Pennsylvania*, two cases about the ACA requirement to provide contraceptive coverage.[10] Though Justice Ginsburg sided with the majority for some issues in *NFIB*, she wrote a dissenting opinion that admonished the majority for not referring an issue affecting interstate commerce (i.e., health insurance) to Congress.[11] In her *Burwell v. Hobby Lobby* dissent, Justice Ginsburg argued that there is a limit to religious freedom when a private employer refuses to provide health insurance coverage for contraception. She famously stated: "'[y]our right to swing your arms ends just where the other man's nose begins.'"[12]

ACA Overview

The ACA's passage in 2010 was a major turning point for health care in the United States. As a result of the ACA, the percentage of Americans under sixty-five who were uninsured or underinsured was almost cut in half, decreasing from 18 percent in 2010 to 10 percent in 2016.[13] This success was largely due to the implementation of an individual mandate, Medicaid expansion, and the creation of health care exchanges and subsidies.[14] The controversial individual mandate and Medicaid expansion are discussed in detail below. The health care exchanges and subsidies help provide a coverage option for individuals of any income who do not receive health insurance through an employer. The ACA created platforms for these individuals to purchase insurance (through "exchanges") and provided funding to subsidize the cost of insurance for people up to a certain income.

The Individual Mandate

The basic premise of the ACA was modeled after previous proposals that had received bipartisan support, including from Republican leadership.[15] Despite President Obama's effort to build consensus, the legislation lost Republican support, in large part because it included an individual mandate.[16] The individual mandate required all Americans to obtain health insurance or pay a fine (defined as a "penalty"). While unpopular, this mandate was thought to be key to the stability of the statute as a whole because it was a way to provide insurance coverage for those who had been unable to purchase health insurance because of preexisting conditions. The addition of healthy people, who otherwise may forgo health insurance without an individual mandate, would help balance the risk pool and thereby keep health insurance prices stable.[17]

However, within a few months twelve states (later joined by fourteen more states) filed suit in *NFIB*, challenging whether the individual mandate exceeded Congress's constitutional authority.[18] In a 5–4 decision, Justice Ginsburg voted with the majority, including Chief Justice Roberts, to uphold the ACA, although she dissented in part.[19] The legal theory that the majority opinion cited to support the individual mandate was under the Constitution's Taxing and Spending Clause. The penalty was deemed a "tax" permissible under Congress's taxing powers because, despite the term "penalty," the fine was collected similar to a tax via the Internal Revenue Service.[20] Justice Ginsburg dissented and offered alternate legal reasoning via the Commerce Clause as both permissible and more appropriate to uphold the individual mandate. She was joined by Justices Breyer, Kagan, and Sotomayor.[21]

The Constitution grants Congress the power to "regulate Commerce . . . among the several States."[22] Justice Ginsburg cited precedent for the Court to defer to Congress and interpret the Commerce Clause broadly, including even indirect activities that "substantially affect interstate commerce."[23] In contrast, the majority distinguished *NFIB* from precedent by concluding that it compelled a person to engage in commerce.[24] Justice Ginsburg rejected this argument and argued that the individual mandate did not compel engagement because it regulated existing markets that everyone participates in.[25]

Reflective of a living constitutionalist perspective, Justice Ginsburg's dissenting opinion also relied on evidence of the intent behind the Framers' use of broad constitutional language.[26] She criticized the majority for attempting to establish a "technical legal conception," citing cases that discourage this practice in favor of considering the actual effects on interstate commerce.[27] "As our national economy grows and changes, we have recognized, Congress must adapt to the changing 'economic and financial realities.'"[28]

While the majority characterized health care as a hypothetical future purchase, similar to that of a car, Ginsburg insisted that all people eventually need health care: the choice is whether or not to pay for it.[29] She emphasized how unique the health insurance market is and why Congress felt compelled to pass the ACA.[30] She noted that the law was designed to address inequities for certain population groups. In particular, the law was designed to protect those with preexisting conditions, who would otherwise be denied access to affordable health insurance coverage, and address free riders, primarily healthy individuals who do not purchase insurance but who rely on the health care system when needed without a way to adequately pay for care.[31] In practice, the individual mandate survived only for a few more years because Congress changed the penalty amount to $0 in 2017.[32]

Medicaid Expansion

Another controversial aspect of the ACA was the incentives provided for states to expand Medicaid, which was also an issue raised in *NFIB*.[33] Medicaid is a government program that pays for the health care of low-income Americans. It is supported by both federal funding and by individual states. Before the ACA, only specific categories of people were eligible to receive Medicaid.[34] For example, low-income childless adults were largely excluded if they were not pregnant, disabled, or otherwise categorically eligible.[35] The ACA expanded Medicaid to include all low-income individuals.[36]

On the issue of Medicaid in *NFIB*, Justice Ginsburg concurred in part but dissented on the main holding, which made Medicaid expansion optional for the states.[37] Medicaid has always been an optional program for the states, but with the passage of the ACA the federal government provided states with substantial additional funding to expand their respective programs and would cease providing existing federal Medicaid funds to states who chose not to expand.[38] The Court ruled that this action by Congress was unconstitutionally coercive and held that the provision exceeded Congress's power under the Constitution's Spending Clause.[39] This was the first law in American history struck down on the basis of an unconstitutionally coercive conditional federal grant to states.[40] As a result of *NFIB*, states have the option not to expand their Medicaid eligibility, and twelve states still have not done so.[41]

Reproductive Health Autonomy and Equity

A third contested section of the ACA was its requirement for employers to cover contraception. Justice Ginsburg emphasized in her speeches, interviews, and judicial opinions that the economic and social consequences of motherhood are so significant that gender equality cannot be achieved without widespread access to contraception and abortion.[42] A study by Nora Becker and Daniel Polsky published in *Health Affairs* highlighted the success of the ACA in reducing cost-related barriers to contraception, finding that the average out-of-pocket costs for contraception dropped from 21 percent to 3 percent after the ACA took effect.[43]

Two Affordable Care Act cases addressed the contraceptive coverage provision: *Burwell v. Hobby Lobby* in 2014 and *Little Sisters of the Poor v. Pennsylvania* in 2020. Both cases permitted employers to seek religious exemption from the ACA's contraceptive mandate. Justice Ginsburg dissented in both cases.

The ACA includes an exemption so that nonprofit religious groups do not have to provide contraceptive coverage. *Burwell* expanded this to owners of for-profit corporations by holding that the contraceptive mandate violated the rights of a privately held company under the Religious Freedom Restoration Act (RFRA).[44] Hobby Lobby, an arts and crafts company, sued, arguing that the mandate violated the RFRA, which prevents the federal government from "substantially burdening a person's exercise of religion unless the action is the least restrictive means of serving a compelling government interest."[45] The majority relied on precedent that defined corporations as people, since corporations are composed of individuals using the business to meet their goals.[46] The contraception requirement therefore compelled religious people to fund something that contradicts their religious principles or pay significant fines, which in the majority's view created a substantial burden that was not the least restrictive method of satisfying the government's interests.[47]

Justice Ginsburg disagreed. Her dissent was joined in full by Justice Sotomayor and in part by Justices Breyer and Kagan. Justice Ginsburg argued that use of contraceptives is determined by a woman and her health care provider and is thus too far removed from employers for the burden to be considered substantial.[48] Furthermore, even if there was a substantial burden, the contraceptive mandate served a compelling interest that could not be achieved by less restrictive means.[49]

Justice Ginsburg's discussion of equality, access to health care, and economic reality was notably stark when she addressed the gravity of the "compelling interest" that the contraceptive mandate intended to serve.[50] For example, the plaintiffs opposed intrauterine devices (IUDs), a method that is more effective and more expensive than other contraceptive options.[51] But, as Justice Ginsburg noted, "the cost of an IUD is nearly equivalent to a month's full-time pay for workers earning the minimum wage; . . . almost one-third of women would change their contraceptive method if costs were not a factor; and . . . only one-fourth of women who request an IUD actually have one inserted after finding out how expensive it would be."[52]

The majority suggested less restrictive alternatives, such as having the government pay for contraceptives if an employer religiously objects. Justice Ginsburg disagreed, arguing that such an alternative would not adequately serve the compelling interests because it would add bureaucratic obstacles to accessing health care. She explained that "[i]mpeding women's receipt of benefits 'by requiring them to take steps to learn about, and to sign up for, a new [government funded and administered] health benefit' was scarcely what Congress contemplated [in the ACA]."[53]

Finally, her dissent also emphasized that precedent requires any application of the RFRA to consider the impact the religious accommodation would have on others.[54] Here, providing religious accommodation to employers would cause too great a harm to employees who do not share those religious beliefs—in this case the very people the ACA intended to help.[55]

A few years later, the Health Resources and Services Administration (HRSA) carved out broad regulatory exemptions from the contraceptive mandate based on religious objections.[56] Those exemptions were challenged in 2020 in *Little Sisters*.[57] Thus, *Little Sisters* was about the limits of the HRSA's statutory authority.[58]

The text of the ACA does not directly state the contraceptive mandate. Instead, it delegates authority to the HRSA by stating that coverage must include "such additional preventive care and screenings . . . as provided for in comprehensive guidelines supported by the Health Resources and Services Administration."[59] In response to the ACA, the HRSA promulgated interim final rules, which offered guidelines that recommended coverage for all FDA-approved contraceptive methods and sterilization procedures, along with related education and counseling.[60] In addition to identifying preventative services, the HRSA later added religious exemptions to the ACA's coverage requirement.[61] After amending the rules several times in response to contraceptive mandate cases, the HRSA settled on an exemption that allowed qualifying organizations to opt out of the contraceptive mandate. This exemption was at issue in *Little Sisters*. Of note, this exemption went beyond what the majority in *Burwell* suggested the RFRA required because it did not provide for an alternative mechanism for women to access contraception.[62]

The majority opinion in *Little Sisters* was delivered by Justice Thomas, who follows a textual originalist philosophy, under which the focus is on the specific words in the Constitution or statute as they would have been understood by a person at the time it was written.[63] As such, it was a technical opinion, which narrowed in on interpretation of specific words in the text and administrative requirements.[64] For example, citing several dictionaries, he wrote:

> "Our analysis begins and ends with the text." Here, the pivotal phrase is "as provided for." To "provide" means to supply, furnish, or make available. And, as the Departments explained, the word "as" functions as an adverb modifying "provided," indicating "the manner in which" something is done. On its face, then, the provision grants sweeping authority to HRSA to craft a set of standards defining the preventive care that applicable health plans must cover.[65]

In contrast, Justice Ginsburg's dissent (joined by Justice Sotomayor) gave more attention to the underlying subject matter.[66] She disagreed with the majority's interpretation of the words themselves and went further to investigate Congress's intent with regard to the statutory language at issue.[67] For example, the dissent identified the Women's Health Amendment, which cited a brief from members of Congress that specified their intent for the provision to "promote equality in women's access to health care."[68]

Finally, the dissent contended that neither the ACA nor the RFRA provided statutory authority for the religious exemptions.[69] It also emphasized the limitations of the RFRA: the religious exemptions at issue in *Little Sisters* did not provide an alternative means for serving the compelling government interest of providing contraception without cost-sharing.[70] As was her custom throughout her tenure on the Court and in her health law jurisprudence, Justice Ginsburg emphasized in her dissent the real-life impact of the majority's holding on the lives of women, particularly those with limited incomes. She explicitly linked barriers for a woman to control her reproduction with equal participation in economic and social life:

> Ready access to contraceptives and other preventive measures for which Congress set the stage . . . both safeguards women's health and enables women to chart their own life's course. Effective contraception, it bears particular emphasis, "improves health outcomes for women and [their] children," as "women with unintended pregnancies are more likely to receive delayed or no prenatal care."[71]

The Court's decisions in *Burwell* and *Little Sisters* opened the door to agency rules promulgated under President Donald Trump allowing any organization to opt out of the ACA contraception coverage requirement if those companies feel that it violates their religious beliefs or, more broadly, moral convictions.[72] Furthermore, employers no longer need to file for exemption with the Department of Health and Human Services; they simply have to notify their employees of their decision not to provide insurance coverage for contraception.

Abortion

There were three highly influential abortion cases decided while Justice Ginsburg was on the Court. These include two "partial birth abortion" bans addressed in *Stenberg v. Carhart (Carhart I)*[73] and *Gonzales v.*

Carhart (Carhart II),[74] in addition to a Texas law requiring bureaucratic restrictions addressed in *Whole Woman's Health v. Hellerstedt* in 2016.[75]

The major judicial framework of abortion law was established before Justice Ginsburg was appointed to the Court, in *Roe v. Wade*[76] and *Planned Parenthood of Southeastern Pennsylvania v. Casey*.[77] *Roe* famously established abortion before viability as a "right to privacy" under the Fourteenth Amendment, and *Casey* established an "undue burden" standard. The "undue burden" test established that a law was unconstitutional if it had the purpose or effect of placing a substantial obstacle on women seeking abortion before viability.[78] This was the legal theory at issue in *Carhart I* and *Whole Women's Health*.[79]

The first major challenge to abortion rights came seven years into Ginsburg's tenure on the Court via *Carhart I*.[80] In this case, the Court narrowly upheld the precedent set by *Roe* and *Casey* in a 5–4 decision by striking down a Nebraska statute that broadly prohibited certain late-term abortion procedures, deemed "partial birth abortions."[81] The Court determined that the statute was unconstitutional under the due process clause because it did not include an exception for the health of the mother and because outlawing the procedures unduly burdened a women's right to choose abortion.[82] Justice Ginsburg drafted a concurring opinion, where she referenced the expertise of physicians, not the state, to use procedures that physicians within their medical judgment felt was the safest for a particular patient.[83] Her opinion reaffirms the role of the medical community, which also provides optimal protection for women's health in obtaining an abortion.

Seven years later, this holding was tested again in *Carhart II*, which addressed a similar federal law.[84] This time, for the first time since *Roe*,[85] the Court changed course and upheld the statute, reasoning that the Constitution does not require an exception for the health of the mother.[86] The majority relied heavily on the argument that abortion harmed women emotionally.[87] Justice Ginsburg, the only female justice on the Court at the time, dissented, writing:

> "There was a time, not so long ago," when women were "regarded as the center of home and family life, with attendant special responsibilities that precluded full and independent legal status under the Constitution." Those views, this Court made clear in *Casey*, "are no longer consistent

with our understanding of the family, the individual, or the Constitution." Women, it is now acknowledged, have the talent, capacity, and right "to participate equally in the economic and social life of the Nation." Their ability to realize their full potential, the Court recognized, is intimately connected to "their ability to control their reproductive lives." Thus, legal challenges to undue restrictions on abortion procedures . . . center on a woman's autonomy to determine her life's course, and thus to enjoy equal citizenship stature. . . . The Court's hostility to the right *Roe* and *Casey* secured is not concealed.[88]

Another abortion law came before the Court again in 2016, and the majority changed course from *Carhart II*. In *Whole Women's Health*, the Court struck down a Texas law that required abortion clinics to meet certain ambulatory surgical requirements and required any physician who performed an abortion to have admitting privileges at a nearby hospital.[89] Justice Ginsburg sided with the majority and drafted a short concurrence in which she called out the dissent's argument on their claims of protecting women. She clearly stated that these additional requirements on abortion clinics would merely create impediments to abortion, and she also stated that the argument that they would protect women "is beyond rational belief."[90] Justice Ginsburg's opinions on abortion consistently asserted that reproductive autonomy is indispensable to equality and that women's health is a priority in accessing these health care services.

In less than two years after Justice Ginsburg's passing, *Dobbs v. Jackson Women's Health Organization*[91] (*Dobbs*) overturned *Roe* and with that fifty years of precedent by holding that the Constitution does not provide a right to an abortion. The majority's opinion attempted to move the issue to Congress and state legislatures, which has led to states passing laws across the country that either restrict abortion or protect abortion access. Justice Ginsburg's influence remains strong as she was cited no less than six times in *Dobbs* by majority, dissenting, and concurring Justices.[92] The first paragraph in the dissent cites Ginsburg's dissent in *Carhart II* and states: "Respecting a woman as an autonomous being, and granting her full equality, meant giving her substantial choice over this most personal and most consequential of all life decisions."[93] While *Dobbs* ended the constitutional right to an abortion, the courts still must determine the future of these new abortion restrictions emerging across the country. Justice Ginsburg's opinions—her legacy—will continue to carry tremendous weight as the country attempts to navigate this polarizing issue with far-reaching ramifications for future generations.

Conclusion

Justice Ginsburg's legacy to health law jurisprudence created a pathway where men and women could have a better future in which Americans are not denied or discriminated against in their attempts to access health care, including health insurance for contraception and the ability to obtain a legal abortion. She persuasively argued for an equitable and humane society in which everyone can fully participate and includes at its core the ability to access health care, including services for reproductive health.

NOTES

The authors wish to thank The University of Arizona James E. Rogers College of Law's Daniel F. Cracchiolo Law Library, especially Alex Clay Hutchings, who provided excellent legal research assistance. The authors are also grateful to Ryan Vacca and Ann Bartow for their generous editorial support, to Slade Smith for his helpful review, and to Toby Friesen for his valuable insights. Warm appreciation to Elena Marks for her mentorship and friendship and for forging new paths for women to achieve their aspirations in life and work. Many thanks to the University of Arizona Mel & Enid Zuckerman College of Public Health for the invitation to present this work.

1 *See* Nat'l Fed'n of Indep. Bus. v. Sebelius, 567 U.S. 519 (2012); Burwell v. Hobby Lobby Stores, Inc., 573 U.S. 682 (2014); Little Sisters of the Poor Saints Peter & Paul Home v. Pennsylvania, 140 S. Ct. 2367 (2020).

2 *See, e.g., Burwell*, 573 U.S. at 746 (Ginsburg, J., dissenting).

3 *Id.; see also* Whole Woman's Health v. Hellerstedt, 579 U.S. 582 (2016).

4 *See generally* RUTH BADER GINSBURG, WITH MARY HARTNETT & WENDY WILLIAMS, MY OWN WORDS (2016).

5 *Id.*

6 The Patient Protection and Affordable Care Act (PPACA), Pub. L. No. 111–148, 124 Stat. 119 (2010).

7 Abbe R. Gluck, Mark Regan & Erica Turret, *The Affordable Care Act's Litigation Decade*, 108 GEO. L.J. 1471, 1472 (2020).

8 *Id.*

9 National Conference of State Legislatures, *Legal Cases and State Legislative Actions Related to the ACA*, www.ncsl.org.

10 *NFIB*, 567 U.S. 519; *Burwell*, 573 U.S. 682; *Little Sisters*, 140 S. Ct. 2367.

11 *NFIB*, 567 U.S. at 589 (Ginsburg, J., concurring in part and dissenting in part).

12 *Burwell*, 573 U.S. at 739 (Ginsburg, J., dissenting, quoting Zechariah Chafee, *Freedom of Speech in War Time*, 32 HARV. L. REV. 932, 957 (1919)).

13 Rachel Garfield et al., *The Uninsured and the ACA: A Primer—Key Facts About Health Insurance and the Uninsured Amidst Changes to the Affordable Care Act*, THE KAISER FAMILY FOUNDATION (Jan. 5, 2019), www.kff.org; Julie Rovner, *Republicans Spurn Once-Favored Health Mandate*, NAT'L PUB. RADIO (Feb. 15, 2010), www.npr.org (listing several Republican U.S. senators who had supported similar proposals).

14 The Patient Protection and Affordable Care Act (PPACA), Pub. L. No. 111–148, 124 Stat. 119 (2010); Matthew Fiedler, *The ACA's Individual Mandate in Retrospect: What Did It Do, and Where Do We Go from Here?* 39.3 HEALTH AFFAIRS 429–35 (2020); George L. Wehby and Wei Lyu, *The Impact of the ACA Medicaid Expansions on Health Insurance Coverage through 2015 and Coverage Disparities by Age, Race/Ethnicity, and Gender.* 53.2 HEALTH SERVICES RESEARCH 1248–71 (2018); David Jones, Sarah Gordon and Nicole Huberfeld, *Have the ACA's Exchanges Succeeded? It's Complicated.* 45 J. HEALTH POL., POL'Y & L. 661–76 (2020).

15 *See* Arthur Nussbaum, *Can Congress Make You Buy Health Insurance? The Affordable Care Act, National Health Care Reform, and the Constitutionality of the Individual Mandate*, 50 DUQ. L. REV. 411, 457 (2012).

16 *See* Julie Rovner, *Republicans Spurn Once-Favored Health Mandate*, NAT'L PUB. RADIO (Feb. 15, 2010).

17 *See* Ilya Somin, *A Mandate for Mandates: Is the Individual Health Insurance Case a Slippery Slope?*, 2012 LAW & CONTEMP. PROBS. 75, 92–93.

18 *NFIB*, 567 U.S. 519.

19 *Id.* at 519.

20 *Id.* at 539, 588.

21 *Id.* 519.

22 U.S. CONST. art. I § 8, cl. 3.

23 *NFIB*, 567 U.S. at 536.

24 *Id.* at 550–55.

25 *Id.* at 604.

26 *Id.* at 600–01.

27 *Id.* at 612.

28 *Id.* at 617.

29 *Id.* at 609–10.

30 *Id.* at 590–91.

31 *Id.* at 593–99.

32 Budget Fiscal Year, 2018, Pub. L. No. 115–97, December 22, 2017, 131 Stat. 2054; 26 U.S.C. § 5000A.

33 *NFIB*, 567 U.S. at 593–99.

34 42 U.S.C. § 1396.

35 *Id.*

36 *NFIB*, 567 U.S. at 519.

37 *Id.* at 589.

38 *Id.* at 541–42, 576–77.

39 *Id.* at 588.

40 Henry J. Kaiser Family Foundation, *A Guide to the Supreme Court's Decision on the ACA's Medicaid Expansion*, www.kff.org.

41 Kaiser Family Foundation, *Status of State Medicaid Expansion Decisions: Interactive Map*, www.kff.org.

42 *See generally* GINSBURG, et al., MY OWN WORDS.

43 Nora Becker & Daniel Polsky, *Women Saw Large Decrease in Out-of-Pocket Spending for Contraceptives After ACA Mandate Removed Cost Sharing*, HEALTH AFFAIRS, www.healthaffairs.org.

44 *Burwell*, 573 U.S. at 688 (citing 42 U.S.C. § 2000bb *et seq.*).

45 *Id.* at 694 (citing 42 U.S.C. § 2000bb).

46 *Id.*

47 *Id.* at 728–29.

48 *Id.* at 760.

49 *Id.*

50 *Id.*

51 *Id.*

52 *Id.* at 762 (internal citations omitted).

53 *Id.* at 765–66.

54 *Id.* at 764.

55 *Id.*

56 82 Fed. Reg. 47812.

57 Little Sisters of the Poor Saints Peter & Paul Home v. Pennsylvania, 140 S. Ct. 2367 (2020).

58 *Id.* at 2379.

59 42 U.S.C. § 300gg–13(a)(4).

60 77 Fed. Reg. 8725 (2012).

61 78 Fed. Reg. 39871 (2013); 78 Fed. Reg. 39873.

62 *See Burwell*, 573 U.S. at 731–32.

63 BLACK'S LAW DICTIONARY (11th ed. 2019) (definition of "textualism" and "originalism"); Lee J. Strang, *The Most Faithful Originalist? Justice Thomas, Justice Scalia, and the Future of Originalism*, 88 U. DET. MERCY L. REV. 873 (2011).

64 *Little Sisters*, 140 S. Ct. 2367.

65 *Id.* at 2380 (internal citations omitted).

66 *Id.* at 2400.

67 *Id.* at 2400–06.

68 *Id.* at 2402 (citing § 300gg–13(a)(4) and Brief for 186 Members of the United States Congress as *Amici Curiae* 6).

69 *Id.* at 2406–09.

70 *Id.* at 2403, 2406–09.

71 *Id.* at 2402.

72 *See, e.g.,* Religious Exemptions and Accommodations for Coverage of Certain Preventive Services Under the Affordable Care Act, 82 Fed. Reg. 47792 (Oct. 13, 2017) (encoded at 45 C.F.R. § 147.133).

73 530 U.S. 914 (2000).

74 Gonzales v. Carhart, 550 U.S. 124 (2007).

75 Whole Woman's Health v. Hellerstedt, 579 U.S. 582 (2016), *as revised* (June 27, 2016).

76 Roe v. Wade, 410 U.S. 113 (1973).

77 Planned Parenthood v. Casey, 505 U.S. 833 (1992).

78 *Id.* at 878.

79 *See id.* at 874; Stenberg v. Carhart, 914 U.S. at 945; *Whole Woman's Health,* 579 U.S. at 607–08.

80 *Stenberg,* 530 U.S. 914 (2000).

81 *Id.* at 929–30.

82 *Id.* at 930.

83 *Id.* at 951–52.

84 *Gonzales,* 550 U.S. at 132.

85 *Id.* at 171 (Ginsburg, J., dissenting).

86 *Id.* at 133.

87 *Id.* at 159.

88 *Id.* at 171–86.

89 *Whole Woman's Health,* 579 U.S. at 591.

90 *Id.* at 627–28.

91 Dobbs v. Jackson Women's Health Org., 142 S. Ct. 2228 (2022).

92 *Id.* at 2312, 2317, 2318–19, 2241, 2345–46, 2279 (2022).

93 *Id.* at 2317 (2022) (Breyer, Sotomayor, and Kagan, JJ., dissenting).

16

Patent Law

A Reliable Compass

W. KEITH ROBINSON

During her time on the Supreme Court, Justice Ruth Bader Ginsburg participated in over forty patent cases. In the intellectual property field, Justice Ginsburg is best known for her support for strong copyright protection. But very little has been written about Justice Ginsburg's views on patent law. In analyzing her opinions and votes in patent cases, several themes emerge, which help paint a clearer picture of the Justice's patent law jurisprudence.

Justice Ginsburg avidly supported innovation. She expressed support for the role small businesses play in shielding innovators from personal risk, rejected imprecision in interpreting patenting requirements, and cautioned that such imprecision could lead to uncertainty and discourage innovation.

Yet Justice Ginsburg did not let her support of innovation override other considerations. Her opinions evidence strong support for due process and statutory interpretation. She admonished lower courts for "forecasting" how Congress might adjust the law to address a novel issue instead of leaving perceived loopholes for the legislature to address. Justice Ginsburg carefully delineated the roles of the judicial and legislative branches and rejected invitations to weaken unpopular patent legislation from the bench.

This chapter is organized into two sections. The first describes the specific legal issues within patent law that were most affected by Justice Ginsburg's writings. Throughout her career, Justice Ginsburg's opinions addressed several important patent law topics, including extraterritoriality, claim definiteness, the doctrine of equivalents, patent exhaustion, and inequitable conduct. Toward the end of her career, she also helped the court wrestle with important constitutional questions raised by inter partes review.

The second section uncovers broader themes that emerge from Justice Ginsburg's decisions. These themes provide additional perspective on the values underlying the Justice's patent law jurisprudence. It concludes by summarizing Justice Ginsburg's impact on patent law. The changes in patent law during her time on the Court presented complex legal questions. Justice Ginsburg's jurisprudence provided the patent system's stakeholders with a reliable compass to navigate the choppy waters of innovation.

The Targeted Patent Jurisprudence of Justice Ginsburg

Due to the length of her career, Justice Ginsburg had the opportunity to hear several important patent cases that touched on a variety of topics. Among her later opinions, she authored a majority opinion and a dissent in two cases concerning inter partes review. Other areas where Justice Ginsburg's writings remain influential concern the concepts of extraterritoriality and patent exhaustion. Her dissent in 2017's *Impression Products, Inc. v. Lexmark International, Inc.*[1] is often discussed in patent and intellectual property casebooks and treatises. This section discusses the patent topics most influenced by Justice Ginsburg's opinions, dissents, and concurrences.

Institution of Inter Partes Review

Toward the end of her tenure on the Supreme Court, Justice Ginsburg heard several cases about inter partes review (IPR). IPR is a procedure that allows the United States Patent and Trademark Office (USPTO) to review the validity of issued patents. The purpose of IPR is to provide a way for parties to challenge the validity of earlier granted patents outside the U.S. district courts.[2] IPR was designed to be cheaper and faster than district court litigation.

The statute specifies the details of the IPR process. Any person other than the patent owner may petition for IPR. In the petition, challengers must specify which patent claims they are requesting be reviewed. Under the IPR process, the validity of claims can be challenged only on certain grounds. If there is a reasonable likelihood of success that a claim may be canceled on these grounds, the director of the USPTO determines whether to institute an IPR.[3] The decision to institute an IPR is not appealable.[4] Once IPR is instituted, the challenger and the patent owner can present written arguments to the Patent Trial and Appeal Board (PTAB). The parties have the opportunity for a hearing in which they present oral arguments before the PTAB. Finally, the PTAB issues a decision on the merits as to whether the challenged claims should be cancelled.

Since its inception, IPR has been controversial. Some patentees viewed the process as fundamentally unfair. A former chief judge of the United States Court of Appeals for the Federal Circuit, Randall Rader, once referred to the PTAB as a "death squad killing property rights."[5] Others have applauded IPR as a way to eliminate low-quality patents without expensive district court litigation.[6]

In many instances, the IPR process has yielded bad outcomes for patent owners. In response, the constitutionality of the IPR process has come under attack. In 2018, the Supreme Court upheld the constitutionality of the IPR process under Article III of the Constitution in a 7–2 majority decision joined by Justice Ginsburg.[7] However, the following two important cases heard by Justice Ginsburg focused on statutory questions surrounding the institution of IPR.

The Scope of Inter Partes Review

In *SAS Institute, Inc. v. Iancu*, the Supreme Court was asked to resolve a dispute concerning the scope of IPR. Specifically, the question was: "When the Patent Office initiates an inter partes review, must it resolve all of the claims in the case, or may it choose to limit its review to only some of them?"[8]

SAS petitioned the USPTO to review a software patent owned by ComplementSoft. The petition alleged that all of the claims in the patent (sixteen in total) were invalid.[9] Because it believed SAS was likely to succeed with respect to at least one claim, the PTAB instituted review of the patent.

However, the PTAB instituted only a partial review. That is, instead of reviewing all sixteen claims SAS had specified, the PTAB authorized review of only claims 1 and 3–10.[10] The PTAB's final decision invalidated claims 1, 3, and 5–10 and found claim 4 to be patentable. But because it did not institute review of claims 2 and 11–16, it made no decision about these claims.

SAS appealed, arguing that the PTAB should have instituted review of all the challenged claims (1–16).[11] The Federal Circuit disagreed. On review, the Supreme Court reversed the decision of the Federal Circuit.[12]

Justice Gorsuch authored the majority opinion of the Court. He declared that SAS was entitled to a decision on all the claims it challenged in its petition.[13] Relying on the absence of any affirmative statutory text, the majority rejected the argument of the USPTO that the director had the power of "partial institution."[14] Further, the Court found that section 314(a) and section 318(a) of the statute did not give the director partial institution power.[15]

Justices Breyer and Ginsburg dissented. Both Justices agreed with the USPTO that it would be more efficient to allow the director to decide which claims would be worthy of the PTAB's time to review.[16] Relying on Chevron, Justice Breyer argued that the director should have the power to institute review of some of the claims challenged by the petitioner.[17]

Justice Ginsburg's short dissent endorsed Justice Breyer's approach. She labeled the majority's reading of the statute as wooden and argued that the agency should be able to determine how best to efficiently resolve the matter.[18] Justice Ginsburg also suggested that the majority's opinion could lead to unintended consequences that would make IPR more burdensome: the director, faced with a decision to institute review of all challenged claims, could decide to reject the entire petition and signal to the petitioner that a more tailored petition challenging fewer claims could be instituted.[19]

Based on her dissent, Justice Ginsburg seemed to be aware that IPR, though it was unpopular among some patent stakeholders, was also useful in eliminating bad patents. If followed, her dissent would make the procedure easier for the USPTO and make IPRs more palatable for patentees forced to defend the validity of their patent claims.

Appealing the Decision to Institute an Inter Partes Review

Justice Ginsburg's desire for efficiency prevailed in *Thryv, Inc. v. Click-To-Call Technologies LP*. This case concerned the statutory bar on review of the USPTO's IPR institution decisions.[20] Specifically, the Court was asked whether institution decisions challenged under section 315(b) are also barred under section 314(d). Under section 315(b), a challenger may petition the USPTO to review a patent in an IPR proceeding if the petition is filed within one year of an infringement complaint being filed in district court. Petitions filed more than one year after a filed complaint are barred.

Relying on an infringement lawsuit that was filed but voluntarily dismissed without prejudice in 2001, Click-To-Call argued that Thryv's 2013 petition for inter partes review was barred by section 315(b).[21] The PTAB disagreed and instituted review on the grounds that section 315(b) did not prevent it from doing so.[22] On appeal, Click-To-Call argued that the PTAB's decision to institute based on section 315(b) should be appealable. The Federal Circuit decided that the time-bar issue raised by Click-To-Call was appealable and held that the PTAB's decision to institute review was in error.[23] The court concluded that "the 2001 infringement complaint, though dismissed without prejudice, started the one-year clock under § 315(b)."[24]

On review, the Supreme Court was tasked with determining whether "§ 314(d)'s bar on judicial review of the agency's decision to institute inter partes review preclude[d] Click-to-Call's appeal."[25] The Court held that the USPTO's determination of whether a petition was barred under section 315(b) was closely related to the institution decision and therefore was not appealable.[26] Writing for the majority, Justice Ginsburg explained that section 314(d) prevented a party from arguing on appeal that the PTAB should not have instituted an inter partes review.[27]

Relying on the Court's decision in *Cuozzo Speed Technologies, LLC v. Lee*,[28] Justice Ginsburg stated that the bar on the appealability of the institution decision extended to any issue closely related to the decision to institute an IPR.[29] Thus, Justice Ginsburg reasoned that if the decision to institute took into consideration the particularity requirement of section 312(a)(3) addressed in *Cuozzo*, then it must also take into account the time bar articulated in section 315(b).[30]

Similar to her dissent in *SAS*, Justice Ginsburg's opinion reflected her understanding that the purpose of the IPR procedure was to eliminate bad patents.[31] In her view, allowing appeals related to section 315(b) would potentially save bad patents from review on the merits. Her majority opinion also asserted that the statute was constructed in such a way that an evaluation of the patent on its merits should take precedence over the section 315(b) timeliness requirement.[32] The *Thryv* opinion also echoes her call in *SAS* for efficiency. Specifically, her opinion argues that allowing appeals related to section 315(b) would be a waste of the USPTO's resources.

Extraterritoriality and Patent Exhaustion

U.S. patent law is territorial in nature. U.S. patent rights cannot be enforced in foreign countries. There are, however, certain provisions in the Patent Act governing conduct in foreign countries. In other contexts, Justice Ginsburg opposed giving similar statutes governing international activity exorbitant extraterritorial effect.[33] Similarly, Justice Ginsburg's patent opinions evidence her reluctance to expand the reach of patent law beyond U.S. borders.[34]

For example, in *Microsoft Corp. v. AT&T Corp.*, the Supreme Court was tasked with interpreting section 271(f) of the Patent Act. Section 271(f) characterizes the supply of a patented invention's components for combination abroad as infringement.[35] AT&T asserted that Microsoft infringed its patent by shipping to foreign countries a master disk containing software that, when installed on computers, infringed its patents. In defense, Microsoft argued that *copies* of the master disk software were installed on foreign computers and therefore Microsoft did not supply a component for combination abroad within the meaning of section 271(f).

The Supreme Court decided that Microsoft was not subject to liability under section 271(f).[36] Writing for the majority, Justice Ginsburg rejected AT&T's argument that software in the abstract qualified as a component.[37] She reasoned that software in the abstract did not become a component capable of being combined with a computer, for example, until the software existed on a physical medium such as a CD-ROM.[38] Justice Ginsburg agreed with Microsoft that the copies of the software installed on computers built abroad were not "components" under section 271(f). Further, relying on the presumption against extraterritoriality, Justice Ginsburg suggested that AT&T's only recourse would be to enforce foreign patents against Microsoft in the countries where the alleged infringing activities took place.[39]

The presumption against extraterritorially was also a theme in Justice Ginsburg's well-reasoned dissent in *Impression Products, Inc. v. Lexmark International, Inc.*, discussed in an earlier section. There, the Court addressed the issue of whether a foreign sale of a patented invention exhausted its patent rights in the United States.[40] The doctrine of patent exhaustion prohibits a patent owner from exercising control over a patented product through patent law once she has sold that product.[41]

There were different views on how the doctrine should apply based on whether the sale occurred domestically or abroad. Concerning domestic patent exhaustion, Justice Ginsburg agreed with her fellow Justices that patent rights were exhausted when the patented product was sold within U.S. borders despite the existence of any contractual restrictions surrounding the sale. However, her views differed with respect to international exhaustion.[42]

Impression Products was the second case in which Justice Ginsburg disagreed with the Court's move toward a principle of "international exhaustion."[43] The majority held that an authorized sale of a product outside the United States could exhaust those rights in the patent under U.S. law.[44] In her dissent, Justice Ginsburg argued that a foreign sale should not exhaust an inventor's U.S. patent rights.[45] Her approach tracked her reasoning in *Kirtsaeng v. John Wiley & Sons, Inc.*, where Justice Ginsburg argued that a foreign sale of a book should not exhaust U.S. copyright protection in that book.[46] In *Impression Products*, she reasoned that it made little sense for one type of sale abroad to implicate U.S. patent law while another did not. That is, if a competitor could sell a product abroad without infringing a U.S. patent, then an authorized sale abroad should not exhaust the patentee's U.S. patent rights.[47] In her view, both Supreme Court decisions departed from the policy position of the United States that an international exhaustion regime was against the country's economic interests.[48]

Claim Definiteness

Justice Ginsburg authored an important majority opinion on claim definiteness. The patent statute requires that a patent's claims particularly point out and distinctly claim "the subject matter which the applicant regards as his invention."[49] Under this statute, a court can invalidate a claim for lack of definiteness.

In *Nautilus, Inc. v. Biosig Instruments, Inc.,*[50] writing for the Court, Justice Ginsburg rejected the Federal Circuit's "insolubly ambiguous" standard for definiteness in favor of a more general framing. The Federal Circuit's test, she opined, failed to serve as a good guide for lower courts and the patent bar. She remarked that the Federal Circuit test fell short of providing a "reliable compass."[51]

Having explained the shortcomings of the Federal Circuit's rule, Justice Ginsburg described a test more probative of the central inquiry. She held that "a patent is invalid for indefiniteness if its claims, read in light of the specification delineating the patent, and the prosecution history, fail to inform, with reasonable certainty, those skilled in the art about the scope of the invention."[52] One rationale for this finding was to enable lower courts to apply a clear test. Justice Ginsburg also made clear that in order to foster innovation the impreciseness of the Federal Circuit's "insolubly ambiguous" test must be rejected. In articulating the Supreme Court's new test, Justice Ginsburg emphasized that clarity in the claims is absolutely required even if absolute precision is unattainable.

Her opinion recognized that the law must balance two competing concerns.[53] On the one hand, too strict a standard could stifle innovation. On the other, claim language serves an important public notice function: alerting the public to what the inventor has claimed. To balance these concerns, Justice Ginsburg's opinion mandated clarity in defining the scope of the invention with reasonable certainty.[54]

The Doctrine of Equivalents

Justice Ginsburg also authored a notable concurrence in a case concerning the doctrine of equivalents. The judicially created doctrine allows the scope of patent claims to be expanded beyond their literal scope to capture infringement where an infringing activity or device is insubstantially different—that is, "if there is 'equivalence' between the elements of the accused product or process and the claimed elements of the patented invention."[55] In *Warner-Jenkinson Co., Inc. v. Hilton Davis Chemical Co.*, the Court adopted the all-elements rule for applying the doctrine of equivalents, which required that infringement under the doctrine of equivalents must be established by an element-by-element comparison of the claims.[56]

The Court also confirmed that the doctrine of equivalents is limited by prosecution history estoppel. Prosecution history estoppel prevents a patentee from applying the doctrine of equivalents to subject matter that was amended during prosecution for reasons related to patentability. In *Warner-Jenkins*, the Supreme Court established a rebuttable presumption that claim amendments made during prosecution were made for reasons related to patentability. The Court placed the burden on the patent holder to establish a reason "sufficient to overcome prosecution history estoppel as a bar to application of the doctrine of equivalents to the element added by that amendment."[57]

Justice Ginsburg, joined by Justice Kennedy, authored a concurrence to guide lower courts in application of the new rule.[58] Justice Ginsburg seemed concerned with how application of the rebuttable presumption articulated by the Court might unfairly disadvantage patent holders that had already completed patent prosecution.[59] Prior to the Court's opinion, these patentees would not be aware of the "clear rules of the game"—the need to establish evidence that could overcome the presumption that any claim amendments made during prosecution were for reasons related to patentability.[60] She warned that lower courts, such as the Federal Circuit, might disadvantage some patent holders if they did not take a patentee's lack of notice into account.[61] In doing so, Justice Ginsburg provided a road map for fair treatment of the litigants and other patent owners in doctrine of equivalents cases.

The Patent System and Justice Ginsburg

This section examines Justice Ginsburg's involvement with patent law from a thematic perspective. From her opinions, we can glean insight into what Justice Ginsburg thought about the patent system. Broader themes of promoting innovation, fairness, efficiency, and preserving the separation of powers permeate her decisions.

Innovation

Justice Ginsburg strongly supported innovation. For example, Justice Ginsburg's opinions reinforce the notion that bad patents stifle U.S. innovation. In *Thryv*, Justice Ginsburg argued that allowing section 315(b) untimeliness appeals would save bad patents, since the only reason a party might appeal under section 315(b) was because its claims were invalidated for reasons related to patentability.[62] Her support for the IPR process as a way to rid the patent system of innovation stifling patents is also on display in her dissent in *SAS*. There, Justice Ginsburg argued that the director of the USPTO should be able to determine which challenged claims would be worthy of review by the PTAB. In doing so, the PTAB would use its resources more efficiently to review the most problematic claims.

Justice Ginsburg also opposed patenting technologies that she viewed as not innovative. She sided with a faction within the Supreme Court that did not believe business methods should be patentable. She, along with Justices Stevens, Breyer, and Sotomayor, argued that U.S. patent law excluded business methods from being patented.[63] Presumably, she and other members of the Court believed that allowing patent rights to exist in "processes for organizing human activity" stifled innovation.[64]

Justice Ginsburg advocated for legal clarity as a way to promote innovation. She rejected imprecision in interpreting patenting requirements. She cautioned that such imprecision could lead to uncertainty and discourage innovation.[65] Accordingly, writing for the majority in *Nautilus*, Justice Ginsburg replaced the Federal Circuit's "insolubly ambiguous" test for claim indefiniteness with the "reasonable certainty" test.[66] She thought that legal formulations should promote certainty, not confusion.[67] Still, her written opinions recognized that "absolute precision" with respect to patent standards were beyond the reach of the Court.[68]

Finally, in one of her earlier Supreme Court opinions involving patents, Justice Ginsburg expressed support for the role small businesses play in shielding innovators from personal risk.[69] In *Nelson v. Adams USA, Inc.*, the patents at issue were owned by a one-person corporation.[70] Nelson was the sole shareholder of the patent owner, OCP.[71] OCP sued Adams for allegedly infringing two patents.[72] The district court dismissed the infringement complaint and granted Adams's motion for attorney fees and costs because Nelson's actions during prosecution of the patents constituted inequitable conduct.[73] Since it knew OCP was insolvent, Adams moved to add Nelson as a party to the suit.[74] The district court granted Adams's motion and simultaneously amended the judgment to make Nelson liable for attorney fees and costs due to Adams.[75] The Federal Circuit affirmed.[76]

On appeal, Justice Ginsburg found that the district court improperly amended its judgment by immediately subjecting Nelson to liability without an opportunity to respond.[77] The Justice went on to explain that the Federal Rules of Civil Procedure require that an adverse party be given an opportunity to respond after being added to a litigation.[78] Despite the fact that the insolvent OCP was a one-person corporation, Justice Ginsburg wrote that due process required that Nelson have an opportunity to respond.[79] She noted that, "where patents are concerned, the one-person corporation may be an altogether appropriate means to permit innovation without exposing inventors to possibly ruinous consequences."[80] In doing so, Justice Ginsburg's opinion reaffirmed the fundamental importance of due process and highlighted the importance of corporate structure to innovation.

Fairness

Justice Ginsburg's desire for fairness is illustrated in her concurrence in *Warner-Jenkins*. The majority opinion announced how two complex patent doctrines—the doctrine of equivalence and prosecution history estoppel—interact. In sum, prosecution history estoppel limits the scope of how broadly the doctrine of equivalents can be applied.[81]

The majority opinion announced that there was a rebuttable presumption that any amendments made during the prosecution of a patent were done for reasons related to patentability. Accordingly, a patentee could not use the doctrine of equivalents to expand the scope of its claims to include the subject matter surrendered by claim amendments unless the patent owner presented evidence to overcome the presumption.

Since the Court was announcing this presumption for the first time, Justice Ginsburg authored a concurrence discussing how the presumption might be applied on remand.[82] Based on the record, it was unclear to the Court why the patentee made specific amendments to the claims.[83] However, the majority's newly fashioned rebuttable presumption necessitated that if the patent owner wanted to assert its doctrine of equivalents argument it had to provide evidence that the amendment in question was not made for reasons related to patentability. Justice Ginsburg warned the lower court against the wooden application of the rebuttable presumption. She noted that at the time of prosecution the patentee would not have had notice of the rebuttable presumption.[84] Justice Ginsburg urged the lower court to take into account the absence of "clear rules of the game."[85] In doing so, Justice Ginsburg advocated for a common-sense application of the law that did not unfairly disadvantage patent owners.

Efficiency

Justice Ginsburg's opinions evidence a preference for efficiency in the administration of justice. Despite controversy surrounding inter partes review, she supported the process and opposed policies making IPR less efficient. In *Thryv*, Justice Ginsburg argued that allowing section 315(b) untimeliness appeals would effectively waste the USPTO's time and resources by possibly resurrecting claims that the PTAB has already reviewed and canceled.[86] Justice Ginsburg also thought that the director should have the discretion to institute partial review of challenged patent claims in an IPR. She agreed that partial institution would allow the PTAB to avoid wasting time on the consideration of less important claims.[87] In the alternative to instituting a review of all the challenged claims in an IPR, Justice Ginsburg suggested, the director might simply reject a petition while also signaling to the petitioner that a more narrowly tailored petition challenging fewer claims might be acceptable.[88] In sum, Justice Ginsburg advocated for reading the statutes related to IPR in a way that would not waste the PTAB's time and would foster the goals the statutory scheme was enacted to achieve.[89]

Separation of Powers

Finally, Justice Ginsburg carefully delineated the roles of the judicial and legislative branches. She rejected invitations to weaken unpopular patent legislation from the bench. While sympathetic to the confusion and potential problems that legal loopholes cause, Justice Ginsburg declined to use the Court's power of judicial interpretation to close them.[90] That, she said, was the job of Congress. In *Microsoft*, she declined AT&T's request to broaden the scope of activities giving rise to liability under section 271(f). This problem, Justice Ginsburg opined, should be solved with "focused legislative consideration" and not by the Court.[91]

Conclusion

Justice Ginsburg made important contributions to patent law. Her opinions addressed key substantive areas of patent law such as inter partes review, extraterritoriality, patent exhaustion, claim definiteness, and the doctrine of equivalents. Notably, Justice Ginsburg argued for interpreting the law such that foreign activity did not diminish domestic intellectual property rights.

Justice Ginsburg's patent opinions also exhibit her jurisprudential values. She was a fierce advocate for fairness. Justice Ginsburg carefully delineated between the Court's role and what tasks were better left to Congress. She also favored legal interpretations that promoted efficiency and legal clarity.

Overall, Justice Ginsburg's actions on the Court indicate a pro-innovation posture. She understood that the primary purpose of the patent system was to incentivize U.S. innovation. As a member of the Court during one of its most active periods in patent law, she sought clear and efficient ways for the law to support the goals of the patent system.

NOTES

1 137 S. Ct. 1523 (2017).
2 See *Thryv, Inc v. Click-To-Call Techs., LP*, 140 S. Ct. 1367, 1370 (2020).
3 *SAS Inst., Inc. v. Iancu*, 138 S. Ct. 1348, 1356 (2018) (explaining that the language of the statute requires likelihood of success on one claim to review them all).
4 *Thryv*, 140 S. Ct. at 1370.
5 AIPLA Annual Meeting, October 2013.
6 See *Thryv*, 140 S. Ct. at 1374 (stating that one purpose of IPR was to weed out bad patents claims).
7 *Oil States Energy Servs., LLC v. Greene's Energy Grp., LLC*, 138 S. Ct. 1365 (2018). After Justice Ginsburg's death, the IPR process survived another more success-

ful constitutional challenge under the Appointments Clause. The Supreme Court held that authority of Administrative Patent Judges is incompatible with their appointment by the Secretary to an inferior office. However, the Court noted that the constitutional violation could be remedied by severing the invalidated portion of the statute to permit direct review of IPR decisions by the director of the USPTO. United States v. Arthrex, Inc., 141 S. Ct. 1970 (2021).

8 *SAS Inst.*, 138 S. Ct. at 1352–53.
9 *Id.* at 1354.
10 *Id.*
11 *Id.*
12 *Id.* at 1360.
13 *Id.* at 1359.
14 *See id.* at 1355.
15 *See id.* at 1357.
16 *See id.* at 1364 (Breyer, J., dissenting).
17 *See id.* at 1360 (Breyer, J., dissenting).
18 *See id.* (Ginsburg, J., dissenting).
19 *See id.*
20 *See* 35 U.S.C. § 314(d).
21 *Thryv*, 140 S. Ct. at 1371.
22 *Id.* at 1372.
23 *Id.*
24 *Id.*
25 *Id.* at 1370.
26 *Id.*
27 *Id.* at 1373.
28 136 S. Ct. 2131 (2016).
29 *See Thryv*, 140 S. Ct. at 1373.
30 *See id.* at 1375 (interpreting the statute such that section 314 encompasses decisions made under section 315).
31 *See id.* at 1374 (arguing that section 315(b) appeals would save bad patents).
32 *See id.* (arguing that timeliness issues do not take precedent over decisions on the merits regarding patentability).
33 *See* Pasquantino v. United States, 544 U.S. 349, 372 (2005) (Ginsburg, J., dissenting); *see also* Kirtsaeng v. John Wiley & Sons, Inc., 568 U.S. 519, 557 (2013) (Ginsburg, J., dissenting).
34 *See* Microsoft Corp. v. AT&T Corp., 550 U.S. 437, 454–55 (2007).
35 *Id.* at 441.
36 *Id.*
37 *See id.* at 448.
38 *See id.* at 449–50 (explaining that code by itself is not a component).
39 *See id.* at 457 (stating "[i]f AT&T desires to prevent copying in foreign countries, its remedy today lies in obtaining and enforcing foreign patents").

40 *See* Impression Prods., Inc. v. Lexmark Intern., Inc., 137 S. Ct. 1523, 1529 (2017).

41 *See id.*

42 *See id.* at 1538 (Ginsburg, J., concurring in part and dissenting in part).

43 *Kirtsaeng*, 568 U.S. at 557 (Ginsburg, J., dissenting).

44 *See Impression Products*, 137 S. Ct. at 1535 (concluding that foreign sales exhaust patent rights in the United States).

45 *See id.* at 1538.

46 *See Kirtsaeng*, 568 U.S. at 557 (Ginsburg, J., dissenting).

47 *See Impression Products*, 137 S. Ct. at 1538. (arguing that a foreign sale of a patented product "should not diminish the protections of U.S. law in the United States").

48 *See Kirtsaeng*, 568 U.S. at 575–77 (Ginsburg, J., dissenting) (asserting that the U.S. government has taken positions on the international stage that are consistent with a national exhaustion position).

49 35 U.S.C. § 112, ¶ 2.

50 Nautilus, Inc. v. Biosig Instruments, Inc., 572 U.S. 898 (2014).

51 *Id.* at 912.

52 *See id.* at 901.

53 *See id.* at 909–10.

54 *See id.* at 910.

55 Warner-Jenkinson Co., Inc. v. Hilton Davis Chem. Co., 520 U.S. 17, 21 (1997).

56 *See id.* at 29.

57 *See id.* at 33–34 (explaining that prosecution history estoppel is a limit on the doctrine of equivalents).

58 *See id.* at 41 (Ginsburg, J., concurring).

59 *See id.*

60 *See id.* at 42.

61 *See id.* at 41.

62 *See Thryv*, 140 S. Ct. at 1374.

63 *See* Bilski v. Kappos, 561 U.S. 593, 613 (2010) (Stevens, J., concurring, joined by Ginsburg, J., Breyer, J., and Sotomayor, J.).

64 *See* Alice Corp. Pty. Ltd. v. CLS Bank Intern., 573 U.S. 208, 227 (2014) (Sotomayor, J., concurring, joined by Ginsburg, J., and Breyer, J.).

65 *Nautilus*, 572 U.S. at 911.

66 *See id.* at 910.

67 *See id.* at 911.

68 *See id.* at 899.

69 Nelson v. Adams USA, Inc., 529 U.S. 460, 471 (2000).

70 *See id.* at 463.

71 *Id.*

72 *Id.*

73 *Id.*

74 *Id.* at 463–64.

75 *Id.* at 464.

76 *Id.*
77 *See id.*
78 *See id.* at 466.
79 *See id.* at 469 (explaining that Nelson should be afforded the opportunity to respond).
80 *Id.*
81 *See Warner-Jenkinson*, 520 U.S. at 33–34.
82 *See id.* at 41 (Ginsburg, J., concurring).
83 *See id.* at 32.
84 *See id.* at 41 (Ginsburg, J., concurring).
85 *Id.* at 42.
86 *See Thryv*, 140 S. Ct. at 1374.
87 *See SAS Institute*, 138 S. Ct. at 1360 (Ginsburg, J., dissenting).
88 *See id.*
89 *See id.*
90 *See Microsoft*, 550 U.S. at 457.
91 *See id.* at 459.

17

Race and the Law

From Consensus-Seeker to Critic

VINAY HARPALANI AND JEFFREY D. HOAGLAND

Justice Ruth Bader Ginsburg is certainly known as an advocate for gender equality, but by the end of her life she was nearly as famous for writing pointed Supreme Court dissents that underscored America's continuing racial inequities. Older generations might remember her as a cofounder of the Women's Rights Project at the ACLU. She played an integral role in *Reed v. Reed*[1]—the first U.S. Supreme Court case to apply the Fourteenth Amendment's Equal Protection Clause to gender classifications. But younger activists know her best as "The Notorious R.B.G."[2]—a moniker given to her after her vociferous dissent in *Shelby County v. Holder*,[3] in which she championed racial justice and criticized the Court for ignoring America's history of racism.

Justice Ginsburg's race jurisprudence illustrates a nuanced, evolving approach to issues of equality. She spent much of her career as a legal advocate arguing against use of putatively benign gender classifications. But during her tenure on the Supreme Court, she opined that benign racial classifications should be used for remedial purposes. Justice Ginsburg long recognized the different measures needed to attain gender versus racial equality. In a 1978 law review article titled "Some Thoughts on Benign Classification in the Context of Sex," she noted that "it takes no buses to put boys and girls together in the same classroom."[4] The Court ultimately rejected her views, applying intermediate scrutiny to gender classifications and strict scrutiny in assessment of all racial classifications.[5]

Nevertheless, there is little doubt that Justice Ginsburg's jurisprudence has been influential in driving the public discourse on the law's treatment of race. Her race jurisprudence is characterized by both consistency and change. From a doctrinal and analytic standpoint, Justice Ginsburg's opinions on race were relatively consistent during her time on the Supreme Court. She accepted the Court's view that government use of race should always be scrutinized carefully, but her perspective was more nuanced. She conceived of strict scrutiny as applied to racial classifications differently than the other Justices. For Justice Ginsburg, the "searching inquiry" that strict scrutiny requires was a first step—a means to sort invidious and benign racial classifications so that courts could strike down the former and allow remedial justifications for the latter. Although she purportedly adopted elements of the anticlassification view of race-based equal protection, her race jurisprudence decidedly espoused an antisubordination perspective—one that underscored the need for acknowledgment of both the history of racism and its continuing effects in the world today.[6] And she consistently called for candor and transparency both in acknowledging racism and in race-conscious government policies designed to address it.

But while Justice Ginsburg's race jurisprudence was doctrinally and analytically consistent throughout her tenure, the tone of her opinions changed. The manner in which she expressed her views evolved dramatically, as she went from emphasizing common ground to articulating pointed critiques of the Court. Her initial opinions, such as the dissent in *Adarand v. Pena*[7] and the concurrence in *Grutter v. Bollinger*,[8] highlighted agreement with the Court's majorities, even as she espoused different views and provided independent analyses of the cases. But Justice Ginsburg's later dissents—particularly those in *Ricci v. Destefano*[9] and *Shelby County v. Holder*—were starkly critical of her fellow Justices who refused to acknowledge racism and the inequalities it created. While her earlier opinions did point to racial inequality, they did so in a general fashion, without delving much into the particular facts of the cases. Conversely, her *Ricci* and *Shelby County* dissents chastised the Court's majority and concurring opinions for ignoring specific facts in the cases and neglecting the long history of racism that established the context for them.

Throughout her transformation from consensus-seeker to critic, Justice Ginsburg's call for candor and her articulation of the antisubordination stance were invaluable. At a time when the Supreme Court grew increasingly hostile to race-conscious policies and curbed the gains of the civil rights era, she became an ardent purveyor of the antisubordination view of race-based equal protection. To be sure, Justice Ginsburg's legacy on race is not without flaws. She missed opportunities to address racial inequities in the criminal justice system, and her public comments on protests against police brutality did not resonate well. Nevertheless, her overall record reflects an individual who championed racial justice, perhaps limited only by the gaps in her own experiences.

Consensus-Seeker

Justice Ginsburg began articulating her race jurisprudence with her dissent in *Adarand v. Pena*. In *Adarand*, the Court struck down financial incentives offered by the federal government for the employment of subcontractors from racial minority groups. *Adarand* was the first case in which the Court ruled that strict scrutiny applied to all racial classifications. It overturned the Court's 1990 ruling in *Metro Broadcasting, Inc. v. FCC*,[10] which had applied intermediate scrutiny to racial classifications by the federal government and limited strict scrutiny to racial classifications by state and local governments.

Justice Ginsburg's dissent affirmed the application of strict scrutiny's "searching inquiry" into racial classifications. She drew upon her experience as an advocate for gender equity:

> Properly, a majority of the Court calls for review that is searching, in order to ferret out classifications in reality malign, but masquerading as benign. The Court's once lax review of sex-based classifications demonstrates the need for such suspicion.[11]

But it is clear that Justice Ginsburg's call here was not an attempt to eliminate government use of race altogether. She emphasized that strict scrutiny need not be "fatal in fact."[12] Rather, she wanted courts to identify and strike down those racial classifications that were "masquerading as benign" so that government could indeed pursue remedial classifications designed to uplift historically oppressed groups. Early in her dissent, she noted explicitly that courts should give "large deference" to legislatures on matters that involve addressing "historic racial subjugation."[13]

Justice Ginsburg's *Adarand* dissent articulates America's history of racism in ironic fashion. She cites Justice John Marshall Harlan's dissent in *Plessy v. Ferguson*[14]—an opinion that has long been revered by advocates of racial justice and viewed as ahead of its time. But Justice Ginsburg cites Justice Harlan to show that even an "advocate of a 'color-blind' Constitution" believed that

> [t]he white race deems itself to be the dominant race . . . [a]nd so it is, in prestige, in achievement, in education, in wealth and in power . . . [and] . . . I doubt not, it will continue to be for all time, if it remains true to its great heritage and holds fast to the principles of constitutional liberty.[15]

Here, Justice Ginsburg subtly asserted that the "color-blind" jurisprudence of anticlassification could not remedy racial inequality and was not even intended to do so. She reinforced this view by highlighting continuing racial disparities, noting that "job applicants with identical resumes . . . still experience different receptions, depending on their race"; that "White and African-American consumers still encounter different deals"; and that racial minorities "still face discriminatory treatment by landlords, real estate agents, and mortgage lenders."[16] She then brought this theme to bear on the issue at hand: "Minority entrepreneurs sometimes fail to gain contracts though they are low bidders, and . . . are sometimes refused work even after winning contracts."[17]

But Justice Ginsburg also sought to forge consensus on the Court. In rare form for a dissent, her *Adarand* opinion noted that she "write[s] separately to underscore not the differences" but rather "the considerable field of agreement—the common understandings and concerns—revealed in the opinions."[18] She cited the majority's acknowledgement of "[t]he unhappy persistence of both the practice and the lingering effects of racial discrimination against minority groups in this country."[19] Justice Ginsburg also quoted Justice Scalia's constitutional ideal that "we are just one race,"[20] though she did so to gently point out that America has not lived up to this ideal.[21] From the dissents by Justices Stevens and Souter, Justice Ginsburg cited the principle that courts should defer significantly to "Congress' institutional competence and constitutional authority to overcome historic racial subjugation."[22] She noted that even the majority acknowledged that Congress has "authority to act affirmatively, not only to end discrimination, but also to counteract discrimination's lingering effects."[23]

Justice Ginsburg continued her attempt to find some level of common ground with her concurrence in *Grutter v. Bollinger*.[24] Here, Justice O'Connor's majority opinion upheld the University of Michigan School of Law's race-conscious, holistic admissions policy, which used race as one flexible factor in conjunction with individualized review of an applicant's entire set of credentials.[25] Justice Ginsburg concurred largely to respond to Justice O'Connor's expectation "that 25 years from now, the use of racial preferences will no longer be necessary."[26] She began on a conciliatory note, noting that the majority's "observation that race-conscious programs 'must have a logical end point' . . . accords with the international understanding of affirmative action."[27] She even added to this point, quoting the International Convention on the Elimination of All Forms of Racial Discrimination, which holds that race-conscious policies "shall in no case entail as a consequence the maintenance of unequal or separate rights for different racial groups after the objectives for which they were taken have been achieved."[28]

However, while she affirmed the principle behind Justice O'Connor's twenty-five-year aspiration, Justice Ginsburg's point here was again to call into question its real-world application. She cited several studies that found that the vast majority of Black and Latina/o K-12 students attended predominantly minority schools and that such schools "lag far behind others measured by the educational resources available to them."[29] In accordance with Justice O'Connor, Justice Ginsburg acknowledged that some minority students succeed in spite of these barriers and that the number of high-achieving minority students will likely continue to increase.[30] But Justice Ginsburg was clear that "one may hope, but not firmly forecast, that over the next generation's span, progress toward nondiscrimination and genuinely equal opportunity will make it safe to sunset affirmative action."[31]

Simultaneous to *Grutter*, the Supreme Court struck down the race-conscious admissions policy of the University of Michigan College of Literature, Science, and the Arts (LSA) in *Gratz v. Bollinger*.[32] Unlike the Law School policy upheld in *Grutter*, the LSA policy used an inflexible, mechanical point system that awarded the same number of points to all underrepresented minority applicants. Justice Ginsburg dissented in *Gratz*, once again referencing strict scrutiny. But rather than emphasizing commonality with the Court' majority, she began to articulate where she believed the Court was wrong:

> [T]he Court once again maintains that the same standard of review controls judicial inspection of all official race classifications. This insistence on "consistency" would be fitting were our Nation free of the vestiges of rank discrimination long reinforced by law[.] But we are not far distant from an overtly discriminatory past, and the effects of centuries of law-sanctioned inequality remain painfully evident in our communities and schools.[33]

She noted that the reason for applying strict scrutiny to race is not because it "is inevitably an impermissible classification, but because it is one which usually, to our national shame, has been drawn for the purpose of maintaining racial inequality."[34] Justice Ginsburg again showed how her view of strict scrutiny differs from the majority. For her, it was a threshold inquiry to eliminate invidious racial classifications, not to preclude benign ones.

Justice Ginsburg then applied her view to the LSA's race-conscious admissions policy. She noted that the groups who benefited from the policy—Black Americans, Latina/os, and Indigenous Peoples—all suffered historic and current discrimination. She also noted that there was no indication that the LSA adopted the policy to limit the enrollment of any racial or ethnic groups and that the policy did not significantly limit the admission of any groups who are not advantaged by it.[35]

Also notable about Justice Ginsburg's *Gratz* dissent was her call for transparency about race-conscious policies. She observed that colleges and universities "may resort to camouflage" by using information from applicants' names, minority student group affiliations, and admissions essays as proxies for race.[36] She asserted that, "[i]f honesty is the best policy, surely Michigan's accurately described, fully disclosed College affirmative action program is preferable to achieving similar numbers through winks, nods, and disguises." Her concern portended the claims of future litigants who have challenged race-conscious admissions policies.[37]

In fact, far before Justice O'Connor's twenty-five-year prognostication in *Grutter*, the Supreme Court heard another challenge to race-conscious university admissions in *Fisher v. University of Texas at Austin* (*Fisher I*).[38] The issue in *Fisher I* revolved around Texas's Top Ten Percent Law,[39] which guaranteed admission to the University of Texas at Austin (UT) to the top students in the graduating classes of every Texas high school.[40] Because many Texas high schools have an overwhelming majority of Black and Latina/o students, this law increased racial diversity at UT. The Texas state legislature adopted the Top Ten Percent Law after the Fifth Circuit's decision in *Hopwood v. Texas*,[41] which precluded the use of race-conscious admissions. *Hopwood* was later abrogated by *Grutter*, and UT reinstated a race-conscious admissions policy for a small percentage of its admitted class, in addition to the Top Ten Percent Law that admitted the majority of the class automatically. The petitioner in *Fisher I* argued that UT could not use the race-conscious policy because the Top Ten Percent Law itself gave UT a racially diverse enough student body. *Fisher I* led to a 7–1 ruling remanding the case for proper application of strict scrutiny.[42]

The lone dissenter was Justice Ginsburg. Her nuanced view of strict scrutiny remained consistent and guided her conclusion. She concluded that the lower courts had properly applied strict scrutiny and that UT's admissions policy should be upheld. She reiterated her view, brought forth several times in prior opinions, that "actors, including state universities, need not be blind to the lingering effects of 'an overtly discriminatory past,' the legacy of 'centuries of law-sanctioned inequality.'"[43] But Justice Ginsburg also acknowledged the deceptive nature of the petitioner's argument. Although the Top Ten Percent Law did not explicitly consider race, relying only on the class rank of students, she contended that "only an ostrich could regard the [Top Ten Percent Law] as race unconscious."[44] She pointed out that the Texas legislature enacted the law "with racially segregated neighborhoods and schools front and center stage[,]" citing the law's legislative history.[45] She made clear her view that "[i]t is race consciousness, not blindness to race, that drives such plans."[46] And reiterating her *Gratz* dissent, Justice Ginsburg asserted that transparency and openness about the use of race was preferable to "deliberate obfuscation."[47]

By the time of *Fisher I*, Justice Ginsburg had moved away from her earlier consensus-seeking on issues of race. But even as a lone dissenter, she tried to find some common ground with the other Justices. She cited Justice Souter's *Gratz* dissent to augment her point about transparency. She also stated that the *Fisher I* majority "rightly declines to cast off the equal protection framework settled in *Grutter*," although she critiques the other Justices for "stop[ping] short of reaching the conclusion that framework warrants."[48]

The Court eventually upheld UT's race-conscious admissions policy in *Fisher v. University of Texas at Austin II*.[49] Justice Ginsburg did not opine in that case.

Critic

Although most of her opinions on race involved affirmative action cases, the culmination of her race jurisprudence came with two dissenting opinions in cases involving other issues: *Ricci*, a Title VII employment discrimination case; and *Shelby County*, a voting rights case.

It was her dissents in these cases that most prominently brought out Justice Ginsburg the critic. Her prior noted opinions were all less than 1,500 words, with *Adarand* and *Fisher I* less than 800. But her *Ricci* and *Shelby County* dissents were both close to 10,000 words long. And unlike her prior opinions, Justice Ginsburg delved into detail about the history, context, and specific facts of each case.

Ricci pitted the city of New Haven, Connecticut, against its own firefighters. To select lieutenants and captains for its fire department, New Haven administered an exam to current firefighters and promoted those who scored the highest. But when the highest scorers did not include Black and Latina/o firefighters, the City discarded the exam results, claiming that it could face Title VII disparate impact liability. In turn, the White firefighters who had scored the highest and stood to be promoted filed a Title VII disparate treatment lawsuit, alleging that New Haven's decision to discard the exam results intentionally discriminated against them. In a 5–4 ruling, the Supreme Court sided with the White firefighters, requiring New Haven to either reinstate the exam results or face a disparate treatment lawsuit.

Justice Ginsburg's dissent was direct and pointed. She stated bluntly that "the Court's recitation of the facts leaves out important parts of the story," noting that "[f]irefighting is a profession in which the legacy of racial discrimination casts an especially long shadow."[50] She cited a 1971 U.S. Commission on Civil Rights report finding that police and fire departments have "barriers to equal employment . . . greater than in any other area of State and local government."[51] Justice Ginsburg also pointed out that "nepotism or political patronage" by government employers had "served to entrench preexisting hierarchies."[52] She noted how decades of Title VII litigation opened up firefighting to members of racial minority groups,[53] and she lamented how the Court now decreed that New Haven's population, which was nearly 60 percent Black and Latina/o, would have few or no members of these groups among the leadership of its fire department.[54]

Justice Ginsburg's opinion laid out the many flaws in New Haven's procedure for devising the promotion exam. She also noted that exam preparation materials were expensive and hard to obtain and that

[w]hile many [White] applicants could obtain materials and assistance from relatives in the fire service, the overwhelming majority of minority applicants were "first-generation firefighters" without such support networks.[55]

Justice Ginsburg continued her insistence on highlighting past and present racial inequities—but with greater detail and specificity to the case at bar than in her prior opinions. She also posited an alternative remedy: she noted that Bridgeport, Connecticut, used a different exam process that yielded fair representation of underrepresented groups for promotion.[56] She gave a long history of Title VII disparate impact litigation to show how its purpose was to open up opportunities for such groups.

Justice Ginsburg fully displayed her shift from consensus-seeker to critic in the last section of her dissent, where she lambasted Justice Alito's concurrence. Justice Alito, who was then in his third full term on the Court, stated that

a reasonable jury could find that the City's asserted reason for scrapping its test—concern about disparate-impact liability—was a pretext and that

the City's real reason was illegitimate, namely, the desire to placate a politically important racial constituency [Black residents].[57]

In response, Justice Ginsburg highlighted Justice Alito's selective use of
facts. She asserted that "Justice Alito compounds the Court's error,"[58] and
she referred to his analysis as a "truncated synopsis" that "exaggerate[d]
the influence of [certain] actors" and ignored "testimony [that] raised substantial doubts about the exams' reliability."[59] She accused Justice Alito
of selectively citing "statement[s] displaying an adversarial zeal" and
"discount[ing] . . . sworn statements" that contradicted his position.[60]

Justice Ginsburg further explained that "Justice Alito's analysis contains a more fundamental flaw: It equates political considerations with
unlawful discrimination."[61] Her critique of Justice Alito here displayed a
marked shift from the consensus she tried to frame in her *Adarand* dissent fourteen years earlier.

This shift reached its apogee with *Shelby County*, Justice Ginsburg's
final opinion that dealt directly with race. Section 5 of the Voting Rights
Act of 1965 (VRA) required certain jurisdictions that had a history of
restricting the ability to vote to obtain federal permission (known as
"preclearance") to implement any legislation affecting voting rights or
practices. Section 4 of the VRA provided the formula to determine
which jurisdictions were covered by section 5's preclearance requirement. This formula has not been updated since 1972 but had been continuously reauthorized by Congress, most recently in 2006.

In *Shelby County*, the Court struck down section 4 by a 5–4 vote, holding that the coverage formula was outdated. It ruled that Congress's 2006
reauthorization of the coverage formula was perfunctory and that Congress had not done any new investigation to see if preclearance was still
necessary. This ruling also effectively rendered section 5 useless. Subsequently, many states implemented voter identification laws[62] along with
other measures that restricted voting.[63] Such restrictions have even more
salience after false claims of voter fraud in the 2020 presidential election.

Justice Ginsburg penned a blistering dissent that essentially laid out
the entire history of voter suppression and voting rights in America—a
history she accused the majority of ignoring. Her opinion was filled with
a variety of metaphors and allusions. She noted how, after ratification of
the Fourteenth and Fifteenth Amendments, nineteenth and early twen-

tieth century attempts to combat voter suppression of African Africans "resembled battling the Hydra,"[64] with states enacting different types of discriminatory laws. Not only did states deny African Americans access to the polls; they also enacted "second-generation barriers" such as racial gerrymandering, vote dilution through at-large voting, and selective annexation to manipulate electoral districts.[65]

Justice Ginsburg described how the Court initially did not intervene and treated voter suppression as a political problem to be resolved by the legislature or executive. This was reflected through cases such as *Giles v. Harris*.[66] Even after the Court shifted course and began to protect voting rights, Justice Ginsburg discussed how "Congress learned from experience that laws targeting particular electoral practices or enabling case-by-case litigation were inadequate"[67] for addressing voter suppression. She described how the VRA "became one of the most consequential, efficacious, and amply justified exercises of federal legislative power in our Nation's history."[68] By "address[ing] the combination of race discrimination and the right to vote, which is 'preservative of all rights,'"[69] the VRA was "the remedy that proved to be best suited to block [voting] discrimination."[70]

Justice Ginsburg also detailed Congress's extensive examination of voter suppression not only when the VRA was passed but at many subsequent junctures. Even though it "recogniz[ed] that large progress has been made, Congress determined, based on a voluminous record, that the scourge of discrimination was not yet extirpated."[71] Justice Ginsburg was critical of how "the Court dismissively brushes off arguments based on 'data from the record.'"[72] She stated pointedly that "[o]ne would expect more from an opinion striking at the heart of the Nation's signal piece of civil-rights legislation."[73]

Justice Ginsburg further noted how Congress found that even the progress in diminishing voter suppression came about precisely because of the VRA.[74] She lamented the "sad irony of today's decision lies in its utter failure to grasp why the VRA has proven effective."[75] Responding to the majority's contention that "history did not end in 1965," she quoted William Shakespeare's *The Tempest*—"what's past is prologue"[76]—and George Santayana's *The Life of Reason*—"[t]hose who cannot remember the past are condemned to repeat it."[77] In perhaps the most recognized quote of her dissent, Justice Ginsburg pointedly asserted that "[t]hrowing out preclearance when it has worked and is continuing to work to stop discriminatory changes is like throwing away your umbrella in a rainstorm because you are not getting wet."[78]

At many other places in her dissent, Justice Ginsburg took sharp aim at the majority. She concluded that "the Court errs egregiously,"[79] and far from her initial consensus-seeking, Justice Ginsburg's culminating opinion on race flatly stated that "[h]ubris is a fit word for today's demolition of the VRA."[80]

Blind Spots

Despite her keen attention to American racism past and present, there were areas where Justice Ginsburg seemed to have blind spots. She missed opportunities to address racial bias in the criminal justice system. For example, Justice Ginsburg wrote the 8–1 majority opinion in *Perry v. New Hampshire*,[81] which opened the door for admission of racially biased eyewitness testimony. In *Perry*, a witness called the police to report that a Black man was breaking into cars at her apartment complex.[82] When questioned, the witness pointed from her window and identified Barion Perry, who was standing in the parking lot next to a police officer.[83] However, a month later, that same witness could not identify Perry in a photo array.[84] Perry moved to suppress the evidence, claiming that a highly suggestive one-person "show up" identification would violate due process.[85] But Justice Ginsburg's majority opinion rejected his claim and allowed the eyewitness testimony. The wider implications of the case are troubling, as studies have shown that white individuals have difficulty positively identifying members of other races.[86]

Justice Ginsburg also joined an 8–1 majority in *Heien v. North Carolina*,[87] where the Court ruled that the Fourth Amendment does not protect against searches based on mistaken police stops. In that case, the police pulled over a car that had one broken taillight because the officer believed this violated a traffic law.[88] While North Carolina law requires only one taillight be working, the Supreme Court held that this was a reasonable mistake of law and thus qualified as a reasonable suspicion, justifying the stop under the Fourth Amendment.[89] This decision gave even more leeway to police officers conducting preemptive stops.[90]

In both *Perry* and *Heien*, Justice Sotomayor was the lone dissenter. Justice Ginsburg did join Parts I, II, and III of Justice Sotomayor's dissent in *Utah v. Strieff*,[91] where the Court limited the exclusionary rule for evidence obtained during illegal police stops. But she did not join Part IV of Justice Sotomayor's dissent—which cited Black scholars regarding the history of racism and racial inequities in the criminal justice system and some have said reads like a "Black Lives Matter Manifesto."[92]

This was not the only time that Justice Ginsburg was unsympathetic to the Black Lives Matter movement. In 2016, she publicly criticized demonstrators across the country who were protesting police brutality against African Americans. These demonstrators had been inspired by the former San Francisco 49ers quarterback Colin Kaepernick to kneel when the national anthem was played at sporting events. Justice Ginsburg referred to those demonstrations as "dumb," "disrespectful," "stupid," and "arrogant."[93] Although she tried to walk back those comments, it was later revealed that she had stated that the demonstrators showed "contempt for a government that has made it possible for their parents and grandparents to live a decent life."[94]

Justice Ginsburg's blind spot might be attributed to gaps in her own experiences. During the oral arguments in *Safford Unified School District v. Redding*,[95] a case involving the strip search of a female middle school student, some of the other Justices seemed to minimize the humiliation felt by the student. Conversely, Justice Ginsburg said pointedly of her fellow Justices: "They have never been a 13-year-old girl . . . [i]t's a very sensitive age for a girl[] . . . I didn't think that my colleagues, some of them, quite understood."[96] But in declining to join Justice Sotomayor's dissents—particularly Part IV of the *Strieff* dissent—and in criticizing the Black Lives Matter movement, Justice Ginsburg herself may not have "quite understood" how Black Americans feel when stopped by the police. While she was aware of past and present racism and concerned about it, her perspective was academic rather than experiential. And this may have also affected her professional relationships: during her entire career as a judge, she hired only two Black law clerks.[97]

Nevertheless, Justice Ginsburg's attunement to racial inequities was unusual on the Court during her tenure, surpassed only by Justice Sotomayor. Overall, her legacy on the Court is of one who championed racial justice as best she understood it and who was willing to be a consensus-seeker or a critic to bring light to it. Although her race jurisprudence was almost always expressed in the Court's minority, Justice Ginsburg's dissenting opinions will long resonate for racial justice advocates.

NOTES

1 404 U.S. 71 (1971). Justice Ginsburg helped to write appellant Sally Reid's brief, and she recognized Pauli Murray, a Black civil rights activist, as a co-author of the brief.

2 IRIN CARMON & SHANA KNIZHNIK, NOTORIOUS RBG: THE LIFE AND TIMES OF RUTH BADER GINSBURG (2015).

3 570 U.S. 529 (2013).

4 Ruth Bader Ginsburg, *Some Thoughts on Benign Classifications in the Context of Sex*, 10 CONN. L. REV. 813, 814 (1978).

5 Craig v. Boren, 429 U.S. 190 (1976); City of Richmond v. J.A. Croson Co., 488 U.S. 469 (1989).

6 The anticlassification view holds that equal protection should serve to eliminate or reduce use of race or gender classifications themselves, while the antisubordination view holds that equal protection should serve to prevent subordination of vulnerable groups rather than eliminate classifications. *See generally* Reva Siegel, *From Colorblindness to Antibalkanization: An Emerging Ground of Decision in Race Equality Cases*, 120 YALE L.J. 1278 (2011); Owen Fiss, *Groups and the Equal Protection Clause*, 5 PHIL. & PUB. AFF. 107 (1976).

7 Adarand Constructors, Inc. v. Peña, 515 U.S. 200 (1995).

8 539 U.S. 306 (2003).

9 557 U.S. 557 (2009).

10 497 U.S. 547 (1990).

11 *Adarand*, 515 U.S. at 275 (internal citations omitted).

12 *Id.*

13 *Id.* at 271.

14 Plessy v. Ferguson, 163 U.S. 537, 552 (1896).

15 *Adarand*, 515 U.S. at 272 (quoting *Plessy*, 163 U.S. at 559).

16 *Id.* at 273.

17 *Id.*

18 *Id.* at 271.

19 *Id.* at 272.

20 *Id.*

21 *Id.*

22 *Id.* at 271.

23 *Id.* at 273.

24 *Grutter*, 539 U.S. at 344–46.

25 *Id.*

26 *Id.* at 343.

27 *Id.* at 344.

28 *Id.* (quoting Annex to G. A. Res. 2106, 20 U. N. GAOR Res. Supp (No. 14) 47, U. N. Doc. A/6014, Art. 2(2) (1965)).

29 *Id.* at 345.

30 *Id.* at 346.

31 *Id.*

32 Gratz v. Bollinger, 539 U.S. 244 (2003).

33 *Id.* at 298 (internal citations omitted).

34 *Id.* at 301.

35 *Id.* at 303 (citing Goodwin Liu, *The Causation Fallacy:* Bakke *and the Basic Arithmetic of Selective Admissions*, 100 MICH. L. REV. 1045, 1049 (2002)).

36 *Id.* at 304.

37 Vinay Harpalani, *Asian Americans, Racial Stereotypes, and Elite University Admissions*, 102 B.U. L. REV. 233 (2022).

38 Fisher v. University of Texas, 570 U.S. 297 (2013).

39 Tex. Educ. Code § 51.803 (1997).

40 *Id.*

41 Hopwood v. Texas, 78 F.3d 932 (5th Cir. 1996).

42 *See Fisher*.

43 *Id.* at 336.

44 *Id.*

45 *Id.*

46 *Id.*

47 *Id.* at 335 (citing *Gratz*, 539 U.S. at 297–98 (2003) (Souter, J., dissenting)).

48 *Id.* at 337.

49 579 U.S. 365 (2016).

50 Ricci v. DeStefano, 557 U.S. 557, 609 (2009).

51 *Id.* at 610.

52 *Id.*

53 *Id.* at 608.

54 *Id.* at 609.

55 *Id.* at 613–14.

56 *Id.*

57 *Id.* at 597.

58 *Id.* at 639.

59 *Id.* at 639–40.

60 *Id.*

61 *Id.* at 642.

62 Ian Weiner, *It's Been 8 Years Since* Shelby County v. Holder. *Congress Needs to Restore the Full Protections of the Voting Rights Act*, Lawyers' Committee for Civil Rights Under Law (June 25, 2021), www.lawyerscommittee.org.

63 Catalina Feder and Michael G. Miller, *Voter Purges After Shelby*, 48 AM. POLITICS RESEARCH 687 (2020).

64 Shelby County v. Holder, 570 U.S. 529, 560 (2013).

65 *Id.* at 563–64.

66 *Id.* at 561.

67 *Id.*

68 *Id.* at 562.

69 *Id.* at 566.

70 *Id.* at 560.

71 *Id.* at 559.

72 *Id.* at 580.

73 *Id.*

74 *Id.* at 575.

75 *Id.* at 592.

76 *Id.* at 576 (quoting W. Shakespeare, The Tempest, act 2, sc. 1).

77 *Id.* (quoting G. Santayana, The Life of Reason 284 (1905)).

78 *Id.* at 590.

79 *Id.* at 594.

80 *Id.* at 587.

81 565 U.S. 228 (2012).

82 Lisa Kern Griffin, *Barriers to Entry and Justice Ginsburg's Criminal Procedure Jurisprudence* in The Legacy of Ruth Bader Ginsburg (Scott Dodson ed. 2015).

83 *Id.* at 105.

84 *Id.*

85 *Id.*

86 Margaret A. Hagen and Sou Hee Yang, *Criminal Defendants Have a Due Process Right to an Expert on Eyewitness Reliability: Why the Court Was Wrong in* Perry v. New Hampshire, 26 S. Cal. Interdisc. L.J. 47 (2016).

87 574 U.S. 54 (2014).

88 Kit Kinports, Heien's *Mistake of Law*, 68 Ala. L. Rev. 121, 125 (2016).

89 *Id.* at 126.

90 *Id.*

91 136 S. Ct. 2056 (2016). Justice Ginsburg also joined Justice Sotomayor's pointed dissent in *Schuette v. Coalition to Defend Affirmative Action*, 572 U.S. 291 (2014), where the Court upheld Michigan's state constitutional ban on race-conscious policies.

92 Marshall Project, *RBG's Mixed Record on Race and Criminal Justice*, Sept. 23, 2020, www.themarshallproject.org.

93 David Zirin, *Ruth Bader Ginsburg Could Not Be More Wrong About Colin Kaepernick*, Nation (Oct. 12, 2016), www.thenation.com.

94 Bruce C. T. Wright, *Examining Justice Ruth Bader Ginsburg's Complicated Legacy on Race*, NEWSONE (Oct. 14, 2021), https://newsone.com.

95 557 U.S. 364 (2009).

96 Joan Biskupic, *Ginsburg: Court Needs Another Woman*, USA Today (May 5, 2009), http://usatoday30.usatoday.com.

97 Wright, *Ginsburg's Complicated Legacy on Race.*

18

Remedies

Justice Ginsburg's Restrained Theory of Remedial Equity

TRACY A. THOMAS

Equity is the power of a court to achieve justice by compelling parties to correct private and public wrongs.[1] Justice Ruth Bader Ginsburg's legacy of remedial equity, perhaps surprisingly, reveals a moderate in liberal's clothing. Her decisions on remedial equity show a tension between the progressive embrace of change that animated her gender equality activism and her deep respect for the limited function of the courts.

Justice Ginsburg came to remedies law early, teaching the course and writing in the field during her pretenure years as a professor specializing in civil procedure.[2] As a judge, she initially leaned toward a broad, flexible, idealized view of a court's equitable power to make systemic change. However, as her tenure on the Supreme Court lengthened, so did her willingness to accept a more limited, restrained role for judicial change and the need, sometimes, to sacrifice remedies for rights.

Ginsburg's theory of remedial equity was driven by three key principles: flexibility over formalism; institutionalism; and judicial restraint. Her emphasis on flexibility expressed a broad, historic notion of "doing equity" as part of a court's mission. This caused her to clash in dissent with the growing conservative formalism of her colleagues, an approach that narrowed the role of equity and its related remedies.

Yet Justice Ginsburg also fashioned her remedial jurisprudence to be most concerned with the institution. Whether she was considering the institutional actor's ability to effect normative social change or the need to defer to that institution's political or functional role, she prioritized the role of that institution over the individual. Finally, Ginsburg's moderate proceduralist view of the courts led her to a position of judicial restraint for remedies.[3] She emphasized pragmatic concerns and accepted minimalist remedies in order to achieve and then protect the more expansive merits rules she sought. Overall, these three principles—flexibility, institutional focus, and judicial restraint—worked together to support her long game: changing the underlying substantive law and social norms.

All three of Justice Ginsburg's principles of remedial equity came together in one of her last great authored majority opinions in *Sessions v. Morales-Santana*.[4] The opinion reads as Ginsburg's swan song to gender equality, retracing and reiterating the leading sex discrimination cases she shepherded as an attorney and judge.[5] The case concerned birthright citizenship for foreign-born children acquired through a parent under the Immigration and Nationality Act when one parent is a U.S. citizen and the other a citizen of another nation. Within its text, Congress established gendered rules for derivative citizenship to children "born out of wedlock" based on whether they were claiming citizenship through their mother or father.[6] There was a much shorter prebirth U.S. residence rule for mothers (one year continuous residence) than for fathers (initially ten years, then five years, total periods of residence including two years after age fourteen).[7] Congress's gendered distinction was based on historical stereotypical assumptions about mothers, believing that an unwed mother would be directly involved in a child's life and caretaking but that most unmarried fathers would not.[8]

Justice Ginsburg declared that the gender line that Congress drew was incompatible with the Fifth Amendment's requirement that the government accord to all persons the equal protection of the laws. She observed that the Court viewed with suspicion laws that rely on "overbroad generalizations about the different talents, capacities, or preferences of males and females," and she wrote that no important government interest was served by laws that position unwed fathers as less qualified and entitled than mothers to take responsibility for nonmarital children.[9] Ginsburg's progressive opinion on the merits was lauded for its reinforcement of the Supreme Court's body of law on equal protection for gender distinctions, an issue that had dominated Ginsburg's career and contribution to the law. It was joined by Chief Justice Roberts and Justices Kennedy, Breyer, Sotomayor, and Kagan; Justice Thomas filed an opinion concurring in part, which Justice Alito joined.[10]

However, the opinion in *Morales-Santana*, shockingly, did not award the actual plaintiff any relief at all. Ginsburg did not apply the shorter one-year rule to fathers but instead extended the longer five-year rule to mothers.[11] Her remedy not only failed to help the individual plaintiff but affirmatively reached out to impose harm on women. Rather than "leveling up" the unequal gendered statuses by extending the statutory benefit to the excluded group, she solved the formal equal protection problem through what commentators called the "mean remedy" of making it harder for all parents.[12] She was content to award relief that simply stopped the government's gender-differentiated treatment prospectively. This focus aligned with her broader concerns of changing systemic norms and social stereotypes of women but seemed to abandon her lifelong commitment to reconstructing norms of masculine caregiving or broader visions of equality.[13] This paradoxical result, however, can be better understood when examined in light of the three key principles of flexibility, institutionalism, and restraint that drove Justice Ginsburg's remedial jurisprudence.

Flexibility Over Formalism

Justice Ginsburg's theory of remedial equity often made her a dissenter. During her tenure, the Court's conservatives adopted a new theory of equity, eroding the accepted understanding of equity as flexible judicial discretion and power. Instead, it was given a reduced, technical meaning found within the formal rules inherited from the English Court of Chancery.[14] In a series of cases, mostly about restitution and sometimes about injunctions, Ginsburg battled to retain the dynamic yet principled power of equity against conservative dilution. More often than not, she lost. However, in one of the last decisions Ginsburg joined, her thinking on remedies may have won the day.

The Supreme Court's foray into a new approach to equity began just as Justice Ginsburg joined the Court, and it was driven by Justice Scalia.[15] In *Grupo Mexicano de Desarrollo S.A. v. Alliance Bond Fund*, a narrowly split Court held that equity did not authorize a preliminary injunction freezing the defendant company's assets to prevent dissipation where the claim was a legal one for money damages.[16] Both sides agreed with the black-letter rule that equity was "an authority" to administer "the principles of the system of judicial remedies" according to "traditional principles of equity jurisdiction,"[17] but they interpreted that rule in materially different ways.

The Court's opinions in *Grupo Mexicano* outlined the range of possible meanings of "equity." At the broadest end of the spectrum, it might mean a court's expansive *power* to aim the conscience and discretion of the judge at the goals of justice and mercy.[18] It might also mean a more positivist approach of the application of *principles* of equity to achieve fairness through flexible, adaptable, and comprehensive remedies.[19] A third, more moderate view might define it as the actual *practice or precedent* of courts.[20] A narrower theory would confine equity to the technical black-letter *rules* of specific claims as summarized by treatise writers.[21] These formal rules could be further modified by a time restriction, either an originalist date of 1789, when equity jurisdiction for the federal courts was established, or 1938 as the date of the merger of law and equity through the Federal Rules of Civil Procedure. It was this narrowest definition—the formal rules of equity as of 1789—that Justice Scalia and the conservative majority adopted in *Grupo Mexicano* to overturn the preliminary enforcement injunction, rejecting judicial discretion and a familiar remedy in modern English law.[22]

Ginsburg dissented and emphatically rejected the majority's hyper-formalism as an "unjustifiably static conception of equity jurisdiction."[23] She argued that it was the *principles* of equity that governed, not the specific practices and rules of centuries past.[24] These principles "valued the adaptable character of federal equitable power," characterized by "flexibility rather than rigidity,"[25] as expressly stated in long-standing Supreme Court precedent.[26] She argued this dynamic and evolving standard of equity was necessary to address the changing complexities of modern legal practice and the "needs of a progressive social condition."[27]

The Court took up the theory of equity again a few years later in *Great-West Life & Annuity Insurance Company v. Knudson.*[28] Again, the conservative majority led by Justice Scalia defined "equity" technically and narrowly to deny the requested specific performance in this case about employee benefits. This time the majority focused on "categories" of relief typically available "in days of the divided bench," as well as the conditions attached to their recovery, as discerned from consulting the "standard current works" of treatises.[29] The majority admitted that its "cases ha[d] not previously drawn this fine distinction,"[30] and scholars criticized Scalia's narrow standard as illegitimate in its application and its "construction of an artificial history" of equity.[31]

Justice Ginsburg, writing for the dissenting four Justices, excoriated the majority for exhuming "an ancient classification unrelated to the substance of the relief sought[] and obstruct[ing] the general goals" of the statute.[32] She chastised the majority for relying on "anachronistic rules" and "recondite distinctions" to equate equity with "the rigid application of rules frozen in a bygone era," thereby producing "anomalous results."[33] She found it "fanciful" to attribute an intent to Congress acting in 1974 to resurrect "those needless and obsolete distinctions."[34] "It is particularly ironic," she wrote, "that the majority acts in the name of equity as it sacrifices congressional intent and statutory purpose to archaic and unyielding doctrine."[35] Instead, she said, equity "eschews mechanical rules" and "depends on flexibility."[36]

Justice Ginsburg repeated her harsh critique of the Court's wrong turn in equity in her short, lone dissent in *Montanile v. Board of Trustees*,[37] in which the majority allowed the defendant to escape a restitutionary subrogation requirement by simply spending the settlement funds quickly on nontraceable items.[38] "What brings the Court to that bizarre conclusion?," she asked.[39] The majority in an opinion by Justice Thomas stated that "equitable relief" is "limited to those categories of relief that were typically available in equity during the days of the divided bench," defined as the period before 1938 when courts of law and equity were separate.[40] It looked only to the "standard treatises on equity" to determine the "basic contours of what equitable relief" meant and rejected any reliance on historical equity practice.[41] And it rejected the argument that equitable relief means "whatever relief a court of equity is empowered to provide."[42] Ginsburg stated emphatically that she would not "perpetuate *Great-West's* mistake" in establishing this formalist path of equity, and she reiterated that "the Court erred profoundly in that case" by reading the statute as "unravelling forty years of fusion of law and equity."[43]

Five years later, however, Ginsburg's lone dissent became the voice of the majority as her thinking found new acceptance on a reshuffled Supreme Court. In *Liu v. Securities and Exchange Commission*, a nearly unanimous Court interpreted a securities statute authorizing "equitable relief" to permit the equitable restitutionary remedy of disgorgement.[44] The majority opinion by Justice Sotomayor nodded to the standard of "those categories of relief that were typically available in equity" but explicitly and resoundingly rejected the technical formalism of the past cases.[45] Instead, the Court focused on "longstanding," "broad and fundamental equitable principles" of the courts.[46] Only Justice Thomas wanted to adhere to a highly formalist definition of equity based on English Courts of Chancery as of 1789 and the technical minutia of an accounting for profits claim.[47] The *Liu* Court did, however, find that the Securities and Exchange Commission had overreached by going beyond these long-standing principles.[48]

Justice Ginsburg's principled approach to equity also emerged in the Court's leading injunction case, *eBay v. MercExchange*.[49] In this patent law case, a unanimous Court endorsed the traditional balancing test for injunctive relief. Justice Ginsburg joined Chief Justice Roberts's concurrence, which articulated the conventional recognition of a court's broad "equitable discretion" to be "exercised consistent with traditional principles of equity" and the "long tradition of equity practice."[50] It reflected Justice Ginsburg's view that equity should be flexible and focused on promoting the basic principle of justice.[51]

The Importance of the Institution

Justice Ginsburg's remedies decisions emphasize the need for governmental entities and institutions to transform, because these powerful institutions play outsized roles in society. She wanted institutions themselves to effectuate change through their own internal or legislative processes. In her view, equality was most readily achieved if all branches of government had a stake in achieving it.[52] Ultimately, she was most concerned with changing the substantive law rather than with specific party outcomes.

Ginsburg's institutional focus makes sense as a classic public law perspective that informs many liberal justices—moving beyond the traditional private law lens of individualized redress.[53] Public law remedies may be aimed at several goals: neutrality of nonarbitrary government action, transformation and reconstruction of legal and social structures, or incorporation of the excluded person or group.[54] In remedies cases, Justice Ginsburg insisted upon neutral, fair action by the government. That neutrality, she thought, would often lead to transformation of the system and the law. And those goals were most important, even at the sacrifice of individual redress.

In *Sessions v. Morales-Santana*, Justice Ginsburg emphasized the need to stop the government's gendered action and wrote a majority opinion that forced the government to adopt nondiscriminatory, fair rules of citizenship for both their legal and social functions.[55] But she overrode the plaintiff's plea for individualized redress and extension of the more lenient citizenship rules. Instead, Ginsburg was attuned solely to the systemic effect on social norms, noting that "discrimination itself . . . perpetuat[es] 'archaic and stereotypic notions'" and their continued entrenchment in society.[56]

Favoring institutional primacy at the expense of the individual seems ironic coming from Ginsburg given her authorship of one of the leading cases of individualized redress, *United States v. Virginia*. In that case, Justice Ginsburg insisted upon the remedy of inclusion for the women excluded from enrollment at the Virginia Military Institute (VMI).[57] The state's all-male military school had been found to have unconstitutionally discriminated against women and was ordered to remedy the violation. The state's proposed remedy was to establish a separate, and allegedly equal, military school for women at a separate college and location. Ginsburg, writing for the majority, rejected the state's proposed solution because it was not equal in offering women the same benefits, opportunities, and reputation as VMI; neither did separation "end their exclusion" from a state-supplied educational opportunity.[58] Even if only a few women wanted to attend the unique program at VMI, those specific women must be included. "A remedial decree," she said, "must closely fit the constitutional violation; it must be shaped to place persons unconstitutionally denied an opportunity or advantage in 'the position they would have occupied in the absence of [discrimination].'"[59]

Justice Ginsburg remained committed to this principle of remedial inclusion, believing that, generally, a court should extend the denied benefit equally to the plaintiff.[60] This had been her approach as an attorney, where she demanded individualized benefits for her clients rather than simply striking down the discriminatory laws.[61] However, this principle of inclusion was tempered by her goal of neutrality and belief in legal process that strongly deferred to the legislature for crafting ultimate solutions. This deference was rooted in Ginsburg's jurisprudence of constitutional federalism, which recognized both a national legislative power and state autonomy and incorporated a pragmatic view of the political process.[62] To her, the proper remedial function of a court was to act as an interim legislature in devising a temporary policy solution until the legislature acted again to correct the wrong.[63] She emphasized that the most important part of the "judicial business" was not to abandon the constitutional review and that the choice of remedy was thus an ancillary issue. In scholarly writing, she expressly rejected as "irrelevant" party choice and the perceived need for individualized benefits, though she acknowledged that such dismissal of interests was likely to "startle and disconcert."[64]

Applying this remedial approach in *Morales-Santana*, Justice Ginsburg deferred to Congress for the remedy, even though the Court refused to defer to the legislature for justification of the unconstitutionally gendered law.[65] In the opinion, she wrote that "we must therefore leave it to Congress to select" the proper time rule "going forward" and that, "[i]n the interim, the Government must ensure that the laws in question are administered in a manner free from gender-based discrimination."[66] For the interim judicial solution, she stated, "the choice between" nullification and extension of benefit is "governed by the legislature's intent, as revealed by the statute at hand."[67] She found that the overall policy, text, and scheme of the statute supported leveling down to the stricter rule for all, although the Second Circuit reached the opposite conclusion in the same case.[68] While it is likely that Ginsburg's retreat from individualized redress in *Morales-Santana* was a consequence of gaining consensus on the merits with conservative Justices Kennedy and Roberts, she also defended it as consistent with her established view of the proper judicial function.[69]

There was a limit, however, to Ginsburg's remedial deference. She would not let the government use it to make an end run around the core substantive values or to eviscerate the core transformative and neutrality goals of remedies. Thus, in the VMI case, she refused to defer to the state legislature's superficial separate-and-unequal remedy, which did not achieve the underlying merits of the equality command.

Her reverence for legislative deference also helps explain her analysis in *Petrella v. MGM*, which at first glance seemed to bend to the Court's new formalistic idea of equity. Ginsburg concluded that the equitable remedial defense of laches for unreasonable delay did not apply to copyright infringement claims seeking legal relief; it applied only to those seeking equitable relief.[70] The dissent of moderates criticized Ginsburg for her formal adherence to premerger equity law and failure to recognize equity as a "correction" that "helps courts avoid the unfairness" of strict doctrinal rules.[71] Ginsburg pushed back, stating that such an expansive role for laches "careens away from understandings[] past and present" of the defense.[72] More tellingly, she rationalized her decision based on legislative intent, emphasizing that laches was "essentially gap-filling, not legislation-overriding."[73] What Congress had prescribed, and what Congress sought to achieve, were key considerations to Justice Ginsburg, for, as she explained elsewhere, courts "do not alone shape legal doctrine[] but . . . participate in a dialogue with other organs of government[] and with the people as well."[74]

A Judicial Restraint Liberal

Justice Ginsburg was radical and reconstructive—but in a restrained and incremental way. She designed acceptable remedies by evaluating a variety of pragmatic factors to cautiously limit the reach and scope of court-ordered relief. Because of this approach, the Supreme Court reporter Linda Greenhouse described Ginsburg as "something of a rare creature in the modern judicial lexicon: a judicial restraint liberal."[75] Though her personal commitments may have been to liberal outcomes, Justice Ginsburg believed that the means by which those outcomes were achieved should be guided by a strong commitment to judicial restraint.[76] For Ginsburg, judicial restraint was "not necessarily the end in itself . . . but rather the best means to achieving her vision of equality."[77] She crafted "minimalist remedies endorsing limited judicial intervention in order to protect the exercise of fundamental rights."[78]

Her restrained approach to remedies reflected Ginsburg's theories about legal process and the function of the Court generally.[79] This restraint was motivated in part by the risk that the Court might rule against positive social change if the result was perceived as too radical in principle or too costly to the defendant.[80] As an attorney, she had been accused of "asking too much" of the courts and losing judicial support by seeking large steps forward. She "recognized that the Court was still sensitive to criticism for what was perceived as 'moving too far, too fast' in the civil rights cases."[81] She understood that a court could be more easily persuaded to take small incremental change, even if it was sometimes two steps forward and one step back.[82]

Ginsburg always preferred "slow but steady forward motion" on the bench.[83] As an appellate judge on the D.C. Circuit, she endorsed using "measured motions" for "third branch decision-making."[84] She wrote that a judge "must be sensitive to the sensibilities and mindsets of one's colleagues, which may mean avoiding certain arguments or authorities," and she cautioned that "doctrinal limbs too swiftly shaped" "may prove unstable."[85] Instead, she argued, more "temperate," interstitial action best "affords the most responsible room for creative, important judicial contributions."[86]

Legal scholars have noted that judicial restraint may be appropriate for equitable remedies because those types of remedies impose greater costs than damages on courts and litigants, interfere with the usual autonomy of business or governance, and are susceptible to abuse.[87] Thus, equitable relief typically will not issue unless an irreparable injury cannot be remedied by money damages and after balancing the burdens to the defendants and third parties.[88] As Justice Ginsburg noted, these "protections in place guard against any routine or arbitrary imposition" of an equitable remedy.[89] She identified pragmatic concerns raised by imposition of a remedy, such as the size of the plaintiff class; the financial costs to a government or to private parties; whether the remedy was a negative or affirmative requirement; and whether the remedy disrupted the legislative solution represented by the original enactment.[90]

Unlike her colleagues, however, Justice Ginsburg did not apply these pragmatic factors rigidly. She reminded them that "flexibility is a hallmark of equity jurisdiction," with the power to "mould each decree to the necessities of the particular case."[91] Thus in *Winter v. Natural Resources Defense Council*, in evaluating a preliminary injunction, she dissented in part to reinforce the importance of flexibility in applying the balancing factors holistically under a sliding scale rather than requiring certainty with respect to each factor.[92]

Yet in *Morales-Santana*, Justice Ginsburg did not apply these pragmatic factors at all. Ironically, had she applied her own factors, she might have reached a different result. There was clearly irreparable injury to the party denied citizenship, as money could not repair the intangible loss; neither could future reforms change the individual's status. There was little administrative burden to the government, and virtually no financial cost, and the affected class was relatively small. The strategically minimalist remedy, however, did achieve Ginsburg's substantive goal of transforming the substantive law of citizenship into something less gendered and discriminatory. Her opinion definitively struck down, at least in a limited context, the perpetuation of antiquated stereotypical notions of women's sole caregiving function and the breadwinner/homemaker dichotomy. An opposite result, even in aid of the plaintiff, would have left in place the stereotypes about women's emotional weakness, maternal role, and need for protection animating the solicitous one-year rule for mothers—a result that was simply untenable to Ruth Bader Ginsburg.[93]

Conclusion: Striking an Equitable Compromise

Justice Ginsburg's theory of remedial equity can be appreciated as a thoughtful, sophisticated understanding of the character and nature of the Court's power. She rejected the technical, formalistic limitations of equity pushed by the more conservative Justices to defend long-standing progressive understandings of the Court's function to impose flexible and fair remedies. Yet her view of equity was constrained by her view of the proper judicial process for social change and letting the institutional actor take the lead. She believed that a deferential, incremental approach was more conducive to persuasive, normative change within the confines of the democratic process. She thus prioritized equitable relief for the public law concern of reforming the bad institutional actor rather than benefiting the particular plaintiff, even though this sometimes meant outcomes that sacrificed the individual for the greater public good.

NOTES
1 DAN B. DOBBS & CAPRICE L. ROBERTS, LAW OF REMEDIES: DAMAGES, EQUITY, RESTITUTION 45–46, 56 (3d ed. 2018).
2 Herma Hill Kay, *Law Professor Extraordinaire*, in THE LEGACY OF RUTH BADER GINSBURG 14–15 (Scott Dodson ed. 2015).
3 *See* Zachary D. Tripp & Gillian E. Metzger, *Professor Justice Ginsburg: Justice Ginsburg's Love of Procedure and Jurisdiction*, 121 COLUM. L. REV. 729 (2021); David L. Shapiro, *Justice Ginsburg's First Decade: Some Thoughts About Her Contributions in the Fields of Procedure and Jurisdiction*, 104 COLUM. L. REV. 21 (2004).
4 582 U.S. ___, 137 S. Ct. 1678, 1686 (2017).

5 Tracy A. Thomas, *Leveling Down Gender Equality*, 42 HARV. J. L. & GENDER 177 (2019).

6 8 U.S.C. § 1409(b)-(c) (1958); 8 U.S.C. § 1401(g) (1958).

7 *Morales-Santana*, 137 S. Ct. at 1686.

8 *Id.* at 1690–91; *see* Kristin A. Collins, *Equality, Sovereignty, and the Family in Morales-Santana*, 131 HARV. L. REV. 170, 172–78 (2017).

9 137 S. Ct. at 1690, 1692.

10 *Id.* at 1686, 1701 (Justice Gorsuch took no part in the case).

11 *Id.* at 1701.

12 *See* Thomas, *Leveling Down*, at 181; Collins, *Equality, Sovereignty, and the Family*, at 175; Deborah L. Brake, *When Equality Leaves Everyone Worse Off: The Problem of Leveling Down in Equality Law*, 46 WM. & MARY L. REV. 513, 515 (2004).

13 Joan C. Williams, *Beyond the Tough Guise: Justice Ginsburg's Reconstructive Feminism*, in DODSON, THE LEGACY, at 64, 66.

14 Samuel L. Bray, *The Supreme Court and the New Equity*, 68 VAND. L. REV. 997, 1014–15 (2015); Samuel L. Bray, *The System of Equitable Remedies*, 63 U.C.L.A. L. REV. 530, 533–34 (2016); *see also* David C. Vladeck, *The Erosion of Equity and the FTC's Redress Authority*, 82 MONT. L. REV. 159, 163 (2021).

15 *See* Mertens v. Hewitt Assoc., 508 U.S. 248, 256 (1993).

16 527 U.S. 308 (1999).

17 *Id.* at 318, 335.

18 *Id.* at 321, 335, 342; DOBBS & ROBERTS, LAW OF REMEDIES, at 54; Doug Rendleman, *The Triumph of Equity Revisited: The Stages of Equitable Discretion*, 15 NEV. L.J. 1397, 1400–01 (2015); John R. Kroger, *Supreme Court Equity, 1789–1835, and the History of American Judging*, 34 HOUS. L. REV. 1427, 1431 (1998).

19 *Grupo Mexicano*, 527 U.S. at 336 (Ginsburg, J., dissenting); Hecht Co. v. Bowles, 321 U.S. 321, 329 (1944); *see* Rendleman, *Triumph of Equity*, at 1401.

20 F.W. MAITLAND, EQUITY AND THE FORMS OF ACTION 1 (1910).

21 *Grupo Mexicano*, 527 U.S. at 322; Guaranty Trust Co. of New York v. New York, 326 U.S. 99, 104–05 (1945).

22 *Grupo Mexicano*, 527 U.S. at 327, 332; *see* Mareva Compania Naviera S.A. v. International Bulkcarriers S.A., 1 All E.R. 213 (C.A. 1975); David Capper, *The Need for Mareva Injunctions Reconsidered*, 73 FORDHAM L. REV. 2161 (2005); Rhonda Wasserman, *Equity Renewed: Preliminary Injunctions to Secure Potential Money Judgments*, 67 WASH. L. REV. 257 (1992).

23 *Grupo Mexicano*, 527 U.S. at 326.

24 *Id.*

25 *Id.* at 326, 342.

26 *Hecht*, 321 U.S. at 329; Seymour v. Freer, 8 Wall 202, 218 (1869).

27 *Hecht*, 321 U.S. at 326–27.

28 534 U.S. 204 (2002).

29 *Id.* at 210, 212, 217.

30 *Id.* at 214.

31 Bray, *New Equity*, at 1014–22; John H. Langbein, *What ERISA Means by "Equi-table": The Supreme Court's Trail of Error in* Russell, Mertens, *and* Great-West, 103 COLUM. L. REV. 1317 (2003); Daniel J. Meltzer, *The Supreme Court's Judicial Passivity,* 2002 SUP. CT. REV. 343, 346–50 (2002); Judith Resnick, *Constricting Federal Remedies: The Rehnquist Judiciary, Congress, and Federal Power,* 78 IND. L.J. 223 (2003); Tracy A. Thomas, *Justice Scalia Reinvents Restitution,* 36 LOY. L.A. L. REV. 1063, 1063 (2003).

32 *Great-West,* 534 U.S. at 224 (Ginsburg, J., dissenting).

33 *Id.* at 223–25.

34 *Id.* at 225.

35 *Id.* at 228.

36 *Id.*

37 577 U.S. 136 (2016).

38 *Id.* at 151 (Ginsburg, J., dissenting).

39 *Id.*

40 *Id.* at 142.

41 *Id.* at 142, 144, 147.

42 *Id.* at 147.

43 *Id.* at 151.

44 591 U.S. ___, 140 S. Ct. 1936 (2020).

45 *Id.* at 1942.

46 *Id.* at 1944, 1946.

47 *Id.* at 1950–51 (Thomas, J., dissenting).

48 *Id.* at 1946–47, 1951.

49 547 U.S. 388 (2006).

50 *Id.* at 394–95 (Roberts, J., concurring).

51 *Id.* at 395.

52 Linda Greenhouse, *Justice Ginsburg and the Price of Equality,* N.Y. TIMES, June 22, 2017.

53 Abram Chayes, *The Role of the Judge in Public Law Litigation,* 89 HARV. L. REV. 1281, 1283–84 (1976).

54 *See* Evan H. Camiker, *A Norm-Based Remedial Model for Underinclusive Statutes,* 95 YALE L.J. 1185, 1202–03 (1986).

55 *Morales-Santana,* 137 S. Ct. at 1686.

56 *Id.* at 1698 n.21.

57 518 U.S. 515 (1996); *see* JANE SHERRON DE HART, RUTH BADER GINSBURG: A LIFE 341–42 (2018).

58 *Virginia,* 518 U.S. at 550–51.

59 *Id.* at 547.

60 *Morales-Santana,* 137 S. Ct. at 1699.

61 *See* Frontiero v. Richardson, 411 U.S. 677 (1973); Weinberger v. Wiesenfeld, 420 U.S. 636 (1975); Amy Leigh Campbell, *Raising the Bar: Ruth Bader Ginsburg and the ACLU Women's Rights Project,* 11 TEX. J. WOMEN & L. 157, 194 (2002).

62 Deborah Jones Merritt, *The Once and Future Federalist*, in DODSON, THE LEGACY, at 172, 196.

63 Ruth Bader Ginsburg, *Address: Some Thoughts on Judicial Authority to Repair Unconstitutional Legislation*, 28 CLEV. ST. L. REV. 301, 317 (1979).

64 *Id.* at 316–18.

65 Thomas, *Leveling Down*, at 179.

66 *Morales-Santana*, 137 S. Ct. at 1701.

67 *Id.* at 1700.

68 Morales-Santana v. Lynch, 804 F.3d 520, 536–38 (2d Cir. 2015).

69 DE HART, A LIFE, at 524.

70 572 U.S. 663, 667 (2014).

71 *Id.* at 688.

72 *Id.* at 680.

73 *Id.*

74 Ruth Bader Ginsburg, *Speaking in a Judicial Voice*, 67 N.Y.U. L. REV. 1185, 1198 (1992).

75 Greenhouse, *Price of Equality*; *see also* Linda Greenhouse, *A Sense of Judicial Limits*, N.Y. TIMES, July 22, 1993.

76 Greenhouse, *Price of Equality*; Melanie K. Morris, *Ruth Bader Ginsburg and Gender Equality: A Reassessment of Her Contribution*, 9 CARDOZO WOMEN'S L.J. 1, 23 (2002).

77 Greenhouse, *Judicial Limits*.

78 Morris, *A Reassessment*, at 23.

79 Tripp & Metzger, *Professor Justice Ginsburg*, at 731; Lisa Kern Griffin, *Barriers to Entry and Justice Ginsburg's Criminal Procedure Jurisprudence*, in DODSON, THE LEGACY, at 102, 104.

80 Campbell, *Raising the Bar*, at 230.

81 *Id.*

82 *Id.*

83 Griffin, *Barriers to Entry*, at 104.

84 Ginsburg, *Judicial Voice*, at 1198.

85 *Id.* at 1194, 1198.

86 *Id.* at 1208–09.

87 *See* Bray, *System*, at 573; Chayes, *Public Law Litigation*, at 1292.

88 *See* eBay v. MercExchange, 547 U.S. 388 (2006); Winter v. Natural Resources Def. Council, Inc., 555 U.S. 7 (2008); Califano v. Westcott, 443 U.S. 76, 90 (1979).

89 *Grupo Mexicano*, 527 U.S. at 341 (Ginsburg, J., dissenting).

90 Ginsburg, *Judicial Authority*, at 318–19, 323–24.

91 *Winter*, 555 U.S. at 51.

92 *Id.*

93 *See* Kristin Collins, *Illegitimate Borders: Jus Sanguinis Citizenship and the Legal Construction of Family, Race, and Nation*, 123 YALE L.J. 2134, 2201–03 (2014).

19

Taxation

The Litigator, the Judge, the Justice

PATRICIA A. CAIN AND JEAN C. LOVE

Ruth Bader Ginsburg is not well known as the author of many Supreme Court tax decisions, but she had important tax connections in her life. This chapter will explore a number of those connections—some personal, some as a litigator, and some as a judge. Perhaps her most important tax decision was handed down when she served as a judge on the United States Court of Appeals for the District of Columbia Circuit. This chapter features that case and concludes with thoughts about her tax decisions as a Justice on the United States Supreme Court.

Ginsburg as Litigator

Ruth Bader met Marty Ginsburg when they were undergraduates at Cornell, the only Ivy League school that admitted women in those days. They wed in 1954. Marty Ginsburg may have been Ruth's most important connection to tax law for two reasons. First, in his day he was one of the most preeminent tax lawyers in the country, and he later became a top-rated tax professor. Second, but for Marty, Ruth might never have read *Moritz v. Commissioner*,[1] the tax case that spawned her historic litigation challenging sex-based classifications.

The story is legend.[2] Here are the highlights. In 1970, Ruth was a professor at Rutgers Law School. She and Marty frequently read advance sheets and did other legal research in their two studies close to each other in their home. One night in 1970, Marty walked into Ruth's study with a case in hand that he had discovered while reading his tax advance sheets. Marty said: "I think you should read this case." Ruth responded: "You know I don't read tax cases." Marty countered: "Read this one."

Marty was absolutely right. What he had handed to Ruth was the Tax Court opinion in *Moritz v. Commissioner.*[3] It turned out that Mr. Moritz had asserted a claim for sex-based discrimination under a provision of the Internal Revenue Code.

Moritz had claimed a tax deduction under section 214 of the Internal Revenue Code[4] that allowed certain taxpayers to claim a deduction for dependent care if the care was required to enable the taxpayer to work outside the home. Moritz, a single man whose job required extensive travel, provided care for his invalid mother, who lived with him. When he had to travel, he paid for a caretaker to come to his home and provide that care. He claimed a deduction under section 214 for these expenses. However, he ran into a problem under the wording of the statute. The deduction was available to all women who claimed it, but it was only available to a man if he qualified as a "widower." The term "widower" was defined broadly in the statute to include "an unmarried individual who is legally separated from his spouse under a decree of divorce or of separate maintenance." But because Moritz had never been married, he could not qualify as a widower under the statute. If a woman was single and had never been married, she could claim the deduction. But if a man was single, he could claim the deduction only if he were a widower.

Mr. Moritz had represented himself pro se (without legal representation) in the Tax Court. He had filed a written brief, which very succinctly argued: "If I had been a dutiful daughter, instead of a dutiful son, I would have gotten the deduction. That makes no sense."[5]

Moritz lost his case in the Tax Court. This is the case Marty Ginsburg discovered that night in 1970 and implored Ruth to read.

Ruth read it. She and Marty then quickly agreed that they would represent Moritz together, pro bono, on appeal to the Tenth Circuit. The ACLU joined them, which turned out to be the beginning of a long relationship between Ruth and the ACLU. This case was perhaps Ruth's first important sex discrimination case. It is certainly the most well-known of her early sex discrimination cases.

If you've seen the movie *On the Basis of Sex*, or if you are a tax aficionado, then you know that the Ginsburgs won their case before the Tenth Circuit.[6] Such a win is very rare in tax cases. It is almost impossible to convince a court that a tax law is unconstitutional because rational basis review typically applies. And while many of us may think that tax laws are frequently irrational,[7] they usually withstand a constitutional challenge due to the significant deference courts give to tax rules under the "tax deference doctrine."[8]

In *Moritz*, the Ginsburgs argued for heightened scrutiny because the discrimination embedded in the tax statute was clearly "on the basis of sex." The appellate brief in *Moritz* was written in 1971, before the Supreme Court had recognized a constitutionally protected right against sex discrimination. Prior to 1971, the Supreme Court had applied low-level scrutiny to multiple statutes and practices that had discriminated against women solely because of their sex, always upholding those statutes,[9] a fact noted in the *Moritz* brief. However, in the fall of 1971, while the Tenth Circuit was still writing its opinion in *Moritz*, the Supreme Court handed down *Reed v. Reed*,[10] the Court's first decision holding that the Fourteenth Amendment prohibited sex discrimination. *Reed* held that the sex discrimination against women under an Idaho probate statute violated the Equal Protection Clause. The Court in *Reed* professed to apply only rational basis review, yet it still struck down the discriminatory statute. While the Tenth Circuit considered the heightened scrutiny argument in *Moritz*, ultimately it chose to rely on *Reed*, ruling that the statute flunked even rational basis review. The distinction between never-married men and women did not "bear a reasonable and just relation to the permissible objective of the legislation," which was to provide relief for taxpayers who had paid for dependent care when that care was required to enable the taxpayer to work outside the home. Because the purpose of the statute was to provide relief, it was appropriate to extend the relief to single, never-married men rather than to strike down the statute.

The other interesting part of the story about the *Moritz* case is that Dean Erwin Griswold, who had been the dean at Harvard when Ruth and Marty were law students there, was serving as Solicitor General of the United States in the early 1970s. He supported a petition for certiorari in *Moritz*. Cert was denied, probably because Congress had changed the text of the statute to remove the language that had created the sex discrimination. But Griswold thought the case was a serious threat to additional federal laws that distinguished on the basis of sex. There were many such statutes, and he used the government's mainframe to identify them and then list them all in his petition. This list was a gift to Ruth. It identified potential plaintiffs that Ruth and the ACLU might choose to represent during their next decade of litigation under the Equal Protection Clause.

Although Ruth's representation of Moritz was stunningly successful in the Tenth Circuit, she did not fare as well in her only tax case before the Supreme Court. The case was *Kahn v. Shevin*,[11] decided in 1974, and it is the only case that she ever argued before the Supreme Court and lost. The case concerned a Florida property tax rule. Widows were given a break on their property taxes, while widowers were not. *Kahn* is often viewed as a case of benign sex discrimination in that women who had lost their husbands were generally thought to be more dependent on their husbands and thus less able to pay their property taxes after the death of their husbands. The Court also justified its decision in *Kahn* on the theory that *Kahn* was a tax case. In the words of the Court: "We have long held that '(w)here taxation is concerned and no specific federal right, apart from equal protection, is imperiled, the States have large leeway in making classifications and drawing lines which in their judgment produce reasonable systems of taxation.'"[12] Tax statutes typically survive constitutional challenge because the courts give so much deference not only to the legislative body that enacted the tax rules but also to the agency that construes and applies them.

Kahn created a challenge for Ruth Bader Ginsburg as a litigator. After *Kahn*, she argued a number of cases before the Supreme Court representing male plaintiffs who, like the widower in *Kahn*, had been denied certain governmental benefits that were available to widows but not to widowers. Overcoming *Kahn*, Ruth won all of these cases, including *Weinberger v. Wiesenfeld*,[13] one of her favorites. The Social Security Act provided survivors' benefits to widows who wanted to stay home to care for their children but not to widowers who wanted to do exactly the same thing. Stephen Wiesenfeld's wife, who had been the couple's primary breadwinner, died in childbirth, and he vowed to stay home and raise their son. Ginsburg won for him the right to the compensation he deserved from the Social Security Administration. And in the process she convinced a unanimous Supreme Court (including five out of six justices who had voted against her in the *Kahn* case)[14] to understand that sometimes discrimination against widowers is "sex discrimination."

Judge Ruth Bader Ginsburg

Ginsburg ended her days as a litigator when she was appointed in 1980 to the D.C. Circuit court of appeals by President Jimmy Carter. Perhaps her most famous tax decision was authored during her tenure on this court. That case, *Wright v. Regan*, was handed down in 1981.[15] A law clerk who was working for her at the time of the decision describes it as a case that she cared about enough to come into her offices earlier than usual to work on the opinion.[16]

To understand the significance of the *Wright* case, one must know more about the background of this litigation. Wright had filed a class action on behalf of all Black parents who had school-aged children, claiming that the Internal Revenue Service (IRS) was granting tax-exempt status to racially discriminatory private schools in violation of its own policy, which stated that private schools were not entitled to tax-exempt status unless the school had a policy of nondiscrimination. The IRS adopted its policy in a 1971 revenue ruling[17] that had been issued in response to an earlier litigated case that was very similar to *Wright*. *Green v. Connally*, filed against the IRS by Black parents in Mississippi,[18] claimed that the IRS could not grant tax-exempt status to private, racially segregated schools as a matter of statutory construction in light of public policy. And the *Green* plaintiffs further claimed that, if the IRS did grant such tax exemptions, it would mean that the government was indirectly supporting discriminatory schools in violation of equal protection principles.

The statutory argument was straightforward. Section 501(c)(3) of the Internal Revenue Code authorized a tax exemption for "charities." An organization could not be considered "charitable" if it discriminated on the basis of race. Charities must be public and open to all. Race discrimination flies in the face of the meaning of "charity."

A federal district court in Mississippi agreed with the statutory construction argument, and it was prepared to rule on those grounds to avoid the constitutional issues. At that point, the IRS concurred with the court's position and promised that, going forward, it would not grant tax-exempt status to discriminatory schools.

But the IRS's promise failed to satisfy the district court, so it issued an injunction against the IRS ordering it to stop granting tax exemptions to any Mississippi private schools discriminating on the basis of race. The injunction applied only to schools in Mississippi.

Despite the published 1971 revenue ruling and the later promulgation of revenue procedures explaining the implementation of that ruling, the IRS continued to grant exemptions to segregated private schools outside Mississippi. In part, this was because the IRS ruling merely required schools to state their nondiscrimination policies. The ruling did not address any actions that a school might take in violation of its stated policy. Many schools enrolled only white students, and yet they could meet the requirement of producing a policy statement against race discrimination. By contrast, exemptions for schools in Mississippi were being monitored closely by the federal district court in accord with its very detailed injunction.

The *Wright* litigants sought to remedy this problem by asking for a nationwide injunction that would prevent the IRS from granting tax exemptions to *any* school if the school was discriminating on the basis of race. The district court in *Wright* had dismissed the case on standing grounds,[19] ruling that a plaintiff does not have standing to pursue a claim against a defendant unless the plaintiff can show that the plaintiff was harmed by the defendant's action. The plaintiffs in *Wright* lacked such standing because they could not show that the IRS action granting tax-exempt status to discriminating schools had harmed them in any way. None of the parents had children who had applied for and been denied admission to a private school.

On appeal, Ginsburg, writing for a majority in a split decision, reversed and found that the plaintiffs had alleged a cognizable harm sufficient to constitute standing. The plaintiffs were not complaining about any failure to admit them to discriminatory private schools. Rather, these plaintiffs were complaining about the harm to their dignity as human beings, a harm that they had experienced because their government, by granting tax-exempt status to discriminatory schools, was devaluing them as Black citizens.[20]

Ginsburg wrote this opinion at a propitious moment during the ongoing saga of the IRS granting tax exemptions to private discriminatory schools. In 1981, there was an important case dealing with this issue on the Supreme Court's docket, *Bob Jones University v. United States*.[21] The IRS had denied the university tax-exempt status because of its alleged racially discriminatory admissions policy. The university challenged that decision. The specific issue in the case was whether the IRS could discourage race discrimination in a case in which the school claimed a First Amendment religious liberty right to engage in that discrimination. While *Bob Jones* was pending, President Ronald Reagan began to question whether the IRS even had the authority to deny tax-exempt status to a private religious school like Bob Jones University. In the absence of any definitive action by Congress clarifying the status of such schools as tax-exempt or not, the president was encouraging the IRS to retract its position under the 1971 revenue ruling. And the IRS was thinking about doing just that: revoking the ruling and granting tax-exempt status to Bob Jones University. If such action were taken, the IRS would be prepared to argue before the Supreme Court that the case was moot and therefore should be dismissed.[22]

Enter Judge Ruth Bader Ginsburg and her 1982 appellate holding in *Wright* that the plaintiffs had standing. On the basis of that decision, the court entered a nationwide injunction.[23] As a result, the IRS could not withdraw its 1971 ruling, and it could not grant tax-exempt status to Bob Jones University, which meant that the Supreme Court was able to hear the case. In *Bob Jones University*, the Supreme Court in 1983 held that the IRS had been correct to deny tax-exempt status because the word "charitable" in section 501(c)(3) of the Internal Revenue Code could not include organizations, such as schools and universities, that discriminated on the basis of race.

As important as the *Bob Jones* case was in the short run, aided by the Ginsburg opinion in *Wright*, the ultimate irony is that the Supreme Court granted a writ of certiorari in *Wright* and reversed on the ground that the plaintiff lacked standing.[24] That action by the Supreme Court had long-term implications. No longer can private citizens readily bring claims against the IRS to complain about its enforcement of its own policy against racial discrimination by charities. Many commentators see this as a significant loss.[25]

Justice Ruth Bader Ginsburg

In 1993, Judge Ginsburg became Justice Ginsburg. As an Associate Justice on the United States Supreme Court, she never was asked to write (or to join) an opinion dealing with the constitutionality of a tax law.[26] And there are no identifiable decisions dealing with sex discrimination and tax law during her tenure. But there is one tax case involving age discrimination. Her vote in this case may strike some as surprising, especially since she did not join the dissenting opinion authored by her only female colleague on the bench, Justice Sandra Day O'Connor.

The case is *Commissioner v. Schleier*,[27] decided in 1995. It raised an issue about the taxation of damages under section 104(a)(2) of the Internal Revenue Code. At the time, that section provided for the exclusion of all damages received "on account of personal injury."[28]

To understand O'Connor's dissenting position in *Schleier*, it is worth considering a case that was decided a year before Ginsburg joined the Court. That case, *United States v. Burke*,[29] did involve sex discrimination. The *Burke* plaintiffs were women who received damages to compensate them for the sex discrimination they experienced in violation of Title VII. Given the text of the tax statute at the time, the taxpayers would have been entitled to exclude the payments, provided the harm caused by "sex discrimination" was considered a "personal injury." The question was whether it is a "personal injury" for a woman to be told, directly or indirectly: "You are worth less because you are a woman." Sex discrimination is, after all, a "dignitary tort."

Nonetheless, a majority of the Court ruled against the taxpayers, finding that the claims were not "tort-type" claims, a standard set forth in the Treasury regulations at the time to help determine whether compensation for a claim was for a personal injury.[30] The problem, reasoned the Court, was that the damages received by the plaintiffs were for back pay. That remedy did not seem to indicate that the underlying claim was sufficiently tortlike. According to the majority of the Court, "one of the hallmarks of traditional tort liability is the availability of a broad range of damages to compensate the plaintiff 'fairly for injuries caused by the violation of his legal rights.'"[31] At the time, however, Title VII permitted only the award of back pay and other injunctive relief. That made Title VII claims appear unlike tort claims, which typically entitled the plaintiff to other forms of compensatory damages. If the underlying claim was not sufficiently akin to a tort claim, then the damages could not qualify for exclusion under section 104(a)(2).

Justice O'Connor, in dissent, opined that sex discrimination was indeed a form of dignitary tort and therefore should qualify for the exclusion, which applied to all damages for personal injury. It seems likely that Justice Ginsburg, had she been a Justice at the time, would have joined Justice O'Conner because this form of dignitary harm was exactly the type of harm she had identified in the *Wright* tax litigation regarding segregated private schools.

Commissioner v. Schleier,[32] decided once Ginsburg had joined the Court, was similar to *Burke* in that it also involved the taxation of damages received for discrimination, although in *Schleier* the discrimination was on the basis of age. True to her prior position, O'Connor found that age discrimination, like sex discrimination, was a personal harm. It, too, was a dignitary tort. Justice Ginsburg, with no explanation, joined the majority, following the *Burke* holding and finding that the damages were taxable. Perhaps she felt bound by the prior precedent in *Burke*.

Ginsburg authored a number of Supreme Court tax opinions, usually ruling in favor of the government.[33] The most important of Ginsburg's tax decisions is *Drye v. United States*.[34] In this case, probably the most cited of her tax opinions, the Court dealt with an apparent conflict between state property law and federal tax law. Throughout our history, federal tax law has relied heavily on state property law to determine the outcome in federal tax cases. Property rights vary from state to state, and federal tax law allocates tax burdens on the basis of state-recognized property rights.

It is often said that, "[a]s a general rule, state law determines the nature and quality of transactions, property rights, and other potentially taxable interests and events, while federal tax law determines the tax consequences of those interests and events."[35] Another way of stating this is that "[s]tate law creates legal interests and rights. The federal revenue acts designate what interests or rights, so created, shall be taxed."[36]

In *Drye*, the conflict between federal and state law was both stark and clear. Drye was the sole intestate heir to his mother's estate. He disclaimed the inheritance from her and the disclaimer was valid under state law, as well as under section 2518 of the Internal Revenue Code. Under state law, the disclaimer had the effect of defeating any creditor's claim to the property disclaimed because the state disclaimer statute treated the disclaimant as having never owned the property. As a result there was no property ever owned by the disclaiming debtor for a state creditor to attach. Section 2518 of the Internal Revenue Code also treated the disclaimant as having never owned the property, but only as to questions of gift and estate tax. In other words, an effective disclaimer cannot be considered a transfer of property to which a federal gift or estate tax might be applied. But the problem in this case was that Drye, the disclaimant, owed federal taxes. Had he not disclaimed, and instead received the inherited property, the preexisting federal tax lien for those delinquent taxes would have attached, and the IRS would have been entitled to reach the property to secure its debt.

So the question in *Drye* was whether or not the state property law (which said that disclaimant never owned the property) could be imposed to avoid the attachment of a federal tax lien to the property that he otherwise would have inherited. This proved to be a very complex question. It had been hotly debated before the *Drye* case arose. This precise issue had arisen in two earlier appellate cases, one decided by the Fifth Circuit[37] and the other decided by the Ninth Circuit.[38] Both courts ruled in favor of the taxpayer. In *Drye*, however, the Eighth Circuit sided with the government.[39]

Ginsburg, writing for a unanimous Court, ruled that the federal tax law prevailed. But she was careful to preserve the ongoing effect and importance of state property law. Questions as to whether or not something created a property interest or a property right were all state law matters. States' rights and interests in property would continue to be given full effect under federal tax law. But it was up to federal tax law to determine whether or not the sum of those state-created rights and interests constituted "property" for purposes of federal tax law. And precedent made clear that, for purposes of the federal tax lien, "property" was to have the broadest definition possible. The federal government had argued that the very right to disclaim was a property interest itself. The tax lien therefore attached to the right to disclaim the moment Drye's mother died because, at that moment in time, he owned that right.

But Ginsburg's explanation went one step further in explaining why the government's position was correct. In rejecting the taxpayer's argument that one who rejects a gift is never thought to own the property, she first agreed that the taxpayer's characterization might well be true for a total rejection of proffered property. But then she explained that, in such a case, the rejection of a gift "restores the status quo ante, leaving the donor to do with the gift what she will." However, she explained that the disclaiming heir or devisee "does not restore the status quo, for the decedent cannot be revived. Thus the heir inevitably exercises dominion over the property. He determines who will receive the property—himself if he does not disclaim, a known other if he does." *Voilà!*—such a seemingly simple explanation, yet so precisely correct, artful, and persuasive. Her most famous dissents are often characterized in the same way.[40]

Conclusion

In Ruth Bader Ginsburg's early career as a litigator for sex equality, she challenged a provision in the Internal Revenue Code on behalf of a taxpayer and won. She then lost a tax case on behalf of another taxpayer. She handed down a crucial decision in favor of the taxpayers in a much publicized race discrimination tax case when on the D.C. Circuit. But during her tenure on the Supreme Court, her decisions were predominantly against the taxpayer.

For someone who professed in 1970 to have no interest in tax law, Ruth Bader Ginsburg ended up participating in a number of interesting and important tax cases. Whether as a litigator or as a jurist, she always made a difference.

NOTES

1 55 T.C. 113 (1970).

2 For Marty's own version, see Martin D. Ginsburg, *A Uniquely Distinguished Service*, 10 GREEN BAG 2D 173 (2006) (published originally in 25:4 ABA SECTION OF TAXATION NEWSQUARTERLY 7 (2006)).

3 *Id.*

4 The deduction has been replaced by a partial tax credit for qualified dependent care expenses currently contained in Internal Revenue Code section 21.

5 Deborah Jones Merritt & Wendy Webster Williams, *Transcript of Interview of U.S. Supreme Court Associate Justice Ruth Bader Ginsburg*, 70 OHIO ST. L.J. 805, 809 (2009) (describing argument made by Moritz).

6 Moritz v. Comm'r, 469 F.2d 466 (10th Cir. 1972).

7 In fact, many of them are irrational because tax laws are often the result of political bargaining rather than rational lawmaking.

8 *See* Andrew C. Weiler, Note, *Has Due Process Struck Out? The Judicial Rubberstamping of Retroactive Economic Laws*, 42 DUKE L.J. 1069 (1993).

9 For example, in *Goesert v. Cleary*, 335 U.S. 464 (1948), the Court upheld a Michigan statute prohibiting women from working in bars. And in *Hoyt v. Florida*, 368 U.S. 57 (1961), the Court upheld a criminal conviction of a woman in which women were not included on the jury.

10 Reed v. Reed, 404 U.S. 71 (1971). *Reed* was the first case in which Ruth Bader Ginsburg had filed a brief in the Supreme Court arguing for heightened scrutiny of laws that discriminated on the basis of sex.

11 Kahn v. Shevin, 416 U.S. 351 (1974).

12 *Id.* at 355.

13 Weinberger v. Wiesenfeld, 420 U.S. 636 (1975) (striking down a Social Security Act provision that made widows, but not widowers, eligible for survivors' benefits, including an allowance for staying home with children).

14 The five were Burger, Stewart, Blackmun, Powell, and Rehnquist. The sixth Justice who had voted against her position in *Kahn* was Justice Douglas, who did not participate in *Wiesenfeld*.

15 Wright v. Regan, 656 F.2d 820 (D.C. Cir. 1981), *rev'd sub nom.* Allen v. Wright, 468 U.S. 737 (1984).

16 *See* Jonathan L. Entin, *Ruth Bader Ginsburg: A Law Clerk's Reflections*, 71 Case W. Res. L. Rev. 1, 8 (2020).

17 Rev. Rul. 71–447.

18 Green v. Connally, 330 F. Supp. 1150 (D.D.C.), *aff'd sub nom.* Coit v. Green, 404 U.S. 997 (1971) (per curiam).

19 Wright v. Miller, 480 F. Supp. 790 (D.D.C. 1979).

20 "The sole injury they claim is the denigration they suffer as black parents and schoolchildren when their government graces with tax-exempt status educational institutions in their communities that treat members of their race as persons of lesser worth." *Wright*, 656 F.2d at 827. Judge Ginsburg emphasized that the federal government had failed to "steer clear" of providing benefits to racially discriminatory local schools. *Id.* at 831–32.

21 Bob Jones University v. United States, 461 U.S. 574 (1983).

22 *See* Virginia Davis Nordin & William Lloyd Turner, *Tax Exempt Status of Private Schools: Wright, Green and Bob Jones*, 35 Educ. L. Rep. 329, 345 (1986).

23 Wright v. Regan, 49 A.F.T.R.2d 82–757 (D.C. Cir. 1982).

24 Allen v. Wright, 468 U.S. 737 (1984). Ironically, the majority opinion was authored by Justice Sandra Day O'Connor, rejecting the "harm in fact" analysis of Ginsburg, despite the fact that she recognized that this sort of injury could be a personal injury for purposes of tax law analysis under section 104 of the Internal Revenue Code. *See* Comm'r v. Schleier, 515 U.S. 323 (1995) (dissenting opinion). And while they did seem to have a difference of opinion—not just in tax cases but otherwise—Justice Ginsburg once said: "We divide on a lot of important questions, but we have had the experience of growing up women and we have certain sensitivities that our male colleagues lack." *See* CBS News, *Ginsburg: Supreme Court Needs More Women*, CBS News (Jan. 29, 2007), www.cbsnews.com.

25 *See, e.g.*, Neal Devins, *On Casebooks and Canons, or Why* Bob Jones University *Will Never Be Part of the Constitutional Law Canon,* 17 CONST. COMMENT 285, 289 (2000); Paul B. Stephan III, *Nontaxpayer Litigation of Income Tax Disputes,* 3 YALE L. & POL'Y REV. 73, 84–85 (1984).

26 Justice Ginsburg did join the majority opinion in *Windsor,* which struck down the Defense of Marriage Act on constitutional grounds as applied to federal tax law. *See* Windsor v. United States, 570 U.S. 744 (2013).

27 Comm'r v. Schleier, 515 U.S. 323 (1995).

28 It was subsequently amended to exclude only damages received on account of personal *physical* injury.

29 United States v. Burke, 504 U.S. 229 (1992).

30 The language in the regulation at the time provided: "The term 'damages received' . . . means an amount received . . . through prosecution of a legal suitor action based upon tort or tort type rights."

31 Burke, 504 U.S. at 235 (quoting Carey v. Piphus, 435 U.S. 247, 257 (1978)).

32 *Schleier,* 515 U.S. 323.

33 She did author two opinions in favor of taxpayers. Both decisions were on procedural points. In *Ballard v. Commissioner,* 544 U.S. 40 (2005), the taxpayer complained that the Tax Court failed to follow its own rules when it refused to share the special trial judge's report on which the Tax Court judge based his decision. Justice Ginsburg ruled that the Tax Court had to follow its own rules and provide the report in accordance with the rules. It could change those rules, of course, but until it did it had to abide by the existing rules.

   In the other case, *United States v. Williams,* a party paid a tax lien that had been assessed against property in her name even though the assessment had been against her ex-husband. She paid the lien and sought a refund. The IRS challenged her ability to seek a refund since she was not the "taxpayer" who had suffered the assessment. Refund suits could only be brought by "taxpayers." Justice Ginsburg reasoned that the party had paid a tax and the IRS had accepted it. That was sufficient to make the party a "taxpayer" for purposes of the refund litigation.

34 Drye v. United States, 528 U.S. 49 (1999).

35 Robert T. Danforth, *The Role of Federalism in Administering a National System of Taxation,* 57 TAX. LAW. 625, 626 (2004).

36 Morgan v. Comm'r, 309 U.S. 78, 80 (1940).

37 Leggett v. United States, 120 F.3d 592 (5th Cir. 1997).

38 Mapes v. United States, 15 F.3d 138, 140 (9th Cir. 1994).

39 Drye Family 1995 Trust v. United States, 152 F.3d 892 (8th Cir. 1998).

40 *See* Sonia J. Buck, *The Brilliant, Legendary, Notorious RBG,* 35 ME. B.J. 178 (2020).

20

Voting Rights

Democracy in a Hurricane

LISA MARSHALL MANHEIM

In one of the last opinions Ruth Bader Ginsburg wrote, she insisted that the Supreme Court's perception of elections "boggles the mind."[1] The Supreme Court had looked into the eyes of a global pandemic—a pandemic that had already caused Wisconsin voters, frightened by the prospect of in-person voting, to overwhelm election officials with requests for absentee ballots—and the Court's conservative majority saw nothing more than a "narrow, technical question" about election administration.[2] In response to this framing, Justice Ginsburg expressed astonishment. The question facing the Court, Ginsburg insisted, was neither narrow nor technical: Wisconsin had structured its elections in a way that forced wide swaths of voters either to vote in person, without any reassurance of personal safety, or simply "lose their right to vote, through no fault of their own."[3] The question facing the Court was therefore "a matter of utmost importance—to the constitutional rights of Wisconsin's citizens, the integrity of the State's election process, and in this most extraordinary time, the health of the Nation."[4]

This was soaring language—written, of course, entirely in dissent. In response, five of Ginsburg's colleagues proclaimed the Justice "quite wrong" and, in a short, unsigned opinion, granted relief to the Republican National Committee.[5]

This 2020 case illuminates much of what Ginsburg contributed to the Supreme Court's voting rights jurisprudence. The Justice voted reliably, and often wrote passionately, in favor of a meaningful and doctrinally grounded right to vote. Yet Ginsburg typically did so in dissent. Moreover, she advanced these positions without clear acknowledgment of just how fundamentally she disagreed with the Supreme Court's growing conservative bloc. Ginsburg seemed to assume that everyone on the Supreme Court shared a central conviction in the context of elections—that, underlying all the abstractions and technicalities, the "paramount concern" of the Justices was ensuring an opportunity for eligible voters to cast a ballot.[6] Over the course of the Justice's career, however, the Supreme Court increasingly belied this assumption of mutual commitment. Perhaps this disconnect helps to explain why, in the world of voting rights, Ginsburg's attempts to counter her colleagues frequently came up short—why her carefully crafted arguments so often failed to persuade.

Throughout her time on the bench, Ginsburg argued powerfully for voting rights on the margins of the doctrine. But the preexisting doctrinal frameworks were not enough to provide voters with the legal protections they required. These deficiencies have only become more pronounced in recent years, as political winds have shifted increasingly in the direction of voter suppression and even election subversion. While Ginsburg insisted on the value of umbrellas in a rainstorm, the electorate was facing a hurricane.

Shelby County as a Tempest

The weather metaphor derives from one of the most famous lines Ginsburg wrote, from her dissenting opinion in *Shelby County v. Holder*.[7] Ginsburg herself identified this opinion as one of her most important: a dissent written to "[appeal] to the intelligence of a future day."[8] She wrote the opinion to serve as a road map for a later time, when the Court could reconsider its analysis. To that end, the *Shelby County* dissent illustrates just how skillfully Ginsburg argued, in the voting rights space, within the analytical frameworks set by the majority. It also exemplifies the Justice's tendency to accept those frameworks on their own terms, even as they proved to be inadequate.

In *Shelby County*, the Supreme Court invalidated a central provision of the Voting Rights Act—a set of voting protections frequently referred to as the "crown jewel" of the civil rights movement. The consequences of the decision were clear, swift, and predictable. Strict voting measures that otherwise would not have been lawful went into immediate effect. The result has been an ongoing transformation of voting practices at a scope and pace that could not have occurred prior to the Court's decision.[9] Many of these changes have had disproportionate effects on Black voters and other racial minorities.[10]

The *Shelby County* majority relied on a jumble of hyper-technical arguments to invalidate the most effective voting rights mechanism American law had ever developed. It did so, moreover, through an opinion that was confusing and loosely reasoned. Ginsburg jumped on these analytical weaknesses with characteristically agile argumentation and ample support. In one of her most memorable parries, Ginsburg first noted that "[i]n the Court's view, the very success of §5 of the Voting Rights Act demands its dormancy." She later completed the countermove: "Throwing out [a central provision of the Voting Rights Act] when it has worked and is continuing to work to stop discriminatory changes is like throwing away your umbrella in a rainstorm because you are not getting wet." In further support of her dissent, Ginsburg described how the Voting Rights Act constituted "one of the most consequential, efficacious, and amply justified exercises of federal legislative power in our Nation's history," explained how "second-generation barriers" continued to undermine minority voting rights, and marched through the "extraordinary" record supporting its reauthorization.[11] Her analysis helped to demonstrate the fundamental weaknesses of the Court's logic.

Yet Ginsburg did not effectively substantiate the conviction that seemed to fuel her dissent: that this should have been an easy case. In her view, *of course* the Constitution allows Congress to reauthorize the Voting Rights Act. While Ginsburg's tone suggested that such a conclusion should be clear, the overall thrust of her dissent remained reactive and bogged down in doctrinal minutia.[12] By ceding this ground to the majority, Ginsburg's dissent inadvertently lent credence to a constitutional framework that, at best, makes it difficult for Congress to enact legislation protective of minority voting rights.

How did the Court—and Ginsburg—get to this point? As suggested by the Justice herself in *Shelby County*, answering questions of this sort often requires a dive into history.[13]

The Development of Permeable Protections

When Ginsburg was in her formative years as a lawyer and professor, American election law was experiencing a fundamental change.

Ginsburg graduated from law school in 1959, the same year that the Supreme Court concluded that the Constitution allowed the disenfranchisement of Americans who could not pass a literacy test.[14] This case, *Lassiter v. Northampton County Board of Elections*, would quickly become an outlier—a relic of a rejected and outdated understanding of voting rights.

Within three years of deciding *Lassiter*, the Supreme Court decided *Baker v. Carr*.[15] Earl Warren later would deem this decision the "most important" of his career.[16] In *Baker*, the Supreme Court altered the role of the judiciary in elections by recognizing the justiciability of redistricting claims. *Baker* soon became a pillar in the Court's increasingly aggressive campaign to protect the right to vote. In rapid succession, the Court required states to make districting decisions that reflected the newly embraced principle of "one person, one vote,"[17] forced jurisdictions to relax residency requirements,[18] struck down poll taxes,[19] and invalidated laws enfranchising only those who held property.[20] As Ginsburg herself later explained, a central rationale for this line of cases was that "when political avenues become dead-end streets, judicial intervention in the politics of the people may be essential in order to have effective politics."[21] While the Supreme Court attempted to fulfill this newly recognized responsibility, Congress bolstered and extended these efforts through statute, including the Voting Rights Act, and constitutional amendment, including the Twenty-Fourth Amendment. Even after the retirement of Chief Justice Warren and a shifting of the political winds, these trends continued: "In the late 1960s and early 1970s, . . . Congress and the Court transformed the right to vote from a formal, theoretical guarantee into a substantive entitlement of citizenship."[22]

These changes required sustained effort and creative, outside-the-box thinking. The U.S. Constitution contains no generally applicable right to vote in its text, so the Supreme Court was forced to develop doctrine around that absence.[23] Voting rights, moreover, are conceptually slippery. They implicate not only the interests of individuals but also the interests of groups (including, most prominently, racial groups) as well as the polity at large.[24] Courts, with their province limited to cases and controversies, have a particularly difficult time navigating this swirling dynamic. To add even further to the challenge, the right to vote is not analogous to the right to free speech, the right to religious exercise, or any number of other fundamental rights, insofar as it is not a negative right. Instead, one's right to vote necessarily depends on the state's willingness to facilitate it.[25] As a result of all these complexities, advances in voting rights required a reconceptualization of the role of the courts, federalism, and constitutional interpretation, among other sweeping concepts. It was difficult work, but the Supreme Court prioritized these issues and managed to push through change.

Helping to fuel this transformation was the ascendance of a new way of thinking about elections in a democracy: "[T]he idea that voting is a universal, individual right of citizens."[26] This conception rejects a view of voting that had been far more prevalent prior to the civil rights movement, when it "was perfectly within the bounds of ordinary political discourse to argue that some citizens were too ignorant, incompetent, corruptible, racially inferior, or poor to deserve the voting rights of full, first-class citizens."[27] Instead, this more modern conception of voting— one insisting that the right to cast a ballot is a substantive and universal right of all citizens—dominated national law and politics, and even popular culture, for decades after Ginsburg first entered the legal field. It appeared, in Ginsburg's words, that "[t]he country was moving together" toward a more inclusive vision of democracy.[28]

Given this appearance of unity, a progressively minded lawyer of the time might be forgiven for not noticing the strong countercurrent running underneath. Fueling the flow were powerful actors who remained skeptical of a universalist conception of voting and were growing increasingly resistant to its implications. These actors held important positions in all branches of government, including at the Supreme Court. There, the "Federalism Revolution" of the Rehnquist Court had already begun putting great pressure on the voting rights precedents set during the 1960s and 1970s. The Court's strict commitment to states' rights inevitably began to clash with voting rights protections emanating from the federal government. Moreover, the Court began to embrace textualism and originalism as preferred modes of constitutional construction. Both these modes sit uneasily with a generally applicable, constitutionally grounded right to vote. As a result of these tensions, where the Warren and Burger Courts tended to interpret the Voting Rights Act broadly, the Rehnquist Court tended to construe it narrowly. And where the Court in earlier years was comfortable with strong constitutionally based voting protections that lacked a clear textual hook, under Rehnquist some Justices began expressing discomfort with constitutional doctrines based on inference—at least when those doctrines protected individuals rather than state governments.

By the time President George W. Bush took office in 2001, the effects of the Rehnquist Court on voting rights were coming into sharper focus. The dispute between the two leading presidential candidates had introduced into the legal lexicon the "independent state legislature doctrine,"[29] a complicated concept applicable to federal elections that potentially privileges state legislatures above others, including state courts construing voter protections emanating from state constitutions. Ginsburg took aim at this theory in her dissent in *Bush v. Gore*,[30] but not in the service of voting rights. Instead, Ginsburg insisted that the theory conflicted with "the core of federalism, on which all agree."[31]

By 2006, the winds had shifted even more forcefully. That year, Congress reauthorized the Voting Rights Act, but it did not update it—a failure that remained baked into the statute like a poison pill.[32] Eyeing this development was the recently confirmed Chief Justice John Roberts, who had argued forcefully against the Voting Rights Act's 1982 expansion while working as a lawyer in the Justice Department.[33]

Several months later in 2006, Roberts joined one of his first election law decisions as a Justice. In *Purcell v. Gonzales*, the Supreme Court reached out in an emergency posture to ensure that Arizona could enforce its newly enacted voter identification restrictions in the upcoming elections.[34] While the Court cited *Reynolds v. Sims*,[35] a landmark 1964 decision of the Warren Court, it did not do so in support of the voters' challenge to the restrictive rules. Instead, the Court cited *Reynolds* for the opposite reason: in support of the idea that the prevention of voter fraud—or even simply the fear of voter fraud—constitutes a compelling interest that states can use to justify restrictions on voters. Without any citation in support, the Supreme Court insisted that "[v]oter fraud drives honest citizens out of the democratic process and breeds distrust of our government"; posited that "[v]oters who fear their legitimate votes will be outweighed by fraudulent ones will feel disenfranchised"; and suggested that, when voters feel such "distrust" and "fear" toward others, *Reynolds*'s commitment to one-person, one-vote principles justifies voting restrictions.[36] Now in her second decade on the Court, Ginsburg did not publicly startle at this counterintuitive reliance on *Reynolds*. Nor did she respond to the discussion with a robust defense of the right to vote. To the contrary, she did not appear to object at all. Instead, without comment, Ginsburg joined the Court's per curiam decision allowing Arizona to go forward with its plan.

It is not clear why the Justice signed on to this decision in *Purcell*. Whatever the case, by the time the Supreme Court issued its next big election law decision, Ginsburg was in dissent, where she so often would remain.[37] Perhaps she recognized, by 2008, that the country's apparent commitment to voting rights lacked the foothold it once had. She also might have recognized that, for her generation, the apex of the Supreme Court's protection of voting rights had already passed and that it did so without establishing a sturdy doctrinal foundation. Through precedents like *Reynolds*, the Warren Court had recognized a generally applicable right to vote contained in the Constitution. But it had done so in a manner that left the right amorphous, untethered to constitutional text, and easily manipulated.[38] Meanwhile, though the Voting Rights Act remained strong—notwithstanding efforts to chip away at its margins—Congress had refused to fortify its provisions against an increasingly hostile Supreme Court. And its vulnerability was already showing.[39] The work of the civil rights movement clearly remained unfinished, and one result was legal protections for voters that remained quite fragile.

The Reactionary Storm

By the time the country held its 2008 elections, the Rehnquist and Roberts Courts had been transforming the Supreme Court's election law jurisprudence for decades. The Court's increased protection of states' rights frequently came at the expense of individual rights, with voting rights proving particularly vulnerable. Among other allowances, the Court at times permitted lawmakers to circumvent voter protections by claiming that political animus, rather than race-based animus, motivated their actions. It also imposed burdens of proof on voters that often were not practicable to meet. And it effectively ignored the phenomenon of intentional voter suppression.[40]

On November 4, 2008, Barack Obama won the race for the Oval Office, becoming the first Black president of a country that had long denied basic rights, including the right to vote, to racial minorities. Simultaneously, the Democratic Party secured control of both chambers of Congress. For a time, the only branch of the federal government dominated by Republicans was the Supreme Court. On that front, it is true, for the entirety of Ginsburg's tenure on the Court, at least five seats remained occupied by jurists selected by a Republican president. Yet by 2010, after a fifteen-year drought, a Democratic president finally had the opportunity to appoint new Justices. As a result, Ginsburg had two new, relatively like-minded colleagues on the bench.

That same year witnessed a backlash against Obama's election so powerful that Republicans "secured control of more state legislative chambers than they had in over half a century."[41] Working efficiently, and often in lockstep, legislators began enacting restrictive voting measures: "From voter ID bills to registration restrictions, from cutbacks in early voting to purging of registration lists, measures making it harder to vote were adopted by approximately two dozen states in less than eight years."[42] Often these suppressive measures correlated to high concentrations of minority voters.[43]

In response, Justice Ginsburg continued to struggle, along with her liberal-leaning colleagues, in a posture that was reactive and defensive. Typically, the strategy was to secure enough votes simply to maintain the status quo.[44] This dynamic was illustrated in 2014 when, in the leadup to the elections, Ginsburg wrote multiple dissents objecting to the Supreme Court's use of the so-called shadow docket.[45] Imploring her conservative colleagues to focus on the procedural posture, she unsuccessfully tried to dissuade the Court from granting last-minute approval to restrictive voting measures.[46] She had more success two years later, when the period prior to the 2016 election saw little activity on the shadow docket. But surely this improvement in performance was not a consequence of heroics behind the scenes. Rather it was almost certainly a result of the conservative wing of the Court playing shorthanded. The death of Antonin Scalia in February 2016 had reduced their numbers to four.

Then, on November 8, 2016, the United States elected Donald Trump as president. Within two years of taking office, Trump nominated two Justices committed to moving the Court even further in the direction of states' rights, including at the expense of voting rights protections. Responding to the shift, Republican-dominated states continued to enact restrictive voting measures while the Supreme Court continued to look the other way.[47] This activity became increasingly frenzied in the months before the 2020 elections, by which time a pandemic had exploded and the shadow docket began bursting with activity. Moving with speed and agility, the Court's conservative majority ensured that their commitment to states' rights remained strong, even when set against suppressive voting measures preserved during a public health emergency.[48]

Ginsburg would not have the chance to witness that year's conclusion. On September 18, the Justice passed away. She, sadly, did not see how millions of people—voters, election workers, activists, and many others—worked to ensure that, against the odds, the November elections would go forward with votes fairly counted and properly certified. Ginsburg also did not have the chance to meet her conservative replacement. Nor did she see the concerted effort by the outgoing president and his allies to subvert the results of the 2020 elections. She did not see the Republican Party's embrace of a democracy-threatening lie fueled by baseless allegations of a stolen election. And she did not witness, in the period that followed, the wave (even larger than the waves after 2000 and 2010) of suppressive and even potentially subversive voting restrictions enacted by state legislatures.[49]

Nevertheless, it was from the trenches of this active and antagonistic battlefield that Ginsburg had insisted, months before her death, that the Supreme Court's election law jurisprudence "boggles the mind."[50] Nearly three decades earlier, during the Justice's confirmation hearings, this confusion might have made more sense. At that time, Ginsburg described America as "a democracy that has, through the years, been opened progressively to more and more people," with a history "marked by an ever widening participation in our democracy."[51] Historians would resist the lack of nuance in this characterization.[52] Still, in the early 1990s—before the New Federalism of the Rehnquist Court had melded with a dramatic rise in reactionary politics—it was understandable that the climate for voting rights might have seemed more progressive to an earnest and optimistic observer. By 2020, however, the Court's election law jurisprudence was hardly a bolt out of the blue. To paraphrase *Shelby County*, history did not end in 1993.[53]

Conclusion: The Limited Legacy of an Iconic Justice

It is difficult to overstate the contributions that Ruth Bader Ginsburg made to American law and culture. Her legacy is deep and multifaceted, and the dedication and talent she brought to her work helped to ensure greater justice for many across the country. It would not be fair to reduce that extraordinary legacy entirely to its shortcomings; even someone as gifted and hardworking as Ginsburg has limitations, including the need to focus her energies and prioritize her causes.

Still, in the context of voting rights, Ginsburg's legacy lacks the creativity and energy that fueled many of her other efforts. Her work in this area largely remains confined within the scaffolding set by the Rehnquist Court and, accordingly, by decades of precedent committed less to the rights of voters than to the rights of state legislatures. At times, Ginsburg was able to squeeze from this framework an important majority opinion—as when she rejected a challenge to the constitutionality of independent redistricting commissions[54] or an objection to the use of total population to draw district lines[55]—but even here, her work was reactive, not forward-looking. Going forward, it is not clear how long these precedents will stand.[56]

A larger body of Ginsburg's voting-related work took place in dissent, where, theoretically, the Justice was writing not only to her colleagues but also to the "intelligence of a future day."[57] But even here, Ginsburg was not creating an alternate set of doctrines to energize and organize a future generation of lawyers; she was not, in other words, following the models of Justices Scalia or Thomas in reconceptualizing American jurisprudence from the ground up. Instead, she was primarily focused on explaining where, even on their own terms, the Justices in the majority had erred. The trouble is that, in the field of voting rights, "that ordinary critique woefully undersells the problem."[58]

What might an alternate vision of voting rights jurisprudence look like? It takes an intellect on par with Ginsburg's to even begin to imagine.[59] But at a minimum, that alternate vision might acknowledge, and seek to counteract, the most obvious failures of current election-related jurisprudence to protect the right of voters—*all* voters—to cast their votes and have them counted.

One can hardly doubt the strength of Ginsburg's commitment to this ideal, that is, of voting as a substantive and universal right. If anything, she seemed to take for granted that others shared this same commitment. Tellingly, she still assumed, even at the very end of her tenure, that her colleagues would wince at an accusation of "massive disenfranchisement."[60] Ginsburg held tight to this assumption even as countervailing winds grew increasingly strong, and even as the Court's doctrinal frameworks grew increasingly weak. The result is a voting rights legacy that is well constructed and technically sound, but that may not be a match for the storm ahead.

NOTES

My gratitude extends to Ann Bartow and Ryan Vacca for their outstanding editorial work, as well as to Tylie Cramer, Cindy Fester, Ramita Kondepudi, Lauren Jaech, and the librarians at the University of Washington School of Law for excellent research and other assistance.

1 Republican Nat'l Comm. v. Democratic Nat'l Comm., 140 S. Ct. 1205, 1210 (2020).
2 *Id.* at 1206.
3 *Id.* at 1211 (Ginsburg, J., dissenting).
4 *Id.* (Ginsburg, J., dissenting).
5 *Id.* at 1207.
6 *Id.* at 1211.
7 Shelby Cnty., Ala. v. Holder, 570 U.S. 529 (2013) (Ginsburg, J., dissenting).
8 RUTH BADER GINSBURG, MY OWN WORDS 285 (Simon & Schuster 2016).
9 *See, e.g.*, Brnovich v. Democratic Nat'l Comm., 141 S. Ct. 2321, 2355–56 (2020) (Kagan, J., dissenting).
10 *See id.* at 2354; *see also The Effects of* Shelby County v. Holder, BRENNAN CTR. FOR JUST. (Aug. 6, 2018), www.brennancenter.org; Alex Vandermaas-Peeler et al., *American Democracy in Crisis: The Challenges of Voter Knowledge, Participation, and Polarization*, PRRI.ORG (Jul. 17, 2018), www.prri.org.
11 *Shelby Cnty.*, 570 U.S. at 559, 562–63, 590, 592 (Ginsburg, J., dissenting).
12 As an illustration, Ginsburg buries a central argument about Congress's voting-related enforcement powers in language that is both indirect and opaque: "Today's Court does not purport to alter settled precedent establishing that the dispositive question is whether Congress has employed 'rational means.'" *Id.* at 569. This assertion represents the closest Ginsburg comes to articulating her own overarching vision of the Constitution. She immediately follows this passage with a discussion of what, ultimately, amounts to an esoteric point: "[L]egislation reauthorizing an existing statute is especially likely to satisfy the minimal requirements of the rational-basis test." *Id.* By contrast, consider, for example, Justice Kagan's dissent in a subsequent decision in which the Supreme Court dramatically weakened

the Voting Rights Act. *See Brnovich*, 141 S. Ct. at 2351–73 (Kagan, J., dissenting) (insisting on her own preferred framing of the case and the doctrinal questions it presents; explaining how, in the alternative, the majority's argument fails on its own terms; and employing highly accessible rhetoric throughout). *See generally* JUSTICE SCALIA: RHETORIC AND THE RULE OF LAW (Brian G. Slocum & Francis J. Mootz III eds. 2019).

13 *Shelby Cnty.*, 570 U.S. at 576 (Ginsburg, J., dissenting).

14 Lassiter v. Northampton Cnty. Bd. of Elections, 360 U.S. 45 (1959).

15 Baker v. Carr, 369 U.S. 186 (1962).

16 EARL WARREN, THE MEMOIRS OF CHIEF JUSTICE EARL WARREN 306 (1977).

17 Reynolds v. Sims, 377 U.S. 533, 558 (1964).

18 Carrington v. Rash, 380 U.S. 89 (1965).

19 Harper v. Va. State Bd. of Elections, 383 U.S. 663 (1966).

20 Kramer v. Union Free Sch. Dist. No. 15, 395 U.S. 621 (1969).

21 *Nomination of Ruth Bader Ginsburg, to Be Associate Justice of the Supreme Court of the United States: Hearing Before the S. Comm. on the Judiciary*, 103rd Cong. 51, 179 (1993); *see also* Ruth Bader Ginsburg, *Speaking in a Judicial Voice*, 67 N.Y.U. L. REV. 1185 (1992) (quoting ROBERT G. DIXON, JR., DEMOCRATIC REPRESENTATION: REAPPORTIONMENT IN LAW AND POLITICS 8 (1968)).

22 Joseph Fishkin, *Equal Citizenship and the Individual Right to Vote*, 86 IND. L.J. 1289, 1322 (2011).

23 *See* Lisa Marshall Manheim & Elizabeth G. Porter, *The Elephant in the Room: Intentional Voter Suppression*, 2018 SUP. CT. REV. 213, 225–27, 240 (2019).

24 *See, e.g.*, Fishkin, *Equal Citizenship* at 1299–1305 (discussing these distinctions).

25 *See* Manheim & Porter, *Elephant in the Room* at 243; *see also* Joshua Sellers & Justin Weinstein-Tull, *Constructing the Right to Vote*, 96 N.Y.U. L. REV. 1127 (2021).

26 Fishkin, *Equal Citizenship* at 1338.

27 *Id.* at 1342–43.

28 *Nomination of Ruth Bader Ginsburg*.

29 *See* Hayward H. Smith, *History of the Article II Independent State Legislature Doctrine*, 29 FLA. ST. U. L. REV. 731, 768 (2001).

30 Bush v. Gore, 531 U.S. 98 (2000).

31 *Id.* at 142 (2000) (Ginsburg, J., dissenting); *see also id.* (arguing that, even in cases implicating federal elections, "[f]ederal courts defer to a state high court's interpretations of the State's own law").

32 *See Shelby Cnty.*, 570 U.S. at 557 ("[Congress's] failure to [update the Voting Rights Act] leaves us today with no choice but to declare [a central provision of the statute] unconstitutional.").

33 *See Confirmation Hearing on the Nomination of John G. Roberts, Jr. to Be Chief Justice of the United States, Before the S. Comm. on the Judiciary*, 109th Cong. 170–71 (2005) (statement of Edward Kennedy, Member, S. Comm. on the Judiciary).

34 Purcell v. Gonzalez, 549 U.S. 1, 2, 5 (2006).

35 Reynolds v. Sims, 377 U.S. 533, 555 (1964); *see also Purcell*, 549 U.S. at 4.

36 *Purcell*, 549 U.S. at 4.

37 *See* Crawford v. Marion Cty. Election Bd., 553 U.S. 181, 209–37 (2008) (Souter, J., dissenting, with Ginsburg, J., joining).

38 *See* Manheim & Porter, *Elephant in the Room* at 224–32.

39 *See, e.g.*, Complaint, Northwest Austin Municipal Util. Dist. No. One v. Gonzales, Civ. No. 06CV01384 (Aug. 4, 2006) (arguing that the relevant provision of the Voting Rights Act is "nothing more than a badge of shame that Congress, without any cognizable justification, has chosen to continue in place"); Northwest Austin Municipal Util. Dist. No. One v. Holder, 557 U.S. 193 (2009) (deciding on alternate theory in favor of plaintiffs, in part due to constitutional avoidance). *See also Shelby Cnty.*, 570 U.S. 529 (relying repeatedly on *Northwest Austin*).

40 *See* Manheim & Porter, *Elephant in the Room* at 229–30, 236, 245. *See also* Lisa Manheim, *Shifting the Burden and Striking a Balance*, TAKE CARE BLOG (Nov 16, 2018), *available at* https://takecareblog.com.

41 Manheim & Porter, *Elephant in the Room* at 232.

42 *Id.*

43 *Id.*

44 *See, e.g.*, Ariz. State Leg. v. Ariz. Redistricting Comm'n, 576 U.S. 787, 824 (2015); Evenwel v. Abbott, 578 U.S. 54, 136 S. Ct. 1120, 1132–33 (2016).

45 In the context of the U.S. Supreme Court, the "shadow docket" refers to "the significant volume of orders and summary decisions that the Court issues without full briefing and oral argument." Stephen I. Vladeck, *The Solicitor General and the Shadow Docket*, 133 HARV. L. REV. 123, 125 (2019). *See also* William Baude, *Foreword: The Supreme Court's Shadow Docket*, 9 N.Y.U. J. L. & LIBERTY 1, 3–5 (2015).

46 *See* North Carolina v. League of Women Voters of N. Carolina, 574 U.S. 927 (2014) (Ginsburg, J., dissenting); Veasey v. Perry, 574 U.S. 951 (2014) (Ginsburg, J., dissenting).

47 *See, e.g.*, Husted v. A. Philip Randolph Inst., 138 S. Ct. 1833 (2018). *See generally* Brennan Center for Justice, *New Voting Restrictions in America*, BRENNAN CTR. FOR JUST. (2019), www.brennancenter.org.

48 *See* Adam Liptak, *Missing from Supreme Court's Election Cases: Reasons for Its Rulings*, N.Y. TIMES (Oct. 26, 2020), www.nytimes.com (describing this period).

49 *See, e.g.*, Nathaniel Rakich & Elena Mejía, *Texas's New Law Is the Climax of a Record-Shattering Year for Voting Restrictions*, FIVETHIRTYEIGHT.COM (Sept. 8, 2021), https://fivethirtyeight.com; *see generally* Lisa Marshall Manheim, *Electoral Sandbagging* (manuscript on file with author).

50 *Republican Nat'l Comm.*, 140 S. Ct. at 1210 (Ginsburg, J., dissenting).

51 *Nomination of Ruth Bader Ginsburg.*

52 *See, e.g.*, ALEXANDER KEYSSAR, THE RIGHT TO VOTE: THE CONTESTED HISTORY OF DEMOCRACY IN THE UNITED STATES (2009).

53 *Shelby Cnty.*, 570 U.S. at 532; *see also id.* at 576 (Ginsburg, J., dissenting).

54 *Ariz. State Leg.*, 576 U.S. at 824.

55 *Evenwel*, 578 U.S. 54, 136 S. Ct. at 1132–33.

56 *See, e.g.*, Andrew Chung & Lawrence Hurley, *Analysis: U.S. Liberals See Dwindling Legal Options to Challenge Voting Curbs*, Reuters (Aug. 31, 2021 4:29 AM PDT), www.reuters.com.

57 Ginsburg, My Own Words at 209.

58 *Brnovich*, 141 S. Ct. at 2351 (Kagan, J., dissenting).

59 *See, e.g., id.*

60 *Republican Nat'l Comm.*, 140 S. Ct. at 1209 (Ginsburg, J., dissenting) ("While I do not doubt the good faith of my colleagues, the Court's order, I fear, will result in massive disenfranchisement.").

21

Teaching the Life and Law of RBG

Exploring Beyond Her Sex Equality Jurisprudence

ELIZABETH KUKURA AND DAVID S. COHEN

When Justice Ruth Bader Ginsburg died in September 2020 at the age of eighty-seven after a long cancer battle, we—along with many others—mourned the loss of this trailblazing advocate, scholar, and jurist. While some nursed their grief by donning homemade dissent collars[1] or stocking personal libraries with children's books about RBG's bravery,[2] we found solace reading various commentaries that emerged in the subsequent days highlighting Ginsburg's accomplishments and her influence on American law and legal culture.[3] As scholars and advocates committed to gender and reproductive justice, we thought we understood Justice Ginsburg's legacy, familiar with her role as the architect of and driving force behind heightened scrutiny for sex-based distinctions under the United States Constitution—a monumental change in the law that opened countless new opportunities for women in public and private life. But we soon discovered how much we did not know about Justice Ginsburg beyond her impact on sex equality jurisprudence.

Eager to learn more about this pioneer in the legal world, we designed a law school seminar that would enable us, along with a group of curious law students, to explore Justice Ginsburg's contributions more deeply. This chapter describes the course and discusses the pedagogical and scholarly value of teaching such a seminar to upper-level law students.

Specifically, we begin with a brief overview of the course itself, including teaching innovations that enabled us to engage in shared learning with our students over the semester. Next, we offer observations about three areas where students acquired substantive knowledge or deeper understanding about different aspects of lawmaking and our legal system through studying the work of this one particular jurist.

These lessons include (1) better understanding the Supreme Court, both as an institution and as an organization comprised of individuals working in a collective enterprise; (2) how identity and individual experience shape the work of judging, despite the common refrain during confirmation hearings that judges are merely neutral umpires "calling balls and strikes";[4] and (3) how the law evolves in complex and unpredictable ways, sometimes as the result of carefully calibrated strategic advocacy and sometimes due to an accidental confluence of circumstances. We also reflect on how a course such as this one can shape the scholarly work of the professors teaching it. Finally, we make suggestions for faculty who might wish to adapt a similar course at their school, including how to use this volume productively for classroom learning.

Course Overview

As we learned more about Justice Ginsburg's impact on legal norms in areas other than sex equality—such as disability law, immigration law, and tribal law—we decided that a primary goal of the course would be to study different substantive areas of doctrine where she made significant contributions. When we began researching her opinions for the course, it became apparent we could not cover all of her interesting opinions in a two-credit seminar. Thus, we decided to select a small number of planned topics that no course on Ginsburg could do without (her sex discrimination litigation and jurisprudence, in particular) while also giving students a role in shaping course coverage based on their areas of interest or expertise. Early in the semester, we asked students to rank their interest in sixteen different topics, and we assigned them areas of law they would be responsible (in pairs) for studying and then teaching to the rest of the class.[5] Because the course was an upper-level seminar with a writing component, the students would also write their final paper on a case that fell within their assigned topic.

We led class discussion for the first five weeks, covering the material that we thought anyone studying Ginsburg must be exposed to: background historical material about women in the legal profession; Ginsburg's early life, family, education, religion, and the beginning of her legal career; her work as an ACLU litigator and her contributions, both as lawyer and judge, to the Court's sex discrimination jurisprudence, including parallels to Thurgood Marshall's legal strategy for dismantling segregation; and Ginsburg's own writing and thinking about the work of judging.[6]

For the next four weeks, our students led class discussion on their specific areas of law. Each team met with their assigned professor two times in advance of their presentation day—first to discuss their proposed reading assignments and then to organize their lesson plan and generate productive discussion questions. The students assigned a combination of opinions and commentaries for their colleagues to read in preparation for class, and they made creative use of slides and audio clips for engaging introductions to new areas of doctrine. Many of the student-led discussions reflected individual students' own passions and areas of professional and personal interest, especially in death penalty law, disability law, and voting rights. Teaching these classes enabled students to bring their own expertise to bear on the conversation, sharing knowledge they had gained in other courses or through their legal work outside the classroom. Toward the end of this section of the course, we invited the editors of this volume as guest speakers to discuss Justice Ginsburg's copyright jurisprudence;[7] we also led discussion on two important areas of the law that had not been covered in the student-led sessions: racial justice and tribal law. The students then spent two classes workshopping drafts of their research papers, with their colleagues and professors offering helpful feedback.

The final section of the course consisted of two classes—one about RBG's status as a pop culture icon, and the last on Justice Ginsburg's legacy. For the pop culture session, the virtual format of our course during the pandemic meant we were able to invite Irin Carmon and Shana Knizhnik, authors of *Notorious RBG: The Life and Times of Ruth Bader Ginsburg*, to talk about how Justice Ginsburg's 2013 dissent in a prominent voting rights case[8] inspired Knizhnik to start an RBG-tribute Tumblr blog, which captured the public imagination and subsequently inspired countless memes and items of memorabilia in homage to RBG as a feminist hero. Students explored upsides to Justice Ginsburg's pop culture stardom in the way it made the Supreme Court more intelligible to the public, served as a source of inspiration for speaking truth to power, and made feminism cool by introducing humorous visual depictions of the ironic contrast between RBG and the rapper known as The

Notorious B.I.G. At the same time, students considered how RBG's pop culture heroism obscured the fact that her fiery dissents represented significant losses, that depiction of RBG as a savior from an unjust majority may have focused too much attention on the Court to the exclusion of political organizing and the power of popular mobilization, and that her connection with The Notorious B.I.G. helped obscure her racial blind spots, such as the fact that she hired only one Black law clerk during her career on the Court.[9]

We closed with discussion of Justice Ginsburg's legacy—both known and still unwritten. Topics for discussion included her decision not to retire under President Barack Obama, her replacement on the Supreme Court by Justice Amy Coney Barrett, and whether the conservative Supreme Court would roll back the gains for which Ginsburg fought so hard. Feedback regarding the course was positive, with students commenting how much they had learned about Justice Ginsburg's personal history and her impact on the law.

Pedagogical Value of Studying the Life and Law of RBG

When we undertook to teach this course, we had a general sense that it would provide a valuable opportunity to explore thematic connections across Ginsburg's personal life, advocacy, and contributions from the bench. We were curious to know what insights students might develop from studying the work of a single Supreme Court Justice and how it might deepen their ability to see connections and analyze law across substantive areas. The value that emerged was slightly different in focus. In particular, we have come to see how the course facilitated student learning about the Supreme Court, about lived experience and the work of judging, and about how legal norms evolve over time.

Understanding the Supreme Court

Student reactions to the course suggest that studying Justice Ginsburg's life and jurisprudence served as a vehicle for learning more generally about the Supreme Court—both as an institution and as a decision-making body of nine individuals. For example, we considered the Court in its lawmaking role and examined instances of the judicial and legislative branches engaging in dialogue. Writing in dissent in *Ledbetter v. Goodyear Tire & Rubber Co.*, Justice Ginsburg explicitly called on Congress to correct what she identified as the majority's cramped reading of Title VII's remedial purpose.[10] And indeed, one of President Obama's first acts in office was to sign into law the Lilly Ledbetter Fair Pay Act,[11] a clear response by Congress to ensure nondiscriminatory pay practices where the Court had declined to do so through enforcement of Title VII.

Other areas for potential judicial-legislative dialogue were perhaps less satisfying to the class, as in *Morales-Santana*, where Ginsburg's majority opinion applied principles of sex equality to eliminate differential treatment in citizenship rights between the children of unwed fathers and the children of unwed mothers.[12] But instead of equalizing their treatment by "leveling up" the rights of children of unwed citizen fathers, the Court applied a remedy that increased the burden on children of unwed citizen mothers—explicitly calling on Congress to change the rules as it sees fit.[13] Students analyzed this outcome favorably as an act of judicial restraint and also unfavorably as a decision that exacerbated an existing injustice, concluding that Congress in its current immigrant-unfriendly composition would be unlikely to take up the issue anytime soon.

Studying the jurisprudence of a single Justice also gave the students a window into the behind-the-scenes work of persuading one's colleagues and reaching consensus for a majority opinion. Reading one decision, a keen Court observer might intuit where compromises were necessary to secure enough votes for the author's position. But looking at Justice Ginsburg's writings in a specific area of law over time crystalized this concept for students. For example, they compared her dissent in the 1998 case *Miller v. Albright*,[14] in which the majority found no unconstitutional sex discrimination in citizenship rules that treated children of unwed fathers differently from children of unwed mothers, with the 2017 decision in *Morales-Santana*, noting how changes in the Court's composition finally enabled her to apply sex discrimination theories to equalize treatment of men and women in the latter case.[15] They puzzled over why Justice Ginsburg, as a fierce advocate for women's rights, would settle on a remedy that increased the burden on mothers of noncitizen children and were able to identify reasons why leveling down might be strategically necessary or advantageous when assembling a Court majority.[16]

Justice Ginsburg's concern for collegiality on the bench and commitment to judicial minimalism were intertwined with her desire for the Court to speak in one voice as often as possible.[17] Reading her own reflections on the value of unanimity helped students think about—some understandingly, others critically—the perspective that compromise in service of a uniform judicial voice enhances the integrity of the Court and, perhaps more important, the clarity of the law for those whose lives it impacts. This surprised some students, who prior to the course were most familiar with Justice Ginsburg through her prominent dissents, while also leading some of them to wonder whether Ginsburg's public statements about unanimity were inconsistent with her opinion-writing practice as a Justice.

For some students, the lens this course provided for evaluating the Supreme Court was their first opportunity to grapple with the idea of the Court as political, whether through the links between judicial identity and the political ideology of the president who appoints the Justice, decisions the Court makes about when to speak and when to remain silent, or the kinds of strategic calculations (and compromises) necessary to attract a majority of Justices to a particular position. While student feedback suggested increased resonance with the view that the Court is a political body, we also heard students profess greater appreciation for the Supreme Court after developing a better understanding of its structure and its impact on society.

Identity, Lived Experience, and the Work of Judging

By all accounts, our students enjoyed learning about Ruth Bader Ginsburg's family, childhood, and education. The biographical excerpts we assigned painted a picture of her origins in a family of immigrants, in which Jewish cultural identity shaped decisions about where to live and where to attend summer camp. They covered young Ruth's close relationship with her mother, Celia, who died on the eve of her high-school graduation, and the way her mother's lack of access to education and professional achievement inspired Ruth's ambition to learn and influenced her decisions about higher education. The students read about Ginsburg's experiences of marginalization as one of a small handful of women at Harvard Law School in the late 1950s, how she balanced caring for a sick husband and young child while earning top grades in law school, and her difficulty landing a job after graduation because she was a woman.

Studying Ginsburg's background served a purpose beyond learning interesting trivia about a prominent figure. Students drew connections between early influences on her life and the approach she took to judicial decision-making.[18] They recognized in her commitment to sex equality principles the personal experiences of being excluded and underestimated, as Ginsburg was so often during her legal training and early professional life. They could see how her demotion to less interesting (and less well-paying) work upon announcing her first pregnancy shaped Ginsburg's nuanced understanding as a Justice about the structural conditions that enable and perpetuate pregnancy discrimination in the workplace. And they read about how her time living in Sweden in the 1960s—where family policies were evolving to promote women's participation in public life—influenced Justice Ginsburg's thinking about gender, caretaking, and parenting under U.S. law, as illustrated in her powerful dissent in *Coleman v. Maryland Court of Appeals*, where she criticized the majority for denying state employees their right under the Family and Medical Leave Act to take time off due to their own serious medical conditions.[19]

Students identified connections between other aspects of Ginsburg's personal history and her judicial decision-making. For example, students were unaware that Ginsburg was an expert in civil procedure, but they came to recognize how Ginsburg's expertise in this area, shaped by her early research comparing American and Swedish procedural rules, influenced the opinions she authored and her commitment to procedural fairness.[20] Examining Justice Ginsburg's jurisprudence through the lens of her civil procedure background sometimes helped students make sense of results they considered surprisingly conservative by focusing their attention on process rather than results.

Perhaps most important, studying Justice Ginsburg's life and jurisprudence together led our students to think critically about how a judge's identity influences—and may be reflected in—judicial decision-making. Students appreciated the humanizing effect of studying a Supreme Court Justice's personal life, noting that doing so makes judges more relatable in general.[21] They also observed that insight into the personal history and commitments of Justice Ginsburg as an author makes her "opinions feel more personal and authentic."[22] Implicit—and sometimes explicit—in this recognition was the idea that judges do not set aside their personal experiences when they engage in the work of judging[23] and that having diverse representation among the judiciary is important for reaching fair outcomes that appropriately reflect the interests and lived experiences of litigants before the court.[24]

How Law Evolves

This course offered students concrete examples of legal norms evolving over time in response to strategic, cultural, and circumstantial forces, with opportunities to think about the power of law in shaping people's lives.

The dominant example of an evolution in legal norms that emerges from studying Justice Ginsburg's life and career is the Court's adoption of heightened scrutiny for sex-based classifications under the U.S. Constitution. From the first case in which Ginsburg argued for strict scrutiny, a tax challenge on appeal to the Tenth Circuit that her husband, Marty, a tax lawyer, brought to her attention,[25] students could see how Ginsburg educated the court about the harms of differentiating based on stereotypes about men and women. They traced this argument through the various cases she litigated before the Supreme Court during her time at the ACLU Women's Rights Project,[26] which culminated with the Court adopting intermediate scrutiny for cases involving sex discrimination—not strict scrutiny, as she had advocated. The students then looked at how, decades later as a Justice, Ginsburg wrote that an "exceedingly persuasive justification" was required for sex-based classifications in *United States v. Virginia*.[27]

In studying this line of argument about heightened scrutiny over time, the students encountered the unpredictability and even haphazardness of how cases reach the Court and become vehicles for legal change. They read about thwarted attempts to control the docket and disagreements with co-counsel at other organizations about how to frame arguments and who should appear for oral argument before the Court. They saw how a half-century-long career fighting for sex equality could be jump-started by a spouse reading a tax journal that just happened to mention a case being litigated thousands of miles away.[28] More strikingly, we considered how the United States Air Force's decision to change its rule that pregnant servicewomen must either terminate their pregnancies or face discharge precluded Ginsburg from arguing Susan Struck's case to the Supreme Court, which would have made it the first abortion case the Court decided.[29] This is especially significant because Struck's case would have been argued on equality grounds under the Equal Protection Clause of the Fourteenth Amendment rather than on the theory of an unenumerated right to privacy adopted in *Roe v. Wade* in 1973[30] and then discarded in *Dobbs v. Jackson Women's Health Organization*[31] in 2022 on the basis that the Constitution contained no right to privacy. And perhaps most significant, we considered how Ginsburg's pursuit of strict scrutiny fell one vote short because of the serendipitous timing of Congress's quick passage of the Equal Rights Amendment and the seemingly imminent ratification by the states, which never actually happened.[32]

We also studied the parallels between Ginsburg's pursuit of heightened scrutiny for sex-based classifications and Thurgood Marshall's legal strategy to secure constitutional protections against race discrimination earlier in the twentieth century. Students learned that Ginsburg owed an intellectual debt to Pauli Murray, the Black lawyer and social justice activist who first argued that the Equal Protection Clause applies to women—an argument later taken up by Ginsburg during her time at the ACLU and for which Ginsburg gave Murray credit by including her name on the brief in *Reed v. Reed*.[33] Studying Ginsburg's pursuit of constitutional sex equality against the backdrop of the legal efforts to dismantle segregation created opportunities for the students to think critically about the similarities and differences between race and sex discrimination, especially when the question becomes one of appropriate remedial measures to remedy the effects of historical discrimination.[34] Throughout, they developed an understanding of how these two important campaigns for legal and social change intersected and influenced each other, with implications for how legal protections against discrimination evolved over time.

Reflections for the Future

Justice Ginsburg's death occurred at a particularly fraught time in our national politics, during the COVID-19 pandemic and two months before a high-stakes presidential election. Designing and teaching the course offered a meaningful opportunity to reflect on the revolutionary advances in the law's treatment of men and women spurred by RBG's efforts, as well as the values she embodied in her judging. Viewed in this light, the teaching experience provided some welcome relief from the sense that our democracy was unraveling (given that the course took place in the immediate aftermath of the January 6 insurrection) and that advances in the protection of vulnerable and minority populations would be undone by an influx of conservative appointees to the federal judiciary.

But the course turned out to be less about a particular snapshot in time than we had imagined at the outset. In their evaluations, students expressed strong support for the law school to offer the course again, and we see how studying the life and law of RBG could be valuable for future generations of law students as the composition of the Court changes and areas of the law where Justice Ginsburg left her mark continue to evolve. Interestingly, some students expressed curiosity about studying the life and legal contributions of other judges in this way, which could potentially help students think critically about other important Justices and their role in American law and society.

The course also gave students the opportunity to think about role models within the profession. Ginsburg's difficulty securing a job after law school, her willingness to take risks and pursue unexpected opportunities, her relentless work ethic, and her unconventional approach to sharing domestic and family responsibilities in an egalitarian partnership with her husband are relatable and inspirational points of connection for students who study her life. In addition, for law students interested in pursuing social change work, it may be particularly valuable to study Ginsburg's contributions to legal reform over many decades, as it encourages students to develop a broad perspective on how legal and social norms evolve, which can otherwise be difficult to grasp when fighting individual battles. Looking ahead, we can also imagine returning to this course after some time has passed, reframed as a seminar about (recent) legal history that will enable students to examine the longer-term legacy of Justice Ginsburg's theories and individual opinions.

Scholarly Value of Teaching the Life and Law of RBG

The benefits of teaching about Justice Ginsburg accrued not only to the students but also to the two of us as law professors and scholars. Having learned more about Ginsburg's life, litigation career, and judicial impact, we will in the future be able to have a more fulsome discussion of Ginsburg and her work in other courses we teach. We will be able to have deeper conversations about the development of the law of sex discrimination under the Constitution and Title VII. Moreover, we will be able to talk about Ginsburg with our students in all classes in a broader way, pointing students to her contributions around civil procedure, disability law, race, immigration, and many other topics we and our students in the course explored.

Teaching a course like this also benefited us as scholars. We saw throughout the course no shortage of commentary about Ginsburg that labels her an incrementalist, claiming that she pursued change through a series of well-planned small steps rather than seeking bold change all at once. By studying all aspects of her career in depth, we saw the many flaws in this narrative and how it has likely been influenced by public perception of Ginsburg's proper demeanor and diminutive stature. Having studied her contributions as an advocate and jurist beyond the headlines, we have begun writing a scholarly challenge to the incrementalist label, arguing that this designation gets Ginsburg wrong in important ways.[35] Teaching this course inspired this scholarly work.

Conclusion

Faculty who are interested in teaching a similar course now have the benefit of this volume of rich commentaries about Justice Ginsburg's jurisprudential contributions, which can provide the foundation for syllabus design. Along with one of the Ginsburg biographies, this book could serve as a required text, with the option to assign individual opinions to supplement each week's readings on different areas of Justice Ginsburg's jurisprudence. If the professor wishes to incorporate student-led instruction for a portion of the course, this book might provide the required background reading for each team of students beginning to research their assigned topic. Rather than relying on Google or the dense law review literature, students could use the relevant chapter in this book as a starting point to decide which opinions their colleagues should read to prepare for class discussion, thus streamlining the workload for students preparing their own presentations.

It is a privilege we enjoy as legal academics to be able to pursue subjects in our research and teaching that interest and engage us. Alongside that privilege rests the responsibility to educate and train new generations of lawyers whose work will shape what the law means and how well it protects the rights we share in society. Our experience teaching "The Life and Law of RBG" contributed in both ways—challenging and inspiring us as scholars and teachers while also providing our students an opportunity to think critically about the Supreme Court, the role of judges, and how legal norms evolve, as well as to grow in their appreciation of RBG's many contributions.

NOTES

The authors would like to thank the students enrolled in their Spring 2021 seminar for the opportunity to teach and learn about Justice Ginsburg together.

1 *Ruth Bader Ginsburg's Favorite Collars in Photo*, TIME (Nov. 24, 2020), https:// time.com.

2 *See, e.g.*, DEBBIE LEVY, I DISSENT: RUTH BADER GINSBURG MAKES HER MARK (2016).

3 *E.g.*, Linda Greenhouse, *Ruth Bader Ginsburg, Supreme Court's Feminist Icon, Is Dead at 87*, N.Y. TIMES, Sept. 18, 2020; Sara Kim, *RBG Fundamentally Shaped the Lives of Women With Disabilities*, BITCHMEDIA (Oct. 16, 2020), www. bitchmedia.org; Marshall Project Staff, *RBG's Mixed Record on Race and Criminal Justice*, THE MARSHALL PROJECT (Sept. 23, 2020), www.themarshallproject. org.

4 Chief Justice Roberts Statement—Nomination Process, U.S. COURTS, www. uscourts.gov; Jennifer Finney Boyland, *Getting Beyond Balls and Strikes*, N.Y. TIMES (Oct. 23, 2018).

5 The topics were: sex discrimination in employment, race discrimination, voting rights, abortion, access to justice, civil procedure, death penalty, prisoners' rights, disability law, immigration, business law, environment, health care, intellectual property, the First Amendment, and education.

6 We required students to buy Jane Sherron de Hart's RUTH BADER GINSBURG: A LIFE (2018) and Ginsburg's MY OWN WORDS (2016), a volume edited by Mary Hartnett and Wendy Williams that contains various speeches and writings over the course of Ginsburg's career. Other readings were made available electronically.

7 See chapter 7 (on copyright law) by Ryan Vacca and Ann Bartow in this volume.

8 Shelby County v. Holder, 570 U.S. 529 (2013).

9 Jonathan H. Adler, *Supreme Court Clerks Are Not a Particularly Diverse Lot*, WASHINGTON POST (Dec. 12, 2017), www.washingtonpost.com.

10 550 U.S. 618, 661 (2007) (Ginsburg, J., dissenting) ("Once again the ball is in Congress' court . . . the Legislature may act to correct this Court's parsimonious reading of Title VII.").

11 Pub. L. 111–2 (2009).

12 Sessions v. Morales-Santana, 137 S. Ct. 1678 (2017).

13 *Id.* at 1701 ("Going forward, Congress may address the issue and settle on a uniform prescription that neither favors nor disadvantages any person on the basis of gender.").

14 523 U.S. 420, 460 (1998).

15 One student noted in their evaluation: "In a constitutional law course, the understanding of the Court is usually shown as justices moving directions over time[,] but this course shows that sometimes the Court moves around the justices." (Spring 2021 Semester Course Evaluations, on file with authors).

16 *See* Deborah Brake, *When Equality Leaves Everyone Worse Off: The Problem of Leveling Down in Equality Law*, 46 WM. & MARY L. REV. 513 (2004).

17 GINSBURG, MY OWN WORDS at 280.

18 One student noted in their course evaluation: "It was interesting because we so often view SCOTUS opinions/dissents in a vacuum—focusing on the content of the words and not the author. But obviously every decision has at least some trace of the author and the life events that led them to come down that way. So I enjoyed viewing the 'background' to these cases and examining them through that lens." (Spring 2021 Semester Course Evaluations, on file with authors).

19 566 U.S. 30 (2012).

20 *See, e.g.*, U.S. v. Bryant, 511 U.S. 738 (2016); M.L.B. v. S.L.J., 519 US. 102 (1996).

21 One student noted in their evaluation: "Knowing their stories would help make sense of their beliefs and why cases are decided as they are. This class served as a reminder that the justices are also human." Another said: "[I]t makes me think more about how all of the justices are just people like me, not these mythical figures that I have imagined them to be in the past. That just gives me more ability to empathize with different justices, to let me think from their perspectives a bit better." (Spring 2021 Semester Course Evaluations, on file with authors).

22 *Id.*

23 One student noted in their evaluation: "I tend to have an idealized view of the Supreme Court (certainly much less so than when I started law school), but learning about the person behind her persona helped me to understand how much goes into judging at that level. The people, their judicial philosophy, and their lived experiences matter more than any set of 'good facts' the Court might hear." *Id.*

24 *See* Linda L. Berger, Kathryn M. Stanchi & Bridget Crawford, *Introduction to the U.S. Feminist Judgments Project, in* FEMINIST JUDGMENTS: REWRITTEN OPINIONS OF THE UNITED STATES SUPREME COURT (Linda L. Berger et al. eds. 2016).

25 Moritz v. Commissioner, 469 F.2d 466 (10th Cir. 1972).

26 Reed v. Reed, 404 U.S. 71 (1971) (striking Idaho probate provision that preferred men over women when naming estate administrators); Frontiero v. Richardson, 411 U.S. 677 (1973) (striking military rule that applied different criteria to benefits for male and female servicepeople); Kahn v. Shevin, 416 U.S. 351 (1974) (refusing to strike as unconstitutional sex discrimination a Florida property tax exemption available only to widows and not to widowers); Weinberger v. Wiesenfeld, 420 U.S. 636 (1975) (finding unconstitutional distinction between widows and widowers in provision of Social Security benefits); Califano v. Goldfarb, 430 U.S. 199 (1977) (same); Duren v. Missouri, 439 U.S. 357 (1979) (striking Missouri county's rule exempting women from jury duty).

27 518 U.S. 515 (1996).

28 RUTH BADER GINSBURG: A LIFE at 124–25.

29 Struck v. Sec'y of Def., 460 F.2d 1374 (9th Cir. 1972).

30 410 U.S. 113 (1973).

31 142 S. Ct, 2228 (2022).

32 *Frontiero*, 411 U.S. at 692 (Powell, J., concurring in judgment).

33 Kathryn Schulz, *The Many Lives of Pauli Murray*, NEW YORKER, Apr. 17, 2017.

34 *See* SERENA MAYERI, REASONING FROM RACE: FEMINISM, LAW, AND THE CIVIL RIGHTS REVOLUTION (2014).

35 Elizabeth Kukura & David S. Cohen, *Rethinking Ruth Bader Ginsburg's Legacy, a Year After Her Death*, PHILADELPHIA INQUIRER (Sept. 20, 2021), www.inquirer.com.

Conclusion

Resting Our Case

The essays in this book paint a complicated portrait of Justice Ginsburg's jurisprudential legacy. In some instances, they reflect the popular image of RBG as the passionate dissenter who carried her fight for gender equality from the bar to the bench. Others portray her as more conservative or overly concerned with the broader structural features of the American legal system. In some chapters, we see her as adhering closely to precedent and engrossed in the facts of the case. In others, we learn that she penned opinions that were bold and driven by the underlying purpose of the law. This book breaks down the popular version of RBG and spotlights the complicated, nuanced, and sometimes contradictory aspects of her jurisprudence.

Synthesizing the contributions in these chapters into an overarching, comprehensive theory that neatly captures and explains what animated Justice Ginsburg's decision-making process and impact as a jurist writ large is an impossible task. But we can draw a handful of observations about Justice Ginsburg's jurisprudential legacy that reoccur across several legal subject areas.

First, we see evolution—how Justice Ginsburg's opinions changed over time. This is illustrated in Jill Gross's chapter on arbitration, which shows how Ginsburg initially authored majority opinions strongly supporting the arbitration process and the Federal Arbitration Act. But over time she became a consistent dissenter and critical of the expansive interpretation of the legislation. We see a similar evolution in Jeffrey Kirchmeier's chapter on the death penalty, in which he describes how Ginsburg began her approach to capital punishment as cautious and restrained but evolved to grow more critical of the death penalty and questioned its constitutionality. Similarly, Vinay Harpalani and Jeffrey Hoagland limn Justice Ginsburg's treatment of racial inequality and note that, although her jurisprudence was doctrinally and analytically consistent during her tenure on the bench, the tone of her opinions evolved. She went from emphasizing common ground to sharp critiques of the Court's decisions involving race. As their subtitle suggests, she moved from consensus-seeker to critic.

Second, we observe incrementalism. Ryan Vacca and Ann Bartow's copyright chapter reveals two types of incrementalism—writing narrow opinions to slowly move the law in her desired direction and acknowledging, but not precipitously deciding, extraneous legal issues for which she planted analytical seeds for the future. Similarly, Tara Sklar and Kirin Goff's chapter on health law discusses how her decisions prioritized targeted, incremental change in lieu of sweeping reforms in the context of congressional authority to regulate health care.

Third, several chapters illustrate Justice Ginsburg's pragmatic approach to the legal issues before her. For example, Elizabeth Porter and Heather Elliott's chapter on civil procedure describes how the Justice refused to privilege formal compliance over the practical impact on litigants and how she attempted to clarify complex procedural questions for future litigants. Likewise, Maria O'Brien's ERISA chapter evidences Justice Ginsburg's pragmatic sensibility tuned toward basic fairness to plan participants and avoiding unpredictable outcomes. Uma Outka's chapter on environmental law illustrates examples of the Justice's pragmatic concerns when she describes how Justice Ginsburg preserved citizen suits and how Ginsburg focused on the practical effects of water pollution. The health law chapter discusses how RBG's dissenting opinions related to contraception focused on the real-life impact of the majority's holding on women with limited incomes. Tracy Thomas, in her chapter on remedies, describes how the Justice emphasized pragmatic concerns and accepted minimalist remedies to protect the expansive rules she sought, such as in *Morales-Santana*. And when considering the propriety of a remedy, she identified pragmatic concerns. Sandra Sperino's chapter on employment discrimination highlights how Justice Ginsburg's opinions were focused not on how the law should be interpreted to reduce litigation but on how the law should be interpreted to best avoid discrimination in transactional and nonlitigation contexts—where the law is most meaningfully applied.

Fourth, we see numerous instances of judicial restraint running throughout Justice Ginsburg's opinions. In Isabel Medina's contribution on citizenship and immigration, she also analyzes the Justice's opinion in *Morales-Santana* and explains how the remedy the Court ordered required judicial restraint to effectuate congressional intent. Mary Jo Wiggins's analysis of bankruptcy law demonstrates instances where the Justice rejected policy arguments and stuck to more textualist analyses. Any changes to the Bankruptcy Code, she reasoned, must be done by Congress rather than the Court. Again, with civil procedure, the authors show that Justice Ginsburg's decision permitting federal courts to decide which jurisdictional tools to use to dismiss a case (rather than requiring them to dismiss on subject matter jurisdiction grounds) is a way to enable courts to restrain themselves and avoid encroaching on congressional powers. The chapter on remedies portrays Justice Ginsburg as sometimes sacrificing a preferred outcome for the prevailing party because of her belief that the Court should exercise restraint and defer to Congress on how best to respond.

Likewise, Patricia Cain and Jean Love describe how Justice Ginsburg declined to join a dissent opining that damages from unlawful discrimination were not a personal injury and thus exempt from taxation. Although this dissent was consistent with her sympathetic views toward discrimination victims, the authors posit that respect for precedent drove her decision.

Keith Robinson's patent law chapter reveals that Justice Ginsburg, despite recognizing the confusion and potential problems that patent legislation created, declined to use the Court's power to fix it. The death penalty chapter written by Jeffrey Kirchmeier demonstrates that Justice Ginsburg, despite her own personal views about capital punishment, closely adhered to precedent and avoided making sweeping pronouncements about the subject as other members of the Court had done. JoAnne Sweeny's chapter on freedom of expression illuminates Justice Ginsburg's critique of the Ninth Circuit for undertaking an analysis raised by the court rather than the parties.

In a number of essays, the reader encounters a common jurisprudential theme: Justice Ginsburg's appreciation of the Court's interactions with other branches of government. In her civil procedure cases, the Justice frequently used federalism and separation of powers concerns to justify her opinions on jurisdictional issues. In copyright law, Justice Ginsburg regularly referenced prior and concurrent actions of the executive and legislative branches as part of an ongoing discussion about the evolution of the law. She wished to avoid overstepping and prematurely cutting off the dialogue with the other branches. She also recognized the Court's institutional capacity constraints and deferred to the political branches because they were better equipped to solve the problems. Similarly, the patent law chapter explains that Justice Ginsburg paid close attention to the needs of the Patent and Trademark Office in more efficiently disposing of challenges to patent claims. She asserted that perceived problems with the patent system could best be addressed by Congress rather than by the Court. In her remedies jurisprudence, the chapter reveals that she took an institutionalist perspective and wrote opinions to permit the other branches to participate in the evolution of the law. And finally, in employment discrimination cases, Justice Ginsburg exhibited respect for and deference to the Equal Employment Opportunity Commission, because she believed it was better situated than the Court to understand how workers experienced discrimination.

These major themes don't tell the entire story. They don't capture other aspects of Justice Ginsburg's jurisprudence, such as the empathy, humanity, and compassion she displayed in criminal procedure cases like Melissa Breger describes; how equality and antistereotyping drove her family law and other gender-based opinions as Joanna Grossman and Deborah Brake explain, as well as influenced her conceptions of the state as Kali Murray unpacks; and how she passionately wrote about voting rights but was ultimately unsuccessful in making a meaningful impact in this area as demonstrated by Lisa Marshall Manheim. And as Elizabeth Kukura and David Cohen detail, these jurisprudential themes, when combined with a study of her personal background as a student, lawyer, woman, and professor, help students of RBG better understand her and her contributions to the law and to society.

Notwithstanding the variety and complexity of themes constituting Justice Ginsburg's jurisprudence, it is fair to say that she was always thoughtful in judging the cases before her. During a 2015 interview, when asked about what she would like to be remembered for, Justice Ginsburg responded: "Someone who used whatever talent she had to do her work to the very best of her ability." This, she certainly achieved.

ACKNOWLEDGMENTS

We would like to acknowledge the terrific group of authors contributing to this volume for their hard work and excellent contributions. This project would have been impossible without your tireless efforts.

We are most appreciative of Professors Lisa Tucker, Sharon Sandeen, and Irene Calboli for their invaluable advice as we first considered this project, and we are indebted to Professor Tracy Thomas for introducing us to the editorial team at New York University Press. The New York University Press team, and Clara Platter, Veronica Knutson, and Martin Coleman in particular, were wonderful to work with, and we are thankful for their enthusiasm for this book and assistance in shepherding it through to publication. We would also like to thank our wonderful colleague and librarian, Kathy Fletcher, for her assistance in locating additional resources relating to RBG, and Professor Mary Heen for her superb review of the manuscript.

This project was made possible in part from a grant from the University of New Hampshire School of Law, for which the editors are grateful.

ADDITIONAL RESOURCES ON JUSTICE GINSBURG
AND HER JURISPRUDENCE

RBG'S PUBLICATIONS

Ruth Ginsburg, *The Jury and the Nämnd: Some Observations on Judicial Control of Lay Triers in Civil Proceedings in the United States and Sweden*, 48 CORNELL L.Q. 253 (1962)

Ruth Ginsburg & Anders Bruzelius, *Professional Legal Assistance in Sweden*, 11 INT'L & COMP. L.Q. 997 (1962)

Ruth B. Ginsburg, *The Competent Court in Private International Law: Some Observations on Current Views in the United States*, 20 RUTGERS L. REV. 89 (1965)

Ruth Bader Ginsburg, *Civil Procedure—Basic Features of the Swedish System*, 14 AM. J. COMP. L. 336 (1965)

Ruth Bader Ginsburg, *Proof of Foreign Law in Sweden*, 14 INT'L & COMP. L.Q. 277 (1965)

Ruth Bader Ginsburg, *Special Findings and Jury Unanimity in the Federal Courts*, 65 COLUM. L. REV. 256 (1965)

RUTH BADER GINSBURG & ANDERS BRUZELIUS, CIVIL PROCEDURE IN SWEDEN (Hans Smit ed. 1965)

Ruth B. Ginsburg, *A Comprehensive Survey of Products Liability Law: Sweden*, 2 INT'L LAW. 153 (1967)

BUSINESS REGULATION IN THE COMMON MARKET NATIONS, VOL. 1 (Ruth B. Ginsburg ed. 1969)

Ruth B. Ginsburg, *Judgments in Search of Full Faith and Credit: The Last-in-Time Rule for Conflicting Judgments*, 82 HARV. L. REV. 798 (1969)

Ruth B. Ginsburg, *Nordic Countries, Service of Process Abroad*, 4 INT'L LAW. 150 (1969)

Ruth B. Ginsburg, *Sweden, Comparative Study of Hearsay Evidence Abroad*, 4 INT'L LAW. 163 (1969)

Benjamin Busch & Ruth Bader Ginsburg, *Summary Adjudication: Sweden*, 4 INT'L LAW. 882 (1970)

Ruth Bader Ginsburg, *Introduction to Women and the Law—A Symposium*, 25 RUTGERS L. REV. 1 (1970)

Ruth Bader Ginsburg, *Recognition and Enforcement of Foreign Civil Judgments: A Summary View of the Situation in the United States*, 4 INT'L LAW. 720 (1970)

RUTH BADER GINSBURG, A SELECTIVE SURVEY OF ENGLISH LANGUAGE STUDIES ON SCANDINAVIAN LAW (1970)

Ruth Bader Ginsburg, *Sex and Unequal Protection: Men and Women as Victims*, 11 J. FAM. L. 347 (1971)

Ruth Bader Ginsburg, *Treatment of Women by the Law: Awakening Consciousness in the Law Schools*, 5 VAL. U. L. REV. 480 (1971)

Ruth Bader Ginsburg, *Comment on Reed v. Reed*, 1:2 WOMEN'S RTS. L. REP. 7 (1972)

Ruth Bader Ginsburg, *The Status of Women*, 20 AM. J. COMP. L. 585 (1972)

Ruth Bader Ginsburg, *Comment:* Frontiero v. Richardson, 1:5 WOMEN'S RTS. L. REP. 2 (1973)

Ruth Bader Ginsburg, *The Need for the Equal Rights Amendment*, 59 ABA J. 1013 (1973)

KENNETH M. DAVIDSON, RUTH B. GINSBURG & HERMAN H. KAY, TEXT, CASES AND MATERIALS ON SEX-BASED DISCRIMINATION (1974)

RUTH BADER GINSBURG & BRENDA F. FASTEAU, COLUMBIA LAW SCHOOL EQUAL RIGHTS ADVOCACY PROJECT, THE LEGAL STATUS OF WOMEN UNDER FEDERAL LAW (1974)

Ruth Bader Ginsburg, *Gender and the Constitution*, 44 U. CIN. L. REV. 1 (1975)

Ruth Bader Ginsburg, *Gender in the Supreme Court: The 1973 and 1974 Terms*, 1975 SUP. CT. REV. 1 (1975)

Ruth Bader Ginsburg, *Women as Full Members of the Club: An Evolving American Ideal*, 6 HUM. RTS. 1 (1976)

Ruth Bader Ginsburg, *Let's Have E.R.A. as a Signal*, 63 A.B.A. J. 70 (1977)

Ruth Bader Ginsburg, *Realizing the Equality Principle, in* SOCIAL JUSTICE AND PREFERENTIAL TREATMENT 135 (William T. Blackstone & Robert D. Heslep eds. 1977)

Ruth Bader Ginsburg, *Book Review*, 92 HARV. L. REV. 340 (1978)

Ruth Bader Ginsburg, *The Equal Rights Amendment is the Way*, 1 HARV. WOMEN'S L.J. 19 (1978)

Ruth Bader Ginsburg, *Sex Equality and the Constitution*, 52 TUL. L. REV. 451 (1978)

Ruth Bader Ginsburg, *Sex Equality and the Constitution: The State of the Art*, 4:3 WOMEN'S RTS. L. REP. 143 (1978)

Ruth Bader Ginsburg, *Some Thoughts on Benign Classification in the Context of Sex*, 10 CONN. L. REV. 813 (1978)

Ruth Bader Ginsburg, *Women at the Bar—A Generation of Change*, 2 U. PUGET SOUND L. REV. 1 (1978)

Ruth Bader Ginsburg, *Women, Men and the Constitution: Key Supreme Court Rulings, in* WOMEN IN THE COURTS 21 (Winifred L. Hepperle & Laura Crites eds. 1978)

Ruth Bader Ginsburg, Bakke *Decision*, 65 WOMEN LAW. J. 11 (1979)

Ruth Bader Ginsburg, *Ratification of the Equal Rights Amendment: A Question of Time*, 57 TEX. L. REV. 919 (1979)

Ruth Bader Ginsburg, *Sexual Equality Under the Fourteenth and Equal Rights Amendments*, 1979 WASH. U. L.Q. 161 (1979)

Ruth Bader Ginsburg, *Some Thoughts on Judicial Authority to Repair Unconstitutional Legislation*, 28 CLEV. ST. L. REV. 301 (1979)

Ruth Bader Ginsburg, *Gender in the Supreme Court: The 1976 Term, in* CONSTITU-
TIONAL GOVERNMENT IN AMERICA: ESSAYS AND PROCEEDINGS FROM
SOUTHWESTERN UNIVERSITY LAW REVIEW'S FIRST WEST COAST CON-
FERENCE ON CONSTITUTIONAL LAW 217 (Ronald K. L. Collins ed. 1980)

Ruth Bader Ginsburg, *American University Commencement Address*, 30 AM. U. L.
REV. 891 (1981)

Ruth Bader Ginsburg, *Inviting Judicial Activism: A 'Liberal' or 'Conservative' Technique?*, 15 GA. L. REV. 539 (1981)

Ruth Bader Ginsburg, *Women's Right to Full Participation in Shaping Society's Course:
An Evolving Constitutional Precept, in* TOWARD THE SECOND DECADE: THE
IMPACT OF THE WOMEN'S MOVEMENT ON AMERICAN INSTITUTIONS 171
(Betty Justice & Renate Pore eds. 1981)

Ruth Bader Ginsburg, *Touring the Law in King Arthur's Court, Book Review*, 61 TEX. L.
REV. 341 (1982)

Ruth Bader Ginsburg, *Women's Work: The Place of Women in Law Schools*, 32 J. LEGAL
EDUC. 272 (1982)

Ruth Bader Ginsburg, *The Burger Court's Grapplings with Sex Discrimination, in* THE
BURGER COURT: THE COUNTER REVOLUTION THAT WASN'T 132 (Vincent
Blasi ed. 1983)

Ruth Bader Ginsburg, *Reflections on the Independence, Good Behavior, and Workload of
Federal Judges*, 55 U. COLO. L. REV. 1 (1983)

Ruth Bader Ginsburg, *The Work of Professor Allan Delker Vestal*, 70 IOWA L. REV. 13
(1984)

Ruth Bader Ginsburg, *The Constitutional Status of Human Rights Here and Abroad*, 3
ANTIOCH L.J. 5 (1985)

Ruth Bader Ginsburg, *The Obligation to Reason Why*, 37 U. FLA. L. REV. 205 (1985)

Ruth Bader Ginsburg, *Some Thoughts on Autonomy and Equality in Relation to* Roe v.
Wade, 63 N.C. L. REV. 375 (1985)

Ruth Bader Ginsburg, *Interpretations of the Equal Protection Clause*, 9 HARV. J. L. &
PUB. POL'Y 41 (1986)

Ruth Bader Ginsburg, *Some Thoughts on the 1980s Debate Over Special Versus Equal
Treatment for Women*, 4 LAW & INEQ. 143 (1986)

Ruth Bader Ginsburg, *A Plea For Legislative Review*, 60 S. CAL. L. REV. 995 (1987)

Ruth Bader Ginsburg & Peter W. Huber, *The Intercircuit Committee*, 100 HARV. L.
REV. 1417 (1987)

Ruth Bader Ginsburg, *Confirming Supreme Court Justices: Thoughts on the Second
Opinion Rendered by the Senate*, 1988 U. ILL. L. REV. 101 (1988)

Lewis F. Powell, Jr. et al., *In Memoriam: Judge Carl McGowan*, 56 GEO. WASH. L.
REV. 691 (1988)

Ruth Bader Ginsburg, *Remarks on Women Becoming Part of the Constitution*, 6 LAW &
INEQ. 17 (1988)

Edward J. Bloustein, Ruth Bader Ginsburg et al., *C. Willard Heckel—In Remembrance*,
41 RUTGERS L. REV. 475, 477 (1989)

John R. Brown et al., *In Memoriam: Judge J. Skelly Wright*, 57 GEO. WASH. L. REV. 1029, 1034–37 (1989)

Ruth Bader Ginsburg, *In Praise of Allan Axelrod*, 41 RUTGERS L. REV. 1047 (1989)

Ruth Bader Ginsburg & Barbara Flagg, *Some Reflections on the Feminist Legal Thought of the 1970s*, 1989 U. CHI. LEGAL F. 9 (1989)

Ruth Bader Ginsburg, *Employment of the Constitution to Advance the Equal Status of Men and Women, in* THE CONSTITUTIONAL BASES OF POLITICAL AND SO-CIAL CHANGE IN THE UNITED STATES 185 (Shlomo Slonim ed. 1990)

Ruth Bader Ginsburg, *On Amending the Constitution: A Plea for Patience*, 12 U. ARK. LITTLE ROCK L. REV. 677 (1990)

Ruth Bader Ginsburg, *On Muteness, Confidence, and Collegiality: A Response to Professor Nagel*, 61 U. COLO. L. REV. 715 (1990)

Ruth Bader Ginsburg, *Remarks on Writing Separately*, 65 WASH. L. REV. 133 (1990)

Ruth Bader Ginsburg, *In Memoriam: Albert M. Sacks*, 105 HARV. L. REV. 16 (1991)

Ruth Bader Ginsburg, *Introduction*, 1 COLUM. J. GENDER & L. 1 (1991)

Ruth Bader Ginsburg, *Sex Equality and the Constitution: The State of the Art*, 14 WOMEN'S RTS. L. REP. 361 (1992)

Ruth Bader Ginsburg, *Speaking in a Judicial Voice*, 67 N.Y.U. L. REV. 1185 (1992)

Ruth Bader Ginsburg, *Styles of Collegial Judging: One Judge's Perspective*, 39 FED. B. NEWS & J. 199 (1992)

Ruth Bader Ginsburg, *Constitutional Adjudication as a Means of Realizing the Equal Stature of Men and Women Under the Law*, 14 TOCQUEVILLE REV. 125 (1993)

Ruth Bader Ginsburg, *Remarks for George Mason University School of Law Graduation*, 2 GEO. MASON INDEP. L. REV. 1 (1993)

Ruth Bader Ginsburg, *Introduction to* THE JEWISH JUSTICES OF THE SUPREME COURT REVISITED: BRANDEIS TO FORTAS (Jennifer M. Lowe ed. 1994)

Ruth Bader Ginsburg, *The Progression of Women and the Law*, 28 VAL. U. L. REV. 1161 (1994)

Ruth Bader Ginsburg, *Remarks for American Law Institute Annual Dinner*, 38 ST. LOUIS U. L.J. 881 (1994)

Ruth Bader Ginsburg, *Remarks for California Women Lawyers*, 22 PEPP. L. REV. 1 (1994)

Ruth Bader Ginsburg, *A Tribute to Justice Harry A. Blackmun*, 43 AM. U. L. REV. 692 (1994)

Ruth Bader Ginsburg, *Communicating and Commenting on the Court's Work, Address*, 83 GEO. L.J. 2119 (1995)

Ruth Bader Ginsburg, *In Celebration of the Life of Vincent L. Broderick*, 16 PACE L. REV. 191 (1995)

Ruth Bader Ginsburg, *Remarks at the Dedication of the Byron White United States Courthouse*, 66 U. COLO. L. REV. 2 (1995)

Ruth Bader Ginsburg, *Remarks at the Rededication Ceremony*, 1995 U. ILL. L. REV. 11 (1995)

Ruth Bader Ginsburg & Laura W. Brill, *Women in the Federal Judiciary: Three Way Pavers and the Exhilarating Change President Carter Wrought*, 64 FORDHAM L. REV. 281 (1995)

Ruth Bader Ginsburg, *Foreword to The Report of the Special Committee on Gender*, 84 GEO. L.J. 1651 (1996)

Ruth Bader Ginsburg, *Supreme Court Discourse on the Good Behavior of Lawyers: Leeway Within Limits*, 44 DRAKE L. REV. 183 (1996)

Ruth Bader Ginsburg, *Supreme Court Pronouncements on the Conduct of Lawyers*, 1 J. INST. STUD. LEGAL ETHICS 1 (1996)

Ruth Bader Ginsburg, *Constitutional Adjudication in the United States as a Means of Advancing the Equal Stature of Men and Women Under the Law*, 26 HOFSTRA L. REV. 263 (1997)

Ruth Bader Ginsburg, *Foreword* to THE SECOND CIRCUIT'S TASK FORCE ON GENDER, RACIAL AND ETHNIC FAIRNESS IN THE COURTS, 1997 ANN. SURV. AM. L. 1 (1997)

Ruth Bader Ginsburg, *In Memoriam: William J. Brennan, Jr.*, 111 HARV. L. REV. 3 (1997)

Ruth Bader Ginsburg, *On the Interdependence of Law Schools and Law Courts*, 83 VA. L. REV. 829 (1997)

Ruth Bader Ginsburg, *An Overview of Court Review for Constitutionality in the United States*, 57 LA. L. REV. 1019 (1997)

Ruth Bader Ginsburg, *Remarks on Women's Progress in the Legal Profession in the United States*, 33 TULSA L.J. 13 (1997)

Ruth Bader Ginsburg, *Tribute to Robert A. Leflar*, 50 ARK. L. REV. 407 (1997)

Ruth Bader Ginsburg & Wendy Webster Williams, *Court Architect of Gender Equality: Setting a Firm Foundation for the Equal Stature of Men and Women*, in REASON AND PASSION: JUSTICE BRENNAN'S ENDURING INFLUENCE (E. Joshua Rosenkranz & Bernard Schwartz eds. 1997)

Ruth Bader Ginsburg, *In Celebration of Charles Alan Wright*, 76 TEX. L. REV. 1581 (1998)

Ruth Bader Ginsburg, *Informing the Public About the U.S. Supreme Court's Work*, 29 LOY. U. CHI. L.J. 275 (1998)

Ruth Bader Ginsburg, *Reflections on Way Paving Jewish Justices and Jewish Women*, 14 TOURO L. REV. 283 (1998)

Ruth Bader Ginsburg, *Remarks for Second Circuit Judicial Conference*, 180 F.R.D. 687 (1998)

Ruth Bader Ginsburg, *Remarks in Celebration of Stetson's Law Library and Information Center*, 28 STETSON L. REV. 231 (1998)

Ruth Bader Ginsburg, *Remarks on Judicial Independence*, 20 U. HAW. L. REV. 603 (1998)

Ruth Bader Ginsburg, *Welcoming Remarks to the Judicial Fellows*, 5 SW. J. L. & TRADE AM. 3 (1998)

Ruth Bader Ginsburg & Deborah Jones Merritt, *Affirmative Action: An International Human Rights Dialogue*, 21 CARDOZO L. REV. 253 (1999)

Ruth Bader Ginsburg, *Introduction to Women and the Law: Facing the Millennium*, 32 IND. L. REV. 1161 (1999)

Ruth Bader Ginsburg, *Remarks on Appellate Advocacy*, 50 S.C. L. REV. 567 (1999)

Ruth Bader Ginsburg, *Charlie's Letters*, 79 TEX. L. REV. 3 (2000)

Harold Edgar et al., *In Memory of Herbert Wechsler*, 100 COLUM. L. REV. 1347, 1359 (2000)

Ruth Bader Ginsburg, *Excerpts From Remarks Given at the International Women's Forum Lunch*, 10 COLUM. J. GENDER & L. 25 (2000)

Ruth Bader Ginsburg, *In Celebration of Kenneth L. Karst*, 47 UCLA L. REV. 1179 (2000)

Ruth Bader Ginsburg, *In Pursuit of the Public Good: Lawyers Who Care*, 52 ME. L. REV. 301 (2000)

Ruth Bader Ginsburg, *Remarks at the New York Law School Law Review Dinner*, 44 N.Y.L. SCH. L. REV. 7 (2000)

Ruth Bader Ginsburg, *The First Female Law Clerks*, in SUPREME COURT DECISIONS AND WOMEN'S RIGHTS: MILESTONES TO EQUALITY 236–37 (Clare Cushman ed. 2001)

Ruth Bader Ginsburg, *Foreword* to MALVINA SHANKLIN HARLAN, SOME MEMORIES OF A LONG LIFE, 1854–1911, vii (2001)

Ruth Bader Ginsburg, *Foreword* to SUPREME COURT DECISIONS AND WOMEN'S RIGHTS: MILESTONES TO EQUALITY (Clare Cushman ed. 2001)

Ruth Bader Ginsburg, *In Pursuit of the Public Good: Access to Justice in the United States*, 7 WASH. U. J. L. & POL'Y 1 (2001)

Susan Low Bloch & Ruth Bader Ginsburg, *Celebrating the 200th Anniversary of the Federal Courts of the District of Columbia*, 90 GEO. L.J. 549 (2002)

Ruth Bader Ginsburg, *Dinner Remarks, Southwestern School of Law*, 9 SW. J. L. & TRADE AM. 1 (2002)

Ruth Bader Ginsburg, *From Benjamin to Brandeis to Breyer: Is There a Jewish Seat?*, 41 BRANDEIS L.J. 229 (2002)

Ruth Bader Ginsburg, *Foreword to Symposium: Women, Justice, and Authority*, 14 YALE J. L. & FEMINISM 213 (2002)

Ruth Bader Ginsburg, *Four Louisiana Giants in the Law*, 48 LOY. L. REV. 253 (2002)

Ruth Bader Ginsburg, *Remarks for the Celebration of 75 Years of Women's Enrollment at Columbia Law School*, 102 COLUM. L. REV. 1441 (2002)

Ruth Bader Ginsburg, *Statement on the Death of Justice Byron R. White*, 55 STAN. L. REV. 3 (2002)

Ruth Bader Ginsburg et al., *Memories of Gerald Gunther*, 55 STAN. L. REV. 639 (2002)

Ruth Bader Ginsburg, *Foreword* to DAVID C. FREDERICK, THE ART OF ORAL ADVOCACY ix (2003)

Ruth Bader Ginsburg, *Looking Beyond Our Borders: The Value of a Comparative Perspective in Constitutional Adjudication*, 40 IDAHO L. REV. 1 (2003)

Ruth Bader Ginsburg, *Remembering Justice White*, 74 U. COLO. L. REV. 1283 (2003)

Ruth Bader Ginsburg, *The Supreme Court: A Place for Women*, 32 SW. U. L. REV. 189 (2003)

Ruth Bader Ginsburg, *The Changing Complexion of Harvard Law School*, 27 HARV. WOMEN'S L.J. 303 (2004)

Ruth Bader Ginsburg, *Looking Beyond Our Borders: The Value of a Comparative Perspective in Constitutional Adjudication*, 22 YALE L. & POL'Y REV. 329 (2004)

Ruth Bader Ginsburg, *Remarks on Women's Progress at the Bar and on the Bench*, 89 CORNELL L. REV. 801 (2004)

Ruth Bader Ginsburg, *Tribute to Yale Kamisar*, 102 MICH. L. REV. 1673 (2004)

Ruth Bader Ginsburg, *University of Hawai'i Law Review Symposium—Comments of Justice Ruth Bader Ginsburg*, 26 U. HAW. L. REV. 335 (2004)

Ruth Bader Ginsburg, *Brown v. Board of Education in International Context—October 21, 2004*, 36 COLUM. HUM. RTS. L. REV. 493 (2005)

Ruth Bader Ginsburg, *A Decent Respect to the Opinions of [Human]Kind: The Value of a Comparative Perspective in Constitutional Adjudication*, 64 CAMBRIDGE L.J. 575 (2005)

Ruth Bader Ginsburg, *A Great Lady and a Little Known Page of Supreme Court History*, 36 U. TOL. L. REV. 849 (2005)

Ruth Bader Ginsburg, *Introduction*, 22 HOFSTRA LAB. & EMP. L.J. 353 (2005)

Ruth Bader Ginsburg, *Tribute to Constance Baker Motley*, 32 HUM. RTS. 26 (2005)

Ruth Bader Ginsburg, *Tribute to John Pickering*, 104 MICH. L. REV. 175 (2005)

Ruth Bader Ginsburg, *The Value of a Comparative Perspective in Judicial Decisionmaking: Imparting Experiences to, and Learning From, Other Adherents to the Rule of Law*, 74 REV. JUR. U.P.R. 213 (2005)

Ruth Bader Ginsburg, *William H. Rehnquist*, 119 HARV. L. REV. 6 (2005)

Ruth Bader Ginsburg, *Women's Progress at the Bar and on the Bench: Pathmarks in Alabama and Elsewhere in the Nation*, 36 U. TOL. L. REV. 851 (2005)

Ruth Bader Ginsburg, *Introduction*, 61 REC. ASS'N B. CITY N.Y. 18 (2006)

Ruth Bader Ginsburg, *Judicial Independence: The Situation of the U.S. Federal Judiciary*, 85 NEB. L. REV. 1 (2006)

Ruth Bader Ginsburg, *Justice Sandra Day O'Connor*, 119 HARV. L. REV. 1239 (2006)

Ruth Bader Ginsburg, *Tribute to Chief Justice William Hubbs Rehnquist*, 74 GEO. WASH. L. REV. 869 (2006)

Ruth Bader Ginsburg, *Closing Remarks for Symposium on Justice Brennan and the Living Constitution*, 95 CALIF. L. REV. 2217 (2007)

Ruth Bader Ginsburg, *Dedication to Chesterfield H. Smith*, 18 U. FLA. J. L. & PUB. POL'Y 3 (2007)

Ruth Bader Ginsburg, *Indiana University School of Law—Indianapolis James P. White Lecture on Legal Education*, 40 IND. L. REV. 479 (2007)

Ruth Bader Ginsburg, *Reflections on Arizona's Pace-Setting Justices: William Hubbs Rehnquist and Sandra Day O'Connor*, 49 ARIZ. L. REV. 1 (2007)

Ruth Bader Ginsburg, *Remarks on Women's Progress at the Bar and on the Bench for Presentation at the American Sociological Association Annual Meeting, Montreal, August 11, 2006*, 30 HARV. J. L. & GENDER 1 (2007)

Ruth Bader Ginsburg & Lee Bollinger, *Letters Honoring Louis Henkin*, 38 COLUM. HUM. RTS. L. REV. 467 (2007)

Ruth Bader Ginsburg, *In Memory of Allan Axelrod*, 61 RUTGERS L. REV. 14 (2008)

Ruth Bader Ginsburg, *Remarks on the Life and Times of Belva Lockwood*, 37 SW. U. L. REV. 371 (2008)

Ruth Bader Ginsburg, *In Celebration of Jack Friedenthal*, 78 GEO. WASH. L. REV. 1 (2009)

Ruth Bader Ginsburg, *In Praise of Judith S. Kaye*, 84 N.Y.U. L. REV. 653 (2009)

Ruth Bader Ginsburg, *Justice Ruth Bader Ginsburg Distinguished Lecture on Women and the Law*, 64 REC. ASS'N B. CITY N.Y. 22 (2009)

Ruth Bader Ginsburg, Muller v. Oregon: *One Hundred Years Later*, 45 WILLAMETTE L. REV. 359 (2009)

Ruth Bader Ginsburg, *A Postscript to Struck by Stereotype*, 59 DUKE L.J. 799 (2010)

Ruth Bader Ginsburg, *The Role of Dissenting Opinions*, 95 MINN. L. REV. 1 (2010)

Ruth Bader Ginsburg, *Remarks in Honour of Patricia M. Wald*, 11 INT'L CRIM. L. REV. 371 (2011)

Ruth Bader Ginsburg, *Women at the Bar—A Generation of Change*, 34 SEATTLE U. L. REV. 649 (2011)

Ruth Bader Ginsburg, *In Celebration of Eva Hanks*, 36 CARDOZO L. REV. 407 (2014)

Ruth Bader Ginsburg, *Keynote Address*, 65 AM. U. L. REV. 525 (2016)

Ruth Bader Ginsburg, *Presentation of AALS Section on Women in Legal Education Ruth Bader Ginsburg Lifetime Achievement Award*, 104 CALIF. L. REV. 575 (2016)

Ruth Bader Ginsburg, *Remembrance of Antonin Scalia*, 41 J. SUP. CT. HIST. 249 (2016)

Ruth Bader Ginsburg, *In Memory of Shirley Mount Hufstedler*, 69 STAN. L. REV. 611 (2017)

Ruth Bader Ginsburg, *Remembrance of Judge Myron H. Bright*, 102 MINN. L. REV. 1 (2017)

Ruth Bader Ginsburg, *In Appreciation of Nina S. Appel*, 49 LOY. U. CHI. L.J. 685 (2018)

Ruth Bader Ginsburg, *Remembrance of Judge Diana E. Murphy*, 103 MINN. L. REV. 1 (2018)

Ruth Bader Ginsburg, *The Progression of Women in the Law*, 53 VAL. U. L. REV. 951 (2019)

Ruth Bader Ginsburg, *The Need for the Equal Rights Amendment*, 104 WOMEN LAW. J. 10 (2020)

Ruth Bader Ginsburg & Deborah Jones Merritt, *Affirmative Action: An International Human Rights Dialogue*, 2020 J. CONST. L. 9 (2020)

RBG TRANSCRIPTS AND INTERVIEWS

Men, Women and the Constitution: The Equal Rights Amendment, 10 COLUM. J. L. & SOC. PROBS. 77 (1973)

Ruth Bader Ginsburg, *The Role of the Equal Rights Amendment in Promoting Legislative and Judicial Change*, 74 F.R.D. 215, 315–21 (1976)

On Becoming a Judge: Socialization to the Judicial Role, 69 JUDICATURE 139 (1985)

Ruth Bader Ginsburg, *Roundtable Discussion—Saturday Afternoon*, 37 RUTGERS L. REV. 1107–11 (1985) (Conference on Civil Rights Developments)

Panel II: Appellate Advocacy Today: What Wins and What Loses, 140 F.R.D. 481, 566–88 (1991)

Nomination of Ruth Bader Ginsburg, to Be Associate Justice of the Supreme Court of the United States: Hearing Before the S. Comm. on the Judiciary, 103rd Cong. 51 (1993)

Ruth Bader Ginsburg, *The Washington College of Law Founders Day Tribute*, 5 AM. U. J. GENDER & L. 1 (1996)

Ruth Bader Ginsburg, *Remarks at the City University of New York School of Law*, 7 N.Y. CITY L. REV. 221 (2004)

A Conversation with Justice Ruth Bader Ginsburg, 53 U. KAN. L. REV. 957 (2005)

Transcript of Interview of U.S. Supreme Court Associate Justice Ruth Bader Ginsburg, 70 OHIO ST. L.J. 805 (2009)

Ruth Bader Ginsburg & Linda Greenhouse, *A Conversation with Justice Ginsburg*, 122 YALE L.J. F. 283 (2012–2013)

Ruth Bader Ginsburg, *A Conversation with Associate Justice Ruth Bader Ginsburg*, 84 U. COLO. L. REV. 909 (2013)

Gillian Metzger, Abbe Gluck & Ruth Bader Ginsburg, *A Conversation with Justice Ruth Bader Ginsburg*, 25 COLUM. J. GENDER & L. 6 (2013)

Jeffrey Rosen, *RBG Presides*, 245 NEW REPUBLIC at 18 (Oct 18, 2014)

Conversation with Ruth Bader Ginsburg: US Supreme Court Justice Live at uChicago (Sept. 10, 2019) *available at* youtu.be/q8L4peUuDU8

Ruth Bader Ginsburg & M. Margaret McKeown, *Searching for Equality: The Nineteenth Amendment and Beyond*, 19 GEO. L.J. 5 (2020)

SCHOLARLY ARTICLES ABOUT RBG

Ruth B. Cowan, *Women's Rights Through Litigation: An Examination of the American Civil Liberties Union Women's Rights Project, 1971–1976*, 8 COLUM. HUM. RTS. L. REV. 373 (1976)

David Cole, *Strategies of Difference: Litigating for Women's Rights in a Man's World*, 2 L. & INEQ. 33 (1984)

Deborah L. Markowitz, *In Pursuit of Equality: One Woman's Work to Change the Law*, 14 WOMEN'S RTS. L. REP. 335 (1992)

Elizabeth E. Gillman & Joseph M. Micheletti, *Justice Ruth Bader Ginsburg*, 3 SETON HALL CONST. L.J. 657 (1993)

Edward A. Fallone, *Neither Liberal Nor Laissez Faire: A Prediction of Justice Ginsburg's Approach to Business Law Issues*, 1993 COLUM. BUS. L. REV. 279

J. Stratton Shartel, *Ginsburg's Opinions Reveal Willingness to Grant Access to Litigants*, 7:8 INSIDE LITIG. 1 (1993)

Eric I. Abraham, Comment, *Justice Ginsburg and the Injury in Fact Element of Standing*, 25 SETON HALL L. REV. 267 (1994)

Joyce Ann Baugh et al., *Justice Ruth Bader Ginsburg: A Preliminary Assessment*, 26 U. TOL. L. REV. 1 (1994)

Jerome McCristal Culp, Jr., *An Open Letter From One Black Scholar to Justice Ruth Bader Ginsburg: Or, How Not to Become Justice Sandra Day O'Connor*, 1 DUKE J. GENDER L. & POL'Y 21 (1994)

William G. Ross, *The Supreme Court Appointment Process: A Search for Synthesis*, 57 ALB. L. REV. 993 (1994)

Christopher M. Shields, Note, Carlisle v. Consolidated Rail Corp. *and Justice Ginsburg's Dissent: Striking an Equitable Compromise Between the Interests of Labor and Management Regarding FELA Liability for Work-Related Stress*, 39 VILL. L. REV. 197 (1994)

Christopher E. Smith et al., *The First-Term Performance of Justice Ruth Bader Ginsburg*, 78 JUDICATURE 74 (1994)

Michael James Confusione, Note, *Justice Ruth Bader Ginsburg and Justice Thurgood Marshall: A Misleading Comparison*, 26 RUTGERS L.J. 887 (1995)

Sheila M. Smith, Comment, *Justice Ruth Bader Ginsburg and Sexual Harassment Law: Will the Second Female Supreme Court Justice Become the Court's Women's Rights Champion?*, 63 U. CIN. L. REV. 1893 (1995)

Michael E. Solimine & Susan E. Wheatley, *Rethinking Feminist Judging*, 70 IND. L.J. 891 (1995)

R. Darcy & Jenny Sanbrano, *Oklahoma in the Development of Equal Rights: The ERA, 3.2% Beer, Juvenile Justice and* Craig v. Boren, 22 OKLA. CITY U. L. REV. 1009 (1997)

Carol Pressman, *The House That Ruth Built: Justice Ruth Bader Ginsburg, Gender and Justice*, 14 N.Y.L. SCH. J. HUM. RTS. 311 (1997)

David Cowan Bayne, S.J., *Insider Trading: The Misappropriation Theory Ignored: Ginsburg's* O'Hagan, 53 U. MIAMI L. REV. 1 (1998)

W. Kent Davis, *Answering Justice Ginsburg's Charge That the Constitution Is "Skimpy" in Comparison to Our International Neighbors: A Comparison of Fundamental Rights in American and Foreign Law*, 39 S. TEX. L. REV. 951 (1998)

Toni J. Ellington et al., Comment, *Justice Ruth Bader Ginsburg and Gender Discrimination*, 20 U. HAW. L. REV. 699 (1998)

Toni J. Ellington, Comment, *Ruth Bader Ginsburg and John Marshall Harlan: A Justice and Her Hero*, 20 U. HAW. L. REV. 797 (1998)

Gerald Gunther, *Ruth Bader Ginsburg: A Personal, Very Fond Tribute*, 20 U. HAW. L. REV. 583 (1998)

Malvina Halberstam, *Ruth Bader Ginsburg: The First Jewish Woman on the United States Supreme Court*, 19 CARDOZO L. REV. 1441 (1998)

Kenneth L. Karst, *"The Way Women Are": Some Notes in the Margin for Ruth Bader Ginsburg*, 20 U. HAW. L. REV. 619 (1998)

Mei-Fei Kuo & Kai Wang, Comment, *When Is an Innovation in Order? Justice Bader Ruth Ginsburg and Stare Decisis*, 20 U. HAW. L. REV. 835 (1998)

Deborah Jones Merritt, *Hearing the Voices of Individual Women and Men: Justice Ruth Bader Ginsburg*, 20 U. HAW. L. REV. 635 (1998)

Barbara A. Perry & Henry J. Abraham, *A 'Representative' Supreme Court? The Thomas, Ginsburg and Breyer Appointments*, 81 JUDICATURE 158 (1998)

Edith Lampson Roberts, *Tribute to Justice Ruth Bader Ginsburg*, 20 U. HAW. L. REV. 595 (1998)

Scott M. Smiler, Note, *Justice Ruth Bader Ginsburg and the Virginia Military Institute: A Culmination of Strategic Success*, 4 CARDOZO WOMEN'S L.J. 541 (1998)

Amy Walsh, Comment, *Ruth Bader Ginsburg: Extending the Constitution*, 32 J. MARSHALL L. REV. 197 (1998)

Susan H. Williams & David C. Williams, *Sense and Sensibility: Justice Ruth Bader Ginsburg's Mentoring Style as a Blend of Rigor and Compassion*, 20 U. HAW. L. REV. 589 (1998)

Elijah Yip & Eric K. Yamamoto, *Justice Ruth Bader Ginsburg's Jurisprudence of Process and Procedure*, 20 U. HAW. L. REV. 647 (1998)

David Cowan Bayne, S.J., *Insider Trading: Ginsburg's O'Hagan: Insider Trading Ignored*, 53 U. MIAMI L. REV. 423 (1999)

Nadine Strossen, *Introduction of Justice Ruth Bader Ginsburg*, 44 N.Y.L. SCH. L. REV. 1 (2000)

Carey Olney, *Better Bitch Than Mouse: Ruth Bader Ginsburg, Feminism, and VMI*, 9 BUFF. WOMEN'S L.J. 97 (2000–2001)

Karen O'Conner & Barbara Palmer, *The Clinton Clones: Ginsburg, Breyer and the Clinton Legacy*, 84 JUDICATURE 262 (2001)

Mary-Christine Sungaila, *Nguyen v. INS and Sex Stereotyping in Citizenship Laws: Building on the Equal Protection Legacy of Ruth Bader Ginsburg*, 10 S. CAL. REV. L. & WOMEN'S STUD. 293 (2001)

Amy Leigh Campbell, *Raising the Bar: Ruth Bader Ginsburg and the ACLU Women's Rights Project*, 11 TEX. J. WOMEN & L. 157 (2002)

Daniel R. Gordon, *Revisiting Erie, Guaranty Trust, and Gasperini: The Role of Jewish Social History in Fashioning Modern American Federalism*, 26 SEATTLE U. L. REV. 213 (2002)

Lenora M. Lapidus, *30 Years of Women's Rights Litigation: An Evolving Constitutional Standard of Review, Remarks Before the 30th Anniversary of the Women's Rights Law Reporter*, 23 WOMEN'S RTS. L. REP. 237 (2002)

Melanie K. Morris, *Ruth Bader Ginsburg and Gender Equality: A Reassessment of Her Contribution*, 9 CARDOZO WOMEN'S L.J. 1 (2002)

Joan R. Tarpley, *An Open Thank-you Note to Justice Ruth Bader Ginsburg for Her Spirit of Belonging*, 24 WOMEN'S RTS. L. REP. 1 (2002)

James A. Kushner, *Introducing Ruth Bader Ginsburg and Predicting the Performance of a Ginsburg Court*, 32 Sw. U. L. REV. 181 (2003)

Laura Krugman Ray, *Justice Ginsburg and the Middle Way*, 68 BROOK. L. REV. 629 (2003)

Samuel R. Bagenstos, *Justice Ginsburg and the Judicial Role in Expanding "We the People": The Disability Rights Cases*, 104 COLUM. L. REV. 49 (2004)

Rebecca L. Barnhart & Deborah Zalesne, *Twin Pillars of Judicial Philosophy: The Impact of the Ginsburg Collegiality and Gender Discrimination Principles on her Separate Opinions Involving Gender Discrimination*, 7 N.Y. CITY L. REV. 275 (2004)

Shira Galinsky, *Returning the Language of Fairness to Equal Protection: Justice Ruth Bader Ginsburg's Affirmative Action Jurisprudence in Grutter and Gratz and Beyond*, 7 N.Y. CITY L. REV. 357 (2004)

Linda Greenhouse, *Introduction: Learning to Listen to Ruth Bader Ginsburg*, 7 N.Y. CITY L. REV. 213 (2004)

Sidney Harring & Jeffrey L. Kirchmeier, *Scrupulous in Applying the Law: Justice Ruth Bader Ginsburg and Capital Punishment*, 7 N.Y. CITY L. REV. 241 (2004)

Kenneth L. Karst, *The Revival of Forward-Looking Affirmative Action*, 104 COLUM. L. REV. 60 (2004)

Herma Hill Kay, *Ruth Bader Ginsburg, Professor of Law*, 104 COLUM. L. REV. 1 (2004)

M. Isabel Medina, *Real Differences and Stereotypes—Two Visions of Gender, Citizenship, and International Law*, 7 N.Y. CITY L. REV. 315 (2004)

Deborah Jones Merritt & David M. Lieberman, *Ruth Bader Ginsburg's Jurisprudence of Opportunity and Equality*, 104 COLUM. L. REV. 39 (2004)

Henry Paul Monaghan, *Doing Originalism*, 104 COLUM. L. REV. 32 (2004)

David L. Shapiro, *Justice Ginsburg's First Decade: Some Thoughts About Her Contributions in the Fields of Procedure and Jurisdiction*, 104 COLUM. L. REV. 21 (2004)

James J. Brudney, *The Supreme Court as Interstitial Actor: Justice Ginsburg's Eclectic Approach to Statutory Interpretation*, 70 OHIO ST. L.J. 1037, 889 (2009)

Courtney Megan Cahill, *Celebrating the Differences That Could Make a Difference: United States v. Virginia and a New Vision of Sexual Equality*, 70 OHIO ST. L.J. 943 (2009)

Martha Chamallas, Ledbetter, *Gender Equity and Institutional Context*, 70 OHIO ST. L.J. 1037 (2009)

Heather Elliott, *Jurisdictional Resequencing and Restraint*, 43 NEW ENG. L. REV. 725 (2009)

David L. Franklin, *Justice Ginsburg's Common-Law Federalism*, 43 NEW ENG. L. REV. 751 (2009)

Carole Goldberg, *Finding the Way to Indian Country: Justice Ruth Bader Ginsburg's Decisions in Indian Law Cases*, 70 OHIO ST. L.J. 1003 (2009)

Pamela S. Karlan, *Some Thoughts on Autonomy and Equality in Relation to Ruth Bader Ginsburg*, 70 OHIO ST. L.J. 1085 (2009)

Kenneth L. Karst, *Those Appealing Indigents: Justice Ginsburg and the Claims of Equal Citizenship*, 70 OHIO ST. L.J. 927 (2009)

Michael J. Klarman, *Social Reform Litigation and its Challenges: An Essay in Honor of Justice Ruth Bader Ginsburg*, 32 HARV. J. L. & GENDER 251, 252 (2009)

Russell A. Miller, *In a Dissenting Voice: Justice Ginsburg's Federalism*, 43 New Eng. L. Rev. 771 (2009)

Neomi Rao, *Gender, Race, and Individual Dignity: Evaluating Justice Ginsburg's Equality Jurisprudence*, 70 Ohio St. L.J. 1053 (2009)

Peter J. Rubin, *Justice Ruth Bader Ginsburg: A Judge's Perspective*, 70 Ohio St. L.J. 825 (2009)

Neil S. Siegel, *Equal Citizenship Statute: Justice Ginsburg's Constitutional Vision*, 43 New Eng. L. Rev. 799 (2009)

Neil S. Siegel & Reva B. Siegel, *Pregnancy and Sex Role Stereotyping: From* Struck *to* Carhart, 70 Ohio St. L.J. 1095 (2009)

Christopher Slobogin, *Justice Ginsburg's Gradualism in Criminal Procedure*, 70 Ohio St. L.J. 867 (2009)

Marc Spindelman, *Toward a Progressive Perspective on Justice Ginsburg's Constitution*, 70 Ohio St. L.J. 1115 (2009)

Tobias Barrington Wolff, *Ruth Bader Ginsburg and Sensible Pragmatism in Federal Jurisdictional Policy*, 70 Ohio St. L.J. 839 (2009)

Catharine MacKinnon, *A Love Letter to Ruth Bader Ginsburg*, 31 Women's Rts. L. Rep. 177 (2010)

Serena Mayeri, *"When the Trouble Started": The Story of* Frontiero v. Richardson, *in* Women and the Law Stories (Foundation Press 2010)

Reva B. Siegel & Neil S. Siegel, *Struck By Stereotype: Ruth Bader Ginsburg on Pregnancy Discrimination as Sex Discrimination*, 59 Duke L.J. 771 (2010)

Stephanie Bornstein, *The Law of Gender Steretotyping and the Work-Family Conflicts of Men*, 63 Hastings L.J. 1297 (2011)

John D. Inazu, *Justice Ginsburg and Religious Liberty*, 63 Hastings L.J. 1213 (2011)

Kenneth L. Karst, *Principles and Persons: Ruth Bader Ginsburg, Raconteuse*, 63 Hastings L.J. 1197 (2011)

Jeremy Waldron, *The Experience and Good Thinking Foreign Sources May Convey: Justice Ginsburg and the Use of Foreign Law*, 63 Hastings L.J. 1243 (2011)

Joan C. Williams, *Jumpstarting the Stalled Gender Revolution: Justice Ginsburg and Reconstructive Feminism*, 63 Hastings L.J. 1267 (2011)

Deborah E. Anker, Grutter v. Bollinger: *Justice Ruth Bader Ginsburg's Legitimization of the Role of Comparative and International Law in U.S. Jurisprudence*, 127 Harv. L. Rev. 425 (2013)

Susan H. Farbstein, *Justice Ginsburg's International Perspective*, 127 Harv. L. Rev. 429 (2013)

Judge Nancy Gertner, *Dissenting in General:* Herring v. United States, *in Particular*, 127 Harv. L. Rev. 433 (2013)

Lani Guinier, *Courting the People: Demosprudence and the Law/Politics Divide*, 127 Harv. L. Rev. 437 (2013)

Vicki C. Jackson, Lee v. Kemna: *Federal Habeas Corpus and State Procedure*, 127 Harv. L. Rev. 445 (2013)

Richard J. Lazarus, Norfolk & Western Railway v. Ayers, 538 U.S. 135 (2003), 127 HARV. L. REV. 451 (2013)

John F. Manning, *Justice Ginsburg and the New Legal Process*, 127 HARV. L. REV. 455 (2013)

Martha Minow, M.L.B. v. S.L.J., 519 U.S. 102 (1996), 127 HARV. L. REV. 461 (2013)

Harriet S. Rabb, *Litigating Sex Discrimination Cases in the 1970s*, 25 COLUM. J. GEN-DER & L. 50 (2013)

Judith Resnik, *Opening the Door: Ruth Bader Ginsburg, Law's Boundaries, and the Gender of Opportunities*, 25 COLUM. J. GENDER & L. 81 (2013)

Reva B. Siegel, *Equality and Choice: Sex Equality Perspectives on Reproductive Rights in the Work of Ruth Bader Ginsburg*, 25 COLUM. J. GENDER & L. 63 (2013)

Carol S. Steiker, *Raising the Bar*: Maples v. Thomas *and the Sixth Amendment Right to Counsel*, 127 HARV. L. REV. 468 (2013)

Julie C. Suk, *"A More Egalitarian Relationship at Home and at Work": Justice Ginsburg's Dissent in* Coleman v. Court of Appeals of Maryland, 127 HARV. L. REV. 473 (2013)

Lawrence H. Tribe, *Respecting Dissent: Justice Ginsburg's Critique of the Troubling Invocation of Appearance*, 127 HARV. L. REV. 478 (2013)

Mark Tushnet, *The Dissent in* National Federation of Independent Business v. Sebelius, 127 HARV. L. REV. 481 (2013)

Wendy W. Williams, *Ruth Bader Ginsburg's Equal Protection Clause: 1970–80*, 25 COLUM. J. GENDER & L. 41 (2013)

Jennifer L. Brinkley, *Ruth Bader Ginsburg: Examining Her Path to the High Court Bench and its Intersection with the ACLU*, 6 LMU L. REV. 1 (2019)

Jonathan L. Entin, *Tribute to Ruth Bader Ginsburg*, 71 CASE W. L. REV. 1 (2020)

Gerald Lebovits, *The Notorious R.B.G.: Lessons on Legal Writing from the Legendary Ruth Bader Ginsburg*, 92 N.Y. ST. B.J. 76 (2020)

Derek Warden, *Canonizing Justice Ginsburg's* Olmstead *Decision: A Disability Rights Tribute*, 2020 U. ILL. L. REV. ONLINE 293

Z. Payvand Ahdout, *Beyond the Notorious: A Tribute to My Justice*, 121 COLUM. L. REV. 577 (2021)

Ginger D. Anders, *Justice Ginsburg's Quiet Example*, 121 COLUM. L. REV. 583 (2021)

John Q. Barrett, *Ruth Bader Ginsburg: Litigating Against Gender Discrimination . . . and Remembering One Such New York Case*, 16 JUDICIAL NOTICE 51 (2021)

Benjamin Beaton, *The Ginsburg Court? A Contrarian View*, 121 COLUM. L. REV. 589 (2021)

Stephen G. Breyer, *A Justice and a Friend*, 121 COLUM. L. REV. 511 (2021)

Hillary Rodham Clinton, *Tribute to Ruth Bader Ginsburg: A Trailblazer for the Ages*, 121 COLUM. L. REV. 513 (2021)

Hon. Harry T. Edwards, *In Tribute to My Friend, Justice Ruth Bader Ginsburg, AKA "Notorious RBG,"* 134 HARV. L. REV. 890 (2021)

Brenda Feigen, *Goodbye, Old Friend: Tribute to Justice Ruth Bader Ginsburg*, 121 COLUM. L. REV. 519 (2021)

Brenda Feigen, *Memoriam: Justice Ruth Bader Ginsburg*, 134 HARV. L. REV. 882 (2021)

Deborah Jones Merritt, *The Music of Ruth Bader Ginsburg*, 134 HARV. L. REV. 886 (2021)

Robert A. Katzmann, *Ruth Bader Ginsburg at Her Quarter Century on the Supreme Court: Brief Reflections*, 121 COLUM. L. REV. 517 (2021)

Goodwin Liu, *Reflections on RBG: Mentor, Friend, Hero*, 121 COLUM. L. REV. 609 (2021)

John B. Owens, *Before She Was Notorious: Reflections on "The Justice,"* 121 COLUM. L. REV. 617 (2021)

Kathleen Peratis, *Memories of RBG*, 121 COLUM. L. REV. 541 (2021)

Daphna Renan, *Untitled*, 134 HARV. L. REV. 899 (2021)

John G. Roberts, Jr., *Remembering Ruth*, 121 COLUM. L. REV. 509 (2021)

Chief Justice John G. Roberts, Jr., *Untitled*, 134 HARV. L. REV. 902 (2021)

Susan Deller Ross, *Early Women's Rights Adventures with Professor Ruth Bader Ginsburg and Our Clinical Teaching at Columbia Law School*, 121 COLUM. L. REV. 553 (2021)

William Savitt, *Some Personal Reflections on Ruth Bader Ginsburg's Contributions to Business Law*, 121 COLUM. L. REV. 623 (2021)

David M. Schizer, *RBG: Nonprofit Entrepreneur*, 121 COLUM. L. REV. 633 (2021)

Margo Schlanger, *Untitled*, 134 HARV. L. REV. 894 (2021)

Alexandra A. E. Shapiro, *Reflections on Justice Ruth Bader Ginsburg and Her Approach to Criminal Law and Procedure*, 121 COLUM. L. REV. 669 (2021)

Arun Subramanian, *A Titan Among Us—On Dissents, Waymaking, and Strong Coffee*, 121 COLUM. L. REV. 719 (2021)

Zachary D. Tripp & Gillian E. Metzger, *Professor Justice Ginsburg: Justice Ginsburg's Love of Procedure and Jurisdiction*, 121 COLUM. L. REV. 729 (2021)

Amanda L. Tyler, *Lessons Learned from Justice Ruth Bader Ginsburg*, 121 COLUM. L. REV. 741 (2021)

Christine M. Venter, *Dissenting from the Bench: The Rhetorical and Performative Oral Jurisprudence of Ruth Bader Ginsburg and Antonin Scalia*, 56 WAKE FOREST L. REV. 321 (2021)

Judge Paul J. Watford, *Untitled*, 134 HARV. L. REV. 896 (2021)

Stephen Wiesenfeld, *My Journey with RBG*, 121 COLUM. L. REV. 563 (2021)

Cesare Cavallini & Stefania Cirillo, *Does Ginsburg's Judicial Voice Get the International Level?*, 22 GLOBAL JURIST 107 (2022)

Orit Gan, *I Dissent: Justice Ginsburg's Profound Dissents*, 74 RUTGERS L. REV. 1037 (2022)

Earl M. Maltz, *The Road to* United States v. Virginia: *Ruth Bader Ginsburg and the Battle Over Strict Scrutiny*, 43 WOMEN'S RTS. L. REP. 5 (2022)

Kim D. Ricardo, *Was Justice Ginsburg* Roe-*ght?: Reimagining U.S. Abortion Discourse in the Wake of Argentina's Marea Verde*, 48 MITCHELL HAMLINE L. REV. 128 (2022)

Julie C. Suk, *Justice Ginsburg's Cautious Legacy for the Equal Rights Amendment*, 110 GEO. L.J. 1391 (2022)

Ryan Vacca & Ann Bartow, *Ruth Bader Ginsburg's Copyright Jurisprudence*, 22 NEV. L.J. 431 (2022)

BOOKS AND CHAPTERS ABOUT RBG

Elinor Porter Swiger, WOMEN LAWYERS AT WORK 50–66 (1978)

Lynn Gilbert & Gaylen Moore, PARTICULAR PASSIONS: TALKS WITH WOMEN WHO HAVE SHAPED OUR TIMES 153–59 (1981)

Edith Lampson Roberts, *Ruth Bader Ginsburg, in* THE SUPREME COURT JUSTICES: ILLUSTRATED BIOGRAPHIES 1789–1995, 531 (Clare Cushman ed. 2d ed. 1995)

Christopher Henry, *Ruth Bader Ginsburg, in* THE JUSTICES OF THE UNITED STATES SUPREME COURT: THEIR LIVES AND MAJOR OPINIONS 1859 (Leon Friedman & Fred L. Israel eds. 1997)

Linda K. Kerber, NO CONSTITUTIONAL RIGHT TO BE LADIES: WOMEN AND THE OBLIGATIONS OF CITIZENSHIP 199–210 (1998)

Barbara A. Perry, "THE SUPREMES": ESSAYS ON THE CURRENT JUSTICES OF THE SUPREME COURT OF THE UNITED STATES 115–25 (Peter Lang Inc. 2d ed. 1999)

Stephanie B. Goldberg, *The Second Woman Justice: Ruth Bader Ginsburg, in* THE SUPREME COURT AND ITS JUSTICES 304 (Jesse H. Choper ed. 2001)

Natalie Wexler & Diedre von Dornum, *Ruth Bader Ginsburg: From Litigator to Justice, in* SUPREME COURT DECISIONS AND WOMEN'S RIGHTS: MILESTONES TO EQUALITY 252 (Clare Cushman ed. 2001)

Joyce A. Baugh, *Ruth Bader Ginsburg: "A Judge's Judge and a Lawyer's Lawyer," in* SUPREME COURT JUSTICES IN THE POST-BORK ERA: CONFIRMATION POLITICS AND JUDICIAL PERFORMANCE 61–80 (Peter Lang, Inc. 2002)

Elizabeth Vrato, THE COUNSELORS: CONVERSATIONS WITH 18 COURAGEOUS WOMEN WHO HAVE CHANGED THE WORLD 175–85 (2002)

Judith Baer, *Advocate on the Court: Ruth Bader Ginsburg and the Limits of Formal Equality, in* REHNQUIST JUSTICE: UNDERSTANDING THE COURT DYNAMIC 216 (Earl M. Maltz ed. 2003)

Amy Leigh Campbell, RAISING THE BAR: RUTH BADER GINSBURG AND THE ACLU WOMEN'S RIGHTS PROJECT (Xlibris 2003)

Diana Klebanow & Franklin L. Jonas, PEOPLE'S LAWYERS: CRUSADERS FOR JUSTICE IN AMERICAN HISTORY 349 (Routledge 2003)

Irin Carmon & Shana Knizhnik, NOTORIOUS RBG: THE LIFE AND TIMES OF RUTH BADER GINSBURG (Harper Collins 2015)

THE LEGACY OF RUTH BADER GINSBURG (Scott Dodson ed. 2015)

Ruth Bader Ginsburg, with Mary Hartnett & Wendy W. Williams, MY OWN WORDS (Simon & Schuster 2016)

Jane Sherron De Hart, RUTH BADER GINSBURG: A LIFE (2018)

Katie L. Gibson, RUTH BADER GINSBURG'S LEGACY OF DISSENT: FEMINIST RHETORIC AND THE LAW (Univ. Alabama Press 2018)

Jeffrey Rosen & Ruth Bader Ginsburg, CONVERSATIONS WITH RBG: RUTH
   BADER GINSBURG ON LIFE, LOVE, LIBERTY, AND LAW (Henry Holt & Co.
   2019)
THE WAY WOMEN ARE: TRANSFORMATIVE OPINIONS AND DISSENTS OF
   JUSTICE RUTH BADER GINSBURG (Cathy Cambron ed. 2020)
RUTH BADER GINSBURG: THE LAST INTERVIEW AND OTHER CONVERSA-
   TIONS (Melville House 2020)
Ruth Bader Ginsburg & Amanda L. Tyler, JUSTICE, JUSTICE THOU SHALT PUR-
   SUE: A LIFE'S WORK FIGHTING FOR A MORE PERFECT UNION (Univ. Calif.
   Press 2021)
Nina Totenberg, DINNERS WITH RUTH: A MEMOIR ON THE POWER OF
   FRIENDSHIPS (SIMON & SCHUSTER 2022)

FILMS ABOUT RBG
RBG (Magnolia Pictures 2018)
ON THE BASIS OF SEX (Participant Media 2018)
RUTH: JUSTICE GINSBURG IN HER OWN WORDS (Kino International 2019)

MISCELLANEOUS RBG MATERIALS
Sarah E. Valentine, *Ruth Bader Ginsburg: An Annotated Bibliography*, 7 N.Y. CITY L.
   REV. 391 (2004)
Derrick Wang, *Scalia/Ginsburg: A (Gentle) Parody of Operatic Proportions*, 38 COLUM.
   J. L. & ARTS 237 (2015)

ABOUT THE CONTRIBUTORS

DEBORAH L. BRAKE is Professor of Law, John E. Murray Faculty Scholar, and Associate Dean for Research and Faculty Development at University of Pittsburgh School of Law.

MELISSA L. BREGER is President William McKinley Distinguished Professor of Law at Albany Law School.

PATRICIA A. CAIN is Professor of Law at Santa Clara University School of Law and Aliber Family Chair in Law Emerita at University of Iowa.

DAVID S. COHEN is Professor of Law at Drexel University Thomas R. Kline School of Law.

HEATHER ELLIOTT is Alumni, Class of '36 Professor of Law at the University of Alabama School of Law.

KIRIN GOFF is Professor of Practice in Law at the James E. Rogers College of Law at the University of Arizona. She is also the Director of Applied Health Policy Institute at the Mel and Enid Zuckerman College of Public Health.

JILL I. GROSS is Senior Associate Dean for Academic Affairs and Law Operations and Professor of Law at Pace University Elisabeth Haub School of Law.

JOANNA L. GROSSMAN is Ellen K. Solender Endowed Chair in Women and the Law and Professor of Law at SMU Dedman School of Law.

VINAY HARPALANI is Lee and Leon Karelitz Chair in Evidence and Procedure and Professor of Law at University of New Mexico School of Law.

JEFFREY D. HOAGLAND is Law Clerk to Judge Megan P. Duffy at the New Mexico Court of Appeals.

JEFFREY L. KIRCHMEIER is Professor of Law at City University of New York School of Law.

ELIZABETH KUKURA is Assistant Professor of Law at Drexel University Thomas R. Kline School of Law.

JEAN C. LOVE is Professor of Law at Santa Clara University School of Law and Martha-Ellen Tye Professor of Law Emerita at University of Iowa.

LISA MARSHALL MANHEIM is Charles I. Stone Professor of Law at University of Washington School of Law.

M. ISABEL MEDINA is Ferris Distinguished Professor of Law at Loyola University New Orleans College of Law.

KALI MURRAY is Professor of Law at Marquette University Law School.

MARIA C. O'BRIEN is Paul M. Siskind Research Scholar and Professor of Law at Boston University School of Law.

UMA OUTKA is Professor of Law at University of Kansas School of Law.

ELIZABETH G. PORTER is Mifflin Professor of Law at University of Washington School of Law.

W. KEITH ROBINSON is Professor of Law at Wake Forest University School of Law.

TARA SKLAR is Professor of Health Law and Director of the Health Law & Policy Program at University of Arizona James E. Rogers College of Law.

SANDRA F. SPERINO is Elwood L. Thomas Missouri Endowed Professor at University of Missouri School of Law.

JOANNE SWEENY is Associate Dean for Academic Affairs and Professor of Law at University of Louisville Louis D. Brandeis School of Law.

TRACY A. THOMAS is Seiberling Chair of Constitutional Law at University of Akron School of Law.

MARY JO WIGGINS is Professor of Law at University of San Diego School of Law.

ABOUT THE EDITORS

RYAN VACCA is Professor of Law at University of New Hampshire School of Law. Prior to joining UNH Law, he served as the David L. Brennan Professor of Law at University of Akron School of Law, as well as Director of the Center for Intellectual Property Law and Technology and Interim Co-Dean of the law school. He has also held visiting professorships at Swinburne University of Technology in Melbourne, Australia, Wuhan University of Technology in Wuhan, China, University of Oregon School of Law, and University of Denver College of Law. His research primarily focuses on intellectual property and federal judiciary reform and has been published in journals such as the *California Law Review, Nevada Law Journal, Temple Law Review, Colorado Law Review, Florida State University Law Review*, and others. He is the author of a copyright casebook, *Copyright Law: Protection of Original Expression* (4th ed. Carolina Academic Press 2021) and has contributed chapters to research handbooks on the economics of intellectual property and 3D printing. Professor Vacca serves on the Editorial Board for the *American Intellectual Property Law Association Quarterly Journal*. A graduate of Amherst College (BA 2001), Professor Vacca earned his JD in 2004 from University of Missouri–Columbia School of Law and his LL.M. in 2008 from New York University School of Law.

ANN BARTOW is Professor of Law at University of New Hampshire School of Law, where she served as Director of the Franklin Pierce Center for Intellectual Property (2015–2020). Prior to joining UNH Law, she served as Professor of Law at Pace Law School and at University of South Carolina School of Law. Professor Bartow has held visiting professorships at Temple University Beasley School of Law, American University Washington College of Law, University of Dayton School of Law, University of Idaho College of Law, and numerous universities throughout China, South Korea, Italy, and Greece, including a year as a Fulbright

Distinguished Lecturer at Tongji University Law School in Shanghai. Professor Bartow is an elected member of the American Law Institute and an internationally recognized scholar in intellectual property and feminist legal theory. Her scholarship has been published in journals such as the *Michigan Law Review, Brooklyn Law Review, Boston College Law Review, Nevada Law Journal, St. John's Law Review, Ohio State Law Journal, Oregon Law Review, Columbia Journal of Gender and Law,* and *Houston Law Review,* among others. Professor Bartow has also contributed chapters to numerous books, including chapters on gender and intellectual property. A graduate of Cornell University (BS 1985), Professor Bartow earned her JD in 1990 from the University of Pennsylvania School of Law and her LL.M. as a Freedman Fellow at Temple University School of Law.

INDEX

abortion, 13–16, 183–85, 215–18; charity
funding restrictions and, 200
absentee ballots, 281
ACA. *See* Patient Protection and Affordable Care Act
access to health care, 207–15, 217–18
access to justice, 3, 39, 44, 77; habeas
corpus and, 129
ACLU. *See* American Civil Liberties
Union
activism, 25, 45; constitutional change and,
28; Supreme Court and, 202
ADA. *See* Americans with Disabilities Act
Adarand v. Pena, 239–41, 245, 247
ADEA. *See* Age Discrimination in Employment Act
adhesive arbitration agreements, 35, 38
administrative law, 20–34; Congress and,
28–29; deference and, 28; macro- and
micro-level models of, 22–25, 27; rationality of state and, 21
administrative state: feminist, 25–30;
gender identity and, 23; interplay of,
27–30; legitimation of, 20
advocates: constitutional change role of,
28; death penalty and, 124; Ginsburg
as, 179–81, 183, 238, 240, 299
AEDPA. *See* Anti-Terrorism and Effective
Death Penalty Act
Aetna v. Davila, 138
Affordable Care Act. *See* Patient Protection and Affordable Care Act
Age Discrimination in Employment Act
(ADEA), 155, 159

agency law, 154
aggravated felonies, immigration and, 72
*Alaska Department of Environmental
Conservation v. EPA*, 170–71
Alien and Sedition Act, 195
all-elements rule, 229–30
all-purpose jurisdiction, 88
Amchem Products v. Windsor, 87
American Civil Liberties Union (ACLU),
6, 13, 123, 181, 296; Moritz and, 269, 271;
Women's Rights Project, 181, 238, 302–3
American Electric Power v. Connecticut,
169–70
Americans with Disabilities Act (ADA),
155; pay discrimination and, 159
anticlassification view, 9, 239, 241, 251n6
antidiscrimination laws, 80, 153
antigay bias, 8
anti-stereotyping, 5–9, 12
antisubordination, 9–10, 12, 239, 251n6
Anti-Terrorism and Effective Death Penalty Act (AEDPA), 81, 126
antitrans bias, 8
appellate review of facts, 82–83
Apprendi v. New Jersey, 128
Arbaugh v. Y&H Co., 80, 86
arbitration, 35–48, 84, 309; federal courts'
role in regulating and supporting, 39–
42; labor, 40, 43; as matter of consent,
not coercion, 44–45; preemption,
36–39
Army Corps of Engineers, 166–67
Article III, 20, 58; environmental plaintiffs'
standing and, 80, 165; IPR and, 224